Thucydides and the
Ancient Simplicity

Thucydides and the Ancient Simplicity

The Limits of Political Realism

Gregory Crane

UNIVERSITY OF CALIFORNIA PRESS
Berkeley　·　*Los Angeles*　·　*London*

This book is a print-on-demand volume. It is manufactured using toner in place of ink. Type and images may be less sharp than the same material seen in traditionally printed University of California Press editions.

University of California Press
Berkeley and Los Angeles, California
University of California Press, Ltd.
London, England

© 1998 by the Regents of the University of
California

Library of Congress Cataloging-in-Publication Data

Crane, Gregory, 1957–.

Thucydides and the ancient simplicity: the limits of
political realism / Gregory Crane.
    p.   cm.
Includes bibliographical references and index.
ISBN 0-520-20789-0 (cloth: alk. paper)
1. Thucydides—Contributions in concept of truth.
2. Human behavior.   3. Objectivity.
4. Realism—Political aspects.   5. Thucydides.
History of the Peloponnesian War.   I. Title.
DF229.T6C88   1997
938'.05—dc2196–29615
CIP

Manufactured in the United States of America

For
Mary
Parker
Thomas

οὕτω πᾶσα ἰδέα κατέστη κακοτροπίας διὰ τὰς στάσεις τῷ
Ἑλληνικῷ, καὶ τὸ εὔηθες, οὗ τὸ γενναῖον πλεῖστον μετέχει,
καταγελασθὲν ἠφανίσθη, τὸ δὲ ἀντιτετάχθαι ἀλλήλοις τῇ
γνώμῃ ἀπίστως ἐπὶ πολὺ διήνεγκεν.

Every form of iniquity took root in the Hellenic countries
by reason of the troubles. The ancient simplicity of which nobility so largely consisted was laughed down and disappeared;
and society became divided into camps in which no one trusted
the next person.

Thucydides History of the Peloponnesian War
3.83.1 (after Crawley)

After a long time, at last though grudgingly, Aristion sent out
two or three of his drinking companions to treat for peace.
These men did not pay attention to anything that could bring
safety, but made high-flying speeches about Theseus and Eu-
molpus and the Persian Wars. To them Sulla responded, "Away
with you, you lucky, lucky people, and take these speeches with
you. I was not sent to Athens by the Romans to get a liberal
education but to crush those who had rebelled."

*Sulla responds to Athenian arguments during the
siege of Athens, Plutarch Life of Sulla 13.3*

Contents

Acknowledgments   ix

Introduction   1

1. Sherman at Melos: *Realpolitik* Ancient
   and Modern   21

2. Truest Causes and Thucydidean Realisms   36
   The Realisms of Thucydides   38
   Thucydides and Political Realism   61

3. Representations of Power before and after Thucydides   72
   Inscribing the Limits of Authority: The Hegemony
      of Herodotus's Spartans   76
   Xenophon's Self-Fashioning Spartans   85

4. Power, Prestige, and the Corcyraean Affair   93
   The Anger of Corinth   97
   The Speeches of the Corcyraeans and Corinthians   105

5. Archaeology I: The Analytical Program
   of the *History*   125
   Views on Human Development   127

The Original Humanity and the Heroic Past 127
The Original Humanity and the Forces of Production 134
The Polis as the Basic Social Unit 138
The Constituent Ties of Society: *Aidôs* and *Dikê* 141

6. Archaeology II: From Wealth to Capital
   The Changing Politics of Accumulation 148

   Wealth in the Archaic Period: Symbolic Rather Than
   Financial Capital 152
   Thucydides and "Symbolic Capital" 161
   Thucydides and Capital 164

7. The Rule of the Strong and the Limits of Friendship 172

   Mytilene 176
   Spartan Traditionalism 187

8. Archidamos and Sthenelaidas: The Dilemma
   of Spartan Authority 196

   Archidamos 199
   Sthenelaidas 212
   Archidamos's Vision and Spartan Practice 221

9. The Melian Dialogue: From Herodotus's Freedom
   Fighters to Thucydides' Imperialists 237

   Herodotus' Athenians and the Politics of Heroism 241
   Thucydides and the Grandchildren of Salamis 246

10. Athenian Theses: Realism as the Modern Simplicity 258

    The Athenians at Sparta: Old Victories, New Lessons 264
    "More Just" Rather Than "Just": Justice as a
    Zero-Sum Game 274
    Problems in the Data: Euphemos at Kamarina and the
    Melian Dialogue 285

11. Conclusion:
    Thucydidean Realism and the Price of
    Objectivity 294

Essentialism, History, and Ideology in Thucydides 295
The City and Man 303
The Funeral Oration and the Price of Objectivity 312

Bibliography 327

Index 343

Acknowledgments

It took a long time to write this book, and I have accumulated many debts, great and small, along the way. Lisa Cerrato, Maria Daniels, Carolyn Dewald, Lowell Edmunds, Jennifer Goodall, Albert Henrichs, Donald Lateiner, Thomas Martin, Robin Orttung, David Smith, Neel Smith, Daniel Tompkins, and Krista Woodbridge all read sections of this work as it evolved over the years. Martin Mueller and Gregory Nagy both suffered through an early version of the manuscript, and their reactions were enormously helpful to its revision and development. More recently, the reviewers for the University of California Press made a tremendous contribution, providing thoughtful criticisms that allowed me to improve this work in many ways. An anonymous reviewer did a great deal to help me sharpen the arguments for classicists and ancient historians. Writing a book that meets the needs of readers beyond my own field has proven particularly challenging. Insofar as I have succeeded in doing so, I owe an enormous debt to Peter Euben, whose own work has made the task of straddling disciplines look deceptively easy. Peter's suggestions caused me to rethink the entire manuscript and to frame it as a study not only of Thucydides, but of Thucydides' contribution to the development of political realism. In particular, Peter prompted me to begin grappling with the difficult but rewarding work of Hannah Arendt. Finally, Thomas Habinek, of the University of Southern California, and Mary Lamprech, classics editor for the University of California Press, deserve a great deal of credit for bearing with this book as it evolved over the past several years.

I have also been privileged to work in an intellectually stimulating and warmly collegial environment at Tufts University. My colleagues both in classics and in other fields have made it easy for me to ask questions and pursue topics that go beyond my traditional expertise. At the same time, my collaborators in the Perseus Project have provided many kinds of support for my research on Thucydides.

Access to the "prepublication" version of the Perseus database has allowed me to make convenient use of many existing translations. Although I have freely modified these to clarify the points that I needed to make, all English translations of Greek texts in this book, unless otherwise indicated, are based on those in *Perseus 2.0: Interactive Sources and Studies on Ancient Greece* (New Haven: Yale University Press, 1996).

Finally, I wish to thank my wife, Mary Thomas Crane, and my children, Thomas and Parker, who have borne with me in my labors on this book and in so much else. I dedicate this book to them—a small gesture in return for what they have given me.

Gregory Crane
Tufts University
Medford, Massachusetts
April 1996

Introduction

Warfare, especially its unpredictable course and unexpected consequences, has often spurred interest in Thucydides and the Peloponnesian
War. As a young professor at the University of Virginia, Basil Lanneau
Gildersleeve, the first great American classicist, spent his summer vaca-
tions campaigning with Robert E. Lee's army and took from this experience a wound that troubled him for the rest of his life. When he wrote
about his experiences more than thirty years later, he playfully entitled
the piece "A Southerner in the Peloponnesian War."[1] Half a world away,
the Boer War, for better or worse, suggested to Francis Cornford that
shadowy commercial interests, barely discernible in Thucydides, were
the real cause of the war.[2] In the early months of the First World War, a
reading of the Melian Dialogue, in which the Germans, British, and
Belgians were cast as Athenians, Spartans, and Melians, was staged at
the University of Toronto. On the other side, Eduard Schwartz dedicated
his book on Thucydides to his son Gerhard, "killed at Markirch, on
November 2, 1914." A generation later, Louis Lord ultimately gave to
his 1943 Martin Classical Lectures the title *Thucydides and the World
War*,[3] and Robert Connor reported that the "shattering experience of

---

1. Gildersleeve 1897, reprinted in Gildersleeve 1915.
2. Cornford 1907.
3. Lord 1945, originally entitled *Thucydides: The First Modern Historian*, derived its
ultimate title from its final chapter (pp. 223–250), which compares the Peloponnesian War
with the two world wars.

the Vietnam War" brought him to focus upon Thucydides with greater intensity.[4] The Second World War increased the prominence of Thucydides outside of classics. Thucydides' generally pessimistic view of human nature and his disdain for pious illusions struck a responsive chord among many who had lived through the struggle with fascism. Observers of contemporary affairs from George Marshall onward compared the standoff between the United States and the Soviet Union to that between Athens and Sparta. Hans Morgenthau's masterful *Politics among Nations*, first published in 1948, made him only the most influential of the new realists who would decisively shape a generation of American foreign policy. Members of this school regularly turned to Thucydides as their earliest member—Robert Gilpin has even questioned whether twenty-four centuries have substantially advanced our understanding of how states relate to one another and of why wars occur.[5]

My own interest in Thucydides intensified during the preliminaries, rather than the actual course or aftermath, of a war. During the fall of 1990, I was teaching a course on Thucydides, sitting in on lectures by Stanley Tambiah about economic anthropology, and observing, with the deep unease prevalent at the time, the diplomatic maneuvers that led to armed conflict. These three strands interacted in ways that I had not anticipated. I had always viewed the world from the vaguely "realist" slant of the cold war. Nations pursued power and interest. Having worked on economic anthropology the previous year with Stephen Gudeman, then visiting at Harvard, I continued to learn from Tambiah's lectures in the fall of 1990 how problematic many of my assumptions about human motivation had been. International morality was a marginal force and constituted, to a large degree, a mere exercise in propaganda. But in listening to Gudeman and Tambiah and in reading such works as Bronislaw Malinowski's *Argonauts of the Western Pacific* (1922), Marcel Mauss's *The Gift* (1990), and Pierre Bourdieu's *Outline of a Theory of Practice* (1977), I began to see how much more complex human motivations were than my rather cynical outlook had allowed. It was not that individuals and groups did not pursue their "interests" or that they were not "rational" actors. Rather, the rationality was often complex, with competing, often mutually inconsistent, systems of value, while different cultures defined vital interests in very different ways.

4. So Connor 1984.
5. Gilpin 1981, 226–227.

Watching the news or reading the *New York Times*, I realized that the definition of interest was not simply an academic pursuit. Many Americans could not, for example, understand how or why the ruling family of Saudi Arabia would, faced with a rampant Iraqi army just across the border of Kuwait, hesitate in the summer of 1990 to call for as many American troops as possible. The Saudis defined themselves as Arabs and as Muslims, linked by blood and religion to the Iraqis, but "national interest" pulled them toward the United States and the industrialized democracies, and the resulting tensions proved foreign to most Western and especially to American sensibilities. The importance of Mecca and of the religious inviolability of Saudi Arabia could be grasped intellectually, but it was hard to assimilate its true significance: the press never ceased to marvel as American soldiers camped in the middle of the Saudi desert were forbidden the open practice of their religions or as the President of the United States, deferring to Saudi sensibilities that trampled on his own constitution, celebrated religious services on an American ship in the Persian Gulf rather than on land. When the dispatch of American troops was linked to the personal friendship between George Bush and Saudi prince Bandar, there was widespread incredulity in the press, and even professional diplomats had difficulty coming to grips with the situation. But if such personal factors clashed with traditional power politics, they nevertheless dovetailed neatly with the forces that the ethnographic literature traced in many non-Western societies.

At the same time, I began to see that many of the same tensions that played themselves out in the *New York Times* were also at work in Thucydides. Classical Greece—untouched by Judaeo-Christian values, precapitalist, a small country that developed late at the periphery of an ancient civilized world—seemed to occupy an intermediary position between modern Western powers and more traditional societies. On the one hand, the power politics that Thucydides articulates in the so-called Archaeology that opens his work and that he puts into the mouths of his Athenians has seemed oddly modern to many readers. Thucydides has attracted attention in part because he includes many sentiments that practitioners of *Realpolitik* take for granted. On the other hand, Thucydides was the product of a society profoundly foreign to modern sensibilities: hundreds of city-states with cultural centers such as Delphi and Olympia but no powerful political union, each vying for individual power while stubbornly grudging much authority to everyone else; extended families that maintained ancestral "ritualized friendship" with their counterparts in other city-states; an amorphous set of alternately vapid and effective ties based on a shared Greek culture; competing subcategories of ethnicity such as Dorian and Ionian, which provided the loose quasi-familial ties that anthropologists term classificatory kinship. Thucydides may marginalize and even mock these phenomena, but his *History* includes them all.

The more I read Thucydides, the more I appreciated the degree to which this apparent familiarity was deceptive. In an earlier book,[6] I tried to quantify the extent to which Thucydides' outlook—and especially the degree to which he marginalized religion and the family in his explanation of events—played into assumptions that many modern readers take for granted. I cannot help but think that Thucydides would be astonished (even dismayed) if he could see how readily later readers accept many notions that were extremely radical in his own day.

In this study, I examine Thucydides' political realism, a particular political outlook that Thucydides did much to shape, and one that has remained a vital force into the twentieth century. Thucydides' *History of the Peloponnesian War* is surely a classic of realist analysis, but the complexity of Thucydidean realism is difficult for us to gauge, because our assumptions are so different from those of the fifth-century elite. First, Thucydides represents as commonplaces ideas that would have stirred angry debate among many. The very sentiments that have become standards of political realism—the anarchic nature of international relations, the domination of the weak by the strong, the primacy of interest over emotional or sentimental considerations—still clashed with the image that Greeks cultivated of themselves. When Thucydides says that the weak endure *douleia*, "slavery," because they desire profit (1.8.3), for example, he highlights the coercive element of, and thus oversimplifies, a client/patron relationship. This account is no more complete than the ideology of *megaloprepeia*, according to which the powerful, because of their inherent goodness and generosity, lavish their wealth on gifts and public displays. When Thucydides' Athenians at Sparta readily concede that they exploit their empire for their advantage, they may be telling the truth, but they are emphasizing a very different aspect of their position than when they see themselves represented as champions of Hellas and protectors of the weak in the suppliant plays of tragedy.

Second, if Thucydides pushes some ideas to the foreground, he also

6. Crane 1996a.

rejects established pretensions. Thucydides wrote to shock. I believe that he would be surprised, if not shocked himself, to discover the broad acceptance his view of the world has won. Vietnam, decades of cold war, and its chaotic aftermath of "Corcyraean" civil wars have made Thucydides' "moral bleakness," to use G. E. M. Ste. Croix's phrase,[7] seem to many a natural state of affairs. Thucydides' vision of history has proven so prominent that the elements of traditional culture that still pervade his work are easily overlooked. To take only one example: Thucydides is notorious for the degree to which he minimizes the role of religion—this despite the fact that impiety was a capital offence that his fellow Athenians persecuted with vigor and that each Athenian army had its own professional seers (with catastrophic results for the Sicilian expedition). This secular bias corresponded to the attitude of more than one Thucydides scholar (including, for example, A. W. Gomme, whose massive commentaries are a monument of twentieth-century Thucydidean scholarship). Not only have modern scholars generally taken the marginal role of religion and especially the great religious sanctuaries for granted, but such religious phenomena as did find their way into the narrative received less attention than they deserved.[8]

In composing the *History*, Thucydides thus pushed many traditional factors off to the side while dragging other phenomena into new prominence. Each of these moves was provocative, and together they lend tension to the text, a tension that the success of Thucydides' outlook has done much to mask. There are really two very different aspects of Thucydides, and much scholarship has constituted a tug-of-war in which scholars seek to redress the balance, stressing one side over the other. On the one hand, there is the "modern" Thucydides—the writer who appeals directly to the changing sensibilities of the twentieth century. The scientific Thucydides of Charles Cochrane and even Jacqueline de Romilly is, in this sense, comparable to the postmodernist Thucydides of Robert Connor, for each of these visions emphasizes an element of Thucydides that speaks to contemporary thought.[9] This is also of course

7. Croix 1972, 23.

8. Hornblower 1992 emphasizes Thucydides' disinterest in the political dimension of religion; for Thucydides' treatment of the sanctuaries themselves, see the chapter on religious space in Crane 1996a.

9. Cochrane 1929 has grown unfashionable and is unjustly neglected; a similar fate has befallen Lord 1945; see also Woodhead 1970; de Romilly has continued to refine her "modernist" view: cf. de Romilly 1963 and 1990. Connor made the characterization "Postmodernist Thucydides" famous in Connor 1977a; he develops this view further in Connor 1984.

the Thucydides whom I will examine in chapter 3 and whose influence lives on among political scientists and philosophers whose field of study is not the ancient Greek world per se.[10] On the other hand, there is a more foreign Thucydides—a Thucydides who is produced by and despite himself reproduces an archaic Greek outlook—whom Francis Cornford's brilliant *Thucydides Mythistoricus* largely established as a subject of scholarship, to which others have continued to contribute.[11] I will not pursue the relationship between Thucydides and Athenian tragedy for which Cornford argued and which John Finley articulated. Some scholars have questioned this relationship,[12] but whatever the impact of tragedy, Cornford's basic thesis, that Thucydides does not escape the outlooks and values of the traditional archaic Greek world, remains valid.

Of course, none of the scholars whom I have cited has completely neglected the other Thucydides. Connor's work, for example, contains much material about Thucydides' cultural background. My goal in this study is to highlight the tension between the archaic and the modern Thucydides. This tension between archaic and modern is linked to the conflict between "real" and "apparent" factors that drives the *History* from beginning to end. If I may oversimplify for the moment, Thucydides spent much of his time critiquing the "apparent" explanations provided by traditional Greek thought and articulating in their place "real" causes (such as the Athenian triad at 1.76 of fear, honor, and advantage) that would fit neatly into the cynical news analyses of the *Washington Post* or *Wall Street Journal*. But Thucydides seems ambivalent. Although his text repeatedly pushes into the foreground the sad fates of those who, like the Plataians and the Melians, depend upon traditional values, Thucydides makes it clear in his description of civil war at Corcyra that he takes a dim view of those who trampled upon such values.[13]

Thucydides was always searching for "the cause that was most true, even if least apparent in public discourse" (1.23.6: *hê men alêthestatê prophasis, aphanestatê de logôi*), and he insisted upon "basing obser-

10. Thucydides has received a substantial amount of attention from scholars outside of classics in recent years. Consider, for example, the following book-length studies: Forde 1989; Palmer 1992; Johnson 1993; Orwin 1994.

11. Cornford 1907; also Stahl 1966; Lloyd-Jones 1971, 140–144; Edmunds 1975a and b.

12. For a skeptical view of the specific influence of tragedy upon Thucydides, see Macleod 1983; for the relationship between ideas expressed in Thucydides and Euripides, see Finley 1967.

13. Euben 1990b, 197–198; White 1984, 68–82.

vations on the actual realities" (1.21.2: *ap' autôn tôn ergôn skopousi*). But if Thucydides felt that he could provide an accurate account of individual events—how many men fought at a given place, the symptoms of the plague, even the general pattern of moral collapse in civil war—to his great credit, he never pretended to resolve the larger ambiguities of his narrative.[14] The ideas that shape his account of early Greek history and of the Archidamian War seem to have little relevance to the events of book 8. The Sicilian expedition, which occupies books 6 and 7, is almost a separate monograph, and book 5, with its complex and messy multipolar politics, anticipates the atomization of events that characterizes book 8. His unfinished account of the war sputters to a close with the desultory warfare of 411. We do not know why the *History* was never finished. Certainly, death with little or no warning may have carried off Thucydides, but I think it at least as possible that Thucydides simply stopped because events diverged from both the vision of history that he articulates in the Archaeology—according to which, Athens, with its sea power, financial reserves, and clear-eyed ruthlessness, should logically demolish its atavistic foes—and the synthesis between public and private interest that Perikles develops in all three of his speeches.

I believe that, like Hobbes, who lived through the Thirty Years War, Thucydides sought to assimilate the decades of brutality that he had observed and that he wished to reconstitute, in a new rationalized form, that "ancient simplicity" (as Crawley renders *to euêthes* at 3.83.1) of which the "well-born" (*to gennaion*)—the old Greek elite to which Thucydides belonged—had enjoyed such a great share. In part, the methodological integrity that Thucydides claims for his text seeks to replace the moral integrity that vanished during the war,[15] but I think that Thucydides attempted to do more. The Thucydidean Perikles and Diodotos each offer syntheses of the old and the new. Neither vision takes root, of course: the forebearance at Mytilene vanishes at Melos, while no one except the ambiguous and brilliantly self-centered Alkibiades can approach Perikles' stature after his death. One of Thucydides' greatest achievements was to help define the problems that would occupy a much more prolific Athenian from the following generation throughout his

14. In this I agree with White (1984, 85–87), who insists that many of the inconsistencies that remain in the *History* reflect structural tensions that Thucydides would not have resolved had he finished the work.

15. So Euben 1990b, 197–198.

life. But if Plato counters the ideas of the Melian Dialogue with his *Republic* and the conditional patriotism of an Alkibiades with Sokrates' submission to the state in the *Crito*, Plato was a philosopher and not a historian. If the world Plato saw was not satisfactory, he could construct an idealized republic, fabricate a symposium that outdid Herodotus's meeting of Solon and Kroisos, or project his ideas onto an Atlantis. Thucydides subordinated himself to a stricter set of rules. He insisted that he wanted to view the world as it really was. We may question how successful he was in this, and indeed much of this study will emphasize the problems of Thucydides' *History*. Some have even questioned Thucydides' honesty,[16] but no one before Thucydides and few since have insisted so firmly on the importance of sticking to the facts.

The model of ideology articulated most prominently by Louis Althusser provides a useful tool with which to measure the goals, achievements, and limitations of Thucydides and his Athenians. According to Althusser, ideology serves, above all, to reproduce exactly the means of production—to ensure that those in dominant positions hand on their privileges undiminished to their children, while the oppressed members of society never rise above their traditional status. In such a scheme, ideology can never be an obvious rationalization cynically exploited by a ruling class. Once the claims upon which privilege are based have been exposed as fictitious and self-serving, they lose their best protection and become powerful targets for resistance. If ideology is to be effective, it must be invisible.[17] "Ideologies are, after all, illusions that are outfitted with the power of common conviction."[18] As the feminist materialist Shakespearean critic, Jean E. Howard, puts it, ideology "is the obviousness of culture, what goes without saying, what is lived as true. It is therefore precisely not a set of beliefs known to be 'false' but cynically sold to others to hold them in an inferior position, nor does it originate from a conspiratorial power group (or author) bent on dominating or deceiving others."[19] Or, as Althusser remarks, "It is indeed a peculiarity of ideology that it imposes (without appearing to do so, since these are

---

16. For an example of extreme skepticism toward Thucydides, see Badian 1990, reprinted as Badian 1993, 125–162; also Hunter 1973.

17. Compare Gramsci (1971, 377), who distinguishes between "arbitrary" ideology, that can "create individual 'movements,' polemics and so on" and "ideologies that are historically necessary" and "create the terrain on which men move, acquire consciousness of their position, struggle, etc."

18. Habermas 1977, 22.

19. Howard 1991, 226.

'obviousnesses') obviousnesses as obviousnesses, which we cannot *fail to recognize* and before which we have the inevitable and natural reaction of crying out (aloud or in the 'still, small voice of conscience'): 'That's obvious! That's right! That's true!' "[20] Ideas that would have been ideological in this sense at certain periods include the following: "Some human beings are destined to be slaves," "European nations have a manifest duty to civilize and improve their less developed brethren," and "Women should devote themselves to child-rearing and other familial pursuits."

Thucydides rejected such fictions and euphemisms. His Athenians act as if they wished to do away with ideology altogether and conduct their affairs according to straightforward if harsh rules.[21] His Athenians call their rule a *turannis* and proudly abandon many illusions about the nature of their power. No extant Greek author before Thucydides had ever subjected human behavior to such cold, reductive analysis, and, for many, this "objectivity" has been Thucydides' distinguishing feature. To take one well-known scholar as an example, in her analysis of the Athenian speech at Thucydides 1.72–78, de Romilly gave eloquent expression to a common reception of this piece in particular and to the work of Thucydides in general. She calls attention to the "objective realism, which, fully recognising the more unfortunate aspects of Athenian imperialism, excuses them only by relating them to the needs inseparable from any imperialism."[22] Thucydides, in de Romilly's eyes, had transcended the particular conditions of his age and begun to work with the timeless truths of the human condition. For her, Thucydides was a kind of heroic realist and pioneering antecedent to the modern, scientific mind.

Thus Thucydides' Athenians do more than critique and break down the old truths that even Herodotus still inscribes in his work. If gratitude and loyalty are secondary emotions, if pity and fellow feeling are wasted, and if traditional justice is irrelevant in international affairs, the Athenians do not, like Jokasta at *Oedipus Rex* 979, fall back in despair and choose to "live at random," abandoning any hope for rationality. They

20. Althusser 1971, 172.
21. The limits of any such attempt to transcend ideology will be pursued during the course of this chapter; on Athenian ideologies, see Ober 1989, passim and esp. 332–333; Ober argues that the masses at Athens exercised "ideological hegemony" over the elite; for the utopian ideologies of the *Oresteia* and of the funeral oration as a genre, see Rose 1992, 185–265, and Loraux 1986a, 328–338.
22. De Romilly 1963, 271.

frame a new, deeply logical system based upon the principle that the strong rule the weak. In modern terms, they seek to ground their empire in natural law and, to this end, assume a transhistorically valid, universal human nature to which I will return in the final chapter.

But, of course, if we accept the view of ideology popularized by Althusser, we can see that the flight from ideology that Thucydides inscribes in his *History* is ultimately futile. More important, though, I argue that Althusserian ideology, with its need to be invisible and to disappear into accepted common sense, allows us to understand some of the unresolved tensions in the *History*.

Thucydides' Athenians never quite succeed in establishing the rule of the strong as an invisible, Althusserian ideology. However hard the Athenian representatives at Sparta in book 1, Cleon and Diodotus in book 3, and the Athenian commissioners on Melos in book 5 may argue, the natural rule of the strong never finds the kind of immediate and spontaneous acceptance that strict ideology should attain. There are always Melians or Syracusans who, with greater or lesser success, refuse to accept the Athenians' self-serving ideological pose.

My argument in general form traces the tension in Thucydides between the ideals toward which he struggled and the goals that he could achieve. For Leo Strauss, however, this tension lay in the gulf between the universalism of the city and the universalism of the *History*. As he puts it, "The longing for sempiternal and universal fame calls for boundless striving for ever more; it is wholly incompatible with moderation. The universalism of Athens, the universalism of the city . . . is doomed to failure. It points therefore to universalism of a different kind"[23] —the universalism of understanding that Thucydides inscribes in his *History*. Strauss continues: "The difference between the sempiternal Memorials of evil things and of good ones and the sempiternal possession which is useful points to the difference beween the brilliant and sham universalism of the city and the genuine universalism of understanding. For Thucydides bases his claim on behalf of his work on the fact that it brings to light the sempiternal and universal nature of man as the ground of the deeds, the speeches, and the thoughts which it records."

There are other points of view. Unlike Strauss, Hannah Arendt, for example, reveled in the vitality of the city—she reversed a traditional opposition of Western thought, subordinating the life of contemplation

23. Strauss 1964, 228.

to that life of action in which human beings define themselves by their
dealings with one another: in her view, the public sphere is the theater
of humankind's highest activities.[24] Arendt's work is especially interesting because she drew a broad distinction that sheds even greater light
upon the tension within the *History*. Thucydides' work occupies an
unstable, indeed uncomfortable, moment where an older force still exerts its pressure, but a newer, still inchoate, force has begun to make
itself felt. Simply put, Greeks had traditionally striven to approach,
insofar as the human condition would allow, that immortality that
their gods enjoyed. Arendt remarks: "By their capacity for the immor-
tal deed, by their ability to leave non-perishable traces behind, men,
their individual mortality notwithstanding, attain an immortality of
their own and prove themselves to be of 'divine' nature."[25] As much
as any figure in Greek literature—the Homeric Achilles not excepted—
Perikles gives eloquent expression to this passion for immortality, not
only in the Funeral Oration but in the heroic vision of Athenian greatness with which he departs from Thucydides' narrative. And Thucydides himself, in the opening pages of the *History*, asserts with transparent pride that Athens's achievement is real, that it requires no
flattering poets to justify its claim to immortality.

But, if, in his feel for immortality, Thucydides plays upon a deep
chord in Greek tradition, his work, albeit less tangibly, gropes toward
a newer vision, one to which Plato would give shape. Thucydides names
himself in the first sentence of the *History* and thus lays a claim to
immortality, but in struggling to efface himself as analyst and to serve
his readers as a pure, transparent lens onto events "as they really happened," he moves to reduce that immortality to an empty name, minimizing his personality and, insofar as he is successful in this project,
calling into question the meaning of that immortality. In fact, Thucydides strives for truth—not only what happened but why, not only the
"Is it true?" and the "Does it exist?" but the "why" and the "cause" to
which Aristotle gives fuller form in book 2 of the *Posterior Analytics*.
Both Thucydides and the Athenians whom he represents struggle to establish for themselves positions that stand beyond ideology. They labor
to ground their actions firmly in a natural law tied to an unchanging
human nature. In this, Thucydides and his Athenians strive to grasp
what Arendt termed "the eternal." Thucydides could go only so far if

24. Arendt 1958.
25. Arendt 1958, 19.

he was to write down his thoughts: "It is obvious that, no matter how concerned a thinker may be with eternity, the moment he sits down to write his thoughts he ceases to be concerned with eternity and shifts his attention to leaving some trace of them. He has entered the *vita activa* and chosen the way of permanence and potential immortality."[26]

But while Thucydides' striving for objectivity and universal knowledge may be clear, he was too honest to claim either that he had himself attained such a vision or even that the antiheroes who dominate his narrative, his Athenians, had established a true, what would once have been called scientific, understanding of events. Thus Thucydides' Athenians seek to annihilate those who disagree with them—the Melians, for example, must die because they refuse to accept the logic of Athenian imperialism and thus undermine the assertion that such imperialism is both natural and self-evident. Likewise, the new logic of power and self-interest proves as ambiguous as any Delphic oracle. In book 6, the Athenian Euphemos even presents us with a dazzling perversion of this logic, boldly adducing cold power politics to argue that Athens's interests in Sicily are limited—when in fact Thucydides' readers know that the Athenians are there to conquer the island. Euphemos's speech is ironic: although Euphemos is lying, his assessment of Athenian interests is actually accurate. The most prudent Athenian strategy would pursue limited goals in Sicily and keep forces potentially hostile to Athens tied up and unable to intervene on the Greek mainland. The consequences are significant. If there is indeed a natural law that governs human relations, no human actors in Thucydides—with the possible exception of Perikles—are able with any reliability to interpret where their true interests lie, and even with Perikles, the plague arrives to dramatize the problems inherent in the best rational planning. The rule of the strong and the pursuit of interest may constitute natural law, but this natural law produces no certainty.

Much of the best scholarship on Thucydides in this century, from Cornford's *Thucydides Mythistoricus* through John Finley's famous essays on Thucydides to Robert Connor's famous "postmodern" Thucydides and Simon Hornblower's emphasis on Thucydides' emotional power,[27] has constituted a reaction against the scientific, even cold,

---

26. Arendt 1958, 20–21.

27. Cornford 1907; Finley 1967; Connor 1977a; Connor 1984; Hornblower 1987; see now also Walker 1993; Howie 1984 is a particularly thorough examination that reads the

Thucydides of scholars such as Charles Cochrane, Jacqueline de Romilly, and F. E. Adcock.[28] Thucydides the Hippokratic observer and Thucydides the proto-Euclid have exerted rather less of a hold upon recent
scholarly imaginations. Nevertheless, these analogies, though inexact,
do capture a crucial element of the Thucydidean project. Like Lowell
Edmunds,[29] I attempt to take seriously Thucydides' quest for objectivity and to treat it as something other than merely an authorial pose.

Nowhere in the exact sciences does any thinker take a greater leap in
the direction of reductive analysis than Thucydides. Operating without
any mathematical models and with only the most rudimentary numerical measures, Thucydides applies a small but powerful set of rules to
human events and, in so doing, transformed his understanding of events.
Two ideas play a particularly crucial role. First, the powerful naturally
dominate the weak, and, second, essential human nature—"the human
thing," as Marc Cogan has neatly rendered it—remains the same in all
cultures and at all times. Thucydides did not discover these principles
(his speakers often refer to it as a piece of general knowledge, and it
certainly influenced Herodotus), but, for better or for worse,[30] he perfected them as an analytical tool and refined them to an unprecedented
and still unsurpassed degree. Much of the *History* is devoted to working
out these ideas, and Thucydides' Athenians are, in some sense, his av-
atars, testing these principles against the different situations that crop
up during the course of the war.

Thus whatever Periklean Athens may have contributed to Hannah
Arendt's vision of a humane society, the universal glory of Athens is, as
Leo Strauss argued a generation ago, in Thucydides' *History*, an illusion.
The great Athenian achievement was not the empire and its fleeting tem-
poral authority (both rather modest achievements by the standards of
the ancient Near East), but the intellectual adventure of Thucydides'
History and of the historian's Athenians as they labor to construct a

---

Archaeology against Pindar and explicates Thucydides' relationship to his Panhellenic
Greek audience.

    28. Cochrane 1929, passim; de Romilly 1963, 271–272; Adcock 1963, 3.

    29. See Edmunds 1993 (which was actually submitted in finished form in 1988).

    30. On the ambiguity of Thucydides' achievement, see, for example, Hornblower
(1987, 30), who points out that Thucydides' influence was "in one way . . . also profoundly
damaging because . . . it was Thucydides who by his influential practice ordained that
history should henceforth be primarily a matter of war and politics"; on the general dominance of the Thucydidean (vs. the Herodotean) model of history, see Lateiner 1989, 220–
224; Momigliano 1990, 44–48 (who is somewhat more cautious).

perfect, Archimedian vantage point from which to understand the world.[31] Fewer scholars would probably accept this praise at face value now than thirty years ago when Strauss first published *The City and Man*. I have no intention of lauding Thucydides for a perfect objectivity to which he never laid claim or of undercutting him for pursuing a chimerical goal. I seek to emphasize at once both the boldness of his objectives and the degree to which he ruthlessly includes in his own narratives the problems and contradictions that he never resolved. Long before Descartes established doubt as the only certainty, Thucydides sensed that "even if there is no truth, man can be truthful, and even if there is no reliable certainty, man can be reliable."[32] No writer ever worked harder to achieve that Archimedian position. No writer ever understood more deeply the impossibility of that quest.

In the first two chapters of this book, I attempt to frame Thucydides within the modern school of realist thought. Machiavelli and Hobbes are regularly enlisted as intermediaries who, closer to us in time and culture than Thucydides, serve to bring the *History* into focus. While I will have occasional recourse to these benchmark figures, I have chosen as a bridge William Tecumseh Sherman, the Union general who earned fame both as a strategist for his daring march from Atlanta to the sea and as a major figure in the development of modern war. I mean, in part, to address a standard bias against figures such as Sherman in the study of *Realpolitik*—the British major general and military historian J. F. C. Fuller argued that European disinterest in the American Civil War generally, and in the achievements of men like Sherman in particular, had contributed substantially to the slaughter of the "European Civil War," as he termed World War I in 1932.[33] At the same time, not only does Sherman offer a surprisingly close point of comparison—both he and Thucydides were conservatives, generals, and authors who helped change the way in which their contemporaries conceptualized armed struggle—but his memoirs also include a strong parallel to one of the most often quoted sections of Thucydides' *History*.

The second chapter sets the stage for much of the remaining discussion, identifying Thucydides as a "realist" in the most general terms—

---

31. So Strauss 1964, 226–236; such an Archimedian point of view is, even insofar as we can realize it, not without its problems: see Arendt 1958, 257–268.
32. Arendt 1958, 279.
33. Fuller 1957, 8, 43–50.

for there are scientific, literary, and artistic as well as political realisms—
and then moving on to those features of Thucydides' work that have
inspired a number of contemporary political theorists to see in this Athenian author the forerunner of their own school of thought.

In chapter 3, I survey the raw cultural materials on which Thucydides
would later build. I begin, however, not with the sophists of the fifth
century but with the discourses of absolute power that appear already
in Homer and Hesiod. Then, to illustrate the contemporary model of
authority that Thucydides would reject, I turn to Herodotus and his
subtly normative account of Sparta's rise in book 1 of the *Histories*.
Even as Herodotus attributes to the Spartans a leading position in the
Greek world, he builds into his account conditions and limitations on
Sparta's authority that both empower and constrain Sparta. For Herodotus, Sparta is a hegemonistic power, whose authority depends in large
measure on the fact that it has only a limited will and ability to project
power beyond its borders. Xenophon, however, writing in the fourth
century and influenced by Thucydides' account of the Peloponnesian
War, has a very different model of Sparta. For Xenophon, Sparta defines
itself. It does not depend so much upon the consent of its fellow Greeks
as upon its ability to project military force and thus to compel respect.
The change in attitude reflects the extent to which Thucydides had
helped develop a new paradigm for power and authority.

In chapter 4, I argue that the debate between the Corcyraeans and
the Corinthians at Athens is programmatic. First, the Corcyraean and
Corinthian representatives illustrate the dynamics of gift and countergift
as well as the value attached to gratitude and to accumulating over long
periods of time moral debts on which individual subjects or whole city-
states could draw. Thucydides' speakers deftly articulate this personalized system of interstate relations, with its roots in the alliances that
bound aristocratic families. These ideas, however, enter the narrative
only to be discarded. Athens ignores the old conventions to which Corcyraeans and Corinthians alike point and demonstrates at the start of
the *History* that it is a new kind of state with a different paradigm for
human relations. Where the Corcyraeans and the Corinthians see exchanges as embedded in long-term, ideally affective relationships, the
Athenians analyze their dealings with other states as if they were simple
market transactions: short-term exchanges that are unaffected by past
dealings and that do not institute any new social relationships.

In subsequent chapters, I demonstrate that Thucydides uses much of
book 1 to flesh out, in programmatic fashion, the revisionist principles

that shape his work.[34] In chapter 5 I trace not only the explicit conclusions of the Archaeology but the implications of Thucydides' method. Thucydides marginalizes the importance of agriculture and of all material production. For him, the rise of agriculture and other arts is not the beginning of human civilization (as it is for other authors of the fifth century). Rather, he takes small farming and basic production as a given that has limited value of its own. For Thucydides, political stability is the true source of prosperity. Human society did not develop because of material technology, but because powerful rulers were periodically able to yoke ever larger groups of states together into well-ordered imperial units. Thucydides' Archaeology presents a world in which city-states are quarrelsome, unfit to govern themselves in isolation and unable to provide that order that is the only true basis for human prosperity. Even as he explicitly revises many traditional ideas that classical Greeks held about their past, he implicitly constructs a world in which empire, *archê*, is necessary and beneficial. The Solonic ideal of balanced production and consumption—the ideal model for maintaining a consistent number of small farmers—yields to the acquisitive logic of empire, for paradoxically empires alone can provide a world in which the small farmers can enjoy their quiet, "steady-state" lives.

In chapter 6, I explore further the new paradigm of wealth that, for Thucydides, shapes events during the Peloponnesian War. I also examine the system of symbolic capital that had dominated traditional Greek relations. Lacking developed and pervasive financial institutions, there were few ways in which accumulated wealth could "bear interest" and grow. Where modern capital is invested and yields a return that augments its value over time, Greeks had traditionally invested surplus wealth as gifts by which to establish alliances and friendships both at home and abroad—a scheme that Pierre Bourdieu has popularized with the phrase "symbolic capital." Such networks of gift and countergift, which were often treated as family treasures and maintained over generations, constituted a powerful store of wealth on which Greeks could draw in times of need. For Thucydides, however, the Athenian empire was a radical departure: while not a financial institution per se, the Athenian empire was a social formation that not only supported itself with money (only tribute made the vast Athenian fleet feasible) but also, because the tribute was greater than the peacetime expenses of maintaining

---

34. On the complex structure of book 1, see now Ellis 1991.

the empire, provided Athens with a steady flow of surplus wealth. This imperial system was so powerful that, at least in Thucydides' view, it upset the traditional balance between repression and ideology: the Athenians no longer felt the same need to advance arguments with their subjects or to wrestle with them in contests for moral high ground. If the allies sought to break off their relations with Athens or to withhold tribute, the Athenians could bring overwhelming naval power to bear. Where Sparta had exercised hegemony over its allies, Athens had constructed a system that could support domination and convert allies into subjects.

In chapter 7, I pursue the consequences for human relations of the power politics described in chapter 4. The traditional language of friendship and reciprocity is found throughout key passages of the *History*, but Thucydides gives his own slant to these traditional ideas. He introduces the mechanisms and assumptions of symbolic capital in order to demonstrate the inadequacy of such conceptual tools. In particular, the often overlooked Mytilenean speech at 3.9–14 articulates a radical reassessment of the limits on friendship. Furthermore, the critique of reciprocal relations that runs throughout the *History* is crucial to our understanding of the eloquent Spartan offer of peace in book 4. Where the Spartans muster a sophisticated argument for the Athenians to show generosity and earn symbolic capital, the *History* as a whole and even the Spartan argument itself undercut the strength of such claims.

In chapter 8, I examine the dilemma that Athens, this new kind of power, constitutes for Sparta, the traditionalist leading state in Greece. Two distinct Spartan types—the old king Archidamos and the blunt government official Sthenelaidas—argue over how best to confront Athens. Both men recognize the dangers that Athens poses to Sparta's position in the Greek world, but each stresses a different side of the problem. Archidamos clearly understands the fundamental difference between Athenian power, with its roots in the empire and in the coercive extraction of wealth by which to maintain a near-professional military force, and Spartan authority, with its reliance upon consensus and upon the willing support of many disparate and touchy allies. Archidamos argues that Sparta should wait before declaring war and accumulate financial reserves of its own. Sthenelaidas, by contrast, delivers a brief but furious harangue in which he calls for immediate action. Scholarly opinion has sided almost unanimously with Archidamos, but I emphasize the degree to which Sthenelaidas stresses a critical aspect of Sparta's position: whatever Sparta's financial reserves, it depends first and foremost upon the respect, more or less freely given, of its many allies. Because Spartan power is qualitatively different from that of Athens, the Spartans must act decisively to dramatize their continuing good faith. The two men thus articulate two sides of a dilemma to which no good solution existed—in Thucydides' eyes, the ultimate Spartan victory was an accident, more the consequence of Athenian errors than of Spartan strength.

With chapter 9, I turn from the Spartans to the Athenians and specifically to the transitional position that they occupy in Thucydides. Athens may, as the Corinthians at 1.68–71 eloquently assert, represent a new kind of power, but this supposed newness has its own history, The Athenians, who, in the name of imperial policy, scorn the heroic defense of freedom, crush Melos, and massacre the population, had themselves established their position in the Greek world by standing up to the Persians in a hopeless cause on behalf of freedom. The parallels between the Athenian position in the Melian Dialogue and the Athenian refusal in Herodotus to accept generous terms from Xerxes illustrate the development that Thucydides posits in his narrative.

The Athenian position is not, however, completely negative, and in chapter 10, I consider the ideology of power that Thucydides' Athenians attempt to construct. Thucydides' Athenians continue to mention the Persian Wars, but the lessons that they draw from these events are very different from those that we find elsewhere. These Athenians have no interest in the morality of their grandfathers' stand against Persia. For them, success against the Persians simply testifies to Athenian military power and resolve. The Greeks should study the Persian Wars well, but only so that they can learn to fear Athenian prowess. Athenian courage and virtue have little intrinsic value and matter only insofar as they contribute to victory. Nevertheless, Thucydides includes clear evidence for the limitations on such a calculus of power. All states may pursue their interests, but the true best interest of Athens is not always clear ahead of time. The Athenian speaker Euphemos and the dialogue at Melos each bring out different problems for this reductionist perspective.

The concluding chapter moves from Thucydides' Athenians to Thucydides himself. The greatest strengths of Thucydides' narrative are also among its greatest weaknesses. On the one hand, he fashioned a model that not only proved extraordinarily compelling and powerful for the events of his own time but also laid the foundations for a realist paradigm that still exerts force today. At the same time, however, Thucydides was able to see some elements by ignoring others: he introduces biases into his work that distract our readerly gaze away from other crucial forces; he creates a story about the decline of Athenian civil society that converts a contested and at best temporary Periklean model of citizenship into a timeless myth; he attempts, I believe, to reconstruct the aristocratic ideology—that "ancient simplicity" to which he was born and in which he was raised—according to the constraints of a more "rational" (or at least more cynical) age but fails to establish that synthesis. Plato would make the pursuit of this synthesis his life's work, but Plato, if he has achieved an even more prominent position in the Western canon, did so by leaving the "real world" behind. Thucydides, more than any extant Greek thinker before him, balanced the general and the particular, following the phenomena wherever they led and refusing to give in to one side or the other. Thucydides never achieved a stable balance—for intellectual closure in human affairs is, of course, an impossibility—but he participated in, and indeed helped fashion, a practice of observation and analysis that we still pursue to this day.

CHAPTER I

Sherman at Melos

Realpolitik Ancient and Modern

> It is more shameful for those who enjoy a good reputation at
> any rate to pursue greed under fair-seeming deception than
> with open violence.
>
> *Brasidas at Thucydides 4.86.6*

"War is cruelty, and you cannot refine it"—it would be difficult to render
this remark exactly into the classical Greek of Thucydides and his contemporaries. A pejorative term, its semantic content shaped by Judaeo-
Christian values, "cruelty" describes a wanton and useless pleasure in
inflicting pain. To refine war, one would, in the usage of the statement's
author, have to render it gentlemanly, to civilize it and make it conform
to Judaeo-Christian values. Nevertheless, William Tecumseh Sherman,
general of the Union army and victor over Atlanta, the "father" of total
warfare, here approaches the spirit, and even the rough aphoristic style,
of his fellow (if decidedly less successful) general Thucydides, the father
of "political realism." If one had to choose a single sentence to characterize Thucydides, Sherman's remark would serve well.

While Machiavelli and Hobbes often serve as reference points for
students of Thucydides, Sherman's memoirs also provide a useful starting point for this analysis of Thucydides. The American general is a good
deal closer to most modern readers in time and in cultural background.
Much of this book will, of necessity, situate Thucydides within a modern
academic framework, but Thucydides was no professor, and he had far
more in common with a Sherman than with those of us who make our
livings as professional students of the past. Each man wrote about a war
in which he had personally participated: Thucydides did most of his
work in exile after the Athenian people had driven him in disgrace from
his home city; Sherman published his memoirs in 1875 when he was

fifty-five, just eleven years after his dramatic capture of Atlanta had restored flagging Union spirits, diverted attention from Grant's bloody and stalled approach to Richmond, assured Lincoln's reelection, and played a decisive role in preserving the Union. Like the elite among Thucydides' Athenians, Sherman faced opponents who shared his language and many of his upper-class values. The Athenian Perikles, for example, was the official "guest-friend" of the Spartan king (Thuc. 2.13), and Thucydides, once exile had removed him from an active part in the war, mingled freely with participants on both sides (5.26.5); in the American Civil War, most of the senior commanders on both sides were West Point graduates who knew each other, directly or indirectly, through service in the Mexican War and the prewar "regular" army.

Each man struggled to preserve the world into which he had been born. Sherman was an avowed admirer of the South and accepted without question the ideology of white superiority common at the time. Thucydides' relationship to the traditional elites of the Greek world is more complex, but I believe that, in demystifying many of the fictions of his time, he was struggling to preserve and reestablish in more defensible form that "ancient simplicity" whose demise he laments at 3.83.1. Sherman sought only to restore the Union and to return the country to a "normalcy" that the Civil War in general and his own tactics in particular buried forever. Placed on the shelf at what proved to be a relatively early stage of the conflict, Thucydides had no direct influence upon events, but he struggled in his brilliantly original, willfully selective, and obstinately biased history to reconcile the naked pursuit of interest with the soothing fictions of the archaic Greek elite.[1] Thucydides was much more successful at debunking the old than in establishing a new set of values—the latter task fell to Plato, who would devote his life to reconciling the ideas of the Greek aristocracy with the rationalistic attitudes of the later fifth century.

But it is as a thinker and observer of events that Sherman deserves particular comparison with Thucydides. At times, Sherman's memoirs approach the ruthless candor with which Thucydides' Athenians articulate their peculiarly rationalized attitude toward force in human affairs. Like Thucydides' Athenians, Sherman was willing to express clearly the logic of warfare. Like Thucydides' Athenians, Sherman laid claim to a

---

1. The biases of Thucydides' history are a major theme of Crane 1996a; two aspects of the ancient world that Thucydides clearly marginalized are the roles of women and of religion, on which, see, for example, Cartledge 1993 and Hornblower 1992.

savagery without passion. Neither applied violence indiscriminately. Their adversaries could come to moderate terms and live with dignity. Most important, like Thucydides' Athenians, Sherman lived in a society that had changed profoundly, and whose changes dictated a revision in the ideology of force: Thucydides understood that monetary exchange had seriously undercut the traditional aristocratic webs of familial ties while the imperial mechanisms of Athens and the development of Athenian democracy had undercut the role of a hegemonic power such as Sparta; Sherman was not the first to confront an entire population "in arms"—Napoleon and the French *levée en masse* had made this strategy familiar—but the presence of railroads, the gross productivity of American industry, and the perfected rifle forced him to rethink tactics and strategy alike. Sherman's success made him famous as a father of "modern" warfare. Thucydides, on the other hand, became the first "realist" thinker in international relations. Sherman was more accomplished as a writer and thinker than Thucydides was as a general, but concrete experiences drove both men to deep and extended analyses of force, justice, and society. And yet, both men were shrewd observers of their times, and, in Sherman's case at least, conclusions from experience had an immediate impact on hundreds of thousands.

Whether or not Sherman read Thucydides at West Point (he probably didn't—the United States military academy was an outstanding school for engineers but devoted surprisingly little time to history),[2] his attitude toward the use of power and the practice of warfare owes much to the tradition that Thucydides inaugurated. One can, of course, trace a line from Melos, where the Athenians annihilated the entire population of a small island, to Sherman's devastating march through the heart of the Confederacy to the firestorms caused by Allied bombing in Dresden and Tokyo that incinerated tens of thousands of children, women, and noncombatants: military necessity, coolly articulated, served to justify ancient and modern actions alike. Indeed, Thucydides continues to occupy a privileged position as the first serious text on international relations and the founding document of the "classical realist" tradition that is exemplified by Machiavelli, Hobbes, Morgenthau, and Kissinger.[3] Within this tradition, Sherman, practitioner and even theorist of

2. Morrison 1986.
3. See, for example, Thucydides' place in such surveys of international relations theory as Votti and Kauppi 1987, 78–84; Vasquez 1990, 16–20; and Knutsen 1992, 30–33.

total war, offers a useful bridge between classical Greece and the late twentieth century.

In particular, Sherman's memoirs include a remarkable exchange of letters that, in spirit and form, comes surprisingly close to Thucydides' Melian Dialogue. For ancient historians, such documentary evidence from a later period serves as a control, reminding us that odd things really do occur. Thucydides does not even pretend that the speeches in his history are precise transcripts. At best, they approach the general spirit of what was said on a given occasion (Thuc. 1.22). Some, however, have gone so far as to doubt whether every speech in Thucydides actually had a historical counterpart. The Melian Dialogue has seemed to one recent commentator too dramatic and stagy to have actually taken place.[4] Improbable discussions do take place, though. The study of ancient history is, in large measure, an exercise in reconstruction, where we necessarily extrapolate to fill in gaps according to our views of what is probable (*kata to eikos*, as the intellectuals of the fifth century put it). In so doing, we run the risk of flattening out events, projecting onto them a predictability that accords too closely with our own assumptions, and retrospectively writing out of history that randomness that baffles all who gaze forward. Specific incidents from better-documented periods are an important corrective, for they direct our attention to the oddities that in fact occur and that shape many events.

As soon as Sherman had captured Atlanta—then a strategic city within the Confederacy—he resolved to "evacuate" ("expel" might be a better term) the civilian population. He complained that he "had seen Memphis, Vicksburg, Natchez, and New Orleans, all captured from the enemy, and each at once was garrisoned by a full division of troops, if not more; so that success was actually crippling our armies in the field." Sherman knew that this move would be unpopular, and on September 4, 1864, he wrote to H. W. Halleck, the Union chief of staff, warning about the reaction in his characteristically aphoristic style: "If the people raise a howl against my barbarity and cruelty, I will answer that war is war, and not popularity-seeking. If they want peace, they and their relatives must stop the war."[5]

Sherman's expectations proved correct. Although he offered to supply

---

4. E.g., Rusten 1989, 15: "In the Melian dialogue the speakers are anonymous, the occasion private (Thucydides was by then in exile in any case), and the sentiments impersonal; it would be difficult to claim that it is not entirely ficitious."
5. Sherman 1984, 2: 111.

food and transportation to Atlanta for refugees who chose to go north, the forced evacuation of Atlanta provoked outrage. His Confederate counterpart, General John Bell Hood, who had finished last in his class at West Point in ethics,[6] nevertheless castigated Sherman with Melian boldness, provoking an extraordinary exchange of letters that ultimately involved the mayor and city council of Atlanta as well. Hood saw in this exchange an opportunity to score rhetorical points, and he accordingly annoyed Sherman by publishing their letters in a newspaper.[7] After the war, Sherman exacted his own revenge by including this exchange within his memoirs, where they are framed by a cover letter from Sherman to Halleck and Halleck's reply, supporting Sherman's action.

These letters synthesize florid nineteenth-century rhetoric with cool calculation of power and interest. In particular, Sherman's language and thought approach the candor and brilliance of the Athenian representatives at Melos. At the same time, Hood's rhetoric recalls, with its appeals to human and divine right in the face of implacable force, the arguments of his Melian counterparts, the members of the local elite (Thuc. 5.84.3), who saw fit to impose their high-minded ideas on the population as a whole. If Hood's sentiments had appeared in the work of an ancient historian, many of us would have assumed that they were a complete fabrication, arguing that no one could seriously have expressed them. The speech would, most likely, be judged a cumbersome literary addition or, if genuinely delivered, proof that the speaker was (as some have called the Melians) naive. But Hood was neither a neophyte nor a rear-echelon staff officer. His combat service included Antietam, one of the bloodiest battles that human beings, until that time, had ever fought. At Gettysburg, he was severely wounded, but within three months he returned to fight, only to be wounded again, losing his right leg to a standardly horrific amputation of the period. By the time he faced Sherman, his aides had to strap him to his horse to ride amidst his army.

When, on September 7, 1864, Sherman announced his determination to empty Atlanta of its civilian population, his offer of aid to refugees did little to soften Hood's reaction. In his letter of September 9, Hood

---

6. McMurry 1982, 13.

7. Hood was famous as a fighting general with uneven judgment on most matters, and it is not clear that the publication of these letters was much of a public relations success: a sympathetic biographer passes quickly over this "undignified correspondence" (McMurry 1982, 157).

could not resist grasping for the moral high ground. After dealing with
the logistics of the evacuation, Hood continues: "And now, sir, permit
me to say that the unprecedented measure you propose transcends, in
studied and ingenious cruelty, all acts ever before brought to my attention in the dark history of war." This rather colorful judgment may make
one wonder what military history Hood had actually studied when he
was at West Point.[8] All the same, Hood had certainly composed his
rhetorical exercises in school, and he concludes this letter: "In the name
of God and humanity, I protest, believing that you will find that you are
expelling from their homes and firesides the wives and children of a
brave people. I am, general, very respectfully, your obedient servant."[9]

Confident as Sherman may have been—basking in the glow of his
recent victory, he was easily the most popular man in the Union—he
refused to let Hood's remarks pass. Sherman expresses nothing but ir-
ritation at the sanctimonious appeals of his weaker adversary. On September 10, Sherman responded: "In the name of common-sense, I ask
you not to appeal to a just God in such a sacrilegious manner. You who,
in the midst of peace and prosperity, have plunged a nation into war—
dark and cruel war—who dared and badgered us to battle." He continues with a list of offences that he charges against the Confederacy and
concludes: "Talk thus to the Marines but not to me, who have seen these
things, and who will this day make as much sacrifice for the peace and
honor of the South as the best-born Southerner among you! If we must
be enemies, let us be men, and fight it out as we propose to do, and not
deal in such hypocritical appeals to God and humanity. God will judge
us in due time, and he will pronounce whether it be more humane to
fight with a town full of women and the families of a brave people at
our back, or to remove them in time to places of safety among their own
friends and people."[10]

Compare the Athenian envoys as they set the terms for the Melian
Dialogue:

> For ourselves, we shall not trouble you with specious pretences (*onomata
> kala*)—either of how we have a right to our empire because we overthrew

---

8. In fact, history played a relatively minor role at West Point, which concentrated on
math and engineering. On the curriculum when Hood was a student, see Morrison 1986,
160–163. Even if Hood had studied a great deal of history, it would probably have mattered little, as he had little affinity for academic work, graduating at the bottom of his
class (forty-fourth of fifty-two).
9. Sherman 1984, 2: 119.
10. Sherman 1984, 2: 120.

the Persians, or are now attacking you because of wrong that you have done us—and make a long speech that would not be believed; and in return we hope that you, instead of thinking to influence us by saying that you did not join the Spartans, although their colonists, or that you have done us no wrong, will aim at what is feasible, holding in view the real sentiments of us both; since you know as well as we do that right, as the world goes, is only in question between equals in power, while the strong do what they can and the weak suffer what they must.

Thuc. 5.89

Unlike the Athenians, Sherman, of course, is anxious to justify himself and unwilling to abandon considerations of morality. Sherman expresses outrage at Hood's appeals to "God and humanity" because Hood, he argues, is at fault, but the exasperation at Hood's moral posturing is very Thucydidean: Sherman's phrase "talk thus to the Marines but not to me" is not so very far from the Athenian insistence that "the strong do what they can and the weak suffer what they must." Were Sherman writing in Greek, the Thucydidean phrase "basing your observations on the facts themselves" (1.21.2: *ap' autôn tôn ergôn skopousi*) would capture the spirit of Sherman's argument, as he lists one piece of evidence after another.

On September 11, the mayor of Atlanta and two members of the city council signed a letter in which they modestly begged Sherman to reconsider his decision.[11] Hood, however, evidently could not let the matter rest, and he refused to back down. Like the aristocratic Melian representatives before him, Hood felt free to claim divine protection and to volunteer the lives of all those under his care—women and children included. He answered Sherman on September 12 with a letter that covers three pages of small print in Sherman's memoirs. It concludes with sentiments that would have earned applause from Thucydides' Melians: "You say, 'Let us fight it out like men.' To this my reply is—for myself, and I believe for all the true men, ay, and women and children, in my country—we will fight you to the death! Better die a thousand deaths than submit to live under you or your Government and your negro allies!"[12] Hood insists upon divine favor for his righteous cause: "Having answered the points forced upon me by your letter of the 9th of September, I close this correspondence with you; and, *notwithstanding your comments upon my appeal to God in the cause of humanity*, I again

11. Sherman 1984, 2: 124–125.
12. Sherman 1984, 2: 124.

humbly and reverently invoke his almighty aid in defense of justice and right."[13]

I have emphasized Hood's explicit refusal to give in to Sherman's withering sarcasm because the Athenian cynicism at 5.89 similarly cannot squelch Melian calls to justice and the gods. Thus the Melians remark at 5.104: "You may be sure that we are as well aware as you of the difficulty of contending against your power and fortune, unless the terms be equal. *But we trust that the gods may grant us fortune as good as yours, since we are just men fighting against unjust.*" The argument continues for several more exchanges before the Melians conclude their case with a final appeal to the morality and gods whom their Athenian counterparts have sought to rule out: "Our resolution, Athenians, is the same as it was at first. We will not in a moment deprive of freedom a city that has been inhabited these seven hundred years; but we put our trust in the fortune by which the gods have preserved it until now, and in the help of men, that is, of the Lakedaimonians; and so we will try and save ourselves." Within the context of Thucydides' calculatedly understated and restrained language, the Melian conclusion is as florid as Hood's.

Sherman wasted little additional time on Hood—a relatively brief note with final arguments on September 14 ends his correspondence on the matter. With the civilian representatives of the city, however, he took greater pains. He addressed to them a letter of which Thucydides' Athenians might well have approved:

> Gentlemen: I have your letter of the 11th, in the nature of a petition to revoke my orders to remove all the inhabitants from Atlanta. I have read it carefully, and give full credit to the distress that will be occasioned, and yet shall not revoke my orders, because they are not designed to meet the humanities of the case, but to prepare for the future struggles in which millions of good people outside of Atlanta have a deep interest.[14]

Sherman makes no attempt to deny the hardships that his order will cause. The "humanities of the case" are noted and dismissed. The "deep interest" of "millions of good people outside of Atlanta" takes precedence. Sherman goes on to clarify what he means with a string of syllogisms that explain the use of force. His explanation is one that Thucydides' Perikles or Athenian representatives at Sparta might have endorsed:

13. Sherman 1984, 2: 124 (italics mine).
14. Sherman 1984, 2: 125.

We must have peace, not only in Atlanta but in all America. To secure this, we must stop the war that now desolates our once happy and favored country. To stop the war, we must defeat the rebel armies which are arrayed against the laws and Constitution that all must respect and obey. To defeat those armies, we must prepare the way to reach them in their recesses, provided with arms and instruments which enable us to accomplish our purpose.[15]

Atlanta, he argues, may need to serve as a military center for years to come, and there will be no way to support a civilian population over the long term. "Why not go now, when all the arrangements are complete for the transfer, instead of waiting til the plunging shot of contending armies will renew the scenes of the past month?"[16]

The sympathy that Sherman expresses does not change his resolve, but it does exert tremendous pressure upon him. The great personal irony of Sherman's career was that he loved the South and had many close friends from that region. Immediately before the war, he had served as president of a small military institute that would later become Louisiana State University. He supported slavery, left the South with only the greatest sadness, and fought the Confederates with mixed feelings throughout the war. And although Sherman became the most hated man in Southern history—in fact, the enmity toward Sherman in many quarters survives undiminished to this day—the mild terms of surrender that he exacted at the war's close outraged many Unionists. Years later, his most distinguished Confederate opponent, General Johnston, insisted on appearing bareheaded at Sherman's funeral, just five weeks before his own death.[17]

But if Sherman's divided personal feelings did not soften his actions, they seem to have forced him, like Thucydides, to reflect passionately upon the nature and meaning of war. Tall, thin, red-haired, heavily wrinkled, and nervous—always pacing back and forth, dashing about the front on horseback, scattering ashes as he brandished the cigars that he smoked one after the other—Sherman's mind was constantly at work, and we can see in the remainder of this letter of September 14 the synthesis that he struggled to maintain and by which he attempted to reconcile his humane longings with the ferocity of his military practice:

You cannot qualify war in harsher terms than I will. War is cruelty and you cannot refine it; and those who brought war into our country deserve all the

15. Sherman 1984, 2: 125–126.
16. Sherman 1984, 2: 126.
17. Howard 1971, 2: 544–547.

curses and maledictions a people can pour out. I know I had no hand in
making this war, and I know that I will make more sacrifices today than any
of you to secure peace. But you cannot have peace and a division of our
country. If the United States submits to division now, it will not stop, but
will go on until we reap the fate of Mexico, which is eternal war. The United
States does and must assert its authority, wherever it once had power; for, if
it relaxes one bit to pressure, it is gone, and I believe that such is the national
feeling.[18]

Like Hobbes, Sherman saw conflict as humanity's natural state and thus
passionately desired order.[19] When Sherman argues that without the Union the United States would dissolve and the result would be "the fate
of Mexico, which is eternal war," he might have been paraphrasing the
famous thirteenth chapter of *Leviathan*, where Hobbes speaks fearfully
of "that condition which is called Warre; and such a warre, as is of every
man, against every man." Like Thucydides' Athenians with their emphasis on fear, honor, and advantage (1.76), Sherman emphasized the
overwhelming forces that constrain human behavior.

Sherman can do nothing else to express his sympathies for the displaced citizens of Atlanta, but he can, like Achilles before Lykaon (Hom.
Il. 21.99–113) and Hesiod's Hawk before the Nightingale (Hes. *WD*
203–212), seek to place the harsh reality of the moment in its more
general context, offering grandeur of vision as a cold anodyne for present pain:

You might as well appeal against the thunder-storm as against these terrible
hardships of war. They are inevitable, and the only way the people of Atlanta
can hope once more to live in peace and quiet at home, is to stop the war,
which can only be done by admitting that it began in error and is perpetuated
in pride.[20]

There is even continuity in the imagery. Patroklos excoriates Achilles for
his coldness to the Greeks: "Harsh one, the horseman Peleus was no
father to you, nor was Thetis your mother. Rather, it was the grey sea
and the jagged rocks, since your mind is unbending" (Hom. *Il.* 16.33–
35).

Achilles, of course, yielded—and, in so doing, he lost Patroklos and
ceased himself to value his own life. He rose to an unprecedented degree

18. Sherman 1984, 2: 125–126.
19. The most recent biography of Sherman, Marszalek 1993, bears the subtitle *A Soldier's Passion for Order*.
20. Sherman 1984, 2: 126.

of fury as he attempted—vainly—to assuage his grief. He cut down every Trojan that he confronted, hunted down Hektor, even slaughtered, in cold blood, Trojan prisoners at the funeral of Patroklos, and then subsided, at once exhausted and forbidding. Sherman, however, did not inhabit an epic poem, and he did not yield. He left Atlanta in flames and drove his army through the South, pursuing over hundreds of miles a campaign of organized pillage and destruction.

Sherman pursued his strategy of total warfare relentlessly, but with remorse as well. The restless general could not help but plead for peace and insist that his cruelty was the limited product of war and not of his own character:

> I want peace, and believe it can only be reached through union and war, and I will ever conduct war with a view to perfect and early success. But, my dear sirs, when peace does come, you may call on me for anything. Then will I share with you the last cracker, and watch with you to shield your homes and families against danger from every quarter.[21]

Sherman was desperately anxious that the war, cruel as it may have been, not destroy the bonds of society. Strictly speaking, Sherman did not pursue total warfare: he did believe that this war was being waged "by total populations" and thus needed to be directed "against total populations." But, unlike the Athenians at Melos, Sherman refused to take the final step and wage "war for total stakes."[22] He seems to have sensed that this step lay just before him and to have profoundly feared its consequences. Sherman could not leave Hood's charge unanswered, not only because he understood full well what he was doing—what he felt needed to be done—but also because he clearly sensed that logical extension to his actions that he refused to pursue. He holds fast to the rhetoric of Christianity, and he challenges Hood to stand beside him for divine judgment.[23] The rebels had begun their war "in error" and continued it "in pride." Sherman insists that he, far more than anyone on the rebel side, is the champion of peace. If Sherman were not to pursue his ruthless course of action, society itself might collapse into a Hobbesian jungle, and any action to prevent such a catastrophe was moral. At the same time, war was dangerous and always carried with it the threat

---

21. Sherman 1984, 2: 127.
22. For the triad, war of total populations, against total populations, and for total stakes, see Morgenthau 1948, 289–301.
23. Sherman 1984, 2: 120.

that violence—Thucydides calls war a "violent teacher"—would destroy the society that the war was supposed to preserve.

Sherman insists that his actions do not, in fact, represent a radical departure from past practice. If Sherman lays waste every factory and farm that he can find, he does what the "rebels have done, not only in Maryland and Pennsylvania, but also in Virginia and other rebel States, when compelled to fall back before our armies."[24] He makes a point of stating that a Union colonel and his Confederate counterpart who arranged a prisoner exchange "harmonized perfectly, and parted good friends when their work was done."[25] Brief as his final letter to Hood may be, he still feels compelled to make two points. He denies that he has with him any "negro allies"—Sherman supported slavery—and he defensively insists that he did not violate the rules of civilized behavior: "I was not bound by the laws of war to give notice of the shelling of Atlanta, a 'fortified town, with magazines, arsenals, founderies, and public stores;' you were bound to take notice. See the books."[26] As Sherman clung fast to his partial vision of total warfare, the people that his armies controlled seemed to change from marauding guerrillas to regular troops to women and children—even to friends, classmates from West Point, and former students whom he had taught before the war.

Where Sherman pulled back, Thucydides—or at least many of the actors in Thucydides' *History*—took the extra step. Each represented a democratic society engaged in ruthless warfare directed at others similar to themselves in language and culture. Sherman agonized over his actions but attempted to justify the harshness of his actions as general. In Thucydides, warfare "for total stakes" begins to emerge. The Athenians restrain themselves after Mytilene, but civil war at Corcyra breaks down all social and moral restraints. In passages such as the descriptions of the plague at Athens and the civil war at Corcyra, Thucydides expresses *in propria persona* his dismay at the brutality of his fellows and the weakness of human virtue. Even when he does not make his judgment explicit, the details that he chooses to include often bring out, in dramatic fashion, the full measure of human suffering during the war—thus a recent book has been justly titled *The Humanity of Thucydides.*[27] At the same time, each writer prized candor and clarity of vision. Sherman

24. Sherman 1984, 2: 128.
25. Sherman 1984, 2: 129.
26. Sherman 1984, 2: 128.
27. Orwin 1994.

explodes at Hood's hypocritical and self-centered appeals to God and humanity. Thucydides virtually excludes high-minded language from his narrative and tends to include these appeals only to undercut them: the plague follows immediately after Perikles' Funeral Oration; calls to Pan-hellenic sentiment do not prevent the Spartans from liquidating their Plataean prisoners.

Harsh as the American Civil War may have been, its conventions were very different from those of fifth-century Greece. In one of the grimmest passages of the *History*, Thucydides describes a militarily trivial, but morally illuminating, atrocity by Thracian mercenaries who capture the small Boiotian town of Mykalessos:

> The Thracians, bursting into Mykalessos, sacked the houses and temples and butchered the inhabitants, sparing neither youth nor age, but killing all they fell in with, one after the other, children and women, and even beasts of burden, and whatever other living creatures they saw; the Thracian race, like the bloodiest of the barbarians, being ever most so when it has nothing to fear.
>
> Thuc. 7.29.4

Thucydides' contempt for these non-Greeks and their unrestrained savagery is obvious. His distaste for this massacre is so close to modern sensibilities that it is easy to forget what the civilized procedure would have been: the Thracians would have butchered all the adult males, then thriftily converted the women and children into cash by selling them into slavery. When the Athenians captured Melos, "they executed all the grown men whom they captured, and sold off as slaves all the women and children" (Thuc. 5.116.4). By contrast, after breaking the siege and capturing Atlanta, Sherman drove families from their homes, providing food and transportation within his own lines and arranging for logistical support for those who crossed over to Hood. Again, any Greek civilians unfortunate enough to encounter a Peloponnesian or Athenian raid could expect little mercy. On the other hand, even when Sherman began his famed march to the sea, cutting a path of destruction twenty miles across, "a great deal of damage was done, but people were generally left alone. Rape and murder were practically nonexistent."[28] For all the rhetorical similarities between Hood and the Melian representatives, the situation was profoundly different: Hood's theatrical remarks cost the

---

28. So Marszalek (1993, 306), who cites as evidence for this Glatthaar 1985.

civilians of Atlanta nothing; the high ideals of the Melian leaders led to the destruction of all.

But, of course, the Thucydidean observer would never accept at face value such a self-serving contrast. The image of Germans racing to surrender to the advancing American forces after the collapse of Germany and Douglas MacArthur's exemplary occupation of Japan have been a source of pride—and justly so—for Americans, while the massacre at My Lai in Vietnam, visually documented in *Time*, or the accidental bombing of a bunker filled with civilians during the Gulf War, graphically covered by CNN, filled them with horror. Nevertheless, democratic sensibilities, weak in imagination, are slaves to the vagaries of representation and relatively insensitive to distanced "push-button" slaughter: the firestorms of Dresden and Tokyo in the Second World War probably killed far more women and children than all the fighting in the Peloponnesian War. Color pictures of the aftermath did not, however, appear on the evening news. Justified or not, the ruthlessness of these actions made little impression upon the American consciousness. Even the mechanics of violence were different. We do not know how many prisoners the Athenians took on Melos—presumably hundreds, since the Athenians sent five hundred colonists to take their place (Thuc. 5.116.4)— but there were no methods of mechanized slaughter. Prisoners needed to be killed one at a time, by hand. Whatever method the Athenians used, there was an intimacy to this slaughter that the nineteenth-century firing squad or even the modern machine gunner does not share.[29]

An intense, at times brutal, candor and an unflinching insistence upon the harshest aspects of war characterize Thucydides. He would have had little patience for any claims of justice that did not also fully stress the costs, in both suffering and brutalization, of any extended recourse to violence. Thucydides and Sherman were influential precisely because they did not avert their gaze from the harsh realities that their contemporaries glossed over or ignored. Each man changed the way in which others viewed the world, because each, in his own way, forced himself to contemplate and to synthesize in his own mind realities that were too

---

29. Thucydides does not explain precisely how mass executions were performed. It is clear that the Spartans executed the captured Plataians one by one because we hear that each captured Plataian was given the "opportunity" to explain what he had done in the past for the Spartans to justify mercy (Thuc. 3.68). At Xenophon *Hellenika* 2.1.32, Lysander cuts the throat (*apesphaxe*) of the Athenian commander Philokles, but Philokles was explicitly exceptional. He was singled out for special treatment on the grounds that he had committed atrocities, throwing Andrians and Corinthians overboard.

painful or discordant for others. Each man was a realist in that each struggled to push aside empty fictions and to concentrate on the world as it was. Of course, reality defies easy definitions and the "realities" of the world are not obvious. What these realities were for Thucydides—what they included, what they left out, how well they accounted for the phenomena—are the main subject of this book. First, however, we must consider realism in general and "political realism," the particular outlook of which Thucydides proved to be a progenitor.

CHAPTER 2

Truest Causes
and Thucydidean Realisms

In concluding the introductory section of his *History*, Thucydides purports to cut through the details and to lay bare the major forces behind the Peloponnesian War:

> [5] To the question why they broke the treaty, I answer by placing first an account of their grounds of complaint and points of difference, that no one may ever have to seek out that from which the Hellenes plunged into a war of such magnitude. [6] The truest cause (*alêthestatê prophasis*) I consider to be the one that was least evident in public discussion (*logos*). I believe that the Athenians, because they had grown in power and terrified the Spartans, made war inevitable (*anankasai*).
>
> Thuc. 1.23.5–6

No one familiar with the practice of scholarship will be surprised that Thucydides' serene analysis has provoked at least as much debate as it has silenced. In particular, students of ancient history have probed almost every nuance of 1.23.6. Monographs have been devoted to individual terms, such as *prophasis*, "cause," and *anankê*, "necessity" (which shows up in the verbal form *anankasai*, translated "made . . . inevitable").[1] Controversy about the actual causes of the war and even about Thucydides' reliability as a source lives on.[2]

---

1. Rawlings 1975; Ostwald 1988.
2. Both Kagan (1969) and Ste. Croix (1972)—in studies more than four hundred pages long—take the origins of the Peloponnesian War as their main theme. Badian (1990, republished in Badian 1993) argues that Thucydides' account is grossly biased, minimizing Athenian responsibility.

Nevertheless, the idea contained in this passage continues to influence students and practitioners of foreign affairs. Thucydides' explanation for the Peloponnesian War has been cited to support the general thesis that war arises when power begins to shift. Thucydides provides the basis for the "balance of power" politics that Western diplomats from Bismarck to Kissinger have explicitly pursued. Academic theorists of international relations still cite Thucydides' judgment on the Peloponnesian War.[3] Even when he has not convinced others that his particular explanation was the best, Thucydides defined "the origins of war" as a topic for academic analysis.[4] In particular, the most recent commentator on Thucydides concludes that this brief passage reflects Thucydides' fundamental contribution to the study of history: "The explicit formulation of a distinction between profound and superficial causes is arguably Thucydides' greatest single contribution to later history-writing."[5]

I have rendered the phrase *alêthestatê prophasis* as "the truest cause" because I wanted to stress the Greek superlative—if there are "truest" causes, then there presumably exist other causes that are true to a lesser degree, and indeed no single cause may even provide a single, comprehensive account.[6] In rendering this phrase "real cause" Richard Crawley may slightly exaggerate, pushing Thucydides' claim of intellectual authority from mere arrogance to absolute omniscience, but the phrase captures Thucydides' goal, if not his claim. Thucydides was obsessed with the need to probe beyond deceptive appearances and to reveal forces that, though often hidden, nevertheless drove events. Thucydides was hardly the first Greek to express this general idea: the late sixth-century thinker Herakleitos remarked that "the hidden relationship (*harmonia*) is stronger than the obvious one" (frag. 54) and "nature (*phusis*) tends to conceal itself" (frag. 123). Thucydides wanted to study the "real world" and was thus a "realist."

Few would then deny that Thucydides was, in some sense, a "real-

---

3. See Wight 1978, 24–25 (quoting a 1947 speech by George C. Marshall on the relevance of Thucydides to contemporary affairs) and 138, where he speaks of Thucydides as "the prototype statement of how we usually express the causes of war"; and esp. Gilpin 1981, 211–230; Keohane (1986b, 143–144) refers to a " 'Thucydides-Gilpin theory' in which war occurs when an equilibrium of power is disturbed"; for critiques of Gilpin's use of Thucydides, see Garst 1989 and Johnson-Bagby 1994.

4. Thus Kagan 1995 takes as its title "On the Origins of War and the Preservation of Peace" and begins with the Peloponnesian War; the phrases "origins of war" and "causes of war" form the titles of Howard 1983, Ferrill 1985, and Blainey 1988, for example.

5. So Hornblower 1991, 65 (on Thuc. 1.23.6).

6. The superlative is not a Thucydidean idiosyncracy: cf., for example, Hdt. 7.233, where both *anankê* and the "truest *logos*" appear.

ist"—indeed, perhaps the first such author whose work survives in the tradition of European writing. But reality is elusive, and there are many kinds of realism. Of course, Thucydides can be viewed as part of a "realist" tradition in academic analysis and the practical conduct of international affairs, and I will return to this crucial aspect of Thucydides' influence. First, however, I want to investigate Thucydides' relationship to a number of more general elements of realisms past and present. Ultimately, I will return to political realism as a particular, if often amorphous, school of thought, but in the meantime I wish to stress that the same balance of theory with practice that makes realism influential in the modern world finds its counterpart in Thucydides' *History*. Every element of realism that Thucydides claims for himself as a historian he also attributes to Perikles. The practices of historian and statesman run parallel to one another.[7]

THE REALISMS OF THUCYDIDES

Thucydides' *History* exhibits four characteristics common to many "realist" schools of thought—not only political, but literary, artistic, and scientific. These four realisms are "procedural" (getting the facts straight), "scientific" (believing that there really are objective facts out there somewhere that can be gotten straight), "ideological" (using your claim to privileged knowledge as a stick to beat your opponents), and "paradigmatic" (seeing some phenomena more clearly and perhaps gaining a better view of the whole, but at the expense of simultaneously minimizing or ignoring other factors on which your predecessors had laid great emphasis). This list is hardly exhaustive, but, like the varying forces that interact with any object, these elements, though complementary and intertwined, need to be distinguished.

First, and above all, Thucydides was a realist insofar as he insisted upon a high level of observational accuracy—I will, for present purposes, call this his "procedural realism." One can argue about how successful Thucydides was in this regard,[8] and since Thucydides never finished the *History*, there are plenty of loose ends in the text. Nevertheless,

7. Students of Thucydides influenced by political theory have been particularly sensitive to the many affinities between Perikles as statesman and Thucydides as historian: e.g., Strauss 1964, 226–230; Edmunds 1975a, 212–214; Euben 1990a, 192–193.
8. Centuries of close study have turned up plenty of objections to Thucydides' narrative, of which Badian, 1993 125–162, is a particularly strong example, in that it charges Thucydides with actively twisting the facts to exculpate Athens.

Thucydides is famous for his insistence upon the importance of careful observation and precise reporting. Consider, for example, one famous passage in which Thucydides sheds some light on his methodological expectations. After he has sketched his own idiosyncratic vision of ancient times, Thucydides castigates the slovenliness of his predecessors:

[1] Having now given the result of my inquiries into early times, I grant that there will be a difficulty in believing every particular detail. The way that most people deal with traditions, even traditions of their own country, is to receive them all alike as they are delivered, without applying any critical test whatever. [2] The general Athenian public fancy that Hipparchus was tyrant when he fell by the hands of Harmodios and Aristogeiton, not knowing that Hippias, the eldest of the sons of Peisistratos, was really supreme, and that Hipparchos and Thessalos were his brothers, and that Harmodios and Aristogeiton, suspecting, on the very day, nay at the very moment fixed on for the deed, that information had been conveyed to Hippias by their accomplices, concluded that he had been warned, and did not attack him, yet, not liking to be apprehended and risk their lives for nothing, fell upon Hipparchos near the temple of the daughters of Leos and slew him as he was arranging the Panathenaic procession.

Thuc. 1.20.1–2

The Athenians are so uncritical that they have utterly misconstrued a central event in their own history, the ouster of the Peisistratids. Thucydides would later return to the Peisistratids and his own reconstruction of their departure in a famous digression in book 6, but here he does not content himself with public opinion. He continues by criticizing the understanding of contemporary history and citing as mistaken two specific beliefs:

[3] There are many other unfounded ideas current among the rest of the Hellenes, even on matters of contemporary history, which have not been obscured by time. For instance, there is the notion that the Spartan kings have two votes each, the fact being that they have only one; and that there is a Pitanate division, there being simply no such thing. So little pains do the vulgar take in the investigation of truth, accepting readily the first story that comes to hand.

Thuc. 1.20.3

Thucydides probably has in mind Herodotus, whose history mentions both the double votes of the Spartan kings and the Pitanate division.[9]

---

9. Herodotus seems to state that the Spartan kings each have two votes (Hdt. 6.57.5), and he refers to the Pitanate company at 9.53.2. In neither case is Herodotus's error quite as unambiguous as Thucydides makes it out: see Hornblower 1991 on 1.20.3. James

The statesman also bases his authority on such procedural realism. Perikles does not so much criticize individual opponents as stress his own unparalleled ability "to recognize and articulate those things which are necessary" (Thuc. 2.60.5). For Thucydides he is a model of accuracy: when the historian chooses to detail Athenian resources at the beginning of the war, he does not do so in an excursus (such as the Archaeology or the Pentekontaeteia) but puts the detailed list of facts and figures in Perikles' mouth (2.13).

It is, however, always easy for a second generation worker such as Thucydides to criticize the weaknesses of the pioneers. Mark Twain's famous 1895 essays that pilloried the earlier American novelist James Fenimore Cooper for his "inadequacy as an observer" were both justified and pusillanimous, in that Cooper largely invented the American novel, laying the foundations upon which Twain would build, just as Herodotus did for Thucydides.[10] And, of course, Thucydides' procedural realism is, in some ways, as disingenuous as that of Twain, for both Perikles' Funeral Oration and the Thucydidean Perikles himself are as romanticized as Twain's Huckleberry Finn or the Jumping Frog of Calaveras County.

Observational accuracy depends upon the existence of a stable, objective reality separate from, and in theory identical to, observers. If equally accurate observers of the same phenomenon produce different results, then procedural realism becomes problematic.

The term "scientific realism," popular among philosophers of science, describes Thucydides' second realism. In the twentieth century, even the physicists—champions of observation, analysis, and prediction—have had to abandon their implicit confidence in a deterministic, predictable world. Einstein showed that time was not absolute but relative to the speed and position of the observer, while quantum mechanics—which Einstein helped to establish—scandalized Einstein himself by suggesting that it was impossible to predict the position and velocity of particles on a very small scale. The label "scientific realist" has been developed

---

Kennelly ("Thucydides' Knowledge of Herodotus" [Ph.D. diss., Brown University, 1994]) has argued, however, that Thucydides wrote without any knowledge of Herodotus. For a recent overview of the possible connections between the two authors, see Scanlon 1994.

10. "Fenimore Cooper's Literary Offenses" and "Fenimore Cooper's Further Literary Offenses" in Twain 1992. Of course, Twain's wit is completely foreign to the humorless Thucydides, and, in this respect, the essays have a much greater affinity with Herodotus. Shi (1994, 107) describes Twain as "at best [a] truant member" of the realist "school," but it is not fair to criticize Twain for not articulating "a concrete literary perspective" (so Shi) without a careful analysis of the Cooper essays.

for those who retain their confidence in an objective world independent of the observer.[11]

The objectivity of human experience was, however, as contested in the fifth century as it is now. Parmenides and Herakleitos had each in his very different way challenged the validity of our perceptions and posited that the ultimate reality was hidden from our view. Experience with alien cultures brought with it the recognition that at least some common assumptions were simply conventions that had no inherent truth. Herodotus, conservative as he may in some ways have been, was acutely aware that people of differing cultures extracted different meanings from the same events.[12] Fifth-century thinkers like Herodotus began to contrast "nature" (*phusis*) and "culture" (*nomos*).[13] Protagoras's most famous saying—"Man is the measure of all things"—was used by some to undercut the authority of traditional ideas and beliefs. Nor was the argument confined solely to such obviously subjective (to us, at any rate) areas as religion and culture: Demokritos, Thucydides' contemporary, questioned the validity of any observation (frag. 9 DK): "sweet by convention (*nomos*), bitter by convention, hot by convention, cold by convention." Demokritos (frag. 11 DK) labeled all sensory information— sight, hearing, smell, taste, touch—"illegitimate." Not all fifth-century thinkers shared this degree of skepticism—Empedocles, for example, urged that we exploit our senses to the full (frag. 3 DK)—but no one familiar with the mainstream intellectual controversies of the fifth century could take for granted the "commonsense" view that careful observation uncovered an unproblematic "real world."

Even when Thucydides explicitly stresses the importance of observational accuracy, his goals presuppose considerable confidence in the validity of observation. Thus Thucydides describes the care with which he constructed his idealized accounts of events:

> [2] And with reference to the narrative of events, far from permitting myself to derive it from the first source that came to hand, I did not even trust my own impressions, but it rests partly on what I saw myself, partly on what others saw for me, the accuracy of the report being always tried by the most severe and detailed tests possible. [3] My conclusions have cost me some

11. On Einstein and scientific realism, see Fine 1986.

12. The classic example is Hdt. 3.38, where Dareios confronts Greeks, who burned their dead, with Indians, who supposedly ate theirs. Each side found the practice of the other abhorrent. For a balanced assessment of the importance of such external stimuli for the development of Greek thought, see Lloyd 1978, 236–239.

13. For a survey of the main passages, see still Heinimann 1945.

labor from the want of coincidence between accounts of the same occurrences by different eyewitnesses, arising sometimes from imperfect memory, sometimes from undue partiality for one side or the other.

Thuc. 1.22.2–3

Thucydides is acutely sensitive to the problems of observational inadequacy and error: he thus insists that he took nothing for granted, refusing even to trust his own observations without corroboration and stressing the time and labor that he lavished on clearing up problems. But when Thucydides deplores the inconsistent descriptions of his informants and promises, without qualification, to deliver in writing an accurate report, he implies that a single, true account of events is possible.[14] The major obstacle to such accuracy is human weakness. Thus Thucydides defends his conclusion that the Peloponnesian War was the greatest in Greek history by contrasting his reasoning with the fickle judgments of others:

> To come to this war; despite the known disposition of the actors in a struggle to overrate its importance, and when it is over to return to their admiration of earlier events, yet an examination of *the facts themselves* (*auta ta erga*) will show that it was much greater than the wars that preceded it.
>
> Thuc. 1.21.2 (italics mine)

If observers can rise above the pressures of the moment and observe "the facts themselves" (*auta ta erga*), a true picture of events will emerge. Our intellectual powers are limited, our expectations biased, but if the disciplined observer can rise above such limitations, a single truth does exist.

But for Thucydides, undisturbed observation is not just a historian's attribute. The first words that he gives to Perikles indicate that it is also an attribute of a statesman:

> I always hold fast to the same intellectual resolve (*gnômê*), Athenians, and that is the principle of no concession to the Peloponnesians. I know that the spirit that inspires people while they are being persuaded to make war is not always retained in action; that as circumstances change, resolutions change. Yet I see that now as before the same, almost literally the same, counsel is demanded of me; and I put it to those of you, who are allowing yourselves to be persuaded, to support the national resolves even in the case of reverses,

---

14. It is admittedly hard to gauge the extent to which Thucydides has thought through the implications of this (1.21.2). Edmunds (1993) and Loraux (1986b) have argued that Thucydides felt that writing could almost perfectly encode experience. I have elsewhere sought to qualify Thucydides' assumptions and to suggest that they are not quite so strong: see "Thucydidean Claims of Authority" in Crane 1996a.

or to forfeit all credit for their wisdom in the event of success. For sometimes the course of things is as arbitrary as human plans; indeed this is why we usually blame chance for whatever does not happen as we expected.

Thuc. 1.140.1

Perikles boasts that whatever the circumstances, he maintains the same *gnômê*, a complex term that implies both an intellectual decision and moral resolve.[15] This proves to be no idle boast: even after the plague has devastated Athens and undermined the moral structure of Athenian society, Perikles fearlessly repeats this claim:

> I am the same man and do not alter; it is you who change, since in fact you took my advice while unhurt and waited for misfortune to repent of it; and the apparent error of my policy lies in the infirmity of your intellectual resolve (*gnômê*), since the suffering that it entails is being felt by everyone among you, while its advantage is still remote and obscure to all, and a great and sudden reverse having befallen you, your mind is too much depressed to persevere in your resolves.
>
> Thuc. 2.61.2

A few chapters later, Thucydides, writing in propria persona about the career of Perikles, gives further emphasis to Perikles' unflappable intellectual resolve. The Athenians first fine Perikles but then soon restore him to power, changing their minds quickly. These Athenians thus prove Perikles' charge (Thuc. 1.140) that his fellow Athenians are unable to maintain a single course of action. Thucydides too says that such fickle behavior is "what the masses (*ho homilos*) are wont to do" (2.65.4). Thucydides designates Perikles' "public esteem" (2.65.8: *axiôma*) and his "intellectual power" (*gnômê*) as the two foundations of his authority. He never flattered the people (2.65.8). Above all, he had the power to dampen their gross swings of mood, instilling fear in them when they had become too elated and restoring their confidence when they gave way to despair (2.65.9). At the center of it all stood Perikles, motionless, beyond passion and personal concerns.[16]

It is almost impossible to stress too much the fascinations that such a detached vantage point offered in the classical period. Ultimately, geometry flourished in large part because it constituted a logically consis-

---

15. The term *gnômê* is a major focus of Edmunds 1975a; Edmunds points out that Spartan *gnômê* tends to emphasize moral resolves, and Athenian *gnômê* has a strong intellectual dimension. Perikles combines the two.

16. When Kleon seeks—without success—to make himself a second Perikles, he echoes Perikles' claim to intellectual constancy (compare Kleon's unchanging *gnômê* at 3.38.1 with Perikles' at 1.140.1 and 2.61.2).

tent system with explicit rules and assumptions in which all rational
observers had to draw identical conclusions. "Give me a place to stand,
and I will move the world," Archimedes is reported to have said,[17] and
it is toward such an idealized position, separate from the world and its
passions, that Thucydides and his Perikles strive. The achievements in
mathematics were immense. Archimedes continues to be considered one
of the great mathematicians of all time.[18] Euclid's *Elements* includes
almost five hundred theorems that Greek mathematicians had proved
with great rigor in little more than a century, a task that the Greeks of
Thucydides' generation had begun in earnest. The Euclidean geometry
remained unchallenged until the nineteenth century, and it continues to
occupy a solid position in the teaching of mathematics. Had Thucydides
been born thirty years later, the great strides in the field of mathematics
might have attracted him in that direction rather than toward history.

The importance of scientific realism emerges when Thucydides describes the collapse of society at Corcyra. One of the most terrible consequences of this warfare was, according to Thucydides, the shift in the
meanings of words:

> Words had to change their ordinary meaning and to take that which was
> now given them. Reckless audacity came to be considered the courage of a
> loyal ally; prudent hesitation, specious cowardice; moderation was held to
> be a cloak for unmanliness; ability to see all sides of a question, inaptness to
> act on any. Frantic violence became the attribute of manliness; cautious
> plotting, a justifiable means of self-defence.
>
> Thuc. 3.82.4

Of course, the change in language reinforces the brutalization of life,
and Thucydides clearly invites his audience to see this phenomenon in
moral terms (although he does not explicitly suggest that they do so).[19]
Yet the degeneration of language has purely practical consequences as
well. If words have no stable meaning, then communication breaks

---

17. There are several variations on the Greek for this: Pappus *Collectio* 8.10.1060;
Simpl. *in Phys.*, Diehls p. 1110; Tzetz. *Chil.* II. *Hist.* 35, 130, *Chil.* III. *Hist.* 66, 62. On
this saying, see Dijksterhuis 1987, 14–18.

18. Hollingdale (1989, 64), for example, ranks Archimedes, Newton, and Gauss together.

19. So Euben 1990b, 169–171; White 1984, 59–92; for White the collapse of Corcyraean society prefigures the extended decline of Athenian culture; I agree with White when
he argues that the ambiguities of language that appear throughout Thucydides are "not
incidental but structural" (p. 87). Thucydides, however, did his best to resolve such problems and to produce a single, unified account.

down, and with it the tasks of historian and statesmen alike become impossible.

It was the undisturbed observer in the ideal, "Archimedean" position from which the fullness of an event can be seen and appreciated—the "scientific" Thucydides—whom Charles Cochrane explored in his 1929 book, *Thucydides and the Science of History*.[20] We are, of course, a good deal more skeptical about the possibility for such detached observation now than we were some sixty years ago—the rejection of such "objectivity" has evolved into a dominant theme of late twentieth-century academic thought. Virginia Hunter's first book on Thucydides focused on the consequences of the author's perspective and labeled him "the artful reporter."[21] Robert Connor stressed the importance of the active reader, who is not simply passive but must endow Thucydides' text with meaning.[22] Nevertheless, objectivity, at least of a particular kind, was a goal for Thucydides, and Jacqueline de Romilly's recent essay, "The View from On High: Discovery of the Sciences of Man," gives proper weight to the success that Thucydides did enjoy.[23]

Furthermore, Thucydides was himself painfully aware that the same events may have very different meanings for different observers. A sudden wind, for example, begins to blow during a naval engagement, throwing the Peloponnesian ships into disorder and providing the Athenians with an opportunity to attack (Thuc. 2.84.3). This represents an "objective" phenomenon—all careful observers on both sides would have detected the same wind from the same quarter at the same time—but each side endows the same event with a very different meaning. Phormio, the Athenian commander, knew that this wind regularly began to blow shortly after dawn, and he delayed battle as he waited for the wind to disturb the Peloponnesian ships (2.84.2). The Peloponnesians, however, did not know Phormio's plans and did not understand that they had been maneuvered into an adverse position: when their commanders attribute their poor showing to "chance" (2.87.2: *ta apo tês*

20. Cochrane 1929, 166–167: "The scientific historian is left merely with the concept of a natural order of which man, like the environment, forms a part, and his problem is to exhibit the relationships which from time to time develop among men in contact with the environmental world. Such relationships being, *ex hypothesi*, uniform and regular, the study of them yields those generalizations about human action which constitute the usefulness of history and give to it the character of science."

21. Hunter 1973.

22. Connor 1984, 12–19.

23. "La vue d'en haut: Découverte des sciences de l'homme," in de Romilly 1990, 105–141.

tuchês), they seem to interpret as accidental the wind on which Phormio had counted.[24]

In this case, the differing interpretations reflect differing levels of knowledge: the Spartan commanders, if they could have read Phormio's mind, might have changed their view of that unfortunate wind. But the meaning of this Athenian battle as a whole is contested. Thucydides clearly sees in Athenian superior naval skill the decisive factor, but the Spartans at home find the whole thing "inexplicable" (Thuc. 2.85.2: *paralogos*) and assume that "some weakness" (*tis malakia*) must have caused the defeat. The Spartans clearly misread the situation (at least as Thucydides sees it), but it is not clear whether more information about the battle would have changed their mind. They were not yet prepared to accept technical matters as an explanation for military events.

Even if Thucydides successfully described who led what force to a particular place, how many men died in the subsequent battle, and what the immediate consequences were, he knew that such data did not, in themselves, necessarily mean the same thing to all parties. Rather, his *History* provides accurate data to serve the interpretations of readers in the future. Thucydides is more than a simple materialist, for he understands the impact of ideas upon events. Adam Parry's 1957 dissertation, "*Logos* and *Ergon* in Thucydides," showed how Thucydides belonged to that tradition of Greek thought that stressed the importance of both words and deeds.[25] Thucydides includes speeches in his *History* (despite the fact that he cannot even pretend to have more than general sources for them) at least in part because they dramatize the degree to which a subject's position shapes perception.

Thucydides' scientific realism had an enormous impact upon his practice as a historian. Thucydides' predecessor, Herodotus, had cultivated an ambivalent relationship toward events that actually took place. Although he seems to have provided us with a reasonably accurate account of the Persian Wars and other fairly recent events, he frequently expresses an agnosticism toward the events he relates. The verb form *legetai*, "it is said," is, for example, a favorite Herodotean term and crops up more than a hundred times in the *Histories*. Herodotus uses the term

---

24. So Stahl (1966, 88), who points out the great emphasis that Thucydides lays on this wind and on the chaos that it created (2.84.3).

25. This was published after Parry's death as Parry 1981; see esp. pp. 15–21. Thucydides' appreciation for *logoi* and their significance is also one of the starting points for Cogan 1981a.

to distance himself from many reports, ranging from those of Kroisos's behavior on the pyre (Hdt. 1.87.1) and Delphi's self-exculpation (1.91.1) to the reports of Pausanias's clever remarks after Plataia (9.82.3) and dried fish miraculously returning to life as they were being cooked (9.120.1). Herodotus, however, does not simply refuse to endorse many of the stories. He seems to relish elaborating events that never took place. Herodotus surely realized that the meeting of Kroisos and Solon, which forms the centerpiece of book 1 and offers in brief an introduction to ideas that shape the history as a whole, was chronologically impossible (Solon's travels would have taken place at least twenty years before Kroisos became king). The conversation between Solon and Kroisos is "true" not because it took place (which it didn't) but because it lets us understand better the parabolic careers that Kroisos, Kyros, Kambyses, Dareios, and Xerxes will all pursue, as each in turn rises and falls. Herodotus refused to let the details of what actually happened distract him from the larger picture. He was an "idealist" for whom stories of the past constituted a means by which to study higher truths.

Thucydides was just as determined as Herodotus to extract the general from the particular, but their methods moved in opposite directions. Rather than rearranging the past so that the data would better reflect his understanding of the world, Thucydides stressed greater rigor and subordination to the facts of the case. Thucydides felt that once he had worked his way through the evidence, he could provide clean and well-digested descriptions of many events. On the level of individual campaigns or episodes, Thucydides seems to have been confident in his method. Nevertheless, this method did not "scale up." On the macroscopic level, contradictions and unresolved tensions pull at Thucydides' history. Herodotus' world is, for all its willfulness, a far more ordered place—almost Newtonian in its predictability—than the messy picture that we find in Thucydides. In Thucydides the plague, Melos, and the Sicilian expedition all undermine the vision offered by Perikles in his Funeral Oration; in Herodotus, by contrast, Solon's analysis of prosperity, which contradicts present phenomena (such as the then good fortune of Kroisos), is validated throughout the *Histories*, as not only Kroisos, but Kyros, Kambyses, Dareios, and Xerxes—all the most powerful figures in the text—all to some extent fit the same Herodotean parabolic curve of rise and decline (cf. Hdt. 1.5.4). At the beginning of the twentieth century, Francis Cornford's *Thucydides Mythistoricus* brilliantly showed that Thucydides' view of the rise and fall of Athens was very similar to that of Herodotus and even Aeschylus—at some level,

Herodotean forces operate in Thucydides' *History*, just as Newtonian
mechanics work perfectly well in virtually all day-to-day circumstances.
Nevertheless, it is equally true that if we follow Thucydides' own historical logic as it plays out in the opening of book 1, Sparta was an
archaic, obsolescent power that should have given way to Athens, with
its sea power, its money, and its dynamism. The accuracy and precision
that Thucydides demanded made it impossible for his work to approach
the intellectual or moral closure of Herodotus's *Histories*. Perhaps this
is why Thucydides' work is, at least in contrast to that of Herodotus,
so humorless, its ironies so harsh.[26] Herodotus could poke fun at his
subjects as well as himself (as he does, for example, when he draws
attention to the implausibility of the constitutional debate at 3.80.1),
because his world, for all its vagaries and contingencies, ultimately made
sense.

Third, both Thucydides and Perikles exploit their procedural accuracy to further a third, subtle, often insidious, project, which I will call
"ideological realism." On this point, Mark Twain's remarks on James
Fenimore Cooper are helpful, for they make explicit a point that neither
Thucydides nor his Perikles had any motivation to highlight. Twain castigated Cooper's inaccuracies for purely practical reasons:

> If Cooper had been an observer, his inventive faculty would have worked
> better, not more interestingly, but more rationally, more plausibly. Cooper's
> proudest creations in the way of "situations" suffer noticeably from the
> absence of the observer's protecting gift. Cooper's eye was spendidly
> inaccurate. Cooper seldom saw anything correctly. He saw nearly all things
> as through a glass eye, darkly. Of course, a man who cannot see the
> commonest little everyday matters accurately is working at a disadvantage
> when he is constructing a "situation."[27]

Twain goes on to develop his famous critique of a scene from Cooper's
Deerslayer, in which five Indians in succession, attempting to jump from
a overhanging tree toward a very slowly moving barge a few feet below,
all manage to fall into the water astern. The reason for Twain's outrage
is clear: his *Huckleberry Finn* and "Celebrated Jumping Frog of Calaveras County," fantastic as they may be taken as a whole, were believ-

---

26. There are relatively few traces of humor in Thucydides: Kleon's embarrassment at
4.28 is probably the clearest. The strategem by which the people of Segesta tricked the
Athenians into overestimating Segesta's wealth has great comic potential, but it is not
clear, given the grim outcome of the Sicilian expedition, whether Thucydides intends for
us to find this story funny.
27. Twain 1992, 184.

able because Twain labored to construct them out of smaller details that were in themselves plausible, and because, to the extent that Twain departed from such a strict canon of objective plausibility, he knew precisely what he was doing. He understood the Hesiodic trick of mixing true things with false (cf. Hes. *Theog.* 26–28), so that he could blur the realistic and the fantastic, making each reinforce the other. His procedural realism was fundamental to his success at creating idealized characters or situations that were at once incredible and convincing, and hence powerful.

Twain's realism is, for the most part, an explicit literary device. It lends power to his prose, but then *Huckleberry Finn* and "The Jumping Frog" are manifestly literary creations. Thucydides wrote a history that purported to be a true account, and the Thucydidean Perikles claimed always to have the best advice for the state. Ideological realism claims for itself a monopoly on truth and opposes itself to "idealism," the pursuit of an attractive, but ultimately ill-founded, vision of the world. This ideological realism has two dimensions. It is, or more properly represents itself as being, emotionally detached. Not only does Thucydides assume that a single objective reality exists and that he is the man to observe it, but he uses these two assumptions to help assert a special authority for himself and his text. Consider the following disclaimer:

> On the whole, however, the conclusions I have drawn from the proofs quoted may, I believe, safely be relied on. Assuredly they will not be disturbed either by the lays of a poet displaying the exaggeration of his craft or by the compositions of the chroniclers that are attractive at truth's expense, the subjects they treat being out of the reach of evidence, and time having robbed most of them of historical value by enthroning them in the region of legend. Turning from these, we can rest satisfied with having proceeded upon the clearest data, and having arrived at conclusions as exact as can be expected in matters of such antiquity.
>
> Thuc. 1.21.1

As the careful observer, Thucydides claims impartiality and the moral authority that comes with it.

The Thucydidean Perikles plays the same game in his three speeches on the war (Thuc. 1.140–144, 2.60–64, and especially the account of Athenian resources at 2.13), where he claims a more detailed vision of the situation than any of his (unquoted) rivals. The same assumptions of direct knowledge shape the Funeral Oration, where an idealized Athens exploits the tension between the state and the individual, drawing on every strength inherent in Athenian democracy. Of course, the Athens of the Funeral Oration never existed; nevertheless, while such a rosy view of the community belongs to the genre of state funeral orations, the Athens that the Thucydidean Perikles conjures up is an extraordinary creation that maintains a place for the Funeral Oration in the general curriculum to this day.[28] Plato's *Menexenus* parodies the genre and derives its strength from the conventional predictability of Athenian funeral orations. The funeral oration of Demosthenes, by contrast, is so insipid that many have doubted its authenticity.[29] The funeral orations of Gorgias (of which only a portion survives), Lysias, and Hyperides have commanded little attention for themselves except as examples of a particular genre and its conventions. The oration of the Thucydidean Perikles has been more successful in part because it dismisses many conventions of the genre (giving, for example, short shrift to Athens's ancient history and even the Persian Wars), basing itself on several of the more compelling traits that shape Thucydides' Athenians. The energy that Perikles attributes to the Athenians (see, for example, 2.39, 40.2, and 41.1) helps account for, and give depth to, the horrified Corinthian vision of Athenian dynamism that preceded the war (1.68–71). At the same time, the energy and dynamism of the Funeral Oration give Alkibiades his opening when he urges the risky Sicilian expedition, which ran against Perikles' strategy (1.144.1, 2.65.11). Above all, the Thucydidean Perikles bases Athenian patriotism on the one motivation that Thucydides always acknowledges: Perikles calls upon the Athenians to gaze upon the "power" (*dunamis*) of their city and thus let themselves be carried away with passion, becoming "lovers" of the city (2.43.1). The admiration for power—whether hypostasized as profit (1.8.3) or as empire (e.g., 6.31.1)—is, with fear (its complement), the only factor that can reliably inspire Thucydides' humans.[30] (Of course, placing the love of power in such a central position raises problems for Thucydides, to which I will return later.)

The plague follows immediately after the idealistic Funeral Oration, and the implied contrast is harsh: Athenian democracy wilts before this

---

28. Edward Everett, who, at a very young age, served as the first Eliot Professor of Greek at Harvard, and later became the most famous orator of his day, had Thucydides in mind when he delivered the "real" Gettysburg address. Lincoln had been invited to deliver a few remarks that would follow the featured speech by Everett. On the influence of the Athenian Funeral Oration in nineteenth-century America, see Wills 1992.

29. For the controversy and demonstration that the speech is, indeed, probably by Demosthenes, see McCabe 1981.

30. On Thucydides' characterization of Athenian character, see Crane 1992a.

disease, and the social virtues that Perikles praises collapse (Thuc. 2.53) as the corpses begin literally to pile up (see 2.52.4). Nevertheless, Funeral Oration and plague are not a self-contained doublet but the opening sections of a three-part sequence: shortly after the plague account, Thucydides brings Perikles back into the narrative so that the statesman can deliver his response to events. Perikles thus speaks before *and* after the plague. He has the last word, and events, terrible as they may be, do not cow him. His speech at 2.60–64 brilliantly synthesizes his own "realistic" assessment of the situation (which Thucydides endorses at 2.65) with the "idealizing" heroic values of the old Greek elite. This final speech is a masterpiece of ideological realism.

On the one hand, Perikles appeals to the pride of his listeners. They inhabit a "great city" and thus constitute a collective aristocracy that must live up to its status (Thuc. 2.61.4). The Athenians have achieved so much, and they are so much superior to their enemies, that they deserve to feel disdain (2.62.4: *kataphronêsis*) for their adversaries. Athens has earned the "greatest name" (2.64.3: *onoma megiston*) because it would not yield to misfortunes (*tais sumphorais mê eikein*). Even if Athens should fall now (as, Perikles concedes, it surely will sooner or later), the achievements of the present will ensure that "memory" of their deeds will survive. Perikles thus appeals to the same "eternal fame" as does Achilles—except that, of course, Athenian fame will rest upon genuine achievements, for which the mendacious poets are unnecessary (2.41.4)—and to which, of course, the plainspoken Thucydides is ideally suited (1.22.4).

At the same time, the heroic exhortation rests upon an appeal to cool judgment and a sound appreciation of the world as it really is. Perikles demands respect on the grounds that he "is second to none at recognizing what things need doing and at explaining these things" (Thuc. 2.60.5). If the Athenians have lost confidence in his strategy for the war, then they have only their own "infirmity of intellect" (2.61.2: *to humeteron asthenes tês gnômês*) to blame. Pain afflicts the Athenians, but their intellects fail to perceive the advantage that is not immediately before them. Their intellect is prostrate (*tapeinê hê dianoia*). Fears about the ultimate outcome of the war are groundless and arise only because the Athenians do not see things as they really are (2.61). "Rational analysis based on what really exists" (2.62.5: *gnômê apo tôn huparchontôn*), which provides the most secure foundation for "foresight" (*pronoia*), justifies Athenian confidence. If the Athenians will only concentrate their minds upon "the future good and present honor" (2.64.6), they will hold out. The speech goes back and forth, playing the "real" and the "ideal" off one another, so that cold calculation appears to call for the pursuit of glory.

Yet the historian Thucydides is a good deal less disingenuous than the author and essayist Twain. Twain makes it clear that procedural realism is important because it lends a text greater credibility. Thucydides even turns the difficult and quirky nature of his text to his own advantage. Readers may find the history slow going or at times somewhat dry in comparison to Homer or (presumably) the unnamed Herodotus, but only because Thucydides has subjected himself to strict intellectual discipline and refused to compromise truth for charm. If Thucydides loses readers in the present, the greater purity of his account will nevertheless strengthen his case in the long run:

> The absence of romance in my history will, I fear, detract somewhat from its interest; but if it be judged useful by those inquirers who desire an exact knowledge of the past as an aid to the interpretation of the future, which in the course of human things must resemble if it does not reflect it, I shall be content. In fine, I have written my work not as an essay that is to win the applause of the moment, but as a *possession for all time* (*ktêma es aiei*).
>
> Thuc. 1.22.4 (italics mine)

Although Thucydides concedes that his history may not win any prizes at first or enjoy wide popularity, he argues that it will nevertheless constitute a permanent heirloom that will be treasured and will even increase in value over time. Of course, such disclaimers are self-serving. While directing our attention to his concessions about charm, Thucydides invites us to concede the far greater point of accuracy and even practical value.

The impact of Thucydides' claim to an austere but authentic account would be immense, for it helped lay the foundations for that rhetorical posture by which so-called technocrats justify their position in society. At the same time, Thucydides is simply varying the hackneyed courtroom persona familiar to all contemporary Athenians. Just as speakers regularly contrast their own inexperience with rhetoric and necessary reliance on the plain, unpolished truth, Thucydides distinguishes himself from others.[31] The protestations of stylistic simplicity culminate a few sentences later when Thucydides provides his explanation for the out-

---

31. Cf. Antiphon 1.1 (*Stepmother*), 5.1 (*Herodes*), 3.2.1–2 (*Second Tetralogy*); Lys. 12.3; for other examples, see Edwards and Usher 1985, 68.

break of the Peloponnesian War (Thuc. 1.23.5–6). Everything that precedes in the *History* is calculated to lend this judgment greater weight, and much of Thucydides' subsequent narrative inevitably serves to reinforce this initial judgment.[32] Thucydides exploits to the full the ideological dimension implicit in the very term "realism," for he claims to portray the "real" world while his counterparts struggle to provoke pleasing but potentially mendacious effects.[33]

Thucydides' ideological realism extends, however, beyond the claims of scientific accuracy. It includes an extra dimension that appeals more openly to the emotions and bullies its audience into submission. The following famous passage from Thucydides' analysis of civil war and its horrifying moral consequences on Corcyra contains an illustration of ideological realism at its most brutal and its consequences:

> [1] Thus every form of iniquity took root in the Hellenic countries by reason of the troubles. The ancient simplicity into which honor so largely entered was laughed down and annihilated; and society became divided into camps in which no person trusted the next. [2] To put an end to this, there was neither promise to be depended upon nor oath that could command respect; but all parties, dwelling rather on the unlikelihood of a permanent state of things, were more intent upon self-defence than capable of confidence. [3] In this contest the blunter wits were most successful. Apprehensive of their own deficiencies and of the cleverness of their antagonists, they feared to be worsted in debate and to be surprised by the combinations of their more versatile opponents, and so at once boldly had recourse to action, [4] while their adversaries, arrogantly thinking that they should know in time, and that it was unnecessary to secure by action what policy afforded, often fell victims to their want of precaution.
>
> Thuc. 3.83

Thucydides makes little attempt to conceal his dismay at the collapse of moral society. The breakdown in trust not only poisons human relations but creates a nightmarish world in which "blunter wits" cut down their cleverer fellows. The practices of intelligence—calm observation and rational analysis—become liabilities, and thus the very conditions necessary for Thucydides as historian disappear. When the "ancient simplicity was laughed down and annihilated," it took with it

---

32. In particular, the restless and insatiably acquisitive character that Thucydides attributes to his Athenians (see esp. the Corinthian speech at 1.68–71 and Alkibiades' speech at 6.16–18, with Crane 1992a) makes Athenian attempts at expansion inevitable and thus strengthens his judgment.

33. On this, see especially Edmunds 1993, 831–852.

anyone who shared Thucydides' intellectual values and left behind a
world antithetical to those values that Thucydides championed.

But if Thucydides invites his readers to share in his horror at this
debased condition, he nevertheless contributes to this corrosive process
as well. Thucydides' *History*, like Machiavelli's *Prince* and Hobbes's
Leviathan, does much to undermine conventional pieties. Thucydides'
Athenians regularly subordinate power to justice, and their example has
ever since served to justify hard-nosed power politics. Perikles' Funeral
Oration remains one of the great visions of democratic freedom, but
Thucydides' account of the plague, which inverts Perikles' values, undercuts his idealization of Athens and forces him to construct a new
argument at 2.60–64. Thucydides allows "the ancient simplicity" to appear in his text only when it can cast discredit upon someone or when
events show the weakness of such traditional values. Even as Thucydides' *History* champions the rational analysis that became untenable at
Corcyra, it adopts the cynicism that helped cause the very condition he
deplores.

This cynicism constitutes a second ideological element commonly
claimed by realists. Not only does realism claim for itself the "real
world," but it adds an emotional charge to this claim and implies that
those who do not share its vision are naive. Realism of this kind relies
for much of its effect upon intimidation, but it is both effective and self-
fulfilling, for it justifies in the name of self-defence the most ruthless
measures. Thus Machiavelli expresses the "realist" position in a celebrated passage of *The Prince*:

> I shall depart from the methods of other people. It being my intention to
> write a thing which shall be useful to him who apprehends it, it appears to
> me more appropriate to follow up the real truth (*verità effetuale*) of a matter
> than the imagination (*imaginazione*) of it; for many have pictured republics
> and principalities which in fact have never been known or seen, because how
> one lives is so far distant from how one ought to live, that he who neglects
> what is done for what ought to be done, sooner effects his ruin than his
> preservation; for a man who wishes to act entirely up to his professions of
> goodness (*professione di buono*) soon meets with what destroys him among
> so many who are not good (*che non sono buoni*). Hence it is necessary for
> a prince wishing to hold his own to know how not to be good (*essere non
> buono*), and to make use of it or not according to necessity.[34]

34. Machiavelli, *The Prince* 15; translation by W. K. Marriott after Machiavelli 1911.

According to Machiavelli, because not all men are good, the ruler, who is responsible for the fate of others, must learn how not to be good. Machiavelli cleverly plays upon the responsibility of the prince, asserting a moral imperative to amorality and espousing an altruism of power politics, whereby the individual gives up something of his personal goodness to further the good of the community. Machiavelli goes on to repeat his distinction between the "real" world and the "imaginary" one: he will speak of those "issues with regard to which an imaginary prince" (*le cose circa uno principe imaginate*) might be praised, and concentrate on those issues that are "real" (*vere*).[35] In this way, "realists," from Thucydides to Machiavelli and Hobbes and on to modern academic theorists such as Hans Morgenthau, John Herz, Kenneth Waltz, and Robert Gilpin, traditionally claim not only for themselves a superior perspective and proprietary vision of the world "as it really is." They undermine the authority of their intellectual adversaries, in modern times applying to them the dismissive label "idealists."

Thucydides' relationship to the bullying ideological realism that he alternately deplores and practices emerges with particular force in the Mytilenean debate. If Thucydides reserves his strongest praise for Perikles (Thuc. 2.65), Kleon, the would-be Perikles, receives equally explicit condemnation, receiving the term "most violent of the citizens" (3.36.6). Kleon opens his speech calling for the liquidation of the Mytileneans with an extended exercise in realist intimidation. When Kleon lashes out at speakers who indulge in intellectual virtuosity at the expense of practical considerations and to the tangible harm of the state (3.37–38), he anticipates countless realist condemnations of idealism. At the same time, in equating the cultivation of anger and the indulgence in retribution with *sôphrosunê*, the "self-control" or "restraint" that Greek aristocrats claimed for themselves (3.37.2–38.1), he illustrates the perversion of language that Thucydides would deplore at 3.82.4. At the same time, however, Kleon's critique of specious intellectualism recalls the charges that Thucydides levels at his own specious predecessors, both poetic and prose.

Thucydides struggled to establish a synthesis that would answer the valid criticisms of Kleon while avoiding violence and brutality. He attempted to constitute the old aristocratic world view, but in such a way

---

35. This ideological realism in both Thucydides and Machiavelli is the subject of Forde 1992.

as to render it impervious to the charges of naiveté. Thus Thucydides gives to his Diodotos, an otherwise unknown figure who answers Kleon and argues for clemency, one of the most admired speeches in Greek literature. Faced with a bitter and venomous diatribe from Kleon, Diodotos concedes to his opponent the rules of debate. He refuses to seek mercy on the grounds of either justice or compassion. He argues instead that mercy is simply more expedient, and thus manages to give the restive Athenians justification to resist Kleon (Thuc. 3.44). But brilliant as Diodotos's speech may be, the Athenians would show no such mercy a decade later when they annihilated the population of Melos. Plato understood the limits of this expediency clearly: in book 1 of the *Republic*, he accepts the same rules of debate as does Diodotos, restricting himself to arguments based upon advantage, but he introduces advantage only to set it aside. The real argument begins in book 2, when Plato's interlocutors insist that justice be defended not because of the advantages it confers but because it is good in and of itself. Plato thus leapt beyond that logic of advantage in which Thucydides remained. But if Plato achieved an intellectual eminence that few thinkers in any culture could equal, Thucydides' disciplined restraint has also attracted admiration.[36]

Finally, I wish to examine as a fourth trend what I will term "paradigmatic realism": new ways of looking at the world may bring overall advantages, but the advance must often be balanced against its cost. Even in the sciences, new schemata that all agree are superior may have serious drawbacks: no one would dispute the superiority of Einsteinian relativity over Newtonian views of time and space, but the increase in understanding came at the price of an enormous increase in complexity, and even now no physicist uses general relativity when, as in most day-to-day circumstances, the old-fashioned view of time and space will do. In the humanities and social sciences, where intellectual progress is far more ambiguous, the benefits of a new realism are almost always problematic. If realists drag new phenomena into the light, they also push other phenomena back into the shadows. The disciplined observer learns not only what to see but also what to ignore—this is as true for painters, novelists, and experimental physicists as it is for political philosophers and historians. No outlook is ever neutral: scientists and scholars alike

36. See, for example, Nietzsche's statement that Thucydides constitutes "my recreation, my preference, my *cure* from all Platonism" (*The Twilight of the Idols*, 106–107, quoted by Derian [1995b, 385]).

see what they expect to see. The historian of science Thomas Kuhn popularized the term "paradigm" as a label for the formalized perspectives of professional scientists,[37] but his concept arguably applies beyond the sciences. It certainly applies to Thucydides.

Kuhn, for example, distinguished "pre-paradigm" science from its more mature counterpart. "In the absence of a paradigm or some candidate for paradigm, all of the facts that could possibly pertain to the development of a given science are likely to seem equally relevant. As a result, early fact-gathering is a far more nearly random activity than the one that subsequent scientific development makes familiar."[38] Kuhn cites Pliny's *Natural History*, with its wide scope and lack of precise focus, as typical of "pre-paradigm" science. Herodotus was no Pliny, nor did Thucydides shape history at all as decisively as did Newtonian physics or Darwinian biology, but the change that Thucydides imposed upon history—for better and for worse—reflects in some degree the sudden narrowing of focus that Kuhn identifies with the rise of a paradigm. Herodotus constructed a brilliant and heterogeneous book—in all probability, the first full-length prose work ever constructed[39]—but, although Herodotus was well known and widely read throughout antiquity, and although Herodotus was, in some ways, arguably more scientific than Thucydides,[40] it was Thucydides—willful, obscure, idiosyncratic but brilliant—who established the ideal canons of the historian. This influence was a mixed blessing, for Thucydides helped limit history to the political and military, while marginalizing social factors and oversimplifying events.[41] Thucydides excluded women from his work to a degree unmatched by virtually any classical Greek author:[42] his was a masculine

37. The classic exposition remains Kuhn 1970; Boyd (1991, 12–14) briefly summarizes Kuhn while placing his work within the broader framework of the philosophy of science. Kuhn was criticized for using the term "paradigm" inconsistently, and he tried in later work to define this concept more narrowly, but many practicing historians of science (e.g., Cohen 1985, xvi-xvii) find the original exposition to be the most useful, perhaps because of its ambiguities and flexibility.

38. Kuhn 1970, 15.

39. So Flory 1980.

40. Momigliano 1990, 29–53.

41. For Thucydides' virtual exclusion of religion, see Hornblower 1992.

42. The decline in the role assigned to women as we move from Herodotus to Thucydides is astounding: women appear only about one-tenth as often in Thucydides as in Herodotus. Even then these few Thucydidean women appear mainly as victims or relatives, whereas Herodotus's women play a far more active role. On Herodotean women, see Dewald 1981; on Thucydides' treatment of women, see Schaps 1977; Wiedemann 1983; Harvey 1985; Loraux 1985; Cartledge 1993. I have explored these topics at length in Crane 1996a, where I point out that Thucydides excludes not only women, but all familial

vision, and he did much to establish the gendered vision that almost all
realists would share for the subsequent two thousand years.[43] He did
more than simply compose a history of the Peloponnesian War. He also
established the starting point for ancient historians. And although few
of those who followed lived up to the standards that Thucydides es-
poused, Thucydides did much more than Herodotus to define ancient
historiography.[44]

This is not the place to go into Twain-like detail about Thucydides'
historical offences. In what follows I will examine those elements of
traditional Greek culture that Thucydides disdained or that modern
readers, going beyond even Thucydides, have overlooked. I will turn to
political realism as a particular paradigm that Thucydides in some measure founded and that, in one form or another, seems destined to flourish. First, however, I wish to consider the degree to which Thucydides
felt that he had established what historians of science might now term
a scientific paradigm.

Successful paradigms, at least within the sciences, allow their users
to predict events with greater certainty. Certainly, Thucydides makes it
clear that he looked for the ability to foresee future events in his statesmen. Consider, for example, his praise of Themistokles:

> Themistokles was a man who exhibited most securely the power of his nature
> (*phusis*); indeed, in this particular he has a claim on our admiration quite
> extraordinary and unparalleled. By his own native capacity (*oikeia xunesis*),
> alike unformed and unsupplemented by study, he was at once the best judge
> in those sudden crises that admit of little or of no deliberation, and the best
> prophet of the future, even to its most distant possibilities. An able theoretical
> expositor of all that came within the sphere of his practice, he was not
> without the power of passing an adequate judgment in matters in which he
> had no experience. He could also excellently divine the good and evil that
> lay hid in the unseen future. Taken as a whole, whether we consider the extent
> of his natural powers (*phuseôs dunamis*), or the slightness of his training,
> this extraordinary man must be allowed to have surpassed all others in the
> faculty of intuitively meeting an emergency.
>
>   Thuc. 1.138.3

The fact that Themistokles himself ended his days as a wanted man,
an exile from Athens and client of the Persian king (Thuc. 1.135–138)

---

relationships—male and female alike. Thucydidean misogyny (if that is the correct term)
contributes to the larger project of reducing the world to individuals and states.

43. Tickner 1995.

44. On the "failure and success of Herodotus," see Lateiner 1989, 211–227.

did not diminish Thucydides' admiration for him. Similarly, Thucydides takes care to inscribe within the *History* his own judgment that Perikles' strategy for Athens was correct. Perikles' own mortality constituted the only flaw in his reasoning, for no one after Perikles' death was able to provide the leadership necessary to keep Periklean strategy on track (2.65.7–12).

The idea that human intelligence could accurately manage the future did, in fact, find expression in the fifth century. Demokritos reportedly said that "human beings invented the image of chance (*tuchê*) as a pretext for their own foolishness, for only rarely does chance conflict with intelligence. Intelligent careful observation makes most things in life run smoothly" (frag. 119 DK). Other texts, such as *Prometheus Bound* 436–506 and the "Ode to Man" at Sophokles *Antigone* 332–375, attest that, in the fifth century, a certain pride in human achievements had at least leavened traditional archaic pessimism about the human condition. Some intellectuals gave full weight to the power of technology and emphasized the possibilities that human intelligence opened up. The optimism visible in the fifth century clearly influenced Thucydides: the Archaeology dismisses early human history and even the heroic age, stressing that modern society had progressed far and that untrustworthy poets such as Homer had grossly exaggerated events of the past (such as the magnitude of the Trojan War).[45]

Thucydides struggled to establish history as what we would now call a scientific discipline, and if he was unsuccessful in this, it is not clear how much farther we have really progressed in the intervening two thousand years. Nevertheless, if history is supposed to generate scientific laws by which we may accurately predict future events, Thucydides was not successful. I have already alluded to the unresolved problems within Thucydides' analysis of the past (for example, "archaic" Sparta's defeat of "modern" Athens). If Thucydides could not even "predict" the past, it is hardly surprising that his *History* ultimately presents a bleak picture of mortal capacity to cope with the future.[46] He begins his *History* with the boast that he wrote so that future generations could scrutinize his account and "judge it useful" (Thuc. 1.22.4), but this confidence seems to evaporate as the narrative progresses. He approaches his superb account of the plague at Athens with marked diffidence:

45. On Thucydides' Archaeology, see chapters 5 and 6 below.
46. This is the main theme of Stahl 1966; Edmunds (1975a) focuses on the unpredictability of events but gives greater emphasis to the power of rationality.

All speculation as to its origin and its causes, if causes can be found adequate to produce so great a disturbance, I leave to other writers, whether lay or professional; for myself, I shall simply set down its nature and explain the symptoms by which perhaps it may be recognized by the student, if it should ever break out again. This I can the better do as I had the disease myself and watched its operation in the case of others.

                                                                        Thuc. 2.48.3

Thucydides can claim a great deal of intellectual authority, since he lived through the plague and suffered from it himself, but his account, however accurate, has few pretentions. He can offer no treatment, much less explanations, for the plague. At most he hopes that others will recognize this disease from his account if it ever crops up again.[47]

By the time Thucydides describes civil war on Corcyra, knowledge of the past becomes even more problematic. On the one hand, he includes in this analysis perhaps his strongest assertion about the predictive power of good observation:

The sufferings that revolution entailed upon the cities were many and terrible, such as have occurred and always will occur as long as the nature of humankind (*phusis anthrôpôn*) remains the same, though in a severer or milder form, and varying in their symptoms, according to the variety of the particular cases.

                                                                        Thuc. 3.82.2

Grim as the subject matter may be, the savagery of the Corcyraeans provides us with a case study in which we see human behavior that is typical for such circumstances. Given the conditions that obtain in Corcyra, human beings anywhere will pursue the same harsh measures. Indeed, Thucydides justifies his analysis of Corcyra as a "case study" on the grounds that what happened at Corcyra repeated itself throughout the Greek world and that Corcyra is a general, not a special, phenomenon. Certainly, every continent, including Europe and North America, has in the past decade produced its own Corcyras, and it would be all too easy to establish case studies eerily similar to Thucydides' analysis of Corcyra.

And yet, even if the Corcyraean excursus constitutes a high-water mark for Thucydidean exposition, the triumph of accurate history

---

47. Even here, Thucydides has enjoyed little success: the identification of the plague with a modern disease remains a perennial source for scholarly speculation, but no explanation has ever won wide support.

proves double-edged. The memory of atrocities is not simply a neutral finding but, like the process of war,[48] takes on a life of its own and begins to exert its own force upon events:

> Revolution thus ran its course from city to city, and the places that it arrived at last, from having heard what had been done before carried to a still greater excess the refinement of their inventions, as manifested in the cunning of their enterprises and the atrocity of their reprisals.
>
> Thuc. 3.82.3

The participants in civil war become students of factional fighting, and by learning of previous struggles they perfect and intensify their own ruthlessness. Memory becomes an incitement to murder and betrayal, as the reputation of past crimes undermines confidence for the future. The self-fulfilling nature of ideological realism finds its way into the *History*.

THUCYDIDES AND POLITICAL REALISM

If historians, ancient and modern alike, have generally found that their work, however rigorous and "scientific" in method, does not consitute a science, Thucydides' aspirations have taken root in the "social" or "human sciences." In particular, Thucydides has earned a remarkable position as an acknowledged creator of the paradigm for political realism. Although more recently "postmodernist" and feminist scholars have subjected realism to searching new analyses,[49] the quest to establish a scientific discipline has remained strong.[50] Although Thucydides did not work with the categories of late twentieth-century criticism and although I believe that his work has close affinities with the project of social science, nevertheless the *History* is remarkable in that it both anticipates a number of elements widely shared by realists and reflects a sense, however imperfectly conceptualized at times, of the weaknesses in political realism. Much of the rest of this book will be devoted to probing these inconsistencies. Here I would like to establish points of connection between Thucydides and the later tradition.

---

48. Thuc. 1.122.1: ἥκιστα γὰρ πόλεμος ἐπὶ ῥητοῖς χωρεῖ, αὐτὸς δὲ ἀφ᾽ αὑτοῦ τὰ πολλὰ τεχνᾶται πρὸς τὸ παρατυγχάνον ("For war of all things proceeds least upon definite rules but draws principally upon itself for contrivances to meet an emergency").

49. A recent anthology of essays on essays about political realism (Derian 1995a) provides an excellent overview of the developing tradition of realist thought.

50. See, for example, Shapiro and Wendt 1992; Wendt 1995.

Thucydides' direct influence on modern political thought begins already with Thomas Hobbes, whose first major work was a translation of Thucydides, and on whose thought Thucydidean influence was substantial. The famous "Athenian thesis" of Thucydides 1.76—that "honour, fear, and profit" (as Hobbes translates *timê*, *deos*, and *ôphelia*) drive all human beings—reappears in the most influential passage that Hobbes ever wrote. The thirteenth chapter of *Leviathan* varies the language, but not the substance, of Thucydides, citing "competition," "diffidence," and "glory" as the three primary human motivations. Hobbes attributes to this triad his famous "warre . . . of every man, against every man," which is the natural state of humanity. If anything, however, Hobbes oversimplifies the picture that we find in Thucydides, presenting us with a much more mechanistic and less nuanced model of human behavior.[51]

In the twentieth century, Thucydides' *History* enjoys a firm position, for better and for worse, as an exemplary analysis of power politics. The struggle between "the expedient" (*to sumpheron*) and "the just" (*to dikaion*), which plays itself out from the opening debate of the *History* (on which, see chapter 3), anticipates such later concepts as the *raison d' état* of Richelieu, the *Realpolitik* of Bismarck, the "big stick" of Theodore Roosevelt, and the cold-war balance of power of which George Marshall was a primary architect.[52] Robert Tucker, writing in the 1960s, explicitly compared Kennedy's July 1961 address to the nation with Perikles' first speech in Thucydides.[53] Thucydides' analysis of the causes of the Peloponnesian War, despite the criticisms of classicists, has remained compelling to many students of international

51. On the relationship between Hobbes's thought and Thucydides, with particular emphasis on the differences that modern observers often overlook, see now Johnson 1993 and Johnson-Bagby 1994.

52. On Richelieu, see Kissinger 1994, 58–59; Church 1973, 495–504; George Marshall explicitly pointed out the resemblance between the emerging cold war and the tensions between Athens and Sparta (see the speech he delivered at Princeton University on February 22, 1947: Dept. of State Bulletin, vol. 16, p. 391). His reading of Thucydides shaped his view of the contemporary affairs in which he exercised tremendous influence.

53. Tucker (Osgood and Tucker 1967, 201) recalls Perikles at 1.140.4–5, when he insists that the real issue is not the Megarian dispute but Athenian independence: "Substitute the surrender of West Berlin for revoking the Megarian decree and Pericles' words [at Thuc. 1.140.4–5] seem entirely analogous to the words of President Kennedy in the summer of 1961: 'West Berlin is more than a showcase of liberty, a symbol, an isle of freedom in a communist sea . . . ; above all it has now become, as never before, the great testing place of Western courage and will, a focal point where our solemn commitments . . . and Soviet ambitions now meet in basic confrontation. . . . If we do not meet our commitments to Berlin, where will we later stand? If we are not true to our word there, all that we have achieved will mean nothing' "(address to the nation, July 25, 1961, Dept. of State Bulletin, vol. 45, pp. 268, 273).

affairs as "the prototype statement of how we usually express the causes of war."[54] Another recent history of international relations theory stresses Thucydides' crucial position for this field: "Thucydides depicts a condition in which power wields the ultimate authority in relations among states, so that 'the strong do what they have the power to do and the weak accept what they have to accept.' "[55] At the same time, the ancient historian Donald Kagan, who published a four-volume history of the Peloponnesian War, used his decades of experience with Thucydides as a foundation for broader work. His 1995 book, *On the Origins of War*, which moves from the Peloponnesian War and Thucydides to the Cuban missile crisis, drew advance praise from, among others, George Shultz, former U.S. secretary of state.

Thucydides has, however, not only attracted considerable attention as a general analyst. He has also become recognized as the first representative of a specific "realist" paradigm for international relations.[56] Realists tend to fall into two groups. The "classical realists," such as E. H. Carr, Hans Morgenthau, and John Herz, emerged when fascism, the Second World War, and the subsequent confrontation with the Soviet Union made the harsh Thucydidean outlook particularly attractive. These writers, like Hobbes, used constants of human nature to explain state behavior. Subsequently, "neorealists," including Robert Gilpin, Kenneth Waltz, and Robert Keohane, shifted the focus from human nature toward the overall structure of the international system. They argued that "unit level factors" (such as individual states) were less important than the overall system, and that the overall system of interstate relations defined the constraints that individual states had to follow. More recently, scholars such as Richard Ashley, James Der Derian, Jean Bethke Elshtain, J. Ann Tickner, and Alexander Wendt have begun to subject realism to a searching critique from a variety of theoretical per-

54. Wight 1978, 138.
55. Knutsen 1992, 32.
56. Vasquez (1990, 3) stressed the influence of Thucydides and Machiavelli on realist thinking in the 1950s and 1960s until Vietnam drove many to focus again upon issues of morality. He includes the Hobbes translation of the Melian Dialogue (pp. 16–20) in his anthology of realist authors. Likewise, Votti and Kauppi 1987 opens its section on the intellectual precursors and influences on realism with Thucydides (pp. 34–36). Even Wayman and Diehl 1994, which concentrates on charts, tables, and heavy quantification rather than historical analysis, begins immediately with Thucydides (p. 5 to be precise).
57. Contributions by these authors are collected in Derian 1995a; to evaluate some of the developments under way, compare this collection (which includes pieces by Hans Morgenthau and Robert Keohane) with Keohane 1986a, where Ashley's contribution plays a far more marginal role. Realism has come under increasing attack: a director of one major

spectives,[57] but even in this revisionist debate Thucydides continues to play a role.[58]

Laurie Johnson (now Johnson-Bagby) has recently dealt at length with the relationship between Thucydides and later political realists;[59] thus I will concentrate on some of the most important assumptions that inspire classical realists and neorealists alike to adopt Thucydides. Writers within and about political realism take pleasure in determining which assumptions define realist thought. These assumptions, though varying slightly, remain reasonably consistent from author to author, and those that I select are fairly standard.[60] These assumptions are important both because they help contemporary realists focus their own intellectual practice and because Thucydides is often cited as a source for one or more of them.[61]

First, political realists, even if they concede to civic life a measure of order and morality, tend to stress the amoral nature of interstate relations.[62] Whatever the religious or political ideology of the time, when nations compete with one another, the powerful dominate the weak. Expressions such as *raison d'état* and *Realpolitik* serve to describe the harsh decisions that actors make when they place the interests of the state over conventional morality. The Melian Dialogue and the "Athenian thesis" propounded at Thucydides 1.76 are commonly cited as examples of this brutal Hobbesian war of all against all. Whatever Thucydides' personal preferences may have been,[63] he makes clear in his

---

university press informed me that it had considered three separate manuscripts critiquing realism in a three-month period in early 1995.

58. E.g., Elshtain 1995, 345–346, stressing "texts as contested terrain"; Derian 1995b, 382–385

59. Johnson (1993) begins from the observation that political theorists often link Thucydides and Hobbes without giving due weight to the differences between the two; she summarizes her model of Thucydides as a realist at pp. 203–229; she restates many of her main points also in Johnson-Bagby 1994; on Thucydides as a realist, see also Garst 1989, Doyle 1990, Forde 1992, Clark 1993, and Derian 1995b, 382–285.

60. See, for example, Johnson 1993, 3; Keohane 1986a, 7. For a synopsis of different sets, see "Core Propositions of Realist Theory," in Wayman and Diehl 1994, 8–13; for a feminist revision of realist assumptions, see Tickner 1995, 66–67.

61. E.g., Gilpin 1981, 211–230; Gilpin 1986, 306; Keohane 1986a, 7; Wayman and Diehl 1994, 5.

62. For a recent attempt to render this outlook more sophisticated, see Wendt 1995.

63. Few students of Thucydides, whether from the field of classics, political philosophy, or international relations, would deny that Thucydides, despite his pose as a detached observer, structured his narrative in such a way as to provoke our horror at the extremes of power politics: e.g. (from among nonclassicists writing on Thucydides), Johnson 1993, 219–220; the title of Orwin 1994, *The Humanity of Thucydides*, boldly asserts its view: this book takes as one of its main themes the attempt in Thucydides to transcend the limits of the Athenian thesis.

analysis of early Greek history that fear (*deos*), honor (*timê*), and advantage (*ôfelia*) (the three qualities that the Athenians cite twice at 1.76)
are fundamental, even dominant, forces that drive international affairs.[64]
Even some ancient historians who express frustration with Thucydides
admire him for this: as Paul Cartledge remarks, "Thucydides has a claim
to both originality of thought and permanency of value in his unswerving insistence, for purposes of historical interpretation, on the amorality
of interstate relations."[65] Even as Thucydides' *History* brings out the brutality of such behavior and does not endorse it,[66] it stresses the gap
between conventional morality and actual practice. Thucydides' insis-
tent demystification of motives and rejection of conventional pieties are
major leitmotivs of this book.

Second, the quest for power—power with which to provide security
and power for its own sake, as a good in and of itself—drives this international free-for-all. For Thucydides, money and power are closely
linked. Thus he represents the accumulation of wealth as a fundamental
engine for the growth of power and prosperity alike. Writing of Greek
experiences under the domination of Minos, Thucydides outlines his
model for the development of power and power relations:

> The coast populations now began to apply themselves more closely to the
> acquisition of wealth (*chrêmata*), and their life became more settled; some
> even began to build themselves walls since they had become richer
> (*plousiôteroi*). For the love of profits (*kerdos*, pl.) would reconcile the weaker
> (*hoi hêssous*) to the dominion of the stronger (*hoi kreissous*), and the more
> powerful (*dunatôteroi*), because they possessed a surplus of wealth (*periousia*
> *chrêmatôn*), were able to reduce the smaller towns to subjection.
>
> Thuc. 1.8.3

---

64. Hornblower (1987, 178–180) objects to any Hobbesian distinction between civil
morality and interstate lawlessness, primarily because the most eloquent expositions of
this perspective appear in Athenian speeches, which do not necessarily reflect the attitudes
of the historian. In this context, see, however, the Archaeology, where Thucydides is explicitly offering his own conclusions. The Archaeology introduces us to the historian's
general methodology and attitudes. See Thuc. 1.8.3, where the desire for profit (*kerdos*)
leads the weak to endure the "slavery" (*douleia*) of the powerful. Note that in this passage,
Thucydides blurs the distinction between individual and state, setting as parallel individuals who seek the patronage of the powerful, and rich states that convert the smaller into
their clients (*hupêkooi*). The classic passage is 1.9, in which Thucydides rejects the traditional view, that loyalty to an oath and *charis* (the formal demands of gratitude) led Greeks
to join Agamemnon in the expedition against Troy. Instead, Thucydides argues at some
length that others served Agamemnon because he was "preeminent in force" (1.9.1) and
that terror (*phobos*) was at least as important as *charis* (1.9.3).
65. Cartledge 1979, 255; see also Ste. Croix 1972, 5–34.
66. Forde (1992) traces in Thucydides the tension between the morality between states
and within states.

Here Thucydides retrojects into the distant past an association of money with power that had gained particular force in his own time. When Perikles analyzes Athenian strength at the opening of the war, he locates Athens's primary strength in its financial reserves and in the continuing revenues from its empire (Thuc. 1.141; 2.13). In the Mytilenean debate, Kleon and Diodotos each stress the importance of keeping the allied cities in good condition lest they become unable to pay tribute and thus useless to Athens (3.39.8, 3.46).

Other figures in Thucydides express a sophisticated awareness that power involves perception as well as material force. Thus Perikles insists that the Athenians must never "yield to the Peloponnesians" on any point (Thuc. 1.140.1). The particular dispute is less important than the act of yielding:

> This trifle contains the whole seal and trial of your resolution. If you accommodate them, you will instantly have to meet some greater demand, as having obeyed because of intimidation (*phobos*) in the first instance; while a firm refusal will make them clearly understand that they must treat you more as equals.
>
> Thuc. 1.140.5

The famous Mytilenean debate turns upon the question of how Athens can best use its material force to make the allies fulfill its own needs. Diodotos, whose opinion carries the day, argues that if the Athenians spare most of the Mytileneans and thus do not exploit their material force to the fullest, they will immediately gain access to more tribute from Mytilene and will in the future waste less of their resources in putting down revolts (3.46). Melos was a small island with negligible resources, but the Athenians insisted on subduing it, because domination of all the islands would have a powerful symbolic effect upon the rest of the allies (5.95, 97). The Thucydidean Alkibiades owes much of his reputation for brilliance to his understanding of the relationship between the appearance and the reality of material power (e.g., 6.15.2).

But if all states and all individuals pursue power to some extent, ambition consumes the Athenians far more intensely than any other group. The qualitatively distinct thirst for power that shapes Athenian character is, in fact, crucial to the *History*. It terrifies the Corinthians, leading them to badger the Spartans into war (Thuc. 1.68–71), and provides Alkibiades with a psychological argument for the Sicilian expedition (6.18). Thucydides even inserts power in the one idealizing vision of Athens that the *History* contains: during the Funeral Oration, Perikles urges his fellow Athenians to gaze upon the power (*dunamis*) of, and thus become infatuated with, Athens (2.43.1). I will return to the ambiguities of this quest for power as Perikles, its most sympathetic exponent, expresses it.

Third, realists have traditionally viewed interstate affairs as an anarchic system in which hegemony or domination alone can bring order. The quest for power, for all its problems, is at least ambiguous, because success in this quest can bring order to a chaotic world.[67] Realism thus brings with it a certain bias toward supranational structures, even empires, as a constructive thing, and for those with more liberal values this can lead to an intellectual tension. The United Nations is only the most prominent example of the compromises that can result from the tug-of-war between the realist fear of anarchy and the liberal respect for multiple sovereignty and decentralized power. Thucydides fits squarely within this tradition: where Perikles' Funeral Oration articulates an almost heroic vision of individual freedom, Thucydides clearly (as I will argue in chapter 5) represents human society as anarchic, almost Hobbesian: without strong imperial superstructures such as those imposed by Minos in the past or Athens in the present, individual prosperity has little chance. Even Perikles, when plague ravages the city and Athenian society starts to come unglued, shifts his focus in his final speech, stressing the primacy of state over individual and reflecting the fear that anarchy is the "state of nature" within, as well as between, citystates.

Fourth, realists generally view the group as the standard unit of analysis. Because for three hundred years the modern nation-state has dominated international relations (by convention, since the Peace of Westphalia in 1648), it provides the focus for most realist work, but virtually all realists acknowledge the nation-state to be a special case—tribes, empires, fiefdoms, virtually any other organized group (such as citystates), would do just as well.[68] This attitude corresponds closely to Thucydides' practice, especially in the early books, which tend to lump together "the Athenians," "the Corinthians," and "the Spartans," representing each as speaking with a single, undifferentiated voice.

Nevertheless, individual actors exercise an increasing influence on

---

67. E.g., Keohane 1986a, 198–199.

68. In the preface to the second edition of *The Twenty Years' Crisis*, E. H. Carr, for example, regrets that his book "too readily and too complacently accepts the nation state, large or small, as the unit of international society" (Carr 1949, viii). See also Gilpin 1986, 313–318; Gilpin 1981, 18; Herz 1951, 29; Wendt 1995, 163–164, Elshtain 1995, 350–351.

events in the later books, and the integrity of the individual city-states grows weaker. I will have more to say about this phenomenon in the conclusion, for I believe not only that Thucydides' attitude genuinely shifts, but also that his attitude does more than reflect what he sees. The fragmented nature of events in book 8 reflects two failures of Thucydides' intellectual expectations. First, the Periklean model of leadership ceases to function, as Thucydides himself points out (Thuc. 2.65.10–11). Even talented men such as Alkibiades and Phrynichos simply cannot place the welfare of the state above their own, and they fail to provide the kind of leadership that Thucydides attributes to Perikles. But there was a second factor at work that Thucydides does not recognize, for it occupies a blind spot in his vision. Thucydides represents the weak leadership that followed Perikles as a decline from a previous state of affairs, but this is only partially correct, for, with the possible exception of Themistokles (cf. 1.138), Perikles towered over his predecessors as well. The politics of Alkibiades, Phrynichos, and the other figures who dominate the end of the *History* are not so much a new phenomenon as a throwback to the traditional politics of the archaic and classical periods, with their emphasis on the connections and alliances of individuals. Thucydides does not make this connection, because he has resolutely excluded from this narrative virtually all of the mechanics that normally governed such behavior. Here his paradigmatic vision is at its weakest, for, as I will argue later, he excludes and underestimates crucial aspects of this system. The reversal of traditional standards thus appears as a decline from Periklean standards.

Thucydides' "tragic vision" of Athenian decline has both an objective and a subjective dimension. On the one hand, there was, as Adam Parry, among others, has argued,[69] the terrible contradiction between Athens's greatness and its fall. Even Perikles in his final speech treats the ultimate fall of Athens as inevitable. I will stress as well the distance that separates the "heroic" Athens of Marathon and Salamis from the ruthless Athens of Melos and the Sicilian expedition. The object of Thucydides' *History* is thus tragic.

But Thucydides' vision is also itself tragic, because it is incomplete, and because this incompleteness, which blinds Thucydides to many crucial elements of history, is also intimately linked to those very strengths that define him. Thucydides has established himself as the first realist

69. Parry 1972.

because he refused to pay court to sentimentalities and pious fictions. His Athenians in particular exhibit an extraordinary candor about their purposes and goals, and although even this candor is at times deceptive and manipulative, the degree of honesty and "self-knowledge" that these Athenians exhibit is at times astonishing. Nevertheless, that very ruthlessness of analysis and refusal to accept surface appearances—the refusal, as he puts it at 1.10.3, to "scrutinize appearances rather than powers" (*tas opseis . . . mallon skopein ê tas dunameis*)—which so characterize his work also rendered many factors difficult for him to assess. It is clear that appearances often are important, actors do not always cast aside their pious fictions, and the bonds of loyalty and friendship do not always break under pressure.

Fifth, realists treat human behavior, at least insofar as it governs the relations between states, as rational. If behavior is rational, then we can expect to determine, through disciplined observation, rules with which to predict what choices actors will pursue in the future. Neorealists differ somewhat in that they push the source of rationality one level up from the "unitary actors" into the international system, and classical realists look to the psychology of the individual actors or the sociology of individual states. The assumption of rationality, to a greater or lesser extent, underlies all serious inquiry—even research into psychoses assumes that scientific analysis can isolate and lay bare the causes for actions that seem bizarre and inexplicable. Nevertheless, both neorealists and classical realists lay particular stress on rationality, because they specifically intend to place the study of international relations on a sounder, more "scientific" basis. E. H. Carr, for example, horrified at the rise of fascism and the breakdown of international order in the 1930s, entitled the opening chapter of *The Twenty Years' Crisis* "The Science of International Relations." Hans Morgenthau published *Scientific Man vs. Power Politics* in 1946. In 1951 John Herz wrote his *Political Realism and Political Idealism* specifically because he wished to help political theory move beyond its " 'pre-scientific' stage." Almost thirty years later, Kenneth Waltz offered his *Theory of International Politics* with the same goal. Frank Wayman and Paul Diehl published the collection of essays *Reconstructing Realpolitik* in 1994 to give realism the most solid foundation that the social sciences could provide.

Sixth, modern realists share Thucydides' desire for a scientific outlook that will provide tangible benefits to those who make decisions in the future. The phrase "utopian realists," recently applied to E. H. Carr, captures a general outlook animating many of the best members of this school.[70] By confronting the realities of human nature, we can, it is argued, learn how to control them and thus avoid the greatest misfortunes. This is the underlying idea behind Hobbes's *Leviathan* (itself influenced by Thucydides) and much of the recent work on political realism. As Robert Gilpin puts it, "Political realism is, of course, the very embodiment of this faith in reason and science. An offspring of modern science and the Enlightenment, realism holds that through calculations of power and national interest statesmen create order out of anarchy and thereby moderate the inevitable conflicts of autonomous, self-centered, and competitive states."[71]

Thucydides, as we have already seen above, is ambivalent about the progress of humankind and the possibilities of reason. He reveals in his Archaeology, the thematic and methodological introduction to his work as a whole, an almost Hegelian sense of history as an ongoing process of development. Early humanity was primitive; life nasty, brutish, and short. Basic human responses, such as greed and fear, have provided a foundation for political structures, and these political structures have, as they have grown in size and power, brought increasing order and prosperity.[72] Against the brutalization of war, Thucydides' Diodotos attempts to provide a rationalized basis for a relatively humane perspective.

But, naturally, events proved almost as problematic for the wary humanism of Diodotos as for the more open idealizations of Perikles' Funeral Oration. Just as the plague undercuts Perikles' bold claims, the Athenians would a decade later use the argument of expediency to justify massacre at Melos. At the same time, no new Perikles or even Diodotos would arise. Instead, the problematic Alkibiades would emerge as the most striking personality in the latter part of the *History*. The tensions between public and private interest would not be resolved, and Athens, the modern sea power, would ultimately fall to its clumsy Spartan adversaries. Thucydides' *History* breaks off in midstream, its tensions unresolved.

Seventh, realists have drawn criticism for their unconsciously gendered view of the world: realist thinkers have conceptualized international relations in terms of masculine aggression, reflecting the over-

---

70. See Howe 1994.
71. So, for example, Gilpin 1981, 226.
72. On this, see chapter 5 below.

whelming predominance of men even now and especially in the governing of state behavior.[73] To a very large extent, this bias toward the masculine and the creation of a world in which men, and men alone, are primary actors were, in fact, something that Thucydides helped fashion: if we move from Herodotus to Thucydides, the frequency of references to women drops by an order of magnitude.[74] I have pursued this particular phenomenon in detail elsewhere;[75] it reflects more than simple misogyny. Women disappear from Thucydides' narrative along with families and households, as Thucydides tries to create a discursive world in which individual citizens and city-states are the sole actors.

To sum up, Thucydides easily meets the rather broad criteria by which political realists define themselves, and he clearly deserves his position as the honorary forerunner of a fluid paradigm for studying groups interacting together. At the same time, Thucydides presents a far darker view of the world than any of his modern academic counterparts, and his work manages to maintain the tensions that he could not resolve, without flattening them or glossing them over. I pursue Thucydides' views at greater length, but first I wish to situate him more firmly in the tradition of Greek thought. Thucydides is hardly the first extant Greek author to give expression to the notion "Might makes right." His Athenians at Sparta or Melos had their own antecedents, whom students of realism need to consider. At the same time, the assumptions of the world into which Thucydides was born—Greece of c. 460 B.C.E.—were clearly different from those that prevailed as he wrote about the war's end some time after 404 B.C.E. The changes were in some ways as momentous as those that separate American society of the 1930s from that of the 1990s. A generation of warfare as well as many individuals—Protagoras, Anaxagoras, Perikles, Kritias, and Sokrates, to name a few—contributed to this process. But Thucydides, the failed general, who mixed with his aristocratic connections from all sides and brooded upon Athens over years of exile, contributed to as well as mirrored the changing times. It is these changes that I will take up next.

73. Tickner 1995.
74. Thucydides: 34 instances; Herodotus: 373. When the differing sizes of the works of these two authors are considered, the main word for woman (gunê) shows up nine times more often in Herodotus than in Thucydides; for references to discussions of this phenomenon, see above, note 42.
75. Crane 1996a.

CHAPTER 3

Representations of Power before and after Thucydides

Thucydidean scholars have traditionally viewed the natural rule of the strong as an idea characteristic of fifth-century sophistic thought and have treated its appearances in Thucydides as a reflection of contemporary interests. This is, to a large extent, true—we can see in the *Clouds* of Aristophanes, as well as in the Thrasymachos of Plato's *Republic* and the Kallikles of Plato's *Gorgias*, that the sophists were seen to have had a particular interest in the rule of the strong and to have given systematic expression to this notion. But in equating the rule of the strong with natural law, the fifth-century sophists were developing an idea that appears already in the earliest surviving Greek texts. Although Thucydides was immersed in the ideas of his time and his work is scarcely conceivable except as a product of the later fifth century, it is important to keep in mind the complex roots that connect even the most radical fifth-century thought with traditional Greek culture.

Consider, for example, a famous scene in the *Iliad*, important not only for its pathos but because as a meditation on the rule of the strong, it points toward Thucydides' Melian Dialogue. At the height of his rampage across the battlefield and as the *Iliad* builds to the climactic killing of Hektor, Achilles encounters the unfortunate Lykaon, a son of the Trojan king Priam. Achilles had taken Lykaon prisoner a few weeks before, and the young man had only recently made his way back home. We hear that "for eleven days he delighted his heart among his friends, but on the twelfth day a god cast him back into the hands of Achilles"

(*Il.* 21.45–47). The desperate Lykaon begs for his life but elicits instead
an emotionally complex but chilling reply:

> Fool (*nêpie*), do not offer ransom to me, and do not make speeches. [100]
> Until Patroklos met his day of fate, even till then was it more pleasing to me
> to spare the Trojans, and many I took alive and sold overseas; but now there
> is not one that shall escape death, whoever before the walls of Ilios a god
> shall deliver into my hands—[105] not one among all the Trojans, and least
> of all among the sons of Priam. No, friend (*phile*), you too die—but why do
> you weep thus? Patroklos also died, who was better far than you. And do
> you not see what manner of man I am, how handsome and how tall? A good
> man was my father, and a goddess the mother that bore me; yet over me too
> hang death and mighty fate. [110] There shall come a dawn or eve or midday,
> when my life too shall some man take in battle, whether he strikes me with
> cast of the spear or with an arrow from the string.
>
> Hom. *Il.* 21.99–113

Lykaon is *nêpios*—a harsh adjective applicable to infants and to profoundly foolish adults—but he is also *philos*—the standard term for
"dear" or "friend." Achilles' tone is elusive. Is he sarcastic? His malicious
treatment of Lykaon's corpse a few lines later gives credence to such a
reading, but Achilles' speech has struck many readers as oddly detached,
as if Achilles' rage had reached such a level that he had progressed beyond personalized emotion and become an almost mechanical engine of
death.

Achilles' speech is also interesting because it articulates an odd justification for his unnecessary brutality. All human beings are subject to
death. Patroklos is dead, and Achilles soon will die. Both men are superior to the insignificant Lykaon, and, for this reason, Achilles implies
that Lykaon should accept his own death, indeed he should not even
weep at his own imminent extinction. The strong are not only superior
to the weak but deserve to expect more out of life. Patroklos and Achilles, by nature of their physical force, are more worthy human beings,
and it is unreasonable for Lykaon to hope for life when his betters expect
death. At the same time, death waits for all, the mighty and the feeble
alike. If Lykaon faces death in battle, the same fate as Patroklos or
Achilles, then he has no reason to complain. Achilles does not deserve
reproach for killing Lykaon, because someone else will, in turn, kill
Achilles. Death becomes a gift that passes in a classic chain of indirect
reciprocity. Not all reciprocal exchange is direct. On the battlefield of
Troy, Patroklos, Achilles, and Lykaon all ultimately receive death as a
final gift. Great as Achilles is, the "gift" of death that he bestows upon

Lykaon will soon be his. The stroke of Achilles' sword renders killer and victim peers.[1]

A similar episode appears in *Works and Days* where Hesiod represents himself as challenging his rapacious brother Perses:

> And now I will tell a fable for princes, since they themselves understand. Thus said the hawk to the nightingale with speckled neck as he carried her high up among the clouds, gripped fast in his talons, [205] and she, pierced by his crooked talons, cried pitifully. To her he spoke disdainfully: "Miserable thing, why do you cry out? One far stronger (*areiôn*) than you now holds you fast, and you must go wherever I take you, songstress as you are. And if I please, I will make my meal of you, or let you go. [210] He is a fool who tries to withstand the stronger (*kreissôn*), for he does not win and suffers pain besides his shame." So said the swiftly flying hawk, the long-winged bird.
>
> Hes. *WD* 203–212

Hesiod's Hawk anticipates the basic position of such hard, sophist-trained men as Plato's Kallikles and Thrasymachos, who argue that might makes right. Already here, in one of the earliest surviving texts of Greek literature, we see expressed the idea that the strong naturally rule the weak and that the weak should therefore accede to their own destruction.

Achilles' remarks and Hesiod's story of the Hawk and the Nightingale are important, for they both demonstrate that many of the ideas that seem most "modern" in Thucydides appear in the earliest surviving Greek texts, composed perhaps two centuries before Thucydides wrote his *History*. When Thucydides' Athenians threaten to massacre the people of Mytilene or actually carry out this threat upon the Melians, their act reflects an increasing brutalization of the conflict in Greece. Thucydides' accounts of the plague at Athens and of the civil strife at Corcyra both argue that moral collapse was progressive, rapid, and extreme, but we must never forget that we can trace the roots of such hard ideas from the start of Greek literature.

At the same time, however, we must also retain a sense of proportion. If there were always Greeks ready to assert the natural rule of the strong, there were always others to argue the opposite side (and, of course, plenty of individuals would doubtless adapt their views to their current

---

1. Note that gifts need not be pleasant: in many cultures, not only gifts but insults and revenge are exchanged only between equals. The response to an affront can thus constitute a recognition of equality, just as silence can loudly proclaim disdain. On this, see Bourdieu 1977, 10–15.

advantage). Tyrants, peasants, and aristocrats all occupied very different subject positions, and no doubt many aristocrats, driven into exile by a ruthless tyrant, later, on driving that tyrant out of power, developed a very different attitude toward the use of force. With hundreds of independent city-states, all vying for prestige, the archaic Greek world was a complex, querulous environment in which many very different parties advanced distinct positions and sought to appropriate traditional values to their own ends. In speaking of archaic Greece, it is particularly important not to assume a single, completely unified set of values or even to suppose that groups that shared common vocabulary (e.g., *sôphrosunê, dikê, aretê*) endowed these terms with the same values—Thucydides, in fact, was particularly sensitive to such semantic warfare (see, for example, Thuc. 3.82.4).

Nevertheless, diversity need not be static—the same ideas do become more or less prominent. There are fascist elements in all the contemporary industrialized democracies, but the Nazi element of 1990 Germany, while disturbing, was very different from that of 1938. Hesiod, for example, does not leave his tale of the Hawk and the Nightingale without context. He continues by casting it into a different light than the isolated passage above might suggest:

> But you, Perses, listen to right and do not foster violence; for violence is bad for a poor man. [215] Even the prosperous man cannot easily bear its burden but is weighed down under it when he has fallen into delusion. The better path is to go by on the other side toward Justice; for Justice beats Outrage when she comes at length to the end of the race. But only when he has suffered does the fool learn this. For Oath keeps pace with wrong judgments. [220] There is a noise when Justice is being dragged in the way where those who devour bribes and give sentence with crooked judgments take her. And she, wrapped in mist, follows to the city and haunts of the people, weeping, and bringing mischief to humanity, even to such as have driven her forth in that they did not deal straightly with her.
>
> Hes. *WD* 213–222

For Hesiod, the Hawk's case is not self-evident. The poet goes on to warn that such ruthless self-assertion is dangerous for the powerful as well as for the weak, and to argue that *dikê*, justice, ultimately serves the interests of all parties. Hesiod thus makes it clear that the Hawk has no monopoly on discourse but espouses only one position in a larger conversation.

The archaic Greek world was remarkable in large measure because it managed to construct a shared political practice in which city-states did not follow the example of Achilles or Hesiod's Hawk. Virtually all

Greeks understood the logic of force—the *Iliad*, after all, captivated the
imaginations of archaic and classical Greeks in a way that few texts,
religious or otherwise, have matched. Nevertheless, during the century
that preceded the Persian Wars, virtually no Greek city-state conquered
another. Conflicts pursued limited goals, and no single polis was able to
accumulate a preponderant level of power. Leadership had far more to
do with hegemony and moral authority than domination and the threat
of overwhelming physical violence.

INSCRIBING THE LIMITS OF AUTHORITY:
THE HEGEMONY OF HERODOTUS'S SPARTANS

Herodotus provides our first detailed picture of Spartan leadership, but
his account, closely studied as it has been, is even more revealing because
of its form, its silences, and its assumptions than because of its tantaliz-
ingly sketchy content. Herodotus's model of Spartan authority is a thick
text that inscribes within itself an idealized set of rules for leadership in
the archaic Greek world. Even as he presents a flattering (and probably
anachronistic) account of Sparta's prestige in the mid-sixth century, he
embeds in his account strict conditions that limit and contain Sparta's
position. He defines a Sparta for which too much power and autonomy
would, paradoxically, endanger its preeminence. In praising Sparta, Herodotus establishes standards that constrain Spartan behavior. His introduction is thus both a panegyric and a cautionary tale.

Herodotus does not flesh out for us the harsh, philistine Sparta on
which Xenophon, Plato, and Aristotle dwell,[2] but his Spartans throughout the *Histories* differ from their fellow Greeks. At the opening of the
two major segments of the *Histories*, books 1 and 5, Herodotus draws
a schematic overview of Athens and Sparta. In the first of these, Herodotus represents his material from a typically oblique perspective, offering
us the account of Sparta as the Lydian Kroisos perceived it. The two
sketches at 1.59–64 and 65–68 encapsulate the leading states of fifth-
century Greece two generations before Xerxes' invasion.

Herodotus's language is often suggestive, but one particular term in
this passage has attracted a great deal of scholarly attention and shaped
perceptions of Herodotus's first account of Sparta. At 1.68.6, Herodotus
remarks that by the time Kroisos made his inquiries in the middle of the

2. Finley 1975, 174.

sixth century "the greater part of the Peloponnese had been subjected by them." Herodotus's choice of language (a form of the verb *katastrephô*, "to subjugate, conquer") is harsh and has caused some embarrassment. Kroisos, for example, "subjected (*katestrepsato*) the Greeks to the payment of tribute" (Hdt. 1.6.2; cf. also 1.27.1), and the term reappears sixty-five times in Herodotus to describe one group subduing another. The commentators W. W. How and J. Wells remark that Herodotus is "exaggerating," though they seem more concerned with the extent rather than the intensity of Spartan control. G. E. M. de Ste. Croix argues that the term would be "fully justified" if Sparta's allies "were obliged to follow Sparta into war at her bidding."[3] More recently, Kurt Raaflaub suggests that the term is a piece of Athenian anti-Spartan propaganda, which sought to portray the Peloponnesian League as analogous to the Athenian empire.[4]

In fact, the verb *katastrephô* is indeed harsh. Herodotus is, in this passage, altering his historical voice, moving from a general view (which brings with it a certain vocabulary) to another, more jaundiced perspective that we may associate with the more cynical, all-knowing historian. The same shift from softened, euphemized language to blunter and harsher rhetoric happens earlier on in book 1. At 1.13, Herodotus quotes in indirect discourse an exchange between Gyges and the Delphic oracle. In this passage, he follows the terminology that the participants, we are to suppose, themselves used, and he uses derivatives of *basileus*, the word for a legitimate king, five times in a single paragraph. When he then goes on to speak of Gyges' dynasty in more generalized language (Hdt. 1.14), he shifts from *basileus* to *turannos*, the term for one who exercises power by force rather than by legitimate right.

If the term *katastrephô* implies that Sparta had harshly subjected the greater portion of the Peloponnese to its will, then Herodotus's "glib generalization"[5] renders ironic the main point of the previous chapters and clashes with the presentation of Spartan authority elsewhere in the *Histories*. Taken as a whole, Herodotus's account of Sparta at 1.65–68 is as remarkable for its silences and for the limits it sets as it is for its contents and its celebration of Spartan power.

First, Herodotus, in this programmatic introduction of Sparta, is silent on two major subjects: the Messenian wars and the helots. This

3. Ste. Croix 1972, 109.
4. Raaflaub 1985, 84, 89 n. 91.
5. Cartledge 1987, 11.

silence is not neutral but conveys a sharp message. The Spartan way of life depended upon the direct control of land within Lakonia and Messenia. Sparta reduced many of the original inhabitants in those districts to the level of "helots," serfs whose labor supported the Spartans. The Lakonian helots had been serfs from time immemorial, but the Spartan conquest of Messene was recent enough that Tyrtaios could give it a permanent (if still somewhat sketchy) place in the poetic record of Greece. The Messenians never forgot that they had been free, and Herodotus several times mentions war with them as a recent event (Hdt. 9.35.2, 64.2) or an ongoing possibility (5.49.8). Likewise, Herodotus elsewhere takes helotage for granted and makes no attempt to minimize its role. We might have expected any description of Sparta's rise to power to have included these two phenomena, the heroized struggle to conquer Messene and the somewhat peculiar institution of helotage.[6]

At 1.65–68, however, where Herodotus sketches the rise of Spartan power, he includes neither the Messenian wars nor helotage in his initial overview of Spartan power and its origins—not a specific judgment, perhaps, but suggestive. He does, however, go on, as we will see, to situate Sparta's final rise to prominence at the point when it ceased expanding and reducing its Greek neighbors to slavery. In Herodotus's model, Sparta achieves its dominant position only when it no longer seeks to dominate others. He complements the silence on Spartan conquest and subjugation of free Greeks with pointed anecdotes from which we may draw our own conclusions.

Second, Herodotus provides us with only a brief description of Lykourgos and his reforms at Sparta. He recalls an earlier time when the Spartans had been the "most ill-governed (Hdt. 1.65.2: *kakonomôtatoi*) of nearly all the Hellenes." This term for "ill-governed," *kako-nomos*, is powerful, for it is the adjectival opposite of the noun *eu-nomia*, "good government," the quality that in later times all—even the unenthusiastic Thucydides[7] —conceded as distinguishing Sparta more than any other state. The term "government" is inadequate: "both *eunomia* and *kakon-*

---

6. Peculiar but not unique: contrast, for example, the serfs of Thessaly and Crete, whom Aristotle compares to the Spartan helots (*Pol.* 1269a35ff.); on the serfs of Thessaly, see Archemachos of Euboea, FGrH 424 frag. 1 (Ath. 6.264a-b); on the Maryandynoi, serfs at Herakleia Pontika, see Poseidonios, FGrH 87 frag. 8 (Ath. 6.263d); Strabo 12.3.4; Ste. Croix 1980, 138–139.

7. See. Thuc. 1.18.1, where Thucydides says that Sparta was "from the earliest times subject to *eunomia* (*eunomêthê*)."

omos characterize a whole way of life, not only (or perhaps not at all)
a form of constitution."[8]

According to Herodotus, however, this early disorder at Sparta had
two dimensions. On the one hand, disorder reigned internally among
the Spartans themselves (Hdt. 1.65.2: *kata spheas autous*), but from the
outset, Herodotus refuses to define the Spartans in isolation or to focus
his attention on strictly internal matters. When Herodotus paints the
dismal situation at Sparta, he combines internal lack of *eunomia* with
the fact that the Spartans were also "unsociable to strangers" (*xeinoisi
aprosmiktoi*). The second feature is significant. Many of our other
sources stress the secrecy and xenophobia of the Spartan state,[9] but here
at any rate Herodotus implies that the Spartans improved not simply
because they adopted a new internal order but because they became
better able to associate with members of other Greek states. No Greek
polis exists in isolation. Even Sparta must establish itself, according to
Herodotus, by its dealings with others.

According to Herodotus, Sparta develops in two separate stages, each
of which receives from Delphi a legitimating oracle: the greatest sanctuary in the Greek world sanctions both Lykourgos's reforms and the
superiority that the Spartans later asserted over the Tegeans. The structure of Herodotus 1.65–69 is typically Herodotean, jumping chronologically backward and forward. The chronology is susceptible to various interpretations, but the narrative seems to proceed as follows. We
first learn that in Kroisos's time the Spartans "had escaped their great
troubles and were already superior to the Tegeans in warfare" (1.65.1),
and Lykourgos was the man who had brought them out of this disordered escape (the verb describing their escape, it might be noted, is in
the perfect rather than the aorist and thus emphasizes that the escape
took place in the past but remains in effect during the present).

From the "present" of his narrative (in this case, the time of Kroisos,
roughly a century before Herodotus was writing), Herodotus moves
back into distant times and discusses the reforms of Lykourgos. The
emphasis of this description is remarkable and has caused many schol-

8. Finley 1975, 164.
9. Thus, at Thuc. 2.39.1, Perikles snipes at *xenêlasia*, Sparta's practice of driving away
foreigners to preserve secrecy; cf. also the Athenian criticisms leveled at Thuc. 1.77.6; at
9.11.2, Herodotus remarks that the Spartans refused to distinguish between "barbarians"
and Greeks who were not Spartan, referring to all non-Spartans, Greek or not, as "strangers" (*xeinoi*).

ars, anxious for early information about Sparta, to grind their teeth in frustration. On the one hand, at 1.65.4 Herodotus summarily alludes to some of the basic institutions attributed in his day to the Lykourgan reforms: the military organization, the ephorate, and the *gerousia*, a council of elders. He does not, however, explain what any of these institutions are, and he dismisses them within a single sentence. On the other hand, Herodotus devotes more than two sections (1.65.2–4) to Lykourgos's visit to Delphi and to the unexpected oracle, which Herodotus quotes, that attributed to Lykourgos a more than mortal status. Herodotus then includes alternate traditions: that the Pythia herself gave Lykourgos the new way of life or that Lykourgos introduced it from Crete. After his death, we learn (1.66.1), the Spartans established a sacred precinct (*hieron*) for Lykourgos where they revere him greatly (*sebontai megalôs*: a strong expression, since the verb *sebô* implies worship rather than simple honor).[10] The precise source of his reforms and their details are, however, less prominent in the narrative than the initial confrontation of Lykourgos and the oracle. The allusion to Lykourgos's ongoing cult concludes this part of the Spartan logos.

Herodotus's emphasis on the trip to Delphi and the cult of Lykourgos is tendentious and imposes on Spartan prestige limits and conditions foreign to the later account in Xenophon's *Constitution of the Spartans*. Xenophon puts far less relative emphasis on this: he praises the sanction of Delphi only in a brief section, and Delphi ratifies, rather than inspires, the reforms (*Lak. Pol.* 8.5). Herodotus's narrative, by contrast, gives cursory attention to the substance, and reinforces instead the legitimacy, of Lykourgos's reforms. Herodotus expresses little interest in Lykourgos's reforms as a set of laws and practices pursued within the Spartan state. He takes much greater care to establish the personal authority of Lykourgos and the official sanction that he and his reforms received from the Panhellenic oracle of Delphi. Thus Lykourgos was not successful in reforming Sparta simply because his institutions were better, but because he had received the advice and support of Delphi, a Panhellenic institution far beyond Spartan control. The Lykourgan reforms are not an autonomous system whereby self-contained Spartans produce power in their isolated city-state. They received their initial origin and legitimacy from a wider Greek society.

Third, once Lykourgos's reforms are in place, Herodotus moves on

---

10. E.g., Hdt. 1.138.2, 2.172.3; when Sophokles' Ajax applies this verb to his contemplated "admiration" of the Atreids (667), the language underlines his bitter sarcasm.

to a further and distinct stage of his story. Lykourgos's reforms do not
by themselves produce Spartan preeminence in warfare. Important as
Lykourgos may have been and however much he was revered, he alone
did not make Sparta the leading state in Greece. Herodotus has already
referred to an intermediate stage in Spartan development, when the
Spartans were successful in the rest of their wars, meeting disaster
against the Tegeans alone (Hdt. 1.65.1). Once again, Herodotus chooses
a remarkable starting point. Blessed with good land and large numbers,
the Spartans "were not content to keep quiet but disdainfully concluded
that they were stronger than the Arkadians" (1.66.1). Although, as we
noted above, Herodotus does not, in this passage, even mention the
bitter warfare in which the Spartans ultimately enslaved the Messenians,
a Greek people who never forgot and ultimately regained their independence, Herodotus does show himself acutely sensitive to the prospect of
Sparta enslaving Arkadian Greeks. There is nothing to be done for the
Messenian helots, as far as Herodotus is concerned, but the historian
refuses to praise Sparta for the conquest of free Greeks (he does not even
acknowledge this loss of freedom at 1.6.3). But Herodotus need not rely
upon silence alone to make his point. By fixing the historical gaze upon
Tegea, the narrative illustrates what it will and will not praise. The story
of Sparta and Tegea firmly establishes the fact that Spartan conquests
of Greek states were a thing of the past. Spartan preeminence is, in fact,
contingent on the shift from expansionism. Herodotus describes Spartan
preeminence in warfare by defining the limitations of this preeminence.

The story of Sparta and Tegea, like that of Lykourgos, begins outside
of the Peloponnese, at the oracle of Apollo at Delphi. The Spartans
consult the god about their prospects of conquering all of Arkadia (Hdt.
1.66.1). (We might note that aggression against landlocked, mountainous Arkadia was never a good idea. The closest classical Greek to that
disclosed in the Bronze Age Mycenaean Linear B tablets are the dialects
of Arkadia, the mountainous center of the Peloponnese, and of Kypros,
the most distant margin of the Greek world. Arkadia seems to have
survived as a backward but defiant fortress of the Mycenaean people,
who once dominated the Peloponnese.[11] The prospects for subjugating

---

11. On the linguistic similarities between Arkadian and the language of Linear B, see
Duhoux 1983, 41–44; Duhoux comments that, despite all the controversy about the relationship between Mycenaean and classical Greek, there is general consensus that Ar-
kado-Cypriote had the closest connection to Mycenaean of any later dialect group (p. 42).
It would appear that the speakers of Mycenaean Greek held out in the poor but rough
fastnesses of Arkadia.

Arkadia were therefore from the outset not encouraging.) The answering oracle limits Sparta's immediate ambitions but seems to endorse warfare against Tegea.

> You ask me for Arkadia? You ask too much; I grant it not.
> There are many men in Arkadia, eaters of acorns,
> Who will hinder you. But I grudge you not.
> I will give you Tegea to beat with your feet in dancing,
> And its fair plain to measure with a rope.
>
> Hdt. 1.66.2

"Measuring the land of Tegea with a rope" sent a strong message. Greek colonists from any polis would initially divide up the new land among themselves, and the oracle seemingly promised Sparta that it would be able to appropriate the territory of the Tegeans and divide it among its citizens. The Spartans naturally assumed that the god had given them his sanction to treat the Tegeans in the same way as they had treated the Messenians. The Spartans happily focused their attentions on Tegea and marched off to war carrying with them the chains with which they planned to enslave the Tegeans.

The oracle, however, proved to be *kibdêlos* (Hdt. 1.66.3), what we might now term "fool's gold," for its true interpretation was hardly favorable to Sparta. The Tegeans defeated the Spartans and made them wear the chains that they had brought with them (66.4). The would-be conquerors measured out the fields of the Tegeans by working on them as prisoners. The chains themselves were preserved and hung in the temple of Athena Alea at Tegea, where, Herodotus tells us, they could still be seen in his own day.

Warfare between Sparta and Tegea continued off and on for some time (Hdt. 1.67.1; note that Herodotus specifies at 1.68.1 that there happened to be free association between Spartans and Tegeans at this period). This warfare seems, however, to have fallen squarely into the inconclusive, limited conflicts that Thucydides at 1.17 and Aristagoras at Herodotus 5.49.8 both treat so dismissively. Nevertheless, during this period, the Tegeans always defeated the Spartans in war (Hdt. 1.67.2). Ultimately, the Spartans asked Delphi which god they should honor in order to achieve military supremacy over the Tegeans. The oracle (which Herodotus quotes at 67.4) tells them that if they physically bring the bones of Orestes, Agamemnon's son, to their own country, they will get the upper hand in their dealings with Tegea.

But if Apollo's oracle predicts that Sparta will, if the bones of Orestes are located, prevail in its struggle with Tegea, the god does not promise conquest or even domination. Sparta is to become *epitarrhothos* of Tegea, and the term sets precise limits on Sparta's success. *Epitarrhothos* appears seven times in Homer, always to describe a god championing a hero. The divine patron can be anonymous (e.g., *Il.* 11.366, 20.453; *Od.* 24.182) or known (Athena as patron of Diomedes at *Il.* 5.808, 828; Zeus as patron of the Trojans at *Il.* 17.339; Poseidon and Athena as patrons of Achilles at *Il.* 21.289). The *epitarrhothos* is thus clearly superior to the hero and serves as his patron, but the relationship does not degrade the subordinate member nor detract from the valor of his acts. Rather, when Athena becomes Diomedes' *epitarrhothos*, she boasts that he will even be able to confront the god Ares (*Il.* 5.826–833). The *epitarrhothos* provides support that allows the hero to earn glory. The *epitarrhothos* is the senior partner in a reciprocal relationship that enhances the prestige of both members.

As the *epitarrhothos* of Tegea, Sparta was therefore not to be the conqueror but the senior partner in a relationship that both sides valued. The two states clearly had their quarrels—even in the fifth century, Sparta had to fight both Tegea and Argos, its two most powerful rivals in the Peloponnese (Hdt. 9.35.2)—but Tegea enjoyed a special relationship with its neighbor to the south. According to Herodotus, the Spartans always made a point of giving the Tegeans the opposite wing, the most honorable place in the line of battle after their own (9.26.1). The Athenians manage to supplant the Tegeans at Plataia (9.28.1), but their successful argument deserves comment. Both the Tegeans and the Athenians base their claims on deeds from both ancient and modern times (9.26.1: *kaina kai palaia parapherontes erga*; 9.27.1: *palaia kai kaina*), but the Athenians end their speech with a gracious acknowledgment of Spartan preeminence:

> Yet seeing that this is no time to engage in stasis about our place in the battle, we are ready to obey you, men of Lakedaimon, and take whatever place and face whatever enemy you think fitting. Wherever you set us, we will strive to be valiant men (*chrêstos*). Command us then, knowing that we will obey.
> Hdt. 9.27.6

The Athenians' generosity and willingness to accept Spartan authority wins resounding Spartan approval, and the Athenians supplant the Tegeans in the place of highest honor among the allies. Nevertheless, the Spartans do not dismiss the Tegeans out of hand (9.28.3) but set the Tegeans next to themselves in line of battle (*timês heneka kai aretês*), on account of their "excellence" (*aretê*) and to show them "honor" (*timê*).

Nor was this respect one-sided: the Tegeans seem not to have nursed bitter hostility or spent their time looking for an opportunity to pay Sparta back for haughty behavior. Sixty years later, when Spartan prestige was at a low ebb and key Greek states were seeking to found a new alliance, representatives of Corinth and Argos asked Tegea to abandon its ties to Sparta. They attached great importance to Tegea's actions, for if Tegea deserted Sparta, then the entire alliance, it seemed at the time, would crumble (Thuc. 5.32.3). Offered the chance to deal a savage blow to Sparta, the Tegeans refused to take any action against Spartan interests (5.32.4). Tegean constancy was a powerful gesture and weakened Corinth's resolve. When, subsequently, word reached Sparta from its friends at Tegea that the city might defect to the Argive alliance, the Spartans, often scorned for their caution and slowness,[12] launched a rapid and unprecedented expedition with all their available forces to secure their support at Tegea (5.64). Ultimately, the Tegeans stood side by side with their Spartan allies and helped them restore their prestige at the battle of Mantinea (5.71.2).

The relationship between Sparta and Tegea seems to have been the cornerstone and grand paradigm for Sparta's relationship with its other allies. Tegea largely accepted Sparta's superiority, and each state publicly dramatized its respect for the other with gestures before third parties such as the Greeks demonstrated at Plataia and the delegations from Argos and Corinth showed. So long as the relationship between Tegea and Sparta retained a strong element of reciprocity, the rest of Hellas could look to at least one case in which Spartan superiority did not mean domination or degradation to the junior partner. Athens, by contrast, could, at the start of the Peloponnesian War, still point to Chios and Lesbos as similar examples, but these islands were the exception in that they were allies, not tribute-paying subjects, of Athens.[13] Herodotus, on the other hand, focuses on Tegea because Tegea, though unusual in the degree of honor that it received from Sparta, was a more general prototype for which Spartan allies could strive.

Herodotus thus circumscribes Spartan power, demarcating its magnitude and limits alike. In the end, Sparta achieved military superiority

12. The classic passages attesting to this are the Corinthian complaints at Thuc. 1.70 and Archidamos's defence at 1.84.

13. Note the apologetic tone of the Mytileneans at Thuc. 3.9–14, who concede that, for all their suspicions, they had received honor from the Athenians in peacetime (ἐν τῇ εἰρήνῃ τιμώμενοι ὑπ' αὐτῶν), even though they elsewhere point out that the Athenians had least to fear from their allies during peace (3.12.1).

over Tegea (Hdt. 1.68.6), the only state that it previously could not defeat (1.65.1). But military superiority over the other Greek states (at least taken individually) did not lead to further Spartan conquest. Spartan expansion was limited to disputed border regions such as Thyrea, which lay between Argos and Sparta. Aristagoras was at least partially correct when he derided Spartan warfare as futile (5.49.8), but such limited goals opened up a space within which other states could safely concede to Sparta its leading position. Since the number of Spartans was finite and since they did not rely upon developed financial mechanisms to support a partially mercenary force analogous to the Athenian navy, the Spartans were, for their part, unable to assert domination much beyond their existing borders. The limits with which Herodotus defined Sparta were, in fact, essential to the existence of Spartan power. Herodotus proved remarkably clear-sighted, for the Spartans proved clumsy imperialists and, used to the subtle devices of hegemony, were, after succeeding the Athenians, unable to master the very different mechanisms of domination.

XENOPHON'S SELF-FASHIONING SPARTANS

If we wish to assess the change in historical attitudes after Herodotus, we might consider Xenophon's *Constitution of the Spartans*. Many forces contributed to a new paradigm for the analysis of international affairs, but Thucydides' particular influence on Xenophon is explicit and pervasive. Xenophon's *Hellenika* literally picks up where Thucydides' unfinished narrative breaks off—it is perhaps the only major history that begins with the words "After these things" (*meta de tauta*). This peculiar mannerism not only offers a seamless connection to Thucydides' broken text but is a gesture of profound respect for Thucydides' achievement and an endorsement for his (rather than Herodotus's) program of history. Xenophon is our most detailed classical source for Spartan customs and society, but we must be cautious in using Xenophon to analyze Thucydides, for Xenophon accepts many of the intellectual assumptions that seem first to take written form in Thucydides and that polemically oppose ideas present in Herodotus.

The concluding sections of the *Hellenika*, however, allow us to gauge even more closely the degree to which Xenophon follows Thucydides rather than Herodotus. For all his overt conservatism, Xenophon takes as assumptions ideas that, if expressed in clear language, would have called the Greeks of his grandfather's generation to arms. Xenophon, for example, gives up his history in apparent despair after the battle of Mantinea in 362, a half-century after its opening in 411:

> When these things had taken place, the opposite of what all believed would happen was brought to pass. For since nearly all the people of Greece had come together and formed themselves in opposing lines, there was no one who did not suppose that if a battle were fought, those who proved victorious would exercise rule (archê) and those who were defeated would be their subjects (hupêkooi); but the deity (theos) so ordered it that both parties set up a trophy as though victorious and neither tried to hinder those who set them up, that both gave back the dead under a truce as though victorious, and both received back their dead under a truce as though defeated, and that while each party claimed to be victorious, [27] neither was found to be any better off, as regards either additional territory or city or rule (archê), than before the battle took place; but there was even more confusion (akrisia) and disorder (tarachê) in Greece after the battle than before.
> Thus far be it written by me; the events after these will perhaps be the concern of another.
>
> Xen. Hell. 7.5.26–27

When Xenophon expresses gloom at the indecisive nature of the battle, he inscribes in his narrative an assumption that would have shocked the Greeks of the early fifth century. Before the Persian Wars, the hundreds of petty Greek city-states maintained, wherever at all possible, the claim that they were free and autonomous. The subjection of the Greek states in the east to Kroisos and then to Persia was unprecedented (Hdt. 1.6.3)—an aberration and, in the eyes of the other Greeks, a disgrace. Even those states that were in some measure subordinate to others sought to frame the hierarchical relationship in some less opprobrious form: they were *apoikoi* and thus owed their mother-city filial respect, or they were friends who owed their benefactors a debt of honor. Open and unambiguous domination was degrading—a relationship dangerous for both sides, since the disgrace would exert constant pressure on the subordinates to revolt, as the Ionians did against Persia, with disastrous consequences.

Xenophon, however, comes to his analysis of Mantinea with an entirely different assumption. More than a century had elapsed since Plataia, and, in that time, one Greek polis or another had exercised domination over a group of weaker states. Even the Peloponnesian War had begun because many Greek states objected to Athenian rule and wished to restore the ancient freedoms that all Greeks had enjoyed. It was ironic that Sparta would, after the Athenian empire was crushed, simply take Athens's place, and Sparta's rule was correspondingly short-lived. Before

the battle of Mantinea, the Greeks had—if we are to believe Xenophon—assumed that one state or another would become the dominant
power. The battle was not fought over freedom versus slavery (as speakers in Herodotus or Thucydides so often claim was the issue in their
wars), but over which power would predominate. The matter-of-fact
way in which Xenophon describes the universal malaise after the battle
of Mantinea is a gauge of the degree to which the situation has changed.
The situation that Xenophon describes after Mantinea, from Xenophon's point of view, violates the expectations and even the hopes of all
who participated. Xenophon implies that the Greeks had not only expected but had desired some preeminent power to emerge. Thus inde-
cisiveness and the lack of a dominant power bring nothing but "confusion" (*akrisia*) and "disorder" (*tarachê*). The production of freedom
(*eleutheria*) and independence (*autonomia*) does not even warrant mention in Xenophon's account. It is almost as if Xenophon had retold the
Greek victories at Salamis and Plataia as a tragedy because they prevented Xerxes from bringing order to Hellas.

Thus even as Xenophon, with his aside to the *theos*, points backward
to Herodotus (rather than to Thucydides, for whom things divine were
of little interest),[14] he shows that the logic of Thucydides had shaped his
own view of history. Already in the Archaeology, Thucydides showed
that he had no use for the system of quarrelsome city-states—predominant *archê* needed to contain these small and selfish entities.

This complex mixture of the traditional and the modern subtly shapes
Xenophon's other works and colors his account of Spartan customs.
Even as Xenophon seeks in his idealizing text to recuperate Sparta's
pristine glory, he cannot even frame his project in terms that would have
made sense to the earlier generation in which he situates his vanished
Sparta. He has lost touch with the earlier Greek world in which Spartan
preeminence was able to flourish.

An Athenian aristocrat and longtime admirer of Sparta, Xenophon
began his fourth-century description of Sparta with a self-consciously
casual remark: "It occurred to me one day that Sparta, though among
the most thinly populated of states, was evidently the most powerful
(*dunatôtatê*) and most celebrated (*onomastotatê*) city in Greece; and I
fell to wondering how this could have happened. But when I considered
the institutions of the Spartans (*ta epitêdeumata tôn Spartiatôn*), I won-

14. See, for example, Hornblower 1992.

dered no longer" (*Lak. Pol.* 1.1). He goes on to provide us with the most detailed picture of Spartan society that has come down to us from antiquity. He tells us how children are begotten (chap. 2) and how children, once born, are raised (3–4). He praises the common messes at which the elite *homoioi*, "peers," the small group of full Spartan citizens, took their meals (5). He approvingly claims that Spartans share children, servants, and goods (6), reject moneymaking (7), obey the laws more rigorously than any other Greeks (8), impose terrible social sanctions upon cowardice (9), and provide an environment in which even the old must aggressively pursue virtue (10). But his analysis of Spartan success is, at least when compared with what we see in Herodotus, as untraditional and distinct as the assumptions about the battle of Mantinea are from hopes of the Corinthians, Mytileneans, and Melians in Thucydides.

For all of Xenophon's interest in and admiration for the personal habits of the Spartans, the practice of warfare constitutes a single, almost Aristotelian goal that unifies and gives meaning to everything in the Spartan state. Women go through vigorous physical training (*Lak. Pol.* 1.4), and sex between husband and wife is restricted so that sexual encounters should be more passionate and produce stronger offspring (1.5). Thus Sparta, we hear, succeeded in producing children that exceeded all others in size and strength (1.10). The growing Spartans toughen themselves throughout their upbringing. They go barefoot because Lykourgos thought that this would allow them to climb hills and steep inclines more easily (2.3). Spartan children wear a single garment, winter and summer, so that they may learn to endure extremes of temperature (2.4), and, for all their exertions, they must get by on a limited ration that leaves them always hungry (2.5) and renders them lean (2.6). The state fosters constant rivalry and competition between young men (4.3–5), and they engage in casual fistfights with whomever they meet (4.6). Older men must continue their physical training so that they may serve in the army as effectively as the young, and, to ward off physical decline, Lykourgos's middle-aged Spartans scampered through the hills and dales of Lakonia hunting (4.7). Lykourgos felt that, left to themselves, many would take their ease, and so imposed physical activity upon all and established a system that produced the healthiest and most physically accomplished men in all Greece (5.8–9). Above all, where other Greeks jealously proclaim their independence from any authority, civil or otherwise, the Spartans revere and take pride in obedience and submission, and even the most important men run, rather than walk, to answer any call (8.1–2). Cowardice leads to systematic and permanent social death (9.3–6).

All of these customs serve conscious purposes, and Xenophon's Sparta is a functionalist's paradise. Courage is not only admirable but practical—courageous fighters suffer fewer casualties than cowards (*Lak. Pol.* 9.2). Physical conditioning and habits of obedience make the Spartan army an instrument that can maneuver quickly and strike hard (chaps. 11–12). All practices within the Spartan state converge: birth, education, and daily life all strengthen the arms and shoulders that will support the heavy shields, spears, and swords of the frontline Spartan hoplites. In the end, Sparta has the greatest reputation (*onoma*; cf. *onomastotatê* at 1.1) because it has the greatest material force (*dunamis*; cf. *dunatôtatê* at 1.1). Antonio Gramsci's distinction between the moral leadership of "hegemony" and the physical power of "domination" applies well to Xenophon's analysis. The extraordinarily methodical pursuit of masculine virtue and the unparalleled subordination of self and family to the state carry to a unique degree tendencies that drew wide admiration in the Greek world, and thus gave the traditional Sparta a claim to moral leadership.

But Xenophon's description of Spartan authority is so teleological and pragmatic that, for him, Spartan moral leadership derives from and is secondary to Sparta's ability to project power. Xenophon is, in fact, not really interested in *ta epitêdeumata* of the Spartans for their own sake, as embodying some set of moral values, but because they are an efficient tool for some further purpose. When provoked, the Spartans can march out and crush any roughly equivalent force of Greeks. Physical toughness makes better soldiers. Obedience allows the Spartans as a group to master group tactics. Courage reduces casualties. Xenophon's analysis renders Spartan prestige conditional on the pragmatic deeds of warfare. The excellences of Spartan life are not praised for their own sakes, but because they allow Spartans to strike faster, harder, longer. Sparta exercises both hegemony and domination, but the two qualities are not equal. Domination produces hegemony. The force of Spartan arms sanctions the Spartan way of life. "The central fact about Sparta," as one historian has recently put it, "was indeed, as Xenophon saw, her way of life, her *epitêdeumata*";[15] yet although Spartan moral excellence

---

15. Xen. *Lak. Pol.* 1.1: *ta epitêdeumata tôn Spartiatôn*; Hornblower 1983, 105.

may reflect the claims with which Xenophon opens his history, it does not reflect the assumptions that actually shaped his text. Sparta's deeds gave this way of life its meaning.

Xenophon's analysis of Spartan power follows Thucydides. Toward the end of the Archaeology, for example, Thucydides offers a simple explanation for Spartan leadership against the Persians: "When tremendous danger loomed near, the Spartans, because they were preeminent with respect to power (*dunamis*), served as leaders of the Greeks who had jointly undertaken war" (Thuc. 1.18.1). Typically for Thucydides, strength is the dominant factor. As elsewhere in Thucydides, a calculus of force designates that the strong lead and the weaker follow in pursuit of their own advantage.[16] Spartan power, by an almost mechanical process, leads to Spartan leadership. In this judgment, Thucydides reveals a fundamental and pervasive interpretive habit that shapes his view of history and that informs such later work as Xenophon's *Constitution of the Spartans*. In classic Marxist terminology, we might say that for Thucydides the base inevitably dominates the superstructure.

The problem for Thucydides—and for Xenophon—is that Spartan preeminence was possible precisely because power alone did not ensure leadership (otherwise, for example, Gelon of Syracuse might well have led Greece against Xerxes). "Such authority as derived from the Spartan preeminence was ultimately extralegal, however much it was validated and objectified by the Spartans' leadership of the Peloponnesian league,"[17] but Thucydides seems never to have been comfortable with such a deliberately vague and unquantifiable position. According to Thucydides' view of history, Athens should have defeated Sparta, and Thucydides never provided a definitive explanation for why things turned out as they did.

Xenophon, too, is sensitive to the problems of his account and openly recognizes the gulf between Spartan power of his day and its previous prestige. But he is less sensitive to symbolic power than Herodotus. He deals with this problem by mythologizing the Spartans of an earlier generation. He concedes that his picture of Sparta is idealized—toward the end of his account (*Lak. Pol.* 14), he hearkens back to an earlier (and, conveniently, extinct) Spartan purity. The Spartans of the mid-fourth century had fallen from the virtue of their forefathers and thus

16. See 1.8.3; cf. 1.76.2, 77.3; note also Thucydides' reinterpretation of Agamemnon's leadership against Troy at 1.9.3.
17. Fornara and Samons 1991, 125.

occupied a less commanding position. But Spartan decadence was not
less problematic than the inadequate assumptions that shaped Xenophon's analysis. For all his emphasis on Spartan customs, Xenophon
remains too utilitarian in outlook. Sparta had "the most power and
greatest reputation in Hellas" (1.1) because the Spartan way of life produced better soldiers. The Spartan way of life is like a steam engine—
valuable because of the power it could generate, a tool whose value flows
from its effects. If Xenophon was uneasy, he may have sensed that his
account was inadequate, but not suspected that the problem lay with
the questions that he thought to put.

   In the sixth and fifth centuries, Sparta enjoyed its position because it
was simultaneously powerful and not too powerful. Kyros became preeminent because he conquered the great nations of the Near East. Sparta,
as we saw, became preeminent because it could not even conquer Tegea.
Spartan power was important not because it set off a chain of conquests,
but because it legitimated the moral claims of the Spartan lifestyle. The
Spartans occupied a position midway between the Great King—who had
a good chance of slaughtering anyone who stood in his way—and Panhellenic athletic stars—admired for outstanding success in contests that
conferred great prestige (and a platform for political advancement to a
string of men from Kylon to Alkibiades) but no legal power. Writing in
the fourth century, Xenophon simply could not imagine the position that
the Spartans occupied a hundred years before. Herodotus, by contrast,
provides nothing like the detail that we find in Xenophon, but the brief
description in Herodotus of Sparta's rise to power gives us a better picture of Sparta's status in the late archaic period than Xenophon's idealizing "Once upon a time." For Herodotus, hegemony far outweighed
domination, and all the aspects of his narrative—its content, its empha-
ses, and its omissions—combined to provide an account of Spartan
power that is, like that of Xenophon, prescriptive. But where Xenophon
reconstructs an idealized previous Sparta, to which his contemporary
Spartans might aspire, Herodotus frames present Spartan preeminence
in terms that, in fact, set conditions for Spartan authority. Herodotus's
Sparta is the leading city in Hellas not because it crushes its enemies,
but because its power is limited and because it does not seek to take full
advantage of such power as it does have.

   Thucydides had little use for such socially conditioned leadership.
The middle-sized states that come to grief—Corcyra, Corinth, Mytilene,
Plataia, and Melos, to name only the most prominent—all assume that
reputation or social values can exert a decisive influence on the great

powers. In this, Thucydides' narrative does not contradict Herodotus but presents a world in which the conditions have changed. The Athenian empire, and its concomitant power, had no real Greek precedent, and the rise of Athens allowed Sparta to command from its frightened allies a new degree of obedience and submission.

But if Thucydides rejected many of the fictions by which poleis of the archaic period tended to shape their affairs, he nevertheless understood them thoroughly. His critique was so powerful that, from Xenophon onward, readers have accepted most tendentious assumptions as if they reflected a set of transcendent laws governing international affairs. We cannot, however, blame Thucydides for this. He carefully sketches the traditional values of the Greek elite. It is the glare of his own idiosyncratic analyses that has generally pushed the other elements into obscurity. In the next chapters we will explore the complex relationship that Thucydides establishes between his own assumptions and those prominent in the late archaic period.

CHAPTER 4

Power, Prestige,
and the Corcyraean Affair

More than one modern reader has been surprised to find at the start of
the *History* a seemingly minor skirmish on the margins of the mainland
Greek world. The issue is not the absolute importance of the Corcyraean
affair (which was certainly substantial), but the role that these events
play in Thucydides. While the historian formally distinguishes this period from the war itself, he lavishes a large amount of time and energy
on the events in book 1. The opening book, with its shifts from one
period to another, its grand thematic speeches outlining the profound
differences in character between Athenians and Spartans, and its climax
with the introduction of Perikles, is, in some ways, a self-conscious tour
de force. The conflict between Corinth and Corcyra, and particularly
the debate at Athens between these two powers, occupies a formally
strategic position within the design of the *History* and sets the stage for
what follows.

A fifth-century audience would have understood this choice of a beginning: where Thucydides himself speaks of a ten-year war, Aristophanes (*Pax* 987–990) refers to the war that ended in 421 as a thirteen-
year war, and Andocides (3.3) and, later, Aeschines comment that the
peace of 447/6 lasted thirteen years. Thucydides specifically differs from
this interpretation, distinguishing the affairs of Corcyra and Poteideia
as the causes (*aitiai*) and disputes (*diaphora*) that preceded and provided
the major pretext (*prophasis*) for the war (Thuc. 1.146).

Many scholars, particularly modern students of ancient history, have
analyzed the debate in moral terms, seeking to determine precisely who

was right and who was wrong. Donald Kagan, for example, sees most
of the Corinthian argument as "very weak and unconvincing," though
he attributes some validity to the arguments that the Corinthians make
about the spirit of the Thirty Years Peace.[1] G. E. M. de Ste. Croix flatly
condemns the Corinthians: "In reality, Corinth was now an unashamed
aggressor."[2] He scorns the Corinthian argument that since they supported the Athenian right to punish Samos, Athens should let them punish Corcyra: "One wonders whether the Corinthians did actually advance such a ludicrous argument, or whether Thucydides put these
words into their mouth by way of demonstrating how weak their case
was. If the latter, he has certainly failed to convey his meaning to most
modern scholars!" He goes on to declare: "I find it incomprehensible
that anyone who has read the preceding narrative in Thucydides should
find the Corinthian speech plausible. Yet many have done so."[3] J. B.
Salmon, in his comprehensive history of Corinth, dismisses the entire
Corinthian argument with contempt: "It is unnecessary to analyse in
detail the speeches of the Corcyreans and the Corinthians as they appear
in Thucydides (1.32–43); the central issues were simple. Scarcely an argument in the whole Corinthian speech carries conviction.[4] . . . There is
but one valid argument presented by Corinth—apart from her references
to past services done for Athens, which she cannot possibly have expected to cut much ice: her discussion of the terms of the Thirty Years
Peace."[5]

Not all recent scholars are so negative. Marc Cogan comments that
the Corinthian speech, which failed to carry the day, "seems a strangely
ineffective one. Yet it was not a weak speech."[6] He faults the legal reasoning by which the Corinthians equate the relationship between Samos
and Athens with that which obtained between themselves and Corcyra,
but sees in this equation a device "to enable the Corinthians to introduce
the one exemplary case of their own aid to Athens."[7] Robert Connor

1. Kagan 1969, 231–232, 235–236.
2. Ste. Croix 1972, 70.
3. Ste. Croix 1972, 71. He cites S. Usher (*The Historians of Greece and Rome* [Nor-
man, Okla.: University of Oklahoma Press, 1969] 48–49) as saying that the Corinthian
argument was very strong: "Arguments based on justice were the strongest that the Corinthians had." Ste. Croix also castigates Kagan (1969) for accepting part of the argument.
4. Salmon 1984, 285.
5. Salmon 1984, 286.
6. Cogan 1981a, 10.
7. Cogan 1981a, 13.

takes a stronger line and sharply criticizes the Corcyraean position that they had been wronged by Corinth: "Under traditional Greek values the Corcyreans were in a very weak position. They had no claim on Athenians either by kinship or by past services. They were Dorians, much more closely tied to the Corinthians and the Spartans than to the Athenians. Their conduct, moreover, had been outrageous. They had refused to help their own colony, Epidamnus. The occasion was not minor or routine, but a desperate appeal to help stop civil strife in which one party was aided by barbarians."[8] Connor then paints the Corcyraeans in dark colors.

Even setting aside the issues of right and wrong, the Corinthians' position has puzzled scholars. The Corinthian attempt to settle a long-standing score with a powerful and wayward colony placed them on a collision course with Athenian interests. Although Corinth's argument very nearly carried the day (Thuc. 1.44.1), and the Athenians refused to accept the Corcyraeans as *summachoi*, Kagan sees their position as a serious problem: "It may seem surprising that the Corinthians did not see the danger of their policy as we do and, apparently, as the Spartans and the Sicyonians did. If we believe the account of Thucydides, they seem to have expected that the Athenians would really desist from aiding the Corcyreans and might even be persuaded to join with Corinth against Corcyra (1.40.4). It is clear, in any case, that they did not want war with Athens and did not expect it. How are we to explain the terrible miscalculation of the Corinthians?"[9] Salmon is even more emphatic: "No rational consideration can have caused them to hope that Athens would reject the Corcyrean appeal."[10] He goes on to excoriate the Corinthians: "Corinthian policy in the Corcyra affair was not based on a miscalculation, but on no calculation at all; doubtless it was hoped that the Athenians would not intervene, but the hope was quite irrational. The hatred and jealousy that Corinth felt for Corcyra did not only cause her to adduce arguments that took no account of reality; they caused her to hope that Athens would share her view that black was white: that aggression was the defence of legitimate interests."

The vehemence of the observations expressed above and the evident *aporia* to which they point indicate how poorly, even now, we under-

8. Connor 1984, 34 n. 33.
9. Kagan 1969, 235–236.
10. Salmon 1984, 288.

stand why primary actors in the late fifth century did what they did. Neither evaluations of the moral positions of Corcyra and Corinth nor analyses of why they became so embroiled have greatly advanced our understanding. The question for Corinthian foreign policy was not whether or not Corinth was willing to go to war with Athens over Corcyra, for it had clearly decided that it was willing to fight with Athens and to push Athens into war.[11] Rather, it was why Corinth attached so much importance to Corcyra that it could subsequently push the Greek world into a far more general and risky war. Human beings attach widely divergent values to different aspects of their existence, and what seems irrational to an outsider may, on closer inspection, reveal a pattern of the greatest sophistication. When the great anthropologist Bronislaw Malinowski described his experiences on the Trobriand Islands in the Pacific, he found the local inhabitants "subjected to a strict code of behavior and good manners" largely foreign to European sensibilities, but "to which in comparison the life at the Court of Versailles or Escorial was free and easy."[12] In analyzing the motivations of people in a foreign environment such as classical Greece, the key is, as another anthropologist recently commented, to "look for rational choice behavior (as opposed to assuming its existence)."[13]

In this chapter we will explore the cultural context of the quarrel between Corcyra and Corinth and attempt thus to explicate the role the episode plays in the history constructed by Thucydides. The affairs of Corcyra and Poteideia reveal basic themes that recur and help shape the account that follows. They provide concrete examples of general principles of historical change outlined in the Archaeology, and, in particular, they illustrate the qualitative changes that underlay the Peloponnesian War and were accelerated and intensified by it. For Thucydides, Corinth, though maritime and as mercantile as any fifth-century state, is in some respects as much Athens's opposite as Sparta.

---

11. See not only their emphatic pronouncements at 1.41.3 and 42.2–3 that Athenian action at this juncture will define the relationship between the two poleis but also the theatrical gesture described at 1.53 with which a small number of men risk their lives to force the Athenians to declare themselves one way or another.

12. Malinowski 1922, 10.

13. Plattner 1989, 15; the context is a controversy in economic anthropology: "Formalists" applied microeconomic techniques to tribal societies without regard to their cultural contexts, and "Substantivists" argued that people from different cultural contexts would not always view the same choice in the same way. Perfectly rational Muslims would, for example, view a decision about whether to consume alcohol very differently from their Christian counterparts.

THE ANGER OF CORINTH

Corcyra founded Epidamnus but, following custom, chose a "founder" (*oikistês*) from its own metropolis, Corinth. Civil war broke out in the 430s, and the common people drove out the "powerful" (*dunatoi*), but the *dunatoi*, together with the local non-Greek inhabitants, "raided those still in the polis by land and by sea." Hard pressed, the people of Epidamnus appealed to Corcyra for aid, but to no avail (Thuc. 1.24.7). The Corcyraeans remained inactive until formally approached by the other faction, the *dunatoi* (1.26.3), who had been driven out of Epidamnus, and whose side the Corcyraeans eventually took.[14]

Meanwhile, the popular faction in Epidamnus, now desperate, sought aid from Corinth and had, after receiving approval from the Delphic oracle, handed over to them their colony. The Corinthians jumped at the offer (Thuc. 1.25.3), both because they thought it just (*dikaion*) to do so and because they hated the Corcyraeans (*misei tôn Kerkuraiôn*). Thucydides is explicit about why the Corinthians felt this way: the Corcyraeans "negelected them, even though they were [Corinthian] colonists." They demonstrated their irreverence in two highly charged religious contexts, the great Panhellenic festivals and local sacrifice at Corcyra.[15]

First, in the common festival gatherings of the Greeks (Thuc. 1.25.4) the Corcyraeans did not confer upon Corinth the settled privileges (*gera*) to which custom entitled them. Sacrifice consisted in the slaughter and preparation of an animal, and the precise cut of meat that one received was a visible token of one's prestige. In a public context such as a Panhellenic festival, the cuts of meat offered at a Corcyraean sacrifice exerted, like many outwardly minor aspects of diplomatic protocol, enormous symbolic power.

The second slight concerns religious activity at Corcyra itself. The

---

14. The sequence of events in 1.26.3 is unclear. Thucydides informs us that the Corcyraeans became angry (ἐχαλέπαινον) when they learned Corinth had chosen to appropriate Epidamnus, but he goes on to inform us that the exiles from Epidamnus had come to Corcyra and presented themselves as formal suppliants. It is not clear whether the Corcyraeans accepted them before news of Corinthian activity arrived, or whether the Corinthian intervention only accelerated a Corcyraean action that had already been decided upon. Since Thucydides picks up the story at Corcyra at the point where news of the Corinthian moves had arrived, the story of the suppliant exiles could have naturally fit into the narrative at this point, and there would have been no need for retrospective and parenthetical explanation of why Corcyra demanded the exiles be accepted back.

15. The following interpretation of the religious terminology at Thuc. 1.25.4 is owed to Albert Henrichs.

Corcyraeans would not, like other colonists, serve as "sacrificial sponsors" (*prokatarchomenoi tôn hierôn*) for Corinthians (Thuc. 1.25.4). The right to sacrifice in a polis was normally restricted to citizens, and outsiders in a state such as Corcyra had no right to perform such rituals.[16] The Corcyraeans thus denied to Corinthians the privileged access to ritual activity that they customarily enjoyed in their other colonies.[17] Though local sacrifice did not occupy the public stage that the Panhellenic festival did, it was also highly charged, for the privilege to sacrifice in another polis was jealously guarded. Overall, the Corcyraeans flatly "looked down upon" (*periphronountes*) their founding city, not only because they had become enormously wealthy but also because they had occupied (and thus appropriated to themselves the prestige of) the land traditionally identified with the Homeric Phaeacians (1.25.4).

Most scholars analyzing the relationship between Corinth and Corcyra have either belittled or even refused to accept this feud and its intensity. R. Sealey comments that "the traditional friction between Corinth and Corcyra had been a small matter; unlike other colonies, Corcyra did not grant perquisites to Corinthians at festivals."[18] Gomme (on Thuc. 1.25.3) thinks it curious that "Thucydides, who in his Introduction is careful to stress political and economic motives, should here mention only sentimental ones. One naturally suspects an economic motive, such as rivalry in the Adriatic trade." De Romilly deprecatingly remarks that "in one form or another the satisfactions of vanity are equally important for anybody," but then goes on to say: "Naturally one cannot too often repeat the fact that these motives complete the idea of material benefit but in no way exclude it."[19] She assumes that material benefit is there somewhere, always lurking, a given, while vanity may or may not be present. Kagan observes that the Corcyraeans had become "puffed up" and "intolerable to the Corinthians. The irrationality of this motive has set off the hunt for better ones."[20] Kagan disagrees with the sugges-

---

16. On the connection between the right to sacrifice or to perform other ritual acts and the status of *politês*, see Manville 1990, 8, 25. Who could and could not sacrifice or participate in such activities often defined who was and was not a member not only of a *polis*, but of a *genos*, *phyle*, or other association.

17. See Stengel 1910, chap. 7, "κατάρχεσθαι und ἐνάρχεσθαι," 40–49; the Thucydidean passage is discussed on pp. 44–46, esp. p. 45.

18. Sealey 1976, 314.

19. De Romilly 1963, 80 and n. 3.

20. Kagan 1969, 219. He cites Beaumont 1936, quoting p. 183: "Is it really credible that the Corinthians disliked the Corcyreans to such an extent as to fight them for the reasons that Thucydides gives . . . ? It is surely justifiable to look for something more

tion of purely economic motives but evidently accepts the analysis of Corinthian hatred as something odd and deserving some better explanation. Ste. Croix does not deny the validity of this resentment over colonial prerogatives, but he sees this as pejorative: "Already we find an unpleasant motive attributed to the Corinthians; and their resentment against Corcyra and desire to humble her play a large part in what follows."[21] Likewise, Salmon accepts the credibility of the explanation that Thucydides gives for Corinth's feelings, but he goes on to belittle the importance of this motive: "Any sober consideration of the issues would have shown that the risk was not worth taking."[22] The stakes in Corinth's quarrel with Corcyra simply did not justify the risks inherent in war with Athens.

Modern scholars have good reason to express such puzzlement, for Thucydides himself, more than any author of his time, ruthlessly penetrates beyond the sentimental and the emotional to harsh and compelling forces that may seem more elementary. Recent critics have emphasized the intensely emotional aspect of the *History*.[23] One reason the text is so powerful is that it illustrates instances in which ambition, blind desire, and, above all, fear drive human beings and subvert established values.[24] In the following two books, Thucydides presents the plague at Athens and the ultimate stasis in Corcyra as case studies in the fragility of human social and affective bonds. He has, already in the Archaeology, sketched a cold and almost mechanistic model of human nature. Heroes such as Odysseus[25] were mere pirates who preyed on unprotected cities "for the sake of their own profit (*kerdos*) and for the sustenance of the weak" (Thuc. 1.5.1). With oblique and cutting force, Thucydides undermines the proud ideology of such predatory heroes, who do not even

concrete." Beaumont's whole purpose, it should be emphasized, was to explore the economic penetration of the Adriatic, and he handles Thucydides only in passing.
21. Ste. Croix 1972, 70.
22. Salmon 1984, 283.
23. For a general discussion of this view, see Connor 1977a and Lateiner 1977a and b; for an illustration of how Thucydides constructs an emotionally charged narrative from seemingly dry details, see Hornblower 1987, 191–197.
24. For a discussion of the role played by fear, see, for example, de Romilly 1956a. For ambition, see, among other passages, Thuc. 2.65.10–11, where Perikles and his successors are contrasted; for irrational desire, see, for example, the remark καὶ ἔρως ἐνέπεσε τοῖς πᾶσιν ὁμοίως ἐκπλεῦσαι at 6.24.3.
25. Thucydides does not mention Odysseus by name, but the phrase "οἱ παλαιοὶ τῶν ποιητῶν" (1.5.2) would have suggested Homer to any fifth-century reader. The following comment about asking travelers if they are pirates might well suggest passages such as Od. 3.69–74, 9.252–255.

know enough to be ashamed when asked if they are pirates and who resemble the most backward members of the modern (i.e., fifth-century) Greek world. The desire for profit laid the material foundations for hierarchical social structures, "for, in striving after profits (*kerdê*) the weak endured slavery to the strong, and the more powerful, having surpluses of wealth (*periousiai*), attached the lesser cities to themselves as subjects" (1.8.3). Thucydides mentions "honorable" motives only to dismiss them (1.9.3): Agamemnon, for example, assembled the expedition against Troy "because with his navy he had far more strength (*ischusas*) than the others," and brought his forces together "less by the use of gratitude (*charis*) than the application of fear (*phobos*)." The *History* begins immediately to exhibit the increased harshness of society that Thucydides exhibits most bluntly in his analysis of stasis at Corcyra: "That good nature, of which nobility has the greatest share, was laughed down and annihilated" (3.83.1). Thucydides' *History* is a polemical document that cuts through the conventional wisdom and beliefs of his time. Its secularism and its model of a cold, calculating, and interested humanity are deceptively familiar. The modern reader can never recover the extent to which the *History* must have shocked and disturbed its original audience.

Thucydides' penetrating analysis of human motivation brings with it, of course, problems of its own. Human society may degenerate as it does in plague-ridden Athens and in the murderous gang-warfare of Corcyra, but fear, hatred, and moral exhaustion do not wholly motivate all human behavior. Thucydides, in emphasizing the hard forces that underlie "the fair appearances" (*to euprepes*), applies a reductive method that can obscure as much as it reveals. The *History* relentlessly discredits the sentimental and probes beneath the self-serving surfaces of events, but the text was polemical, and it needed to strike hard at social pretensions if it was to make its point. Spartan *moral* prestige, for example, exerted real influence on those inside and outside of the Peloponnesian League, and the current force of that prestige determined how many poleis sent how many men to challenge Athenian power. Thucydides constantly undercuts the persona that Sparta has constructed for itself, brutally juxtaposing rhetorical postures and his own analyses.[26]

---

26. Contrast the rhetorical pose of Sthenelaidas at 1.86 with the analysis offered at 1.88; the Athenians themselves are reported not to have believed ὁ βελτίων λόγος that the Spartans offered when they sent back Athenians who came to their aid against the helots a generation earlier (1.102.3–4); Thucydides likewise attributes Spartan behavior after the fall of Plataia to their desire to please the Thebans (3.68.4).

The Corinthians embody many of those qualities and draw strength from those cultural patterns, which the Peloponnesian War devalued. The marks of prestige that its colonies conferred on Corinth were not empty symbols. When a Corinthian citizen came forward to begin a sacrifice, or when Corinthians received public tokens of respect before the rest of the Greek world in Panhellenic gatherings, these were not vacuous gestures, useful only insofar as they led to preferential treatment in trade or help in times of war (though both of these objectives were doubtless important). The symbolic performance of rank was an end in itself, and the accumulation of wealth and allies can properly be seen as a means to attain such public signs of prestige. Material and symbolic power are symbiotic and reinforce each other.

The relationship between the great tyrants of Sicily and mainland Greece reveals clearly enough the complex relationship between material power and intangible prestige. On the one hand, the massive temples built in Sicily and Magna Graecia were a clear attempt to convert the wealth of these states into a form that would command admiration and respect. Albert Speer, Hitler's personal architect, visited the temples of Sicily and Magna Graecia while planning to rebuild Berlin on an enormous and unprecedented scale. He remarked later, in his memoirs, that he knew precisely what the western Greek architects had wanted to accomplish. Herodotus describes how the mainland Greeks, faced with Xerxes' invasion, sought assistance from Gelon, the tyrant of Syracuse and probably the single most powerful man in the entire Greek world (Hdt. 7.153–163). In Herodotus's account, Gelon offers a staggering level of support (7.158), but only on condition that he be granted the overall command of the Greek forces. Rebuffed by the Spartan delegate, he declares that he will accept command of either the land or the sea forces. At this point, however, the Athenian delegate, fearing that the Spartans would hand over command of the sea, intervenes and expresses his indignation at the idea.

The assumptions that underlie this exchange are important and deserve emphasis. Both the Spartans and the Athenians, in Herodotus's account at any rate, feel that their lineage and history entitle them to precedence over Syracuse or any such "derivative" Greek state. Even defeat at the hands of the Persians and subjugation to a foreign empire are preferable to such an immediate loss of prestige within the Greek world. The identity of the general was of great practical importance and could, of course, decide the war (even at Athens, the generalships were among the few offices not chosen by lot), but the argument as presented in Herodotus turns wholly on issues of prestige. Whatever our feelings as to the historicity of this episode, the story makes sense only if it at most exaggerates the kinds of values according to which Greeks guided their behavior.

Both the architectural program and Gelon's request for the general-ship reflect a phenomenon that anthropologists term "spheres of ex-change."[27] In most societies, value alone does not determine whether or not an exchange is appropriate. A bouquet of flowers would be an appropriate gift for someone recovering in a hospital, but an envelope containing an amount of cash equivalent to the cost of a bouquet would be, at best, out of place. Such spheres of exchange are often organized in a hierarchical manner: in one society analyzed in these terms, subsistence items, prestige objects, and personal loyalties each occupy separate "spheres." Foodstuffs and subsistence items may be exchanged, but no amount of food may equal the value of a prestige object such as a weapon or family heirloom. At the same time, no combination of prestige objects may, in theory, purchase the loyalties that bind established clients to their patron. In offering to exchange massive help against the Persians for leadership of all or part of the enterprise, Gelon seeks to violate established spheres of exchange, using his material wealth to acquire a prestige that is, technically at least, not for sale. Hence the Spartans and Athenians do not merely reject his offer; they do so with a great show of indignation and without regard to the consequences. Had they accepted Gelon's offer, they would have subverted the relative hierarchy of the Greek world and thus, in their own eyes, have lost more status than if they were subjugated to an external power.

At the same time, however, even those on the "margins" of the Greek world whose prestige may be lower than their material power would suggest manipulate the existing value system to legitimate and establish themselves. Pindar's *Olympian 6* celebrates the victory of Hagesias from Syracuse in the mule chariot race at Olympia and emphasizes the victor's illustrious family connections in the Peloponnese. The text explores in detail the birth of Iamos, an ancestor of Hagesias and the founder of the Iamid clan, and documents the fact that Hagesias is also associated by birth with Stymphalus in Arkadia. *Pythian 1* praises Hieron, successor to Gelon as tyrant at Syracuse, and it pushes to the fore the ancient connection between the city of Aetna, which Hieron has just founded,

27. The society in question is that of the Tiv of Nigeria, as described by Bohannen (1955, 60–69); for a recent discussion, see Plattner 1989, 175–178.

with Lakonia. The Greeks at Aetna are still the successors to the Her-
aclidae, and Pindar proudly links them to their emphatically Dorian
ancestors (*Pyth.* 1.62–66). Even in praising the Rhodian Diagoras, one
of the greatest athletes of his time, the poet formally establishes that
Tlepolemus, founder of Rhodes, was originally from Tiryns (*Ol.*
7.20ff.). When the powerful men of Syracuse, Acragas, or any Greek
state competed in the Panhellenic games and, in particular, commissioned a victory ode from a famous poet such as Simonides, Pindar, or
Bacchylides, they expended enormous amounts of wealth and energy to
increase their prestige in the Greek world as a whole, and they expected
to use their pedigrees in the Greek mainland to the best possible advantage.

Returning now to Thucydides, the bitterness of Corinth should be
seen not against the hard and brutal events that follow in the *History*,
but against the rough-and-tumble world in which hundreds of city-states
competed for respect and honor, and in which no one state could predominate too much—no one state, in any event, until Athens began to
perfect its *archê* as a self-perpetuating engine. Corcyra's contempt for
Corinth may or may not have affected the volume of trade with western
markets or similar interests—Thucydides simply does not see fit to inform us on this point. Corcyra's contempt for Corinth does, however,
strike at the heart of Corinth's standing and self-image as an ancient and
consequently central Greek state. Corcyra threatens the basic ideology
by which Corinthians defined themselves, and the Corinthians, doubtless terrified at the long-term consequences, naturally lavished hatred on
their wayward colony.

Thucydides clearly, if succinctly, explains the twofold strategy by
which Corcyra challenges the moral hegemony of Corinth. First, Corcyra is rich, and its wealth translates into a powerful fleet:

> Since they were at that time with respect to the power (*dunamis*) of wealth
> (*chrêmata*) on an equal footing with the richest of the Greeks and as far as
> military resources (*paraskeuê*) are concerned still more powerful
> (*dunatôteroi*), and when their navy was considered, they were even more
> outstanding.
>
> Thuc. 1.25.4

As with Gelon of Syracuse, the material power of Corcyra was out
of proportion to its position in the social hierarchy (at least, in the hierarchy as the Corinthians saw it).

The second reason adduced for Corcyraean pride is perhaps even
more intriguing:

At times, they were puffed up (*epairomenoi*) because the Phaeacians had previously inhabited Corcyra and had enjoyed fame (*kleos*) for their naval position—and for this reason they lavished even more attention on their navy and were by no means lacking in power (*adunatoi*). Indeed, they possessed 120 triremes when they began this war.

Thuc. 1.25.4

The Corcyraeans are "carried away" (*epairomenoi*: a negative word that suggests lack of emotional balance or control)[28] because the Phaeacians—characters from the Homeric *Odyssey*—had supposedly inhabited Corcyra before them. The mythical tale of Phaeacia exerted, according to Thucydides, a tangible influence on the self-image that the Corcyraeans had of themselves, and this self-image intensified their interest in building a navy. The modern scholar may skip this portion of Thucydides in search of more important phenomena, but Thucydides, by and large a reductive and materialistic analyst of power, presents the Corcyraean ideology as a patent force.

For the Corinthians, the association with Phaeacia was a clear and doubtless polemical threat, since, in appropriating the mythical Phaeacians, the Corcyraeans had created for themselves a new pedigree, as venerable as that offered by Corinth. The appropriation of Phaeacia gave the Corcyraeans the symbolic weaponry with which to deflect the kinds of attacks leveled against Gelon by the Spartans (Hdt. 7.159) and the Athenians (7.161.3).

Thucydides' fairly brief account provides a revealing picture of how an established power such as Corinth operated within the Greek world. When the Corinthians assemble a convoy to Epidamnus, Thucydides names ten states that come to its aid, offering everything from money (the Thebans and Phliasians) to matériel (hulls from the Eleans) to fully manned ships (ten from Leucas, eight each from Megara and Ambracia, five from Epidaurus, four from Pale in Cephallonia, two from Troezen, and one from Hermione). We know of no formal treaty that commanded this assistance. While we may look for some economic or mercantile motive for the participating states,[29] there is no reason, when interpreting Thucydides' view, to look beyond the system of "good services"

---

28. Thucydides often uses the term *epairô* to describe people who let foolish considerations carry them away (e.g., 1.81.6: *elpis*, "hope"; 1.83.2: "the arguments of the allies"; 3.38.2: *kerdos*, "profit").

29. Hammond (1967, 318) assumes that states such as Epidaurus and Hermione "were less interested in the fate of the volunteers than in the re-establishment of naval control in the Ionian Sea."

(*euergesia*) and "pleasure/gratitude" (*charis*), which dominates Thucydides' account of the Corcyraean and Corinthian debate at Athens. The Corinthians are masters of traditional Greek diplomacy, and they present the network of colonial ties as the centerpiece of their standing.

The Corinthians make no bones about their relationship with their *apoikiai*:[30] they supported these colonies precisely because they expected to be their *hêgemones* (Thuc. 1.38.2) and to receive the respect that they deserved (*ta eikota thaumazesthai*). At the same time, however, it would be incorrect to reduce Corinth's idealized relationship between colony and metropolis to one of simple power and subjugation. The Corinthians go on to claim that the proof of their worth is not mere obedience but the affection that their colonies pay them: "The rest of our colonies (*apoikiai*), anyway, confer honor (*timê*) upon us, and we are loved (*stergometha*) most of all by our colonists (*apoikoi*)" (1.38.3). This is the only place in Thucydides where the emphatic verb *stergô* appears, and it is one of the very few passages in which Thucydides adduces affection as a real and potent force in the world. Such a "distinctive moral quality of reciprocal obligation and affections characterizes . . . relationships of inequality" in other societies as well.[31] The relationship between metropolis and *apoikia* is, to use a contemporary phrase, a "total social fact": it is not legal, religious, or emotional but unites all these aspects. Or, to use another term, economic or political exchanges are, for the Corinthians, not separate and self-contained, but *embedded* in a larger social context. The debate between Corcyra and Corinth and the subsequent actions of the Athenians allow us to document this attitude.

THE SPEECHES OF THE CORCYRAEANS AND CORINTHIANS

The scholiast on Thucydides 1.32 summarizes the debate between the Corcyraeans and Corinthians succinctly: "The speech of the Corcyraeans places greater emphasis upon expediency (*to sumpheron*) than on what is just (*to dikaion*), that of the Corinthians justice more than expediency." Eduard Schwartz opens his own discussion of these

30. On the relationship between Corinth and its colonies, see Graham 1964, 139–142; for the religious background, see Malkin 1987, esp. 189ff. for a discussion of the cult of the founder, a primary ritual mechanism by which to maintain the link between *apoikia* and metropolis.

31. Abu-Lughod 1986, 85, discussing the way in which the family model structures hierarchical relationships within and beyond the family.

speeches with a virtual paraphrase of the scholiast but goes on to say that while one quality or the other dominates the two speeches, each side makes its own claims to *to sumpheron* and *to dikaion*.[32] Certainly, just a survey of the terms that each side employs supports this view. The Corcyraeans open their speech by stating generally that those seeking a new alliance must, above all, demonstrate that they are seeking things that will be of advantage (32.1: *hôs kai sumphora deontai*), and they consciously refer to this theme again three times (35.5, 36.1, 36.2). Indeed, *to sumpheron* seems for them to be not merely a rhetorical device to persuade the Athenians, but a basic category by which they measure their own actions, for they regret their neutrality as "inexpedient (32.3: *asumphoron*) at the present." Their presentation begins and ends with the material advantages an alliance with Corcyra would confer upon Athens.

On the other hand, the idea of *dikê*, "justice," both as moral category and as juridical process, permeates the harsh Corinthian speech. The Corinthians snidely remark on the negative way in which the Corcyraeans portrayed them (Thuc. 1.37.1) and thus justify their counterattack. Although eighteen words containing the stem *dik-*, indicating "just," appear in the Corinthian speech, only two are in any sense positive. The Corinthians warn the Athenians that they would be "just" (*dikaioi*) if they remained neutral in the quarrel with Corcyra (40.4), and they urge the Athenians not to accept their arguments as "just" (*dikaia*) while following instead what is "expedient" (*sumphora*) (42.1). Otherwise, they focus on injustice: the Corcyraeans, the Corinthians allege, have no allies because they want no witnesses to their "injustices,"*adikêmata* (37.2), and twice they warn the Athenians not to become accomplices to Corcyraean injustice (*sunadikein*, 37.4, 39.3). The simplex verb *adikeô*, "to act unjustly," appears seven times (37.1, 37.4, 38.4, 39.3, 42.2, 42.4, 43.4). Although the Corinthians once cite the "things that were owed them according to justice" (41.1: *dikaiômata*), they refer to the Corcyraean offer for mediation (39.1: *dikê*, "justice" as a legal proceeding) only to scorn the Corcyraeans for cynically pursuing

---

32. Schwartz 1929, 252: "Das Redenpaar der Korkyraeer und der Korinther dreht sich um die κεφάλαια des συμφέρον und δίκαιον; jenes beherrscht die Reder der Korkyraeer, dieses die der Korinther. Aber nicht ausschliesslich." Schwartz goes on to show how Thucydides lets each group seize the strong points of the other. The Corcyraeans turn to *to sumpheron* only after securing *to dikaion* for their side. For a similar analysis, see Kurt von Fritz, *Die griechische Geschichtsschreibung* (Berlin: de Gruyter, 1967) 1:631–635; White (1984, 64), by contrast, sees little or no difference between the two sides.

"the fair appearance of justice" (39.2: *to euprepes tês dikês*). In vilifying Corcyraean behavior at home, they sarcastically refer to the way in which the Corcyraeans prefer to be "judges over those whom they harm" rather than to decide matters according to "settled agreements" (37.3). The Corinthians thus constantly appeal to justice but use this concept in all its aspects as a stick with which to pummel their adversaries.

Both sides situate their arguments in the framework chosen by their adversaries. Anticipating what the Corinthians will say,[33] the Corcyraeans open their speech with the word *dikaion*, "it is just," and introduce one of the debate's few references to what people should do (rather than what they should not do). The Athenians should support them because they "suffer injustice (*adikomenous*) and do not harm others" (Thuc. 1.33.1). Corcyra is a colony "alienated" (34.1: *allotrioutai*) from its metropolis because it has suffered injustice (*adikoumenê*). "Thus it is clear that the Corinthians were acting unjustly" (34.2: *edikoun*), and it is outrageous that they should regard it as "an injustice" (35.3: *adikêma*) for the Athenians to side with Corcyra. It is certainly "just" (34.1: *dikaion*) for Athens to accept a Corinthian colony as an ally, and it is not "just" (35.4: *dikaion*) for Athens to stand by while Corcyra is attacked. For their part, the Corinthians, as they begin to wind down their own speech, urge the Athenians not to accept those "expedient things" (42.1: *sumphora*) offered by Corcyra, but to adhere to the "just things" (*dikaia*) offered by the Corinthians, since in the long run "what is expedient" (42.2: *to sumpheron*) and just behavior are identical.

Scholars are divided as to whether the Corinthians, like the Athenians (Thuc. 1.44.2), accept the premise of the Corcyraean argument (36.1), that war with Sparta is inevitable and that Athens must keep Corcyra out of the Peloponnesian camp,[34] but most discussions of this debate and of Thucydidean debates in general assume that "in both cases, the argument turns on personal advantage clothed in the terms of justice" and that beneath all three cases are "entirely material ends."[35] One his-

33. Schwartz (1929, 252) specifically alludes to the formal rhetorical strategy προσδεχομένων γενήσεσθαι βλαβερῶν διακώλυσις, for which he cites Anaxim. p. 14t Hammer.
34. De Romilly (1963, 21) focuses her brief discussion of the debate on the "true cause" of the war, Spartan fear of Athens and the inevitable conflict between the two; she points out that the Corinthians do not deny the probability of war but only emphasize that a war remains ἔη éfane (42.2).ἐν ἀφανεῖ. Cogan (1981a, 14) believes that "the appeal was genuine, at least at the moment it was given, even though it is impossible to say that a favorable Athenian decision would have avoided the war."
35. Finley 1967, 12–13.

torian, speaking generally, concludes that "Thucydides has a claim to
both originality of thought and permanency of value in his unswerving
insistence, for purposes of historical interpretation, on the amorality of
interstate relations."[36] By contrast, the "postmodernist" outlook on Thucydides stresses his emotional connection to the events that he relates.
But in this view of Thucydides, the amoral events in the *History* often
provide the dark background against which Thucydides' emotional and
principled attitudes stand out.

Expediency and advantage do, of course, play a decisive role in both
speeches, but the two sides portray advantage in very different terms,
and we lose much that is substantial if we immediately reduce them both
to their material foundations. The Corcyraeans and Corinthians are engaged in a public, theatrical contest with deep roots in Greek thought
and complex rules that all the players are expected to understand. To
the speakers in the debate, expediency and justice frame their arguments,
but the drama of this historical event turns, as we will see, on another
term, which runs throughout both speeches: these brief speeches contain
a full 17 of the 110 instances of the verb *dechomai*, "to receive," in
Thucydides, with 8 occurrences in the Corcyraean speech and 9 in the
somewhat longer Corinthian response.

RECIPROCITY AND STATUS

The rhetoric that the Corcyraeans and Corinthians employ in their
speeches is that of *xenia*, "ritualized friendship." It should not surprise
us that Greeks depict an alliance between poleis, a *summachia*, in much
the same way as an alliance between individual citizens or families of

different poleis. Gabriel Herman, for example, has recently shown that
the term *proxenos* is modeled on *xenos*, and that *proxenoi* are, in a
sense, *xenoi* of a polis.[37] An inscription describing the alliance between
Athens and Egesta, tentatively dated to 458/7, mentions that official
representatives from that state are to be offered *xenia*, presumably at
the *prutaneion*;[38] the representatives of Egesta thus became, in effect,
xenoi of the Athenian demos as a whole. As Virginia Hunter has noted,
Thucydides in particular tends to treat aggregate groups of people as if

36. So Cartledge (1979, 225), who presents this as a summary of the view put forward
by Ste. Croix (1972, 5–34).

37. Herman 1987, 130–142; Herman documents the importance of reciprocal guest
friendships within the classical period as a whole.

38. Meiggs and Lewis 1988, no. 37.14–15.

they were individuals, and thus projects individual psychology onto what we would now call sociology.[39] As poleis became more developed and their relations more complex, Greeks naturally turned to the ideas and structures governing institutions such as *xenia* when they explored the rights and responsibilities inherent in *summachia*.

The Corcyraeans seek to establish a new relationship with the Athenians while the Corinthians seek to capitalize on their existing relationship with Athens. The offer of a *summachia* is a classic example of a gift exchange as described by anthropologists such as Bronislaw Malinowski and particularly Marcel Mauss in his influential book *The Gift*.[40] Briefly put, Mauss argues that there is no such thing as a free gift, and that any gift from one individual to another establishes an expectation of something sometime in return. Mary Douglas, in her discussion of *The Gift*, observes that "though we laud charity as a Christian virtue, we know that it wounds," and states that by working for a charitable foundation she learned "that the recipient does not like the giver, no matter how cheerful he may be."[41] A gift offered without expectation of return in any form or at any time is an assertion of power and in many societies degrades the recipient. The "free gift" as assertion of power appears quite clearly in the Funeral Oration, where Perikles proclaims: "As far as virtue (*aretê*) is concerned, we are distinct from the multitude: for we acquire friends not by having good things done for us, but by doing good things" (Thuc. 2.40.4). The greatness of Athens allows it to indulge its generosity freely and to win friends by its actions. Perikles immediately proceeds, however, to undercut his own statement, as if to support the thesis of Mauss (and Douglas): "The one who performed *charis* [an act that demands gratitude] is more reliable so that he can preserve this *charis* that is owed him (*opheilomenê*) through the goodwill (*eunoia*) of the one to whom he gave it; the person who owes this debt in return (*antopheilôn*) is slower to repay this virtue (*aretê*), since he knows that he is contributing not to *charis* [an act that demands gratitude] but to the payment of a debt." Athenian aid, generously given,

---

39. Hunter 1989; Morrison 1994.

40. Mauss 1990, first published in 1950 as *Essai sur le don*. The study of exchange, especially as explored by Karl Polanyi, was developed in classical studies by Moses Finley, in such works as Finley 1954. For Polanyi and classics in general, see Humphreys 1978, 31–75. Recently, interest in the ethics and pragmatics of exchange has grown considerably: see, for example, Herman 1987; Compagner 1988; Kurke 1991. For the application of these ideas in an archaeological context, see, for example, Renfrew and Cherry 1986.

41. See Mauss 1990, vii.

is an assertion of power and superiority, and the recipient accepts a subordinate position in prestige.[42]

Both the Corcyraeans and the Corinthians are as concerned about status as they are about material power. The Corcyraeans open their offer by attempting to define their position as that of an equal partner. They represent themselves as something more than the helpless suppliants of Attic tragedy, who beg and flatter the Athenian demos. They come as a state proudly offering as much as it requests. Few, they declare, come in search of an alliance offering to give no less than they seek in return (Thuc. 1.33.2). The fact that they are not in absolute terms equal to the Athenians is not important: they argue, in effect, that they hold a balance of power on the seas, and their strength will determine whether the Athenians can maintain the maritime power on which they depend (36.3).

If the Corcyraeans attempt to define their relationship with Athens as one of equality, they may be overstating their case, but their attitude is consistent. Status is at the root of the Corcyraean quarrel with Corinth. The duties they refuse to fulfill with regard to their metropolis are materially small—these obligations surely cannot compare with the tribute that Athens levied from its allies or even with the inconvenience, danger, and expense of serving with Athens as allies—but as symbols of subordination they were intolerable. The Corcyraeans draw their proposed position in harsh terms: colonists "are sent out on the condition that they be not slaves (*douloi*) but equals (*homoioi*) to those left behind" (Thuc. 1.34.1). In their eyes, such subordination is morally unacceptable: "Every colony (*apoikia*) that is treated well confers honor (*timê*) upon its metropolis but becomes alienated if it suffers injustice (*adikoumenê*)." The Corcyraeans emphasize reciprocity: the respect that a colony confers on its metropolis balances the respect that the colony itself receives. The Corinthians, for their part, defend their status vis-à-vis their colonies. They sponsored the colony at Corcyra precisely because they expected to receive tokens of their superior position: "We

---

42. See Loraux (1986a, 81), who vividly depicts the Athenian allies smothered with Athenian largesse: "Forced to leave all initiative to Athens and laden with its benefits, these 'friends' had no alternative but the weakness of the debtor—rather like Euripides' Herakles, described in the last lines of the tragedy (Eur. *Her.* 1424) as 'following Theseus like a boat being towed by another.' "MacLachlan (1993, 151) suggests that Perikles' usage "reflects the dramatic change in social conventions which took place during the mid fifth century BCE;" yet though the bluntness may be peculiar to Thucydides, I doubt competition was ever absent from *charis*.

ourselves would not say that we founded it so that we could be abused by these men, but so that we could be the leaders (*hêgemones*) and receive such admiration (*thaumazesthai*) as is appropriate" (38.2). In founding (*kaitoikisai*) the colony, they earned for themselves, as we saw above, a permanent and inalienable right to be *hêgemones* and to receive the kind of respect that was their due.

The ethics and expectations of hierarchical status, particularly when such status is interlinked with an ideology that stresses freedom and self-sufficiency, are complex; their function in Thucydides deserves a separate study. Nevertheless, we can note in passing that one argument presented by the Corinthians is typical of other strongly hierarchical societies. The Corinthians assert that even if they had wronged the Corcyraeans, the Corcyraeans should have accepted this treatment: "If we were in error (*hêmartanomen*), it would be honorable (*kalon*) of them to give way to our wishes and shameful (*aischron*) for us to trample on their moderation (*metriotês*)" (Thuc. 1.38.5). The proper course (*kalon*) for subordinates is to yield (*eikô*), thereby employing their restraint (*metriotês*) as a weapon to heap shame upon the dominant. Other passages in Thucydides similarly describe the moral virtue of the strong not exploiting their advantage to the full. Later in book 1 the Athenians claim credit because they exercise restraint in their dealings with their subjects;[43] during the Melian Dialogue, the Athenians outline the basic system: "It is certain that those who do not yield (*eikô*) to their equals, who deal nobly (*kalôs*) with their superiors and are moderate (*metrioi*) toward their inferiors, on the whole, succeed best" (5.111.4). Although our fifth-century sources largely reflect the attitudes of Athens or other great states, most of the 700 odd, for the most part small poleis known from this period surely identified themselves by who was above, equal to, and below them in the complex bonds that linked states together.

The Corinthian appeal at Thucydides 1.38.5 is perfectly reasonable, and Pierre Bourdieu, in fact, documents precisely this phenomenon in his analysis of Kabyle society: "The man who finds himself in a strong position must refrain from pushing his advantage too far, and should temper his accusation with a certain moderation, so as to let his adversary put himself to shame. . . . His opponent, for his part, can always try to turn the tables by leading him on to overstep public limits." Where the offender is clearly stronger, "the offended party is not required to

---

43. Thuc. 1.77.2: καὶ οὐδεὶς σκοπεῖ αὐτῶν τοῖς καὶ ἄλλοθί που ἀρχὴν ἔχουσι καὶ ἧσσον ἡμῶν πρὸς τοὺς ὑπηκόους μετρίοις οὖσι διότι τοῦτο οὐκ ὀνειδίζεται.

triumph over the offender in order to be rehabilitated in the eyes of public opinion: the defeated man who has done his duty incurs no blame. The offended party is even able to throw back 'extreme humiliation publicly inflicted' on his offender without resorting to a riposte. He only has to adopt an attitude of humility which, by emphasizing his weakness, highlights the arbitrary and immoderate character of the offense."[44] Such a course is precisely what the Corcyraeans seek to avoid, since in their eyes the underlying issue is their status relative to the Corinthians. To adopt the moral position of the weaker party would be to lose the whole game.

The language of reciprocal exchange runs throughout both speeches. The Corcyraeans try to portray their offer as a rare windfall within this system: Corcyra is "giving itself without risks (Thuc. 1.33.2: *kindunoi*) and expenditure (*dapanê*)." They offer, as we saw above, as much as they seek (33.2). Corcyra and Athens should act "with us, the Corcyraeans, giving and you, the Athenians, receiving" (33.3). The Corcyreans should prove their good character in reciprocal dealings with others, "giving and receiving things that are just (*ta dikaia*)" (37.5). They draw on a rich vocabulary for evaluating such relationships at 39.3 (as indicated by italics):

> But it was when they stood firmest that they should have made overtures to you, and not at a time when we have been wronged, and they are in peril, nor yet at a time when you, who never *took a portion of* (*metalabontes*) their power then, will now *give a portion of* (*metadôsete*) present advantage, but, having had *no part of* (*apogenomenoi*) their misdeeds, *you will have an equal share* (*to ison hexete*) of the blame. They should have *shared* (*koinôsantas*) their power with you before they asked you to *share* (*koina . . . echein*) their fortunes.

The Corinthians sketch an elaborate program of costs and benefits that they apply to an alliance such as that offered by the Corcyraeans. The Corcyraeans have themselves made such a critique possible: had they come, like the exiles from Epidamnus who begged their own aid at Thucydides 1.26.3, as simple suppliants, the above argument would not hold. The Corcyraeans, however, disdain such abject pleas and frame their request as if they did not have to pay for Athenian help by yielding some of their own carefully hoarded status. (The Athenians, it should

---

44. Bourdieu 1977, 12–13. In this passage, Bourdieu actually uses the term *elbahadla*, and I have substituted for this the phrase "extreme humiliation publicly inflicted," which Bourdieu uses to define *elbahadla* on p. 12.

be noted, are not fooled: they give the Corcyraeans only an *epimachia*, a defensive alliance and one far less valuable than the *summachia*, but the Corcyraeans serve them as clients thereafter.)

DISCREDITING THE CORCYRAEANS

Reciprocity, in both a positive and a negative sense, is the cornerstone of the Corinthian argument. Their attack on the Corcyraeans has struck many readers as odd. The Corcyraeans had appealed to traditional elite values in defending their lack of political alliances. They describe their previous policy as now "that which seemed before to be our self-restraint (*sôphrosunê*)" (Thuc. 1.32.4)—an attempt at virtue. They deserve sympathy: "It warrants forgiveness if we make bold a policy opposed to a previous political inactivity (*apragmosunê*) that resulted not from moral turpitude (*kakia*), but rather from an error (*hamartia*) of judgment (*doxa*)" (32.5). They had previously acted not through moral turpitude (*kakia*) but through a miscalculation. Only now do they turn their backs on their previous *apragmosunê*, and in choosing this loaded term they appropriate yet another conservative value to legitimate their position.[45] The Corinthians move quickly to discredit this image of the "genteel" (*apragmôn*) Corcyraeans. Corcyra's position on the edge of the mainland Greek world made its inhabitants unusually self-sufficient (37.3), and outsiders had to visit Corcyra while Corcyraeans could remain at home. The Corcyraeans could thus pass judgment on others without having to undergo the same process. If the Corcyraeans had refused all offers of alliance, they did not do so "on account of their self-restraint" (37.2: *dia to sôphron*). Rather, they had "cultivated this habit" (37.3: *epetêdeusan*) so that they might perpetuate base deeds (*kakourgia*), and not because of any moral virtue (*aretê*). They preferred isolation because they were ashamed (*aischunesthai*) to have witnesses of their crimes.

Neither the Corcyraeans nor the Corinthians adduce any ongoing bilateral relationships between Corcyra and the rest of the Greek world. According to the argument that the Corinthians construct, this at most discredits the Corcyraeans, or, perhaps more accurately, it provides them with no credit by which they can withstand the insinuations against them. A bit later, the Corinthians present the following reason for Athens to support them. The Athenians are "bound by a treaty" (*enspondoi*)

---

45. The classic discussion of *apragmosunê* vs. *polupragmosunê* in Greek society is Ehrenberg 1947; for more recent analyses, see Carter 1986; Demont 1990.

with the Corinthians (Thuc. 1.40.4), but they have not even arranged a
"suspension of hostilities" (*anokôchê*) with the Corcyraeans. Gomme,
commenting ad loc., remarks that this is "an illogical point," but the
argument is serious and revealing. The Corinthians imply not only that
it would be better to be *enspondoi* than to be subject to a mere suspension of hostilities, but that a state with whom one has gone to war in
the past (and with whom one has shared the ritual of butchering one
another's citizens) is more trustworthy and deserving of support than a
state with whom one has had no relations. The absence of bilateral
exchanges of any kind, even hostility, means that a state cannot be
trusted.

This attitude underlies another theme that appears in the two
speeches: actions must be open and public to have their full effect. The
Corcyraeans promise that if they only accept the power that the Corcyraean alliance offers, this *dunamis* will, among other things, "contribute to [Athenian] *aretê* in the eyes of the world" (Thuc. 1.33.2). Athenian
help consists of more than men and ships: the public act of support has
its own value. The Corcyraeans thus urge the Athenians "to accept and
aid them *publicly*"(35.4) so that Corinth and its potential allies will
know what they are facing. Whether the Athenians are fearful or courageous is less important than the impression that Athenian power will
have upon their adversaries. The surfaces of things, whether they are
deceptive or not, have real impact. Thucydides constantly wrestles with
the contrast between appearance and reality. While he can dismiss the
physical show of an Athens (1.10.2), his Corinthians bitterly accuse the
Corcyraeans of cynically appropriating first "the fair appearance (*to eu-
prepres*) of nonalignment" (37.4) and then a few lines later "the fair
appearance (*to euprepes*) of justice (*dikê*)" (39.1). The self-serving moral
veneer is a weapon that speakers throughout the text of Thucydides
fear.[46] Moral values matter primarily when they are on display, and hidden qualities are adduced primarily to discredit the surface.

The Corinthians bring this attitude to bear during their attack on

---

46. Thuc. 3.38.2: Kleon vilifies the venal speaker τὸ εὐπρεπὲς τοῦ λόγου ἐκπονήσας,
and Diodotos takes up this language in his response (3.44.4: καὶ οὐκ ἀξιῶ ὑμᾶς τῷ εὐ-
πρεπεῖ τοῦ ἐκείνου λόγου τὸ χρήσιμον τοῦ ἐμοῦ ἀπώσασθαι). During the stasis of Corcyra μέλλησις δὲ προμηθής is damned as δειλία εὐπρεπής (3.82.4), and demagogues
from all sides push themselves forward (3.82.8) μετὰ ὀνόματος . . . εὐπρεποῦς (3.82.8).
Thucydides is particularly fond of the term εὐπρεπής, which appears twenty times in his
History, as opposed to six times in the somewhat longer work of Herodotus.

Corcyra. They declare that the power of Corcyra's natural position places a strong moral burden on it:

> And yet if they were the good (*agathoi*) men they pretend to be, the less hold that others had upon them, the stronger would be the light in which they might have put their honesty by giving and receiving what was just (*ta dikaia*).
>
> Thuc. 1.37.5

They thus link three themes. First, poleis are to be regarded as dishonorable and untrustworthy unless proven otherwise. Second, exchanges between parties are an index of the reliability and moral worth of the participants. Third, these exchanges must be conducted in full view for the public inspection of the Greek world.

The Corinthian attitude is an important one. Individuals (and poleis when they are described in terms applicable to individuals) are not autonomous entities, with a worth inherent in themselves. They are social beings whose character is, in a sense, only the sum total of all dealings that they have ever had with others. Inner feelings, where they count at all, can be a sign of duplicity and bad faith. This conception of the self finds parallels in other societies and is at least as common as the Western view of the disembodied individual as atom and building block of society.[47] The Corcyraeans have no allies because they do not want to be ashamed (Thuc. 1.37.2: *aischunesthai*). Thucydides, of course, is particularly sensitive to the gap between external appearance and inner feelings (see, for example, his ruthless analyses of Spartan actions). Yet even as Greek poets fret over who is and is not a true friend, the issue primarily boils down to the question of who can and cannot be trusted to stand by their friends or *do* something in a time of need.

The Corinthian attack is odd. They not only deny that the Corcyraeans had anything to do with *sôphrosunê*, but they attribute their base behavior in part to *autarkeia*, or self-sufficiency, and, although they do not use the word itself, they attack the Corcyraeans for their *apragmosunê*. Their criticism is more than standard rhetorical opportunism, in which the speaker picks and chooses which qualities deserve praise at any given time according to the needs of the moment. *Apragmosunê* is not absolute, but relative. Elites do not pride themselves on having nothing to do with anything or anyone, but with anything or anyone

---

47. For analyses of alternate ways in which societies organize their views of self, see, for example, Dumont 1970; Geertz 1973, 360–411.

outside of their own sphere, and an admired *agathos* should maintain
relationships with *philoi* at home and many *xenoi* scattered throughout
the Greek world. *Apragmosunê* is an ideological weapon to discourage
members of established elites from consorting with those outside their
proper sphere and from thus implicitly legitimating those who seek to
join the chosen few.

ESTABLISHING CREDIBILITY

Social credibility is the foundation on which the Corcyraean offer rests,
for if the Athenians do not trust them in the future, they will have no
motive to advance them the help that they need now. The Corcyraeans
offer the Athenians *charis*, a store of gratitude that can, on need, be
converted to active use. As with the ties that bind *xenoi*, the Corcyraeans
seek an *euergesia* (Thuc. 1.32.1), and on this basis the Athenians will
obtain lasting *charis* (*charis bebaios*.) The Corcyraeans are confident
that they can provide the Athenians with "securities" for this gratitude
(32.2). The Athenians for their part stand to receive a rare *eupraxia*
(33.2) for which they would themselves have exchanged "considerable
wealth and *charis*." In case the Athenians did not quite grasp the earlier
point, the Corcyraeans quickly assert that the Athenians will, if they
come to the rescue in this hour of need, "deposit for themselves a store
of *charis* for which they can always claim witnesses" (33.1). The Corcyraeans and Athenians share the same enemies, and this is "the most
obvious guarantee of good faith" (35.5). Athenian interests suggest that
they should either maintain a monopoly on sea power or, if necessary,
make sure "to have as their friend (*philos*) this one who is most trustworthy" (35.3). By contrast, the Athenians would bitterly regret showing *charis* (34.3: *charizesthai*) to their enemies.

Both the manner and the rhetoric of the debate are largely traditional.[48] The Theognidean corpus, for example, exhibits a fascination
with the bona fides of *hetairoi*, "companions." Do not, we are told,
associate with the "ignoble" (*kakoi*), but cling fast to the "noble" (*agathoi*) (Theog. 31–32). Keep to yourself affairs of any importance (73–
74), since few have a "mind that can be trusted" (*pistos noos*). Trust few
people when you begin an enterprise if you wish to avoid irreparable

---

48. See Donlan 1985.

harm (75–76). A "man worthy of trust" (*pistos anêr*) is worth his weight in gold (77–78). You will find few "companions worthy of trust" (*pistoi hetairoi*) who will dare (80) in "difficult matters" (*chalepa pragmata*) to have a "heart that shares your feelings" (81: *homophrôn thumos*) and "to share equally" (82: *ison . . . metechein*) the good and the bad.

The phrase "symbolic capital," made famous by Bourdieu,[49] aptly describes the intangible but essential power that one's personal reputation exerts, as the noun *axiôsis* describes this kind of dynamic and effective moral standing. Despite (or more likely because of) his tough and unflinching view of human nature, Thucydides uses the verb *axioô*, literally, "to calculate the worth of something," approximately 100 times, and the noun *axiôsis*, "an estimate of worth," 14 times. Often difficult to render into English, these terms do not point to some absolute measure but describe a calculation of worth that is open to public scrutiny. To use the verb *axioô* is to assert that, in the speaker's opinion, a given action deserves to be done. To use the noun *axiôsis* is to presume a widely shared judgment. The Athenians choose as speaker of the Funeral Oration "whoever seems to be distinguished in mental abilities and is outstanding in 'public estimation' (*axiôsis*)" (Thuc. 2.34.6). Likewise Perikles comments during the Funeral Oration that Athenians receive honor "in accordance with public estimation (*axiosis*)" rather than according to their social class (2.37.1). The public estimation in which a man is held is a source of power that can be used at will. Perikles is able to oppose the masses when they are angry *ep' axiôsei*, because of the estimate that the people have formed of him. The Mytileneans nervously guard against losing part of their own *axiosis* (3.9.2) because they offer to revolt from their allies, the Athenians. When Thucydides ultimately describes how stasis destroys Corcyraean society, he cites a change in the customary public estimation (*axiôsis*) of words (3.82.4) to gauge the broader change in society as a whole.

Neither *axioô* nor *axiôsis* shows up in the Corcyraean speech. The Corinthians, on the other hand, five times ask the Athenians to form their estimate (*axioô*) and consider the moral assessment (*axiôsis*) that they offer. They open their speech by directing the Corcyraeans to learn "their own estimate (*axiôsis*) of the situation" (Thuc. 1.37.1). The Corcyraeans, according to the Corinthians at 39.2, have come to Athens

---

49. Bourdieu 1977, 171–183.

"estimating (*axiountes*) that you Athenians now would not become allies (*sunmachein*) but would share in injustice (*sunadikein*)." Assuming the stance of a friendly adviser,[50] they urge upon the Athenians their advice and their estimate (*axiôsis*) of the *charis* between them (41.1). They call upon the basic mechanism by which values are maintained in a traditional, largely oral society: let the young learn from the old and then "see fit" (*axioutô*) to repay Corinth for what Corinth had done in the past (42.1). At the conclusion of their speech (43.1), they formally "assert their claim" (*axioumen*) to receive the same kind of aid that they themselves once gave. With each repetition of this term, whether in nominal or verbal form, they call upon the Athenians to measure the situation against the precedents of Greek society as a whole and of their dealings with Corinth in particular.

In establishing its own credibility, Corinth reveals much, both in those arguments that have impressed modern critics and those that have annoyed them. Twice the Corinthians had been of service to Athens. Before the Persian Wars, Corinth had sided with Athens against Aegina and provided Athens with twenty desperately needed ships. Later, when the Samians had revolted against Athenian control, the Corinthians had openly (Thuc. 1.40.5: *phanerôs*) supported the Athenian position and argued that "anyone should be able to punish their own allies." Each of these acts was an *euergesia* (41.1), on which the Corinthians may base "their claim" (*axiôsis*) for *charis*. They demand "to be given something in return" (*ant-dothênai*), and enter into an elaborate accounting of the relations between the two powers. The Athenians are not so firmly "hostile that they should harm" Corinth, but they are also not "such firm friends that they can now trade upon their friendship" and put off repaying their debt to another day. The Corinthians discuss in some detail how Athens and Corinth have reached "one of those critical periods"(41.2) in which victory was all important, and which can redefine friend and foe (41.3). Athens and Corinth had had their recent differences, but proper Athenian conduct now would remove these, "for the final *charis* occupies the most effective position and can cancel out a greater claim (*enklêma*)" (42.3). The Corinthians appeal to both the positive and negative rhetoric of "self-restraint," *sôphrosunê*. The Athenians must not be "carried away" (42.2: *eparthentas*, from *epairomai*); the Athenians would show *sôphrosunê* (42.2: *sôphrôn*) if they disproved

---

50. The Corinthians do this again in their first speech at Sparta (1.69.6–70.1).

Corinthian suspicions, and they must not be seduced (42.4: *ephelkes-thai*) by the Corcyraean offer nor, again, "be carried away (*eparthentas*) by what was obvious at the moment."[51]

One argument raised by the Corinthians has stirred substantial modern surprise. They assert that since Corinth supported Athens's right to punish Samos, they have established a precedent by which they can now punish Corcyra. Since Samos was an ally and did not pay tribute to Athens, Corinth argues that the relationship between itself and Corcyra is equivalent. Since Corcyra was, however, by admission of all concerned, the ally of no Greek state, modern analysts have found the Corinthian assertion troubling at best.[52] Nevertheless, the language that the Corinthians use at 40.5 is carefully chosen: anyone (*auton tina*) is free to punish "those allies belonging to them." The critical term for the Corinthians is not just "allies" (*summachoi*), but the participle *prosechontes*, "belonging," which qualifies *summachoi*. Later on, the Melians contrast their position with that of people of other islands already subject to Athens:

> Is that your subjects' idea of equity, to put those who do not belong (*hoi mê prosêkontes*) to you in the same category with peoples that are most of them your own colonists (*apoikoi*), and some conquered rebels?
>
> Thuc. 5.96

Those who are in fact colonists (*apoikoi*) are thus those who are properly *hoi prosêkontes*, "the ones who belong," and the Melians, in defending their independence, concede that Athens would have a claim of some kind if they were in fact Ionian and thus looked to Athens as their ancient metropolis. The Corinthians thus probably push their case

---

51. The overall argument is a variation of the traditional "near and the far" topos. Foolish mortals, impelled by hope and desire, throw away a present situation for a distant (and ultimately unattained) future; on this, see Young 1968, 116–120.

52. Gomme, commenting ad loc., emphasizes the difference between Samos, the Athenian ally, and Corcyra, which was one of the ἄγραφοι πόλεις , when the Thirty Years Peace was signed. Ste. Croix (1972, 71) states that "Athens was certainly entitled to ally herself with Corcyra" and dismisses the Corinthian "specious provisos" to equate Samos and Corcyra; Cogan (1981a, 12) notes that the Corinthian argument is "so peculiar and periphrastic that it must lead us to believe that no such qualification existed in terms of the treaty," but he goes on to remark that "the Corinthians do not raise the point as a *legal* point, they raise it as a political one." Salmon (1984, 275) comments that "the argument is plainly false" and that it "flies in the face of the facts" (pp. 285–286). Kagan (1969, 234), however, does accept the Corinthian position: spheres of influence had been established for Athens and Corinth, and "the Corinthians were surely not mistaken in their understanding that the Athenians had accepted this *modus vivendi*."

as a whole too far, but they can properly argue that the Corcyraeans are their *prosêkontes*, and this fact does strengthen their argument.

To a reader in the fifth century, for whom the text of Thucydides is not the primary lens through which to view Athenian imperialism, the Corinthian position might not have seemed flawless, but it would not have appeared as weak as it does to us, for Corinth is appealing to a real side of Athenian power that played a prominent role in the fifth century and that Thucydides, "the artful reporter," polemically chooses not to mention.[53] When Corinth equates Corcyra and Samos, it is pointing not to Athens the ruthless exponent of *Realpolitik*, but to the Athens that compelled its allies to send the panoply and cow[54] to the Panathenaia, and that incorporated the delivery of tribute into the Dionysia.[55] Athens did not simply exploit "religious propaganda"; it sought to subsume its power relations within traditional ties of extended kinship and *apoikia*. The Athenians did not base their empire solely upon force but exploited the relations and symbols that already existed to create an imperial ideology, a set of ideas that justified their authority to their subjects and, perhaps even more importantly, to themselves.

Thucydides, however, peered deep into this system and found behind the familiar trappings of hierarchy and subordination something cold and, if not new, then more important than it had been. Relations between groups tend, in the absence of developed bureaucratic states, to be ambiguous. Participants see their positions not as fixed, but as a complex set of options from which they can pick and choose. In his work on head-hunting in the Philippines, Renato Rosaldo provides a telling example of how such systems work.[56] Two fishing parties from different lineage groups that were engaged in a long-standing feud accidentally encountered one another. Technically, violence should have broken out, but neither side had any interest at the time in pursuing the matter: "The Peknars rose to the occasion, ingenious in their use of the

53. Meiggs (1972, 305) concludes his chapter on religious sanctions as follows: "It is interesting, however, that almost all our evidence for Athens' religious policy towards the allies derives from inscriptions. This is perhaps an indication that religion played only a superficial part in determining the attitude of the allies." The lack of literary evidence may more properly reflect the prejudices of our literary sources and especially of Thucydides, who in many ways set the tone for accounts of the Athenian empire.

54. For the panoply and the cow required from all colonies, see Meiggs and Lewis 1988, no. 49.11–12; schol. ad Ar. *Nub.* 386; for the panoply and the cow demanded from the allies as well, see Meiggs and Lewis 1988, no. 46.41–42.

55. See, for example, Goldhill 1990.

56. Rosaldo 1980, 252–253.

unrestricted mode of category name transmission. Tukbaw said that he had only one category name, true Rumyad, handed down from his father—hence he denied any connection with the killers, who were identified as Peknars (his mother's name). Kadeng, on the other hand, invoked his mother's name, Payupay, in order to affirm his kinship with those who had confronted them. . . . Though nobody was fooled, the issue was aired and then dropped so that they could cooperate during the fishing trip. . . . When people feud it can be a matter of life itself to muddle things, claiming to be a little on this side and a little on that, somewhat attached to both parties but not necessarily and unambiguously involved." The traditional situation in Greece had been just as fluid and fuzzy. The Poteideians were tribute-paying members of the Athenian empire, but they also received yearly magistrates (Thuc. 1.56.2: *epidêmiourgoi*) from Corinth and thus occupied an ambivalent position.

The Athenian empire was qualitatively different from the older alliances and ties that bound colony to mother-city. It rested on a financial system that extracted money from its subjects and converted this money into an engine that could, in turn, project brute physical force to keep the allies in their subordinate position. Athens had developed an imperial mechanism that could exert far greater and more overwhelming force than any other Hellenic power in Greek memory, and the more power it exerted, the greater its power could become. Sparta, for its part, exerted influence as much because of its weakness as because of its strength. Preoccupied with its internal security and already overextended, it could simply digest no more territory. Although they were useful as shock troops and as a rallying point, the Spartans themselves could not seriously threaten many of their allies. States such as Corinth and Boiotia yielded to Sparta its hegemony only because they were confident that the Spartans could not exploit this position too far. After the Peace of Nikias and particularly after the fall of the Athenian empire, Corinth and Boiotia grew rapidly disenchanted with a Sparta no longer balanced by Athenian power.

The Athenian empire thus disrupted the balance between material force and ideology. Athens had greater and more thorough powers of coercion at its disposal than any Greek state had ever had, and it no longer needed to rely as completely on the ideological minuet in which client and patron exchanged favors and services for their mutual benefit. The hard logic of the empire overwhelmed the old system, and Athens had the power to resolve ambiguities that challenged its interests. Thus the Athenians demand that the Poteideians refuse to accept their Corinthian magistrates (Thuc. 1.56.2). They resolve, by sheer force, the ambiguous position of that city and by this public act celebrate the impotence of the ties by which Corinth defined its position.

When the Corinthians state their case at Athens, they frame their position in the traditional language of bilateral relations. In essence, they assume that exchanges between different parties cannot be divorced from emotional and affective ties. Their colonies do not merely give them their proper respect (Thuc. 1.38.2) but feel an emotional attachment to them (38.3). Good services, even though performed generations before (as with the help against Aegina), have vitality and are handed down from old to young (42.1). The main basis of their attack on the Corcyraeans is, as discussed above, that the Corcyraeans have not had dealings with Athens and thus have forged no ties on which they can build. In traditional exchange systems, exchanges are not simple occurrences but establish a social relationship that supports future solidarity and cooperation.

As the economic historian Karl Polanyi and others have emphasized, market exchanges based on coinage or abstract schemes of value differ fundamentally from traditional transactions. In a pure market exchange, each side struggles to get the best deal possible, and the transaction, once completed, is complete. No emotional ties or commitments other than those associated with the exchange are involved, and the participants sharply separate the transaction from their social lives.

For Thucydides, coldness and emotional detachment openly characterize the Athenians in their dealings with other states. These qualities permeate the Athenian speech at Sparta later in book 1 and provide the logic behind their remonstrances to the Melians in book 5. Thucydides dramatically substantiates this general principle in the Corcyraean and Corinthian debate that begins the narrative. The Corcyraeans appeal to *charis*, to their trustworthiness and good character, to the mutual benefits that each side will confer on the other over time. The Corinthians point backward to their *euergesiai*, call upon their own *charis*, and appeal for a new birth of friendship that will bring Corinth and Athens together. Thucydides has enumerated the many friends that helped the Corinthians in the first battle with Corcyra (Thuc. 1.27.2), and the Corinthians themselves speak of how well they satisfy their colonies (38.4: *areskontes, apareskoimen*). They are honorable and trustworthy partners.

The Athenians accept neither argument, and their final decision,

though it rescues Corcyra, is not intended to favor either side.[57] After
two days of debate, in which they initially favored Corinth, they ultimately decide to establish a defensive alliance with Corcyra. Thucydides
does not report who led the debate or argued for each option, but he
does provide us with several reasons for the final decision. Corcyra, as
its representatives argued, occupied a strategic position on the path to
Italy and Sicily, and war with Sparta did indeed seem inevitable to Athens. The third motivation is, however, of particular importance to this
discussion. The Athenians accepted neither mother-city nor colony as
friend but sought to damage them equally so that if war should come,
both these possible competitors would be as weak as possible (Thuc.
1.44.2). They neither value Corinth's services in the past nor seek future
charis from either Corinth or Corcyra. In the final analysis, the claims
of loyalty, good character, and friendship fall upon deaf ears for Thucydides' Athenians. The complex equation of power and material advantage alone determines their decision. The Athenians, at least in Thucydides' eyes, refine and push to new limits the materialism embodied
in such phrases as *chrêmata, chrêmat' anêr*, "Money, money makes the
man!"[58]

Earlier in this discussion, I mentioned that 17 of the 110 instances of
dechomai, "to receive," appear in the relatively brief Corcyraean debate.[59] The term *dechomai* is loaded and dramatic in this context. Bourdieu[60] has emphasized that systems of exchange, whether to accord
honor or to exact retribution, may seem mechanical and deterministic
if viewed schematically, but that within such systems individual actors
have diverse strategies that they can employ. When will a gift be repaid?
How much will be returned? Will the gift be ignored and protocol violated? Or will the return be perhaps too little, or, conversely, will its
generosity challenge the recipient to exhaust himself when his turn

57. For an analysis of the reasons behind Athens's decision, see Stadter 1983.
58. Pindar *Isthm.* 2.11 quotes this as ⟨τὸ⟩ τὠργείου ῥῆμα, the saying of the Argive
man, and the scholia attribute a simpler form of this saying to Alkaeus. A quick glance
through the Theognidean corpus would illustrate the ambivalent and demoralizing effect
that archaic and classical elites could attribute to material wealth. For the corrosive effects
of money on Sparta, see already Thucydides' younger contemporary Xenophon, *Lak. Pol.*
14. On *Isthm.* 2, see Nagy (1990, 341 and 429), who illustrates how this proverb is
employed when the speaker feels betrayed; also Kurke 1991, 240–256.
59. Seven times in the Corcyraean speech: 33.1, 33.4, 34.1, 35.1, 35.4, 36.1, 36.3;
nine times in the somewhat longer Corinthian speech: 37.1, 37.2, 37.3, 37.5, 39.2, 40.1,
40.2, 40.4, 43.3.
60. See "From the Mechanics of the Model to the Dialectic of Strategies" in Bourdieu
1977, 3–9.

comes to respond? To the actors engaged in such exchanges, the system affords many possible outcomes.

The Corcyraeans come to Athens offering to give it an alliance; and they urge that Athens reciprocate, accept the alliance, and complete the exchange (Thuc. 1.33.4): we are giving, and you should accept. But the action is not automatic, and both Corcyraeans and Corinthians wait anxiously to see whether the gift will be formally accepted. Forms of the verb *dechomai* recur like a drumbeat, mesmerizing both speakers. Corcyraeans and Corinthians both know the rules and the protocol, but the Athenians have begun to play a different game, one in which a power such as Corinth has little place. The rebuff over Corcyra and the subsequent cancellation of the Corinthian magistrates at Poteideia open the eyes of Corinth to the strange new threat that it faces. With good reason, the chastened and terrified Corinthians later in book 1 present a perceptive analysis of the relative characters of Athens and Sparta.

CHAPTER 5

Archaeology I

The Analytical Program of the *History*

The nineteenth-century European notion of "primitive society," with its links to Darwinism and its confidence in progress (culminating in its own culture), has recently drawn a good deal of attention.[1] Yet the development of such a concept by nineteenth-century anthropologists, who established their own self-serving image of "less advanced" peoples, was not something completely unprecedented. A transformation in attitudes toward early humanity is documented as early as the fifth century B.C.E. In *Works and Days*, Hesiod had presented an idealized vision of the distant past. Greek myth and literature had generally assumed a heroic age far superior to the present, and well into the fifth century art and literature alike used the glorified past to discuss the present.[2] A variety of sources from the fifth century, however, point to a very different attitude, which postulated a rather bleak vision of early humanity.[3] Thucydides reflects this attitude, but, similar as he may be to other sources, his analysis is on several points distinct, and this distinctness reflects general themes that shape his view of the present.

1. See, for example, the work of Kuper (1988) and Tambiah (1990), who begin their analyses with the work of Henry Maine and Lewis Henry Morgan.
2. Castriota (1992, 3–16) offers a survey of mythical analogues for the present; his book as a whole explores the way in which physical monuments representing mythical events were used to glorify the recent Athenian role in the Persian Wars.
3. On the possible role of Demokritos, see Cole 1967, which develops a thesis earlier advanced by Reinhardt 1912; on Thucydides and Demokritos, see more recently Hussey 1985.

Thucydides opens his *History* with the "Archaeology," which, in this case, means literally "an account (*logos*) of ancient things (*archaia*)." In the Archaeology, Thucydides analyzes human development from the earliest past to his own time. Eduard Schwartz's study of Thucydides, published in the early twentieth century, proved to be one of the most influential publications on Thucydides, but Schwartz's judgment on the Archaeology found little favor. He saw it as an "incomplete patchwork," published only because a pious editor could not bear to excise it.[4] Most other readers of Thucydides have seen the Archaeology as a tour de force of Thucydidean analysis.[5] The Archaeology surely functions, in some degree, as a "manifesto of rationalism"[6] and deserves particular attention because in it we can see Thucydides wrestling not only with problems of presentation, but with the construction of his own synthesis and the way in which he analyzes sources.[7] In the Archaeology Thucydides articulates indices by which to measure human civilization, internal problems such as stasis, which can bring down political structures and reverse human development, and recurrent patterns, which clusters of the indices form.[8] In so doing, he introduces several major themes that run throughout the *History*, themes that have been widely recognized.

The Archaeology suggests first that "settled life and material progress are possible only through political unification, which in practice meant forcible control by some central authority."[9] Second, it makes clear that sea power plays a crucial role in Greek history.[10] Third, it indicates that Athens represents in some sense a culmination, or at least a logical product, of Greek history and by the logic of Thucydides' own account should have defeated Sparta.[11] Above all, there is the sense here that history for Thucydides is not static but evolves over time. Whether or

---

4. Schwartz 1929, 173.

5. For an elaborate argument that the Archaeology is also a tour de force of ring composition, see Ellis 1991.

6. De Romilly 1956a, 244–251; e.g., p. 251: "C'est un manifeste rationaliste dans tous les senses du mot, puisque les diverses méthodes qu' il instaure impliquent à la fois rigueur critique, déduction logique, et même, dans une certaine mesure, établissement de grands principes généraux permettant la comparaison et l'analogie."

7. De Romilly 1956a, 242–243; Connor 1984, 27; Hunter 1982, 17.

8. Hunter 1982, 44–45.

9. Finley 1942, 87; Connor 1984, 25.

10. Finley 1942, 88; de Romilly 1956a, 266: "Il n'est point douteux que ce système ait été la grande originalité de Thucydide"; Hornblower 1987, 80; on the influence of sea power, see Starr 1989, esp. 29–49.

11. Finley 1942, 91.

not we choose to assume that Thucydides believed in human progress (thus implicitly appropriating a modernist program to his *History*),[12] there is no doubt that human society has, in Thucydides' eyes, generally grown larger and more prosperous. This "evolutionary" view of history is not new to Thucydides, but his interpretation of the general idea is unique and particularly revealing of his own analytical project.

VIEWS ON HUMAN DEVELOPMENT

By the time Thucydides composed his *History*, the concept of "social evolution" (for want of a better term) was nothing new. Xenophanes, Protagoras, Demokritos, the author of the *Prometheus Bound*, Sophokles in the *Antigone*, and Euripides in the *Suppliants*, among others, had given expression to the idea that humans had developed from a primitive state not unlike that which Hobbes outlines in *Leviathan*, in which there was "no place for industry because the fruit thereof is uncertain, and consequently no culture of the earth, no navigation nor use of the commodities that may be imported by sea, no commodious building, no instruments of moving and removing such things as require much force, no knowledge of the face of the earth, no account of time, no arts, no letters, no society, and which is worst of all, continual fear and danger of violent death; and the life of man, solitary, poor, nasty, brutish and short."[13] Enough survives to reveal that Thucydides' picture of humans rising from weakness to strength fell squarely within a growing intellectual tradition. At the same time, however, our other sources, scattered and difficult to assess as they are, share many elements that set them apart from Thucydides and, in fact, emphasize how different and unique Thucydides' analysis was.

THE ORIGINAL HUMANITY AND THE HEROIC PAST

First, Thucydides attacks the vision of early times found in Homer, the strongest source of authority for the heroic period, and begins to develop his own model in its place. The Archaeology immediately demonstrates

12. See, for example, Hunter 1982, 42; Hornblower 1987, 87; on the general issue of "progress" in Greek thought, see Edelstein 1967; Dodds 1973; for a survey of the ancient materials, see Cole 1967, 1–10; for a review of the controversy surrounding this idea, see Connor 1984, 26 n. 19.

13. Hobbes, *Leviathan* 1.13, "On the Natural Condition of Mankind as Concerning their Felicity and Misery."

the revisionist and reductive stance that Thucydides will strike throughout the *History*. On the other hand, all of the evolutionary theories
preserved in other authors supplement but do not directly alter the conventional picture of a heroic past. At Euripides *Suppliants* 195–215,
Theseus looks back from the heroic period to a period of human weakness in which the standard indices of culture—language, agriculture,
shelter, seaborne commerce, prophecy, and religious worship—did not
yet exist. Likewise at *Prometheus Bound* 436–506, Prometheus reflects
upon a similar state of nature from which he delivered humankind, and
the Chorus at Sophokles *Antigone* 334ff. envisions a comparably grim
past. The stories that appear in Plato's *Protagoras* and in book 1 of
Diodoros exist in a timeless past that stands outside of or before the
heroic traditions that constituted a part of Greek identity. The original
humans may live in a primitive or inglorious state, but this primitive
existence does not impinge upon the proud image of the heroic age.

Thucydides' Archaeology approaches the problem of human development from a completely different, and far more controversial, direction. He does not insulate the prestige of the heroic period from his
analysis of early human weakness. He builds by first demolishing the
conventional vision of the heroic past, and then constructing his picture
from the rubble. He sees the weakness of humankind in the heroic age
itself. The proudest heroes of Greek tradition flourished before the Trojan War: Panhellenic figures such as Herakles, the greatest of the heroes
and the dominant mythological subject of Greek art, and local heroes
such as Theseus or even Triptolemos of Eleusis, who brought the secret
of agriculture to humans. Thucydides does not choose to include such
individual men in his narrative. He obliquely dismisses them by equating
common action with strength and by pointing to the lack of such common actions as a sure sign of weakness: "Another circumstance contributes not a little to my conviction of the weakness of ancient times. Before
the Trojan War there is no indication of any common action in Hellas."[14]
Prior to that time, "the Greeks accomplished nothing as a group on
account of their weakness (*astheneia*) and lack of contact (*ameixia*) with
one another" (Thuc. 1.3.4). The Trojan War itself was a crude affair. It
dragged on far too long, not so much because Agamemnon lacked men
as for want of money (*achrêmatia*) (1.11.1). Agamemnon always had

---

14. Thuc. 1.3.1: δηλοῖ δέ μοι καὶ τόδε τῶν παλαιῶν ἀσθένειαν οὐχ ἥκιστα· πρὸ γὰρ
τῶν Τρωικῶν οὐδὲν φαίνεται πρότερον κοινῇ ἐργασαμένη ἡ Ἑλλάς.

to keep much of his forces busy gathering supplies and thus could not concentrate the force necessary to take Troy quickly.

Thucydides does, however, raise the issue of labor power and population. Without attacking the veracity of Homer, he devalues Homer's strongest claims for the glory of the Trojan War. In so doing, Thucydides does not naively accept Homer at face value but instead accepts Homer's testimony as a starting point for historical analysis.[15] Homer's account may or may not be accurate, but, in Thucydides' view, Homer's account will err only on the high side, exaggerating its subject. If Thucydides can accept Homer's exaggeration and still demonstrate that the expedition to Troy is inferior to the Peloponnesian War, then he can make his point even without attacking the bias of the epic account. Thucydides attempts a rhetorical and analytical tour de force. His analysis of Homer has, at least in recent times, encountered considerable criticism and thus, at least as a rhetorical exercise, is not entirely successful.

In the Catalogue of Ships (*Il.* 2.484–760), the epic poem provides a list of the Greek states that contributed ships to the Trojan expedition. Twenty-nine contingents sent roughly 1,200 ships (1,186 by my calculation). Quantitative measures are important to Thucydides: who went where, with how many men, for how many days, with what number of casualties—these are the kinds of figures that Thucydides painstakingly collects for his own narrative. He thus subjects this kind of evidence in Homer to close analysis:

> He has represented it as consisting of 1,200 vessels; the Boiotian complement of each ship being 120 men, that of the ships of Philoktetes 50. By this, I conceive, he meant to convey the maximum and the minimum complement: at any rate he does not specify the amount of any others in his catalogue of the ships. That they were all rowers as well as warriors we see from his account of the ships of Philoktetes, in which all the men at the oar are bowmen. Now it is improbable that many supernumeraries sailed if we

---

15. See Hunter 1982, 32: "What Thucydides does in chapter 9 is accept both Peloponnesian oral tradition and the Homeric poems as factually accurate, and then go on to interpret the data in such a way as to prove his own personal thesis that fear motivated the other Greeks to accompany Agamemnon to Troy;" p. 33: "While admitting to the probability of poetic exaggeration, he accepts Homer's figures." It is important to emphasize that this acceptance is skeptical and constitutes the basis for what we would now call a working hypothesis. Note carefully qualified comments such as Thuc. 1.9.2: οἱ τὰ σαφέστατα Πελοποννησίων μνήμῃ παρὰ τῶν πρότερον δεδεγμένοι, i.e., the best available evidence; note also 1.9.4: ὡς Ὅμηρος τοῦτο δεδήλωκεν, εἴ τῳ ἱκανὸς τεκμηριῶσαι. Homer may or may not be correct, but he must, for better or for worse, serve as the starting point for Thucydides' analysis.

except the kings and high officers; especially as they had to cross the open
sea with munitions of war, in ships, moreover, that had no decks but were
equipped in the old piratical fashion. [5] So that if we strike the average of
the largest and smallest ships, the number of those who sailed will appear
inconsiderable, representing, as they did, the whole force of Hellas.

Thuc. 1.10.4–5

Assuming that Homer will have, if anything, exaggerated his subject,
Thucydides accepts Homer's figures as an upper limit. The number of
ships would probably, in Thucydides' eyes, have been considerably
smaller, but he lets that pass. Furthermore, he assumes that the Boiotian
complement (120 men per ship) would have been as typical as that of
the smaller ships brought by Philoktetes (50 men each), and thus assumes 85 men per ship. But as G. S. Kirk has recently noted, "Actually
the Boeotian number is likely to be as exceptional as their other statistics,
and fifty is a more realistic ship's complement."[16] Again, Thucydides
gives Homer the benefit of the doubt and, like a careful statistician,
conservatively chooses a high figure. If 1,200 ships each had a complement of 85, then the Greek expeditionary force contained 102,000 men.
Thucydides does not multiply 85 by 1,200 and make this final calculation in his narrative. He just gives the figure for ships and men per ship
and concludes that the total number was an "inconsiderable" number
of men, if it is to represent all of Hellas.

Thucydides' dismissive treatment of a 102,000 man force (far larger
than any marshaled in the Peloponnesian War) has provoked harsh
words and nervous apologies from modern scholars. Thucydides, according to V. J. Hunter, comes to "a conclusion that is patently absurd
and generally recognized to be so."[17] "Thucydides cannot," comments
Gomme, "in fact be acquitted of a certain inconsequence; this excursus,
like most of the others, has not been fully thought out."[18] De Romilly
seeks only to change the focus of the analysis: "Even if there were no
contradictions between this figure and the analysis given by Thucydides,
one could at least say that this is hardly conclusive and that the method
is here more original than the result."[19]

Such criticisms of Thucydides' analysis are misplaced. Thucydides'

16. Kirk 1985, 168.
17. Hunter 1982, 35.
18. Gomme on 1.10.5.
19. De Romilly 1956a, 248.

point, though it may shock the modern reader, is consistent and defensible. The gap between military forces of the industrial age and those of the ancient period has made many scholars skeptical of the distinction that Thucydides might draw between the fifth century and the heroic period.[20] But Thucydides has good reasons for his observation. First, the Catalogue of Ships does not cover all of fifth-century Hellas, but only the Greek world of the Bronze Age. (The Catalogue of Ships, in fact, paints a surprisingly faithful picture of which sites were and were not important in the Bronze Age, and thus is a prime example of how retentive oral tradition can, in some cases, be.)[21] Since that time, Hellas had expanded both to the east and to the west. Ionia, Magna Graecia, and Sicily, as well as individual settlements scattered throughout the Mediterranean basin (such as Kyrene in North Africa, Massilia in France, Olbia in the Crimea), had greatly increased the scope of "Hellas." Syracuse, founded long after the heroic period, was the greatest city in Sicily and as powerful as any other single Greek state.[22] The Bronze Age Greece outlined in the Catalogue of Ships was no more than a "rump Hellas" and constituted a subset of the classical Greek world.

Second, if we look beyond the impressive total of 102,000 and examine the individual contingents that form the basis of this calculation, Thucydides' analysis does not seem nearly so outlandish. Agamemnon contributed the largest single contingent in the Trojan War, 100 ships (*Il.* 2.576), but, by Thucydides' reckoning, this force would have in-

---

20. See, for example, Gomme's comment on αὐτόθεν πολεμοῦντα βιοτεύσειν at Thuc. 1.11.1. Thucydides criticizes the Trojan expedition for taking more men than could live off the country. Gomme lumps the Trojan War together with the Sicilian expedition in its logistical sophistication: "This was a general principle of all Greek warfare—armies took a few days' supplies with them and for any longer campaign expected to live on the country. The Athenians took no more than that with them to Sicily (6.30.1, etc.: the wheat was to be made into bread in Sicily), but even so the great bulk of their supplies were to be purchased or seized on the island." Gomme thus dismisses as inconsequential the entire logistical apparatus of the Athenian empire in particular and the importance of monetary trade (which allowed Athenians to purchase supplies in-country) in general. The complex palace economies of the Bronze Age were clearly sophisticated administrative centers, but Thucydides and his contemporaries knew the heroic age only from Homer and other traditional sources.

21. See Simpson and Lazenby 1970, 156–157: "The probability is, then, that the political divisions implied by the Catalogue reflect a real situation which once obtained in Greece, and, if this is the case, it is most likely that this real situation obtained in the Mycenean era, for we can hardly account for the differences between the political map drawn by the Catalogue and that of historical times except by supposing that the changes occurred when Mycenean civilization collapsed."

22. The power of Sicily is a major theme throughout books 6 and 7 of Thucydides, but see also the offer made by Gelon at Hdt. 7.158.4.

cluded no more than 8,500 troops. Only six contingents provide more than 50 ships to the Trojan War (Nestor with 90, Diomedes and Krete as a whole with 80 each, and 60 from Menelaus and all of Arkadia). The remaining twenty-three contingents range from 50 ships (c. 4,250 men) from Boiotia, the Myrmidons, and Athens down to 3 ships (c. 255 men) led by Nireus.

By contrast, the Athenian fleet of 300 ships available at the opening of the Peloponnesian War implies a crew of 60,000. Even though a majority of the oarsmen may have been metics (resident aliens) or mercenaries (as the Corinthians assert at Thuc. 1.121.3, a charge that Perikles does not deny; see 1.143.1),[23] the Athenians also fielded 13,000 frontline hoplites, 16,000 garrison troops drawn from the very young and old, 1,200 cavalry, and 1,600 unmounted archers. How would Agamemnon's 8,500 men have stacked up against the 100 triremes (with 20,000 crewmen), 4,000 hoplites, and 300 cavalry that the Athenians themselves dispatched against Sicily? Even if Athens is exceptional and more dominant than Agamemnon's Mycene, the Greek forces of the Peloponnesian War overmatch those enumerated in the Catalogue of Ships. A powerful regional fleet such as that deployed by the Corcyraeans (Thuc. 1.29.4) could, just before the war began, simultaneously maintain 120 ships and thus a crew of c. 24,000 oarsmen (not counting hoplites or other categories of fighter). Agamemnon would have been hard-pressed to contend against the 50 ships that Lesbos and Chios (neither of which, of course, appear in the Catalogue of Ships) sent to accompany the Athenian expedition against Sicily (Thuc. 6.31.2).

Agamemnon may have assembled a large number of troops, but his expeditionary force could not, on serious scrutiny, compete with the *potential* resources available in fifth-century Hellas as a whole. Thucydides wrote for the Greek elite,[24] and those who read his *History* would have been veterans, wealthy enough to have served as hoplites or horsemen for various city-states. All of Thucydides' contemporaries must have had some experience of the war that raged on and off for twenty-seven years. It is hard to imagine that such men would not have spent considerable time during their lives speculating on how many ships, hoplites, or horsemen a given polis could bring to bear. Likewise, Greeks

---

23. Note that the number of Athenian citizens is a hotly contested topic, but most estimates place the figure at roughly 25,000–50,000.

24. On the audience for Thucydides in general and the Archaeology in particular, see Howie 1984.

were very conscious of what role their city-state did (or did not) play in the Catalogue of Ships,[25] and would thus have been well prepared to compare its present and past capacities.

Furthermore, Thucydides' analysis goes beyond raw numbers, obliquely undercutting the dignity of the Trojan expedition. The Greeks in the Trojan War made no distinction between oarsmen and infantry. Philoktetes' ships included nothing but archers, and Thucydides seems to assume that the only specialized foot soldiers would have been the "kings and those most in authority," that is, the heroes mentioned by Homer. The ships themselves were, of course, not modern triremes but "equipped in the old piratical fashion" and would have been helpless in any serious naval encounter. They were useless except as transports that moved men from one place to another. Technically, the Greek ships sent to Troy were primitive, and their military organization was undeveloped. Thucydides scarcely deigns to mention the individual heroes and ignores the individual exploits around which epic tradition was built. From a qualitative point of view, the entire expedition was backward in conception and execution.

The Peloponnesian War does offer one parallel for a massive invasion, comparable in magnitude to the 102,000 Greeks who descended on Troy, but Thucydides' parallel is barbarian, not Greek. The Thracian Sitalkes' vast horde of plundering foreigners reportedly swelled to 150,000 men (Thuc. 2.98.3). This terrifying force threatened northern Greece, but only as far south as Thermopylai (2.101.2), and it departed after just thirty days. In future centuries the Greeks would learn how devastating such mass invasions could be, but for now the Athenians did not take Sitalkes altogether seriously, failing to send the forces that they had promised because they did not expect that he would actually materialize (2.101.1). Thucydides clearly sees in the earlier Greeks a group little different from the disorganized foreigners of his own day.

The point of Thucydides' analysis is sharp and clear. He attacks

---

25. The classic example is the meager Athenian entry: the Athenian hero Menestheus plays at best a tertiary role in the *Iliad* as a whole and receives a brief mention at *Il.* 2.552–555, where he is briefly praised for his ability, second only to Nestor, to marshal chariots and warriors. At Hdt. 7.161.3, an Athenian envoy at Syracuse is represented as citing this passage to justify Athens's contemporary status as a leader of the Greeks and as superior to the Syracusans. There may be some understated Herodotean irony when the Athenians place so much weight on such a slight textual basis during such a crisis, but the Athenians took their appearance in the Catalogue very seriously: see the official Athenian inscription that refers to Menestheus in the Catalogue, quoted at Aeschin. *In Ktes.* 3.185; Plut. *Kimon* 7.5. On the importance of this inscription in Kimonian Athens, see Castriota 1992, 6–7.

Homer on his strongest point, the massive size of the Trojan expedition. When he is finished, the great Trojan expedition proves that it can compete neither in size nor in organization with the forces available in Thucydides' own day. Thucydides is not naively accepting a vast Greek force at Troy, but conceding the figures implied by Homer so as to make his larger point all the more forceful.[26]

THE ORIGINAL HUMANITY
AND THE FORCES OF PRODUCTION

Most classical analyses of early humanity portray a Hobbesian "state of nature," in which human beings, naked and unarmed, fall prey to the elements and to the depredations of beasts. "Listen," Prometheus tells the Chorus of Oceanids, "to the miseries that beset humankind—how they were witless before and I made them have sense and endowed them with reason. . . . First of all, though they had eyes to see, they saw to no avail; they had ears, but they did not understand; but, just as shapes in dreams, throughout their length of days, without purpose they wrought all things in confusion" (*PV* 442ff.). Prometheus attributes this condition to the absence of technical skills, and he goes on to list the skills that humans lacked: they could not build homes out of brick (450–451), did not know how to fashion things from wood (451: *xulourgia*), lived in caves like ants (452–453), and had no way to predict the changing of the seasons (454–456). "They did everything without any rational plan (*ater gnômês to pan / eprasson*)" (456–457). Theseus in Euripides' *Suppliants* likewise pictures humans leading lives that were "confused" (*Supp.* 201: *pephurmenos*) and "bestial" (202: *thêriôdês*) before some unnamed god intervened to change their condition. Diodoros's account echoes the language of Theseus: the first people "established themselves in a disordered and bestial life" (Diod. 1.8.1: *en ataktôi kai thêriôdei biôi kathestôtas*) and were "warred upon" by wild beasts (1.8.2: *polemoumenous hupo tôn thêriôn*). In Plato's *Protagoras*, Prometheus observes that humans, in their initial incarnation, had nothing to protect them, being "naked, shoeless, with no proper place to rest, and unarmed" (*Prt.* 321c: *gumnos te kai anupodêtos kai astrôtos kai aoplos*).

---

26. Within the rest of the narrative, the Mytilenean debate offers a comparable example: there, Diodotos accepts the terms of debate that his opponent Kleon has established, arguing for mercy on the grounds of pure self-interest. When he subsequently carries the day, defeating Kleon, his rhetorical triumph is all the greater because he has defeated Kleon at his own game.

In the Hippokratic treatise *On Ancient Medicine*, human beings initially ate the same raw products of the earth as cattle, horses, and other beasts and "suffered many terrible things from the harsh and savage lifestyle, consuming things that were raw, unmixed, and possessed of very strong qualities." This led quickly to suffering, disease, and then ultimately death.[27] Only those with tough constitutions could survive for very long on such a harsh diet.

Each of the Greek "anthropologies" offers its own explanation of how the human race emerged from this feckless state, and most emphasize the manner in which humans learned to control their environment and to produce the things that they needed. In the *Prometheus Bound*, Prometheus provides humankind first with astronomy (*PV* 457–458, so that they can discern the seasons), then numbers (459–460) and writing (460–461), and the ability to domesticate animals (462–466) and to build ships (467–468). After a brief pause and exchange with the Chorus, Prometheus goes on to name the other skilled activities of humans: medicine (478–483), prophecy (484–499), and metallurgy (500–504). Plato's Prometheus steals from Hephaistos and Athena not only fire but the technical skill to use it (*Prt.* 321d: *hê entechnos sophia sun puri*), and from this theft mortals acquired all their material needs for existence (321e: *ek toutou euporia men anthrôpôi tou biou gignetai*). The Chorus in the *Antigone* skips primitive life and immediately praises human achievements: travel by sea (335–337), agriculture (338–340), and fishing (344). In Euripides' *Suppliants*, Theseus praises the unnamed divinity who rescued humans from their condition. The first gift was intelligence (*Supp.* 203: *sunesis*), followed by language (203–204), agriculture (205–207), shelter (207–208), seaborne commerce (209–210), prophecy (211–214), and worship of the gods (215). The Hippokratic treatise *On Ancient Medicine* concentrates on food: the needs inherent in such a primitive state drove humans to seek out (*zêteô*) food that matched their constitution (*trofê harmazousan têi phusei*).

Thucydides' perspective is entirely different. First, he has no interest in the kind of primitive existence from which the other accounts proceed. He takes as exemplars of the "original human" those "who cultivate each individually their own property enough so as to live and who do not possess any surplus wealth" (Thuc. 1.2.2: *nemomenoi te ta hautôn*

---

27. Hippok. Corpus *On Ancient Medicine* 3: ἔπασχον πολλά τε καὶ δεινὰ ἀπὸ ἰσχυρῆς τε καὶ θηριώδεος διαίτης, ὠμά τε καὶ ἄκρητα καὶ μεγάλας δυνάμιας ἔχοντα ἐσφερόμενοι.

hekastoi hoson apozên kai periousian chrêmatôn ouk echontes). Thucydides thus provides one of our earliest descriptions of the classic subsistence farm, the peasant household that produces what it needs with little or no surplus. Thucydides' category of primitive human does not exist far off on the edge of time but in fact applies to the vast majority of his contemporaries, who lived on their land and had as little contact with the money economy as possible. In Thucydides' way of thinking, the Peloponnesians are above all small farmers, sufficiently autonomous so that they can imagine themselves as independent of trade and market forces.[28] Recent scholarship on Aristophanes has emphasized the extent to which Dikaiopolis in the *Acharnians*, with his disdain for monetary exchange and his affection for the nonmonetary economy of his farm (*Ach*. 29–36), reflects typical Athenian attitudes. Thucydides does not situate his *Urmensch* in a distant and politically neutral never-never land. A large number, perhaps a majority, of Athenian citizens would have scored low according to Thucydides' "indices of civilization."

Second, Thucydides does not glorify the means by which humans provide themselves with their sustenance.[29] Good farmland is the obvious source of agricultural wealth, and agriculture itself is taken for granted. In primitive forms of life, however, fertile land was simply an incentive for civil strife and invasion: "The richest soils were always most subject to this change of masters; such as the district now called Thessaly, Boiotia, most of the Peloponnese, Arkadia excepted, and the most fertile parts of the rest of Hellas. The goodness of the land favored the aggrandizement of particular individuals and thus created factions that proved a fertile source of ruin. It also invited invasion" (Thuc. 1.2.3–4). Athens itself derived much of its early strength from the very poorness of its soil, because Attika, being an unattractive prize, became a safe haven for refugees from without (1.2.5). Thucydides not only minimizes

28. On the distinction Thucydides draws between the Athenians and Peloponnesians, see Crane 1992a.

29. Thucydides' attitude in part anticipates that of Weber (1958, 68–70, 143–149; 1988, 162–164), who argued that the ancient city was designed to emphasize consumption rather than production. Thus Austin and Vidal-Naquet (1977, 6) comment that "he approached the subject from the angle of the institutions and laid stress on the particular characteristics of Greek history; his aim was to define the ancient Greek city as oppposed to the medieval city. The Greek city was an aristocracy of warriors—or even of sailors— and a city of consumers, whereas the medieval city was a city of producers. A craftsman in fourteenth-century Florence, a city which exercised its sovereignty over the countryside (*contado*), was a citizen insofar as he belonged to one of the *arts*, and he exercised his share of sovereignty through the *art* of which he was a member" (italics mine). In Athens, on the other hand, citizenship depended entirely upon birth.

the role of agriculture but subjects it to an apparently polemical analysis as he demystifies agricultural toil.

Third, Thucydides does not generally include in his outline of human development the growth of *productive* forces at all. Thucydides singles out exchange, rather than production, as the source of prosperity. Other analysts of "human progress" mention seafaring as a major human activity,[30] and conservative poets such as Hesiod and Solon had singled out seaborne trade for skeptical consideration long before the fifth century.[31] Thucydides, however, is unique in singling out maritime commerce and the free intercourse of people by land and sea as critical elements for prosperity—their absence is a fundamental cause of the weakness described at 1.2.2. Trade is the basis for increased prosperity. To Thucydides and others of his time, prosperity derived primarily from the different products of different regions and the trade that allowed these to circulate freely.[32] Stability and security are, however, the key elements on which all else depends, and centralized, authoritarian rule, *archê*, appears as the best framework by which to provide stability and security.

Thucydides' use of the *prôtos heuretês*, "the first discoverer,"[33] illustrates his attitude toward progess. Greeks tended, as they constructed histories of human society, to identify specific advances with particular individuals. Sophokles' first play was about Triptolemos, who introduced from Demeter cultivated wheat and became the teacher of humankind (frags. 596–617). In Aristophanes' *Frogs*, we hear that Orpheus invented cultic ritual (*Ran.* 1032: *teletai*), and Mousaios was responsible for medicine and prophecy (1033: *exakeseis te nosôn kai chrêsmous*). *Homeric Hymn* 20 attributes to humans the cave-dwelling, bestial existence (3–4) that we have seen elsewhere, but praises Hephaistos for providing humankind with the skills they need to pass their lives at their ease in their homes (5–7). The *Prometheus Bound* and Plato's *Protagoras*, both possibly influenced by Protagoras, develop the traditional figure of Prometheus as fire giver, responsible for making

30. Fishing: Soph. *Ant.* 345–346; seaborne trade: [Aesch.] *PV* 467–468; Eur. *Supp.* 209–210 mentions fishing but not seaborne trade.
31. Hesiod *WD* 663ff.; Solon 13.43–46 West.
32. At Thuc. 2.38, Perikles praises Athens because it attracts good things from all over the world; the "Old Oligarch," at 16–18, more cynically points out how much money visitors to Athens, forced to do business at the imperial city, pump into the local economy. Modern economic theory would in addition point out that the circulation of goods through markets facilitates the specialization of labor and thus increases overall productivity.
33. On this, see Kleingünther 1933.

human existence possible. Theseus in Euripides' *Suppliants* does not name anyone, but he makes it clear that some individual divinity was responsible for human progress (*Supp.* 202–203: *ainô d' hos . . . theôn*). Thucydides expatiates on only one such *prôtos heuretês*: roughly three centuries before the end of the Peloponnesian War (i.e., c. 700 B.C.), Ameinokles of Corinth constructed for the Samians the first four triremes ever built, and thus opened new possibilities for the application of naval power.[34] To Thucydides the trireme was not just a tactical instrument for individual sea battles, but a strategic resource on which naval empire could depend. On a less technical level, Thucydides presents Minos as the first man known to have created a navy (Thuc. 1.4: *Minôs gar palaitatos hôn akoêi ismen nautikon ektêsato*) and to have exerted mastery (*ekratêse*) over the Aegean. Neither of these individuals contributes anything to the actual process of growing food, building shelter, fashioning useful things from metal, predicting the future, or caring for the sick—none of which are of any interest to Thucydides in the Archaeology. Other people, unnamed and unconsidered, produce useful things. Thucydides focuses on the means by which to extract[35] or, at best, exchange wealth. He seems to assume that increased seaborne trade generates as its by-product an overall increase in wealth.[36] While he does not spell out the mechanism that links trade and wealth, Thucydides sees that these two phenomena drive each other. If naval power creates the climate in which wealth can accumulate, wealth can be invested in further naval power[37] and thus form a system that reinforces itself. The only cultural heroes who merit Thucydides' praise are those who can contribute to this process of redistribution and extraction.

THE POLIS AS THE BASIC SOCIAL UNIT

The analyses of human society in Sophokles' *Antigone* and Plato's *Protagoras* both begin with the means of material production, but both

34. Our understanding of the ancient trireme has been vastly expanded since the reconstruction and testing of an entire trireme: see Morrison and Coates 1986.

35. Thus Minos quells piracy so that his revenues may increase: τό τε λῃστικόν, ὡς εἰκός, καθῄρει ἐκ τῆς θαλάσσης ἐφ' ὅσον ἐδύνατο, τοῦ τὰς προσόδους μᾶλλον ἰέναι αὐτῷ (Thuc. 1.4).

36. E.g., Thuc. 1.7: τῶν δὲ πόλεων ὅσαι μὲν νεώτατα ᾠκίσθησαν καὶ ἤδη πλωιμωτέρων ὄντων, περιουσίας μᾶλλον ἔχουσαι χρημάτων; 1.8.3: καὶ οἱ παρὰ θάλασσαν ἄνθρωποι μᾶλλον ἤδη τὴν κτῆσιν τῶν χρημάτων ποιούμενοι βεβαιότερον ᾤκουν.

37. Thuc. 1.13.1: τῶν προσόδων μειζόνων γιγνομένων (πρότερον δὲ ἦσαν ἐπὶ ῥητοῖς γέρασι πατρικαὶ βασιλεῖαι). ναυτικά τε ἐξηρτύετο ἡ Ἑλλάς, καὶ τῆς θαλάσσης μᾶλλον ἀντείχοντο.

explicitly emphasize that society consists of more than material production. For Sophokles, Plato, and almost certainly Protagoras, the polis is the crowning achievement of human social evolution. The hundreds of city-states scattered throughout the Mediterranean provided more-or-less autonomous societies for their citizens. Both Sophokles and Plato take the polis as the basic, ideal unit for human society.

The first three strophes of the chorus at *Antigone* 334–364 focus on humanity's ability to dominate nature, but the climax of the chorus focuses on society itself. Whoever maintains the laws of the land (*Ant.* 367–368: *nomoi chthonos*) and the "sworn justice of the gods" (369: *chthonos theôn t' enorchon dikan*) has a lofty polis (370: *hupsipolis*). Whoever seeks what is ignoble (370: *to mê kalon*) has no polis at all (*apolis*) and is excluded from any hearth in the community (372). Whatever humans can produce, they are nothing outside of the framework provided by the polis.

The *Protagoras* draws the distinction between material and social aspects of life even more explicitly. From the start Plato makes the technical skill stolen by Prometheus a second-best gift—Prometheus enters the house of Athena and Hephaistos only because he cannot evade the guards who watch over Zeus's home (*Prt.* 321d). Once mortals possessed this skill, they went about building altars and offering dedications to the gods. Then, after acquiring language, they created for themselves "dwelling places, clothes, footgear, places to sleep, and food from the soil" (322a). This material progress—which encompassed those skills conventionally viewed as necessary for the physical maintenance of life—was only a beginning, and a poor one at that. Human beings lived scattered about (322b: *sporadên*), and poleis did not exist. Although human beings could produce what they needed, individually they could not ward off the depredations of wild beasts, and so they banded together, founding poleis for their own preservation. But this expedient served only to replace one set of problems with another. People living together but "lacking the skill necessary for a polis" (*ouk echontes tên politikên technên*) now began to wrong one another. They left these imperfect communities and began again to perish (*skedannumenoi diephtheironto*) (*Prt.* 322b). Only the institution of *dikê*, "justice," saved humans in the end and permitted them to live in the polis communities necessary to their survival.

A citizen of and long-time exile from Athens, descendant of Thracian kings, and, as an exile in midst of the Peloponnesian War, comfortable with Greeks from any state, whether friend or foe of Athens (Thuc.

5.26.5), Thucydides does not present the polis as a triumphant and climactic social formation. Thucydides starts his analysis with Hellas as a
whole, not with any particular polis (1.2.1: *phainetai gar hê nûn Hellas
kaloumenê*). Early Greece was weak because there was no seaborne
trade and because individuals could not safely travel by land or by sea
(1.2.2). One could see the "weakness of ancient times" (1.3.1: *tôn pa-
laiôn astheneia*) in lack of common action on the part of the Greeks
before the Trojan War (1.3.2). Until recently, in fact, they did not even
call themselves Hellenes. Here, Thucydides cites Homer, "who lived long
after the Trojan War . . . and calls them in his poetry Danaans, Argives,
and Achaians, but not collectively Hellenes" (1.3.3). Concepts such as
"Hellas" and "Hellene" had not emerged, because no clear line yet divided barbarian from Greek. The Greeks had not yet begun to define
themselves as a separate group, and Thucydides spends some time at
1.6 explaining that Hellenic culture was a relatively recent product.

     As far as Thucydides was concerned, the polis was not the product
of an evolutionary process that began in the eighth century; it was instead the primeval unit of Greek society. Thucydides calls the groups
that preyed upon one another and thus never grew strong *poleis*, not
ethnê or some other name.[38] Where Plato's *Protagoras* describes people
preying upon one another within the polis, Thucydides opens his spectacle of history with organized groups driving each other from their
homes (Thuc. 1.2.1). Agricultural wealth in individual states served to
increase the risk of stasis or of external invasion (1.2.4). Attika pros-
pered only because its low-quality soil rendered it a poor prize (1.2.5),
and the victims of stasis or war took refuge there (1.2.6). The scattered
Greek states were capable of little individually: "weakness and lack of
contact with each other" (1.3.4: *astheneia kai ameixia allêlôn*) prevented
them from accomplishing anything.

     If other accounts emphasize the polis governed by *dikê*, Thucydides
counters with his poleis restrained by force from devouring one another.
Against the harsh and dangerous landscape of 1.1.2, Thucydides sets
Minos, whose naval forces controlled the Aegean sea by force, who
exerted imperial power (Thuc. 1.4: *archê*), and who became the personal
founder, the *oikistês*, of most of the islands, drove out the Karian inhabitants, and placed his own sons in charge of the new societies (see
also 1.8.2). Without such an iron hand, international anarchy reigned,

---

38. Thuc. 1.2.2: οὔτε μεγέθει πόλεων ἴσχυον οὔτε τῇ ἄλλῃ παρασκευῇ.

and piracy flourished: since poleis lacked walls and were dispersed into small villages, those who were armed easily extracted their livelihood from plunder (1.5.1). Worst of all, they felt no shame at such behavior. Thucydides maliciously points to the manner in which speakers pose the question "Are you pirates?"—as if those who are asked the question would have no idea of disclaiming the imputation, or their interrogators of reproaching them for it (1.5.2). The scorn for those who are unashamed at their piracy illustrates better, perhaps, than any other passage that Thucydides did not view interstate relations as "amoral."[39] People continued to live in their separate poleis, but, under the protection of imperial control, they were able to accumulate wealth and even to develop walls and other resources whereby to defend themselves more effectively (1.8.3). Indeed, it was only because Minos had used his authoritarian rule to instill some initial organization in the Greek world that the Greeks had the means whereby to conduct the Trojan War at all (1.8.4).

Unlike Sophokles, Protagoras, or Plato, Thucydides did not see in the independent polis a viable social unit (an opinion that fourth-century history might seem to confirm). The force majeure of archê is, in the final analysis, necessary if states are not to degenerate into impoverished and fearful chaos.

THE CONSTITUENT TIES OF SOCIETY: AIDÔS AND DIKÊ

Plato's *Protagoras* emphasizes at least one other major theme that sharply contrasts with Thucydides: the attitudes toward "shame" and "respect." If Plato is accurately representing views held by Protagoras and widely known in the Greek world, then Thucydides may well have had them in mind when he composed his Archaeology, and seen his own analysis as an argument against the Protagorean position. Even if no

---

39. This idea, derived in modern scholarship ultimately from Hobbes, is argued by Ste. Croix (1972, 16): "I believe that in practice he drew a fundamental distinction—though he never names it explicitly, in general terms—between, on the one hand, the relations of *individuals inside the State*, where there are laws, enforced by sanctions, which may enable the weak to stand up to the strong from a position of approximate equality and where ordinary ethical consideration can apply, and on the other, the relations *between States*, where it is the strong who decide how they will treat the weak, and moral judgments are virtually inapplicable" (italics mine). See, however, Hornblower (1987, 178–190), who is "reluctant to admit that Thucydides made any 'Hobbesian' distinction between the morality which prevails between individuals and the 'war of all against all' which prevails between states."

such connection exists, the tale in the *Protagoras* sheds light upon an attitude that plays a central role in Thucydides' *History* and that emerges in a particularly clear form in the course of the Archaeology. Thucydides does not portray an entirely amoral world, in which interest alone determines the choices that individual actors make, but the problems of human motivation are a major theme in the *History*.

Consider what unifies society in the *Protagoras*. Fearing lest mortals be utterly annihilated, Zeus sends Hermes to provide them with *aidôs* and *dikê* ("shame" and "justice," *Prt.* 322c) so that they might be the ornaments of poleis and the unifying bonds of friendship (*hin' eien poleôn kosmoi te kai desmoi philias sunagôgoi*). In this passage, *dikê*, "justice," seems to be insufficient: the formula *aidôs kai dikê* is repeated four times in 322d-e. If *dikê* describes justice as an objectified system, *aidôs* describes the manner in which individual social actors respect the boundaries of *dikê* in their own lives. *Aidôs* is that quality which makes people respect both those who are stronger and those who are weaker than they. *Aidôs* restrains individual subjects from pushing their immediate interests too far. *Aidôs* is also a social phenomenon, shame rather than guilt:[40] one feels *aidôs* before other people, not in the privacy of one's own heart. *Dikê* and *aidôs* are meant to combine with one another and together bind the members of a community together with *desmoi philias sunagôgoi*, "ties of affection." The myth in the *Protagoras* locates the strength of a community in a moral and emotional framework.

No quality is more problematic in Thucydides than "shame" and the general importance of ties based on affection or social judgments. Before examining Thucydides' analysis of human motivation in the Archaeology, a brief survey of "shame" in Thucydides as a whole will help us frame the problem. Thucydides understands perfectly well that emotional factors other than raw self-interest and fear do affect human behavior, and gentler possibilities provide the background for some of the most brutal action in the *History*. Thucydides sketches an apocalyptic vision of society torn by stasis on Corcyra (Thuc. 3.83.1), in which old-fashioned "good nature (*to euêthes*), of which nobility (*to gennaion*) had such a great share, was mocked out of existence." Yet the whole point

40. On the distinction, see Dodds, "From Shame-Culture to Guilt-Culture," in Dodds 1951, 28–63; for essays analyzing this distinction in other cultures of the Mediterranean, see Peristiany 1966; for a detailed analysis of the distinction in Bedouin culture, see Abu-Lughod 1986.

of the description is to reveal the extent to which stasis could spread "evil character" (*kakotropia*). Thucydides expatiates upon the sufferings at Corcyra because they provide what we might now call a case study in behavior and reflect events that took place in many parts of Greece (3.82). Thucydides argues that human nature, placed in circumstances such as obtained in Corcyra, will always react in much the same way. At the same time, however, he implies the existence of an earlier, less brutal society from which Corcyra degenerated.

For all of his emphasis on what is expedient and on the harsh calculus of self-interest, Thucydides uses the main Greek terms for shame, *aidôs* and *aischunê*, substantially more often than the more conventional Herodotus (nineteen vs. eleven times, just over twice as often when the differing sizes of their works are factored in).[41] Shame is, as noted above, a social phenomenon: it consists not in the internal feelings of guilt, but in the pain that one suffers at a loss of public esteem. Thus the Corcyraeans, according to their Corinthian detractors, refuse to be entangled in alliances, because they do not wish to have witnesses to their crimes and thus to feel shame (Thuc. 1.37.2: *aischunesthai*). Archidamos urges his fellow Spartans not to let the insults of their allies fill them with shame (1.84.1: *mê aischunesthai*). According to Perikles, shame binds Athenian society together more firmly than force: Athenians yield not only before written laws but before those that are not written (and thus have no legal penalty) but that bring with them "shame in the common opinion" (2.37.3: *aischunê homologoumenê*). The participants in Corcyraean stasis are morally bankrupt, but they have a keen sense of shame: "they prefer to be called (*keklêntai*) clever evil doers than noble fools, because they are ashamed (*aischunontai*) of the latter and take pride in the former" (3.82.7).

Thucydides puts shame at the center of the martial ethos and thus echoes in at least one regard Homeric values that he otherwise treats with disdain.[42] The dead Athenians praised by Perikles held firm "under the influence of shame" (Thuc. 2.43.1: *aischunomenoi*) in the heat of battle. This valorization of *aischunê* is not, however, an Athenian prerogative. A Boiotian general urges his younger troops "not to cast shame

---

41. Note 1.84.3, where Thucydides uses *aidôs* and *aischunê* as virtual synonyms; on the different forms: *aidôs*: (1 time), *aideomai* (4 times), *aischunê* (2), *aischunô* (2) in Herodotus; *aidôs* (1), *aischunê* (11), *aischunô* (7) in Thucydides; on the differing ratios: we possess c. 180,000 words of Herodotus vs. 150,000 of Thucydides.

42. For *aidôs* as a rallying cry in the midst of battle, see, for example, *Il.* 13.95; 15.502, 561–562, 662; for *aidôs* as one of the constituent virtues of battle, see *Il.*15.129, 657.

upon those virtues that are theirs" (4.92.7: *mê aischunai tas prosêkousas aretas*). The Spartan Brasidas, faced with battle against barbarians, reminds his troops that barbarians feel no *aischunê* at running away in battle (4.126.5), just as, a bit later, he urges his own men "to feel shame" (5.9.9: *to aischunesthai*) when they fight.

One specific passage, however, does raise some questions about and dramatizes the dangers of the efficacy of a "shame" ethos. Four times, speakers on both sides of the Melian Dialogue cite *aischunê*. Melos is a Spartan colony, and the Melians accordingly express confidence that the Spartans will come to their defence, because if they do not, their "shared kinship" (Thuc. 5.104: *suggeneia*) would bring *aischunê* upon the Spartans. The Athenians ridicule such hopes (5.105.3). The Spartans, they argue, exercise the utmost virtue (5.105.4: *aretê*) in defence of themselves but follow expediency in dealing with others. The Athenians perform for us here the action schematically described at 3.83.1, for they mock the old-fashioned good nature that characterized the well-bred members of Greek society. The ruthless negotiators for Athens acknowledge *aischunê* but see in it a force of secondary influence.

If the Athenians challenge the effect of *aischunê*, they also explicitly question its inherent value. Reasonable men, the Athenians argue, do not let mere matters of *aischunê* influence them when survival is at stake. The Melians face a life-and-death decision, and they have more to worry about than "nobility" (Thuc. 5.101.1: *andragathia*) and *aischunê*. A few sections later, they repeat this idea: "Surely you will not," they urge the Melians at 5.111.3, "be caught by that idea of *aischunê*, which in dangers that are disgraceful, and at the same time too plain to be mistaken, proves so fatal to mankind!" Disgrace "by the mere introduction of a seductive name" (*onomatos epagôgou dunamei*) leads people on to a real and manifest destruction. If the Melians yield to the influence of words (*hêsseitheisi tou rêmatos*) and in very fact willingly encounter irrevocable disasters, they will incur shame that is all the more disgraceful precisely because it could have been avoided. In effect, the Athenians argue here that no abstract notion of honor is worth dying for. This is not to say that nothing is worth one's life (just as the Athenians do not deny that the Spartans can exercise the utmost *aretê*). But mere words and ideas do not constitute anything so substantial that they justify desperate acts.

Thucydides, of course, does not himself express this cynical view of "shame" but puts these sentiments in the mouths of the Athenian ambassadors. Nevertheless, the Archaeology analyzes human motivation in equally cold-blooded terms. From the very beginning, material conditions determine behavior: early inhabitants of Greece could easily be pushed out of their territory, because they made no permanent investment in any particular territory and knew they could meet their day-to-day needs anywhere (Thuc. 1.2.2).[43] Greeks from many states invited the sons of Hellen into their countries "for their advantage" (1.3.2: *ep' ôpheliai*), presumably as allies in local struggles for power. Minos cleared the seas of piracy "so that revenues could more readily come to him."[44] When the Greeks began to devote themselves to piracy, they also organized themselves into simple but hierarchically structured units: "The most powerful men led both for their own profit (*kerdos*) and for the support of those who were weak (*tois asthenesi trophês*)."[45] When sea travel—and with it wealth—increased, the Greeks began to surround themselves with walls and those (such as the Corinthians) who could seize any available isthmus "for the sake of trade and because of the strength that it gave them with respect to their neighbors."[46] As trade continued to grow, the simple differentiation of people according to power intensifed. "The weak, seeking profits, endured slavery (*douleia*) under those who were more powerful, and stronger men, because they had surpluses of wealth, rendered weaker cities subordinate to them."[47] At Troy, for example, raw power was more influential than emotional attachments. Agamemnon controlled the greatest number of forces, and this surplus of military power was the basis for his authority: "He assembled this expedition just as much by means of terror (*phobos*) as by . . . debts of friendship (*charis*)."[48]

Human beings act according to their own advantage, seeking money,

43. By contrast, see Hanson 1983 and 1989, which forcefully argue against such a view. Hanson analyzes the effects of invasion and devastation of crops by hoplites. The Peloponnesian forces regularly ravaged Attika during the war, but according to Hanson (1989, 4), "even the somber historian Thucydides . . . presumes that actual long-term losses to Athenian agriculture were not great. Why then did men march out to fight when the enemy entered their farms?" Hanson goes on to conclude that "the mere sight of enemy ravagers running loose across the lands of the invaded was alone considered a violation of both individual privacy and municipal pride."

44. Thuc. 1.4: τοῦ τὰς προσόδους μᾶλλον ἰέναι αὐτῷ.

45. Thuc. 1.5.1: ἡγουμένων ἀνδρῶν οὐ τῶν ἀδυνατωτάτων κέρδους τοῦ σφετέρου αὐτῶν ἕνεκα καὶ τοῖς ἀσθενέσι τροφῆς.

46. Thuc. 1.7: ἐμπορίας τε ἕνεκα καὶ τῆς πρὸς τοὺς προσοίκους ἕκαστοι ἰσχύος.

47. Thuc. 1.8.3: ἐφιέμενοι γὰρ τῶν κερδῶν οἵ τε ἥσσους ὑπέμενον τὴν τῶν κρεισσόνων δουλείαν, οἵ τε δυνατώτεροι περιουσίας ἔχοντες προσεποιοῦντο ὑπηκόους τὰς ἐλάσσους πόλεις.

48. Thuc. 1.9.3: τὴν στρατείαν οὐ χάριτι τὸ πλέον ἢ φόβῳ ξυναγαγὼν ποιήσασθαι.

power, and sustenance, while avoiding other actions in the interests of fear. Ultimately, Thucydides describes human beings as products of hard, material forces. He does not altogether deny the impact of debts of gratitude (*charis*) on the assembly of the Greek expedition against Troy, but the rhetorical form of his language suggests that *phobos* was in fact not equal to, but much more important than, *charis*.[49] Although *dikê* and *aidôs* are the qualities that make human society possible and that represent the climax of human evolution in Plato's *Protagoras*, the same cannot be said of these qualities in Thucydides' Archaeology. "Shame" appears only once (Thuc. 1.5.1), while neither the noun *dikê* nor its corresponding adjective *dikaios*, "just," appear at all. By contrast, words for power reappear in every chapter of the Archaeology. The term *dunamis*, "power," shows up ten times, and related terms for physical force bring the total up to thirty-five.[50] The same terms that appear so often in the Archaeology recur throughout the *History*, for a total of 931 times. The same group of terms appears in Herodotus, on the other hand, 285 times, or less than one-third as often. There can be little doubt that this fascination with power is conscious and polemical. Thucydides was not the first person to analyze historical events in terms of self-interest and a calculus of forces, but his *History* does so with greater intensity and thoroughness than any earlier surviving document. Thucydides in some measure anticipates the classic Marxian position, that material conditions (the "base") determine the intellectual forms and ideas of a society (the "superstructure").

Thucydides' insights are complex, and he did not attempt to develop a coherent philosophical system. His *History* explores events and their causes, but he was acutely conscious that historical events did not follow the (to him at any rate) most logical path—otherwise, the sea power Athens would have defeated its atavistic Peloponnesian rivals—and the speeches in the *History* are designed to let us see the same events from very different and competing analytical perspectives. Nevertheless, money and its effect upon wealth are primary themes in the Archaeology

49. The technical term is *litotes*: thus "not more because of *charis* than *phobos*"would imply that *phobos* is far the more powerful; likewise at 1.5.1 οὐ τῶν ἀδυνατωτάτων clearly means τῶν δυνατωτάτων; for examples of litotes in Thucydides, see Rusten 1989, 27.

50. See Parry 1972, 52: "The historical facts which make up the object of intellection appear primarily as words meaning *power*. History in fact is movements of power." The words that Parry cites are δύναμις, δύνατος, ἰσχύς, βιαζόμενοι, ἔκρατησαν, and κρεισσόνων.

as elsewhere in Thucydides. Thucydides' understanding of money and power is fundamental to his working "model of history." Thucydides displays attitudes that contrast sharply with those of earlier sources, and he self-consciously presents a culture in transition. To approach Thucydides' distinct vision, I will begin by examining his analysis of wealth and of tyranny, a major cultural phenomenon of archaic Greece.

CHAPTER 6

Archaeology II

From Wealth to Capital:
The Changing Politics of Accumulation

Thucydides does more in the Archaeology than demystify the heroic age and argue that early Greece, far from being a glorious heroic age, was disorganized and materially weak. He extracts for historical analysis definite principles that he then treats as generally applicable.[1] At one point, for example, Thucydides argues that land power had proven unable to develop large political structures:

> Wars by land there were none, none at least by which power (*dunamis*) was acquired; we have the usual border contests, but of distant expeditions with conquest (*katastrophê*) of others as object, we hear nothing among the Hellenes. There was no union of subject cities round a great state, no spontaneous combination of equals for confederate expeditions; what fighting there was consisted merely of local warfare between rival neighbors.
>
> Thuc. 1.15.2

The logic of this analysis is clear enough: power, *dunamis*, comes from the conquest of others (*allôn katasrophê*). Thucydides, in part, anticipates the Marxian analysis of feudal expansion. The only way for feudal lords to expand their power was "by forcefully *redistributing* wealth away from the peasants or from other lords. This meant that they had to deploy their resources (surpluses) towards building up their *means of coercion* by means of investment in military men and equipment, in

---

1. On the generalizing tendencies of Thucydides in the Archaeology and elsewhere, see Hunter 1982, esp. 17–49.

particular to improve their ability to fight wars. A drive to *political accumulation*, or state building, was the feudal analogue to the capitalist drive to accumulate capital."[2]

But Thucydides diverges from the Marxian analysis in one crucial regard. In the Marxian paradigm, political accumulation was necessary because feudalism imposed economic stagnation. If nothing could be done to increase the productivity of land or labor per se, one could only acquire a greater share of the limited wealth available. "In view of both the lords' and the peasants' restricted ability effectively to allocate investment funds to improved means of production to increase agricultural efficiency, both lords and peasants found that the only really effective way to raise their income was by forcefully *redistributing* wealth away from the peasants or from other lords."[3] Thucydides, by contrast, assumes that "political accumulation" increases security, contact between people, and wealth in general (Thuc. 1.7, 8.3, 13.1). Thucydides does not provide a "moral" framework insofar as he does not apply criteria of justice to this process, but he does imply that political accumulation serves the interest of society as a whole.

Once Thucydides establishes political accumulation as a primary value, his analysis of the Greek tyrants follows logically:

> Again, wherever there were tyrants, their habit of providing simply for themselves, of looking solely to their personal comfort and family aggrandizement, made safety the great aim of their policy and prevented anything worthy of consideration (*axiologos*) proceeding from them, though they would each have their affairs with their immediate neighbors. Those in Sicily, as proof of this, attained to the greatest power (*dunamis*) of any. Thus for a long time everywhere Hellas was restrained so that it could not accomplish any public action as a group, while it remained, when considered as separate poleis, rather lacking in daring (*atolmotera*).
>
> Thuc. 1.17

This section of the Archaeology has not attracted as much attention as some others, but its dismissive treatment of the Greek tyrants has sparked interest among readers.[4]

---

2. Brenner 1987, 174 (italics mine).
3. Brenner 1987, 173–174 (italics mine).
4. This statement about the Sicilian tyrants has caused considerable concern, for Gelon and Hieron were, in their time, the most powerful individuals in the entire Greek world. Stahl, Classe, Steup, and Hude all bracketed this sentence "as a marginal note by a reader." Gomme remarks ad loc. that "the sentence is unnecessarily obscure. . . . Thucydides is thinking of the period before 480, and possibly Phalaris rather than of the Deinomenidai." But Thucydides, himself born c. 460, must have had Gelon and Hieron in mind when he referred to the power of Sicilian tyrants. Likewise, Hunter (1982, 29 n. 17), who does not

Thucydides' dismissive analysis of the tyrants is polemical and provocative. With his offhand remark on tyranny, the historian willfully
dismisses the obvious physical achievements of the tyrants and brings
to the fore his revisionist perspective of history. The tyrants were more
successful than any other individuals or groups of their time at exploiting the nature of archaic Greek society. But the Thucydidean judgment,
however shocking it may have been at the time, so perfectly anticipates
many modern attitudes that it raises little comment. Even those who
have studied the most successful tyrants have echoed Thucydides' contempt.[5]

Consider two other well-known and equally polemical passages. At
1.9.3, Thucydides concludes that Agamemnon employed not merely
charis, which we might here term a "debt of honor," but *deos*, "fear,"
to assemble the Greek host. A bit later, he considers the impression that
a desolate and ruined Sparta and Athens might make on visitors in the
distant future. No one would deduce the true power of Sparta from its
material remains, since "the city had not been combined into a single
political unit, nor did it make use of sanctuaries and buildings but was
settled in scattered villages according to the old Greek fashion" (Thuc.
1.10.2). Athens, on the other hand, was a single, massive city, heavily
built up with impressive structures, and a later observer would "estimate
from its obvious appearance the city's power to be twice that which it
really is." Neither of these comments has provoked much surprise.[6] Thucydides' analysis here strikes a blind spot in modern scholarship, which,
influenced by Hobbes, has often taken such cold-blooded calculation for
granted.[7] Nevertheless, these two judgments in effect reject fundamental

---

accept Gomme's analysis, suggests: "Thucydides, it seems to me, wants to keep Sicily in
the background, a distant, rather unknown place with a history, or more precisely, an
Archaeology of its own, saved for its proper place at the beginning of Book 6." "One can
get the impression," Täubler (1927, 83) wrily observes, "that Thucydides does not do
justice to the increase of all non-political interests, not just economic but even power
politics, which were caused by the tyrants." Täubler then runs through an impressive list
of achievements associated with the tyrants in the archaic period.

5. See, for example, Shapiro 1989, 6: "The building of temples was in fact an activity
always closely associated with tyrants, who thereby gratify the ego which had driven them
to seize power in the first place."

6. Hunter (1982, 34) argues that architectural development is in fact a proper index
of the relative financial power of Athens and Sparta, but Thucydides—who was acutely
sensitive to Athens's financial resources—has general military power in mind in this passage; Hornblower (1991), in his comments on 1.10.2, primarily contrasts Herodotus's
interest in religious sanctuaries with Thucydides' indifference to such phenomena.

7. As Peter Euben has pointed out to me, Hobbes himself (like Thucydides) understood
how radical and reductive his analysis was. Hobbes was prescriptive: he wanted us to be

assumptions on which much activity in the archaic Greek world was based. Thucydides' method is self-consciously reductive, in that he assigns minimal impact to phenomena that were, in fact, important. His model of human behavior, with its calculus of fear and interest, deliberately simplifies reality, and the original readers of Thucydides—even those who shared this perspective—would have understood the degree to which the historian was outraging an earlier set of values.

At 1.10.2, Thucydides rejects two kinds of influence. First, he obviously denies that buildings, statues, and other material artifacts can serve as a reliable index of power, and his comparison of Sparta and Athens strongly supports this assertion. The second point is perhaps less obvious, but equally important. Thucydides dismisses Athenian architectural splendor to make a more general point, that symbolic values are, in his view, unimportant and irrelevant in the calculus of power. Thucydides does not acknowledge the fact that material goods do not simply mirror, but can themselves *produce*, power. The building of temples, the dedication of costly statues or of large quantities of bullion—all of these can serve as manifest symbols, which instantiate power and generate prestige in the public eye. The tyrants in particular consumed their wealth extravagantly to publicize their power in a kind of Greek potlatch.[8]

Thus the Deinomenids not only competed in horse racing on a Panhellenic level—the most expensive avenue of competition—but they subsequently used their wealth to memorialize their victories and to make them a fixed and tangible part of Greek tradition. Pausanias saw a chariot and portrait statue of Gelon executed by Glaukias of Aigina (Paus. 6.9.4–5).[9] Deinomenes, Gelon's grandson, dedicated at Olympia a chariot by the Aiginetan artist Onatotos, with racehorses by Kalamis on either side. Polyzalos, brother of Gelon, who became tyrant of Gela when Hieron assumed control of Syracuse, dedicated a chariot group at Delphi of which the charioteer, buried in the earthquake of 373, survives to the present day.[10] The tyrants used every tool at their disposal to

---

and tried to make us calculating beings as an antidote to the religious enthusiasms that led to civil war.

8. On the allusion to such tyrannical largesse in the carpet scene of the *Agamemnon*, see Crane 1993; on the competitive generosity of the *turannos*, see Kurke 1991, 195–224.

9. Note that Pausanias (6.9.4–5) tells us that he disagrees with previous authority, and deduces that the statue could not have been dedicated by Gelon. Gelon had moved to Syracuse in 491, and his victory at Olympia took place in 488—the tyrant Gelon would not therefore have signed himself as a citizen of Syracuse. The dedicant must, Pausanias concludes, be another Gelon, who also just happened to have a Deinomenes as his father (and who also just happened to win a major victory in the chariot race).

10. See Stewart 1990, 1: 149.

publicize their victories. From the sixth century the coins of Syracuse had portrayed a four-horse chariot, but with Gelon's triumph they begin to include a flying Nike that crowns the horses.[11] The poet Simonides invented the genre of epinician poetry, to celebrate such victories and designed to become part of the public and international canon of Panhellenic poetry. Hieron commissioned not only Simonides, but the younger poets Pindar and Bacchylides, to make sure that their literary texts would provide a framework within which his victories would survive—a wise choice, since four poems by Pindar (*Ol.* 1, *Pyth.* 1–3) and three by Bacchylides (poems 3–5) survive to praise Hieron for modern audiences.

If we now lay emphasis upon material display and its symbolic value, we are only describing as best we can in modern idiom forces that shaped the actions and perceptions of Greeks in the archaic and classical periods. Nor does Thucydides deny this—the Corcyraeans and Corinthians still frame their arguments within the traditional scheme of symbolic capital and *charis*. Before we can appreciate Thucydides' reductive analysis, we need to consider more closely those factors that were pushed aside.

WEALTH IN THE ARCHAIC PERIOD: SYMBOLIC RATHER THAN FINANCIAL CAPITAL

Why, one may ask, did men such as Hieron lavish such wealth and attention on matters that, to Thucydides at least, seemed of secondary importance? The answer to this question is simple enough and consistent with Thucydides' analysis of the past. The tyrants of Sicily, and of Greece in general, had, we might say, great "wealth," but not "capital." Precious metals could store surplus wealth, whether as bullion or as coinage, but it is easy to forget that such resources are effectively inert. Almost all of us—whether we live in North America or mainland China—live in a world where accumulated wealth automatically and as if by its inner nature produces additional wealth. Capital generates interest or dividends or rent or some other form of wealth. If we accumulate money, we put it in banks, stocks, or bonds, and our money reproduces some fraction of itself as a return on our investment. For many of us, it is hard to imagine the instincts that a different system, which lacked these now

11. See, for example, the coins illustrated in Mildenberg and Hurter 1985, 1: 47, nos. 689–693.

pervasive financial mechanisms, would have stirred. Even those of us who grew up in formerly Communist nations understood interest payments existed, since Communist society was, in part, a reaction against such a financial system. Marx denounced "the wealth of the few that increases constantly, although they have long ceased to work."[12] This condition, in which capital not only reproduces but also augments itself, is the hallmark of capitalist production: "As soon as capitalist production stands on its own two feet, it not only maintains this relation but reproduces it on a constantly expanding scale."[13]

Until financial mechanisms became more pervasive and reliable, the precapitalist lord could, as we have seen, expand his power only by recourse to "political accumulation." Capital did not automatically grow and increase its value in archaic Greece. We know, of course, that money was loaned for interest,[14] and in this sense money could generate money, but loans were a special case, not the natural form in which to store accumulated wealth. Herodotus, for example, records a story about a certain Milesian in the early part of the sixth century (Hdt. 6.86a). Although oppressed by the instability of Ionia and the rapidity with which money changed hands, the Milesian knew that the Peloponnese was securely settled. He converted one-half of his wealth into silver (6.86a.4) and decided to deposit it with Glaukos, a Spartan renowned for justice at the time. The Spartan was supposed to safeguard the silver in its original form until the Milesian or one of his heirs returned for it, and the silver cache would, in an ideal world, simply be returned to its owner. There was no question of interest. The Milesian was grateful if he could guarantee the security and integrity of his wealth.

Another story from Herodotus illustrates the function of surplus wealth stored as precious metal. In book 7, Pythios is portrayed as the richest man in the entire Persian empire after Xerxes (Hdt. 7.27.2). He offers to Xerxes all of the money he has accumulated—two thousand talents of silver and almost four million Daric staters of gold (7.28.3). After announcing this gift, he makes a revealing comment: "All this I freely give to you: for myself, I have a sufficient livelihood from my slaves and my lands." He keeps surplus wealth in the form of metal, but this surplus wealth is not productive. Land and labor produce wealth, and so long as Pythios controls these productive forces, he can live per-

12. Marx 1977, 873; Halpern 1991, 64–65.
13. Marx 1977, 874; Halpern 1991, 62–63.
14. E.g., *tokos* as "interest" at Pindar *Oly.* 10.9.

fectly well without recourse to monetary wealth at all. The story, as it unfolds, reveals three tiers of wealth, each separate from the other. At one extreme stand the land and labor of Pythios, which he retains and does not offer to Xerxes (nor does Xerxes anticipate such a gift). These forces of production stand outside the normal exchange between king and subject. Next comes Pythios's monetary wealth, and it is this wealth that he offers. His gift is wildly generous in quantity but only exceeds the amount that he might have owed in tribute.

Later in the book, however, Herodotus delimits the sphere of exchange in which monetary gifts pass from one person to another. Pythios asks to have one of his sons excused from military service. Yet the fortune of precious metals that he had offered does not justify this request. Not only does Pythios fail to get what he requests, but the request itself outrages Xerxes and provokes him to execute Pythios's son in brutal and spectacular fashion. In a classic example of "spheres of exchange," no amount of middle-rank gifts (e.g., money) can equal the smallest top-rank gift (in this case, military service by a single member of Pythios's family).[15] Xerxes' behavior is extreme, and his cruelty here characteristic of the "oriental despot," but the underlying framework is Greek. Money thus occupies an ambiguous position, for while it provides the material for a spectacularly generous gesture, the value of monetary exchange faces qualitative limits that no quantitative amount can transcend.

For a tyrant such as Hieron, money in the storeroom was an important thing to have, and he accumulated as much as he could, but as long as it sat in his treasury it did nothing. It was of potential use and could be expended on any number of things, but the entire time he kept it hidden away, it remained unchanged. Where capital is a living entity that grows of itself, wealth is inanimate and inert. The effective price of gold may well rise or fall, but ten talents of silver in the back room will not transmogrify itself into eleven talents no matter how long one waits.

Pythios's generosity was, in fact, not an idle or extravagant act, but, despite his subsequent miscalculation, in fact the best possible avenue of investment. When money does not earn financial interest, it is best invested in personal relationships. The only way in which wealth could produce more wealth was through investment in some action that strengthened the relationship between the giver and some individual or group. In archaic societies, gifts must be repaid *with interest*, and gifts

15. On spheres of exchange, see Bohannen 1955.

are, in fact, the normal productive avenue of investment. In Greek, *charis* is the term used to describe various facets of this reciprocal relationship of gratitude.[16] Pythios's story commands attention because it is a special case, given the generosity of the initial gift, the importance of the subsequent request to himself (his eldest son), and the unimportance, by some criteria, of the request to Xerxes (a single, utterly insignificant soldier). Its point comes from the fact that both Pythios and Xerxes can be seen as having transgressed separate norms: in Xerxes' eyes, Pythios violates the implicit ranking of gifts, while Xerxes, of course, reacts to Pythios with the savagery that Herodotus repeatedly uses to characterize foreigners.

To sum up, if Pythios's gold and silver had formed capital in a modern sense, his gift would have been grotesque, for he would have given away the source of additional wealth. But, to use Marx's phrase, Pythios's money was "petrified into a hoard, and it could remain in that position until the Last Judgement without a single farthing accruing to it."[17] For the capitalist, money generates money, and things are commodities that serve only as a means to be converted into and out of money at a profit. The noncapitalist sells one commodity to acquire money with which to purchase another useful item, while the capitalist buys commodities only to sell them again at a profit.

In an archaic society, symbolic capital takes the place of modern capital, which does not, properly speaking, exist.[18] Money is not in itself a *source* of wealth, but a temporary repository that must be cashed in and invested in some social relation before it can generate any returns. In many cases, symbolic capital represents "a disguised form of purchase of labor power, or a covert exaction of corvées."[19] In the Archaeology, Thucydides is not so much analyzing inner workings of the polis as an individual social unit as he is exploring the interaction of poleis. As we noted above, Thucydides has little interest in individual states, viewing them as the constituents out of which larger, more viable units can be assembled. Archaic Greek culture gave enormous value to balance and moderation in personal behavior, but balance was the keystone of all

---

16. On the workings of this as it appears in Pindar, see Kurke 1991, 66–70; for the general practice of such exchanges in the classical period, see Herman 1987.

17. Marx 1977, 252; Marx attributes to the capitalist the fundamental relation money-commodity-money (M-C-M) and to the noncapitalist commodity-money-commodity (C-M-C). The steps are the same, but the capitalist sees acquisition as an end, while the noncapitalist sees it as a means.

18. Bourdieu 1977, 171–183.

19. Bourdieu 1977, 179.

interstate relations as well. Sparta had considerable power in continental Greece, and the mainland provided a prestigious theater in which to showcase Sparta's status, but the Greek in Olbia or Rhegion, or even on Naxos, had little to fear from direct Spartan force. No Greek state could exert its authority over a critical mass of the Hellenic world. Thus no polis or league was large enough to set off a chain reaction of growth. Each was, in Thucydides' view, mired in skirmishes with its neighbors (Thuc. 1.15.2). Sparta, by contrast, did win complete and decisive victories over Messenia but then found itself almost as debilitated as strengthened by the constant effort of exerting this mastery over a brutalized and recalcitrant population.

The "rhetoric of wealth" matches its function. Pindar, writing for the elite of the early fifth century, reflects an ideology according to which wealth, *ploutos*, must be displayed and expended socially: "If someone hoards hidden wealth at home and attacks others with mockery, he fails to consider that he is giving up his soul to Hades without glory" (*Isthm.* 1.66–68). "I take no pleasure in keeping great wealth hidden away in my hall, but in using what I have to be successful and to win a good name by helping my friends. For the hopes of men who toil much come to all alike" (*Nem.* 1.31–32). "Wealth is widely powerful, whenever a mortal man receives it, blended with pure excellence, from the hands of fortune, and takes it as a companion that makes many friends" (*Pyth.* 5.1–4). The expenditure of wealth (*dapanê*) is good. At *Isthm.* 1.42, financial expenditure (*dapanê*) commands as much admiration as the physical stress of training (*ponoi*). The *genos* of the Theban Melissos delights in the expenses (*dapanê*) of horse racing on an international level (*Isthm.* 4.28–31), and they have not let these expenses (*dapanai*, pl.) wear out their reverence for their hopes (*Isthm.* 5.57–58).

Financial profit, *kerdos*, clearly exists by the fifth century—the coinages that began to emerge in the sixth century were popular in large measure because they could efficiently store such financial surpluses. We can see, however, that at least some of those who accumulated wealth took great pains to present themselves as the exponents of the earlier premonetary world. The relatively small island of Aigina could support roughly 4,000 people at bare subsistence, but in the first half of the fifth century it regularly fielded fleets of fifty ships or more, requiring a complement of 10,000 adult men, suggesting a population of c. 40,000.[20]

20. Figueira 1981, 22.

Aigina clearly generated the vast majority of its wealth through nonagricultural means, primarily seaborne trade. Starting in the sixth century, Aigina was a leading producer of coined silver and thus could afford to tie up large quantities of its wealth in precious metals. *Kerdos* is always a dangerous thing in Pindar[21]—unless it is used metaphorically and converted into a special case that reverses its original nature.[22] Raw monetary exchanges are degrading and threaten to turn even the Muse into a whore.[23] The elite of Aigina did not, however, shun Panhellenic athletic contests or the elite medium of epinician poetry. Eleven of the forty-five complete surviving epinician poems by Pindar celebrate Aiginetan victors, and Aiginetans were far and away Pindar's most common patrons. These men generated wealth by nontraditional means (i.e., not by agriculture), but with this monetary wealth they paid the poet Pindar to create an image that set them in a traditional position to which they held a dubious claim. The Aiginetans invested some of their surplus wealth first in supporting the training needed for international competition and then in commissioning epinician poems. But the epinician poems, it should be noted, are still read. The Aiginetans converted their silver into symbolic capital that is still paying them dividends long after they and their world have vanished.

Archaic Greece was constantly, as Marshall Sahlins, quoting Hobbes, observed of archaic societies in general, at "war with warre," but a war in which status and prestige, rather than absolute dominance and possession of territory, were the primary goals. The weapons were less spear and sword than the public display and consumption of property, especially at the great Panhellenic gathering places. Participation in and victory at the games, the dedication of costly monuments, the building of lavish sanctuaries with temples and impressive offerings, the glorification of a city's role (or, for colonies, the role of their founding city) in

---

21. *Nem.* 7.18: σοφοὶ δὲ μέλλοντα τριταῖον ἄνεμον ἔμαθον, οὐδ᾽ ὑπὸ κέρδει βλάβεν; *Nem.* 9.33: αἰδὼς γὰρ ὑπὸ κρύφα κέρδει κλέπτεται; *Pyth.* 1.92: μὴ δολωθῇς, ὦ φίλος, κέρδεσιν εὐτράπλοις; *Pyth.* 3.54: κέρδει καὶ σοφία δέδεται; *Pyth.* 4.140: ἐντὶ μὲν θνατῶν φρένες ὠκύτεραι κέρδος αἰνῆσαι πρὸ δίκας δόλιον.

22. *Pyth.* 8.13: κέρδος δὲ φίλτατον, ἑκόντος εἴ τις ἐκ δόμων φέροι; *Nem.* 11.47: κερδέων δὲ χρὴ μέτρον θηρευέμεν; *Isthm.* 1.50–51: ὃς δ᾽ ἀμφ᾽ ἀέθλοις ἢ πολεμίζων ἄρηται κῦδος ἁβρόν, εὐαγορηθεὶς κέρδος ὕψιστον δέκεται, πολιατᾶν καὶ ξένων γλώσσας ἄωτον.

23. *Isthm.* 2.1–11; see the analysis at Kurke 1991, 240–256; on one point, I would part company with Kurke. She argues that Pindar is integrating money into the ideology of the aristocracy, but her argument treats money and wealth interchangeably. The rest of the ode expatiates upon the fact that Xenokrates embeds his dealings with others in the emotional and social ties that pure monetary exchange excludes.

the poetic record, and the production of new poems translate a particular occasion—a victory in the games, the founding of a city, or simply
a particular celebration of a local festival—into the permanent and international poetic record.[24]

The prestige of a Greek state differed absolutely in one fundamental
respect from that enjoyed, for example, by the leaders of the various
empires that had flourished in Near East. If Xerxes did not receive the
public respect and subordination he desired, he might be expected to
appear at the head of a devastating force to annihilate those at fault. He
could *extract* respect by command. Greek poleis could not bring such
force to bear. They needed to *win* respect from their fellows, to move
their fellow Greeks to yield this respect freely. Herodotus dramatizes
how suspicious and prickly states could be: those Greek states willing
to oppose Xerxes did so conditionally. In book 7 of Herodotus, the
Argives and Gelon of Syracuse preferred surrender to Persia to acceptance of the hegemony of Sparta and Athens. Status was, with the occasional exception of basic survival (cf. the Melians), the single most
important factor in international relations. In the end, even the Persian
Wars became a contest over status. After Salamis and before Plataia,
Persia no longer threatened Athens with annihilation but offered favorable terms (Hdt. 8.140). But even though it no longer needed to fear the
disasters that had overtaken Miletos in 494 (Hdt. 6.18–22) or Eretria
in 490 (Hdt. 6.100–102), Athens chose to continue the struggle. The
desire for autonomy and respect among Greek poleis now emerged as a
passion for freedom: "We will defend ourselves," the Athenians boast,
"because we long for freedom (*eleutheria*)" (Hdt. 8.143.1). Prestige won
from Greek states was always conditional and could be denied if the
claimant pushed too hard or demanded too much. The Athenians in
Herodotus's narrative constructed their opposition to Xerxes, with all
of its harsh risks, as a dramatic claim for respect and prestige among
their fellow Hellenes. But if Athenian resistance was perhaps the
grandest such gesture, the game to which it contributed was well established.

The contest for prestige affected the rhetoric by which the elite of the
archaic period presented themselves. The epinician poets portrayed ty-

---

24. See Sahlins 1972, 182, quoted by Kurke (1991, 93–94) as part of her discussion
(at pp. 85–97) of the ideology of exchange; the classic discussion of this sublimation of
conflict in the exchange of gifts is Mauss 1990.

rants in different ways than they did private victors, adopting for the tyrants "a rhetoric of extremes which suits the preeminent position and gestures of [their] patrons."[25] Yet each of Pindar's odes to Hieron also incorporates sections that stress the limits of power and thus modulate the claims of his patron.[26] Hieron deserves praise from others, according to Pindar, because of his selfless generosity:

> You are the guardian (*tamias*) of an ample store. You have many faithful witnesses of both good and bad. But abide in a blossoming temper, and if you are fond of always hearing sweet things spoken of you, do not be too distressed by expenses (*dapanai*), but, like a steersman, let your sail out to the wind. Do not be deceived, my friend, by glib profit-seeking (*kerdos*). The loud acclaim of renown that survives a man is all that reveals the way of life of departed men to storytellers and singers alike. The kindly excellence of Kroisos does not perish, but Phalaris, with his pitiless mind, who burned his victims in a bronze bull, is surrounded on all sides by a hateful reputation.
>
> Pind. *Pyth.* 1.88–98

The underlying logic here is that of the potlatch, in which the wealthy publicly consume vast quantities of wealth. Hieron is a great man and wealthy, but he deliberately expends that wealth without regard to self-ish concerns, and he thus lays a claim to praise and social approbation. Pindar equates Hieron with the kindly Kroisos and contrasts him with the murderous Phalaris. The tyrant wins praise beyond the borders of his immediate domain because he exploits his enormous powers in benevolent and socially acceptable ways. Listeners in Olbia or Olynthos, outside of Hieron's direct control, can yield to him their jealously guarded admiration. Or, to use Bourdieu's terminology, Hieron applies portions of his material wealth first to horse racing and then to the victory ode, but only because he thereby converts this material wealth into symbolic capital.

The pose that Pindar sketches for Hieron is not, however, confined to poetry, nor should we divide the archaic Greek world into serious/

---

25. Kurke 1991, 224; on the self-presentation of tyrants in epinician poetry, see Kurke 1991, "Envy and Tyranny: The Rhetoric of *Megaloprepeia*," 195–224; Race 1987; Race 1986, 36–66.

26. *Oly.* 1.55–57: Tantalos unable to "digest his prosperity" (καταπέψαι μέγαν ὄλβον οὐκ ἐδυνάσθη); *Pyth.* 1.1–20: Typhos subdued by Zeus; 47–55: combined weakness and strength of Philoktetes; *Pyth.* 2.25–41: Ixion who could not "withstand his great prosperity" (26: μακρὸν οὐχ ὑπέμεινεν ὄλβον); *Pyth.* 3.15–23: Koronis, who "conceived a passion for things that were distant, as happens to many" (20: ἤρατο τῶν ἀπεόντων· οἷα καὶ πολλοὶ πάθον); 54–60: Asklepios who let his knowledge be bound by profit (54: ἀλλὰ κέρδει καὶ σοφία δέδεται).

political and frivolous/literary spheres. The same rhetoric of self-presentation appears in the historical record. Diodoros, following the historian Timaios of the third century B.C., describes the aftermath of Gelon's spectacular victory over Karthaginian forces at Himera in Sicily. Although anachronisms from the Hellenistic period may embellish this account, its overall tenor corresponds very closely to the picture from the archaic period.[27] When Diodoros emphasizes the general consequence of this victory, he focuses upon the "respect" (Diod. 11.23.3: apodochê) and "goodwill" (eunoia) that Gelon earned. Diodoros goes on to describe an elaborate theater of power and self-effacement. Gelon's victory earned him respect and goodwill not only in Syracuse but throughout Sicily (11.25.5). His former adversaries on the island approached him now "asking for forgiveness for their previous errors, announcing that they would in the future do everything that he ordered."[28] Not to be outdone, Gelon responded by concluding an alliance but exercising great restraint (11.26.1: epieikôs chrêsamenos). He "bore his good fortune as a mortal should" (tên eutuxian anthrôpinôs epheren). Perhaps Gelon could consolidate his power and bring down his enemies by force, and so they approached him for reconciliation. On the other hand, military action is expensive, time-consuming, and risky, so Gelon played an appropriately gracious role in response. Both sides disguise their new calculations of material power in an elegant and dignified social minuet.

Gelon reserved his greatest gesture for his own polis. Tyrants who cared to live long carefully disarmed their subjects and surrounded themselves with bodyguards. More than one tyrant had been murdered by a vengeful populace once he lost control of armed force. Gelon thus staged a scene that transgressed the behavior normally attributed to a tyrant, and legitimated his rule. He commanded all citizens to assemble under arms, and then appeared among them, not only unarmed, but wearing only the simplest of clothing, and in this vulnerable condition he delivered a verbal defence of his entire life and of his dealings with the Syr-

---

27. Diod. 11.26.6: μιᾷ φωνῇ πάντας ἀποκαλεῖν εὐεργέτην καὶ σωτῆρα καὶ βασιλέα; Hornblower 1983, 48: "The interest of this triple acclamation is that it is emphatically and oddly Hellenistic (cp. OGIS 239, 301, etc., inscriptions of the Seleucid and Pergameme kingdoms)." The term euergetês, "benefactor," is, however, central in archaic society.
28. Diod. 11.26.1: εὐθὺς δὲ καὶ τῶν πρότερον ἐναντιουμένων πόλεών τε καὶ δυναστῶν παρεγένοντο πρὸς αὐτὸν πρέσβεις, ἐπὶ μὲν τοῖς ἠγνοημένοις αἰτούμενοι συγγνώμην, εἰς δὲ τὸ λοιπὸν ἐπαγγελλόμενοι πᾶν ποιήσειν τὸ προσταττόμενον.

acusans.[29] The crowd was amazed that he had put himself at the mercy of so many men who wished to kill him. Far from taking vengeance, they showered him with praises, and his control over Syracuse was never afterward challenged. Gelon then turned to the standard material rhetoric of the period (Diod. 11.26.7), instantiating his prestige by building temples to Demeter and Kore, dedicating a golden tripod of sixteen talents' weight at Delphi, and beginning work on a temple to Demeter near Delphi.

Diodoros also tells us about Gelon's death (Diod. 11.38). Gelon had instituted strict sumptuary laws limiting the wealth that could be expended on funerals—a measure that was common in the archaic period and that was an attempt to weaken the solidarity of powerful aristocratic clans. He left strict instructions that his own funeral should conform to these regulations and specified that he be buried in a particularly fertile field a number of miles outside of the city. The common people (11.38.5: *ho dêmos*) spontaneously erected an impressive grave (*taphos axiologos*) for Gelon and subsequently offered to him the cult due to a *heros*.[30] No act could confer greater legitimacy on a Greek ruler. Whether or not we believe Diodoros's account, its shape aptly describes the goal for which a Greek tyrant might strive and to which wealth would properly be subordinated. If the Aiginetans and Hieron enjoy the continuing audience that Pindar's odes command, Gelon acquired sufficient symbolic or cultural capital that his subjects—and the literary tradition embodied by Timaios and Diodoros—paid dividends to his grave long after his death.

THUCYDIDES AND "SYMBOLIC CAPITAL"

Both the temples of Demeter and Kore erected by Gelon (Diod. 11.26.7) and his grave are termed *axiologos*, "worthy of note" (11.38.5). Events in Sicily are, in fact, characterized as among the most *axiologos* (11.26.8) of a particular year, and this term, a common one that appears almost 300 times in Diodoros, generally designates what we might call in a slightly different context "all the news fit to print." Thucydides uses

29. Diod. 11.26.5: αὐτὸς δὲ οὐ μόνον τῶν ὅπλων γυμνὸς εἰς τὴν ἐκκλησίαν ἦλθεν, ἀλλὰ καὶ ἀχίτων ἐν ἱματίῳ προσελθὼν ἀπελογίσατο μὲν περὶ παντὸς τοῦ βίου καὶ τῶν πεπραγμένων αὐτῷ πρὸς τοὺς Συρακοσίους.
30. Diod. 11.38.5: ὁ μὲν δῆμος τάφον ἀξιόλογον ἐπιστήσας ἡρωικαῖς τιμαῖς ἐτίμησε τὸν Γέλωνα.

this same term in much the same way as Diodoros, but he employs it to dismiss the collective achievements of Greek tyrants: with few exceptions, he notes, "no achievement was brought to fruition by them that was *axiologos*."[31] In the this one term, Thucydides distills his rejection of an entire habit of thought, and even of the archaic world.

Before analyzing the new, however, let us consider the way Thucydides portrays the old. At 1.17, Thucydides uses the expression *tas poleis ôikoun* to describe the rule of the tyrants. This phrase is often treated as if it meant "they dwelled in their poleis," with the verb *oikeô* given a colorless meaning. In fact, the verb, as Thucydides uses it, is a loaded word: *oikeô* literally means "to treat as one's *oikos*." When it describes someone living in a larger unit, it is used with a preposition to indicate that someone has their *oikos* in a larger space.[32] When *oikeô* is used with a simple accusative, it often implies that the subject has appropriated this space entirely and converted it into an *oikos*.[33] The verb *oikeô* does not just imply habitation but the control, even if conditional, of the space occupied.[34] In several important passages, the verb clearly means "govern": thus Kleon boasts that the "worser sort of men for the most part *govern* (*oikousi*) their cities better than their more clever fellows";[35] and the revolution of 411 draws up laws "so that the city will be *governed* (*oikêsetai*) in the best possible manner."[36] If Thucydides had wanted to say that the tyrants merely lived in their home cities, he would have said *en tais polesin ôikoun*. In writing *tas poleis ôikoun*, he implies that the tyrants appropriated their poleis and controlled them as an extension of their own household. Thus the Athenian Euphemos, in a speech remarkable for its cold-blooded acknowledgment of Athenian ruthlessness, states that "having become leaders of those previously under the Great King, we control them (*oikoumen*)" (Thuc. 6.82.3).

It is important to stress that in many cultures (and in most of those cultures with which Greeks had contact), rulers were expected to treat

---

31. Thuc. 1.17: ἐπράχθη δὲ οὐδὲν ἀπ᾽ αὐτῶν ἔργον ἀξιόλογον.

32. Thuc. 2.16.1: ἐν τοῖς ἀγροῖς . . . γενόμενοί τε καὶ οἰκήσαντες; Thuc. 4.120.1, 5.34.1, 5.42.1, 6.2.1.

33. Thus the displaced Aiginetans occupy Thyrea (Thuc. 2.27.2: *Thurean oikein*); see also Thuc. 2.17.1, 2.102.5, and 5.18.6.

34. See the collocation of *oikeô* with *autonomos* at 2.71.2 and 4, 3.39.2.

35. Thuc. 3.37.3: οἵ τε φαυλότεροι τῶν ἀνθρώπων πρὸς τοὺς ξυνετωτέρους ὡς ἐπὶ τὸ πλέον ἄμεινον οἰκοῦσι τὰς πόλεις.

36. Thuc. 8.67.1: τούτους δὲ ξυγγράψαντας γνώμην ἐσενεγκεῖν ἐς τὸν δῆμον ἐς ἡμέραν ῥητὴν καθ᾽ ὅτι ἄριστα ἡ πόλις οἰκήσεται; see also 2.61.4 and 6.18.7, where the ideas of "control" and "inhabit" are also intermixed.

their territory as a part of their own *oikos*. Such a posture can be portrayed as intrusive and can outrage sensibilities, but it can also be subsumed as part of a larger strategy in which power relationships are expressed in terms of an extended family. "When domination can only be exercised in its *elementary form*, i.e. directly, between one person and another, it cannot take place overtly and must be disguised under the veil of enchanted relationships, the official model of which is presented by relations between kinsmen; in order to be socially recognized it must get itself misrecognized."[37] The ruler becomes the paterfamilias of a vast extended family. All members of the Persian empire are the servants of its emperor, just as the *oiketai* of an *oikos* must subordinate themselves to the head of the household. The palace is the center of such a social formation.

Instead of a palace, Greek poleis each had their agora, a neutral space corporately owned and controlled by the polis, for assembly and (as the economy evolved) for market exchanges. Just as individual poleis fiercely defended their autonomy, individual *oikoi* retained as much control as possible. Greeks would, in the best case, subordinate themselves to, freely lay down their lives for, *nomos*, but never for another mortal.[38] But this attitude was not self-evident, or a matter of natural law—the great empires to the east loomed dangerously on the horizon and threatened to subsume Greece. Thus successful tyrants (such as the Peisistratids) carefully declined to change the form of law or openly to appropriate power. Some were extremely successful in this regard: both Periander of Corinth and Pittakos of Mytilene found themselves at one time or another among the Seven Wise Men of archaic Greece.[39] Thus though many systems of domination may express themselves in terms of kinship and use family roles to misrecognize the raw power of a ruler, Greek tyrants did well to avoid this model. When Thucydides claims that they ran their poleis like an *oikos*, he is demystifying the understated position that clever tyrants might adopt. Thucydides does not, however, object to appropriation or domination on principle—as we have seen, Thucydides does not object to empires per se. Thucydides objects to the tyrants because they did not actually treat the polis as they should treat an *oikos*. They used the polis and governed it, but "they looked out to augment (*auxein*) their own interests insofar as they affected their own persons (*es te to*

37. Bourdieu 1977,191.
38. See, for example, Demaratos's advice to Xerxes at Hdt. 7.104.
39. Diog. Laert. 1.13.

sôma) and their own *private* household (*es to ton idion oikon*)" (1.17). Thus though the tyrants might seem to control their poleis as large-scale *oikoi*, they in fact exploited the poleis for the small-scale interests of themselves and their personal *oikoi*. This is a very harsh judgment by Thucydides, for he treats nothing with more scorn than the emphasis of private concerns (*idios*) over those shared by a wider audience.

Thucydides dismisses the entire system of honors and polite restraint that tyrants such as Gelon manipulated so skillfully. He has little interest in polite surfaces and relentlessly pushed beyond to hard calculations of force and interest. When Thucydides claims that Agamemnon used fear (*deos*) just as much as *charis* to assemble the Greeks, he is passing judgment not only on the epic tradition, but on the self-effacing stratagems and polite theatrics that concealed the harsh edges of authority. The acquisition of power (*dunamis*) and its application to the world in concrete deeds (*erga*) fascinate Thucydides.[40] Thucydides simply ignores much (though not all) of what we have called symbolic capital.

THUCYDIDES AND CAPITAL

It is easy to see what Thucydides rejects—the old world had not developed the large-scale political bodies that he admired. And it should be clear by now that Thucydides has little patience for the self-serving fictions of the Greek elites. But what was it that had changed? Was the Athenian empire only an accident? Or did it reflect a fundamental change and the emergence of possibilities that had not previously existed?

Thucydides was able to dismiss symbolic factors almost entirely from his analysis, because he perceived the emergence of a new force. Where material wealth had previously been inert and could return "interest" only when handed over as a gift, Thucydides saw imperialism as a mechanism that could, as it were, make money out of money. The Athenian empire was analogous to modern financial capital in that it earned a regular rate of return (tribute taking the place of interest). Thus Thucydides traced in the Peloponnesian War a major theme familiar from recent studies of the impact of modern capitalism on traditional societies. Once financial and technological systems give dominant figures unprecedented levels of control, they can begin to dispense with the ex-

40. On this, see especially Parry 1981.

pensive and tiresome obligations they had previously needed to win the loyalty of those on whose services the great depended. Thus, in the modern ethnographic record, we might turn to James Scott's work[41] to see how a technological tool such as a combine harvester could reduce the need for human labor in Indonesia and allowed the landlords to forgo many of the obligations they had formerly had toward the peasants who worked their land. The mechanized harvester was not simply a technological innovation, but a catalyst that allowed the powerful to increase their power and redefine the balance between themselves and those less powerful than they. The landlord-dependent relationship became tangibly less personal. Power increased in significance as social bonds became correspondingly less important. Scott describes a shift in what Bourdieu calls "modes of domination."[42] The same kind of shift took place when Athens established its empire in the fifth century. Thucydides directs our gaze relentlessly at the impersonal calculations of his Athenians, who repeatedly turn to an objectified logic of power, rather than to traditional values or obligations.

Thucydides could not have differed more completely from Marx and Adam Smith alike in one fundamental respect: he had, as we noted earlier, remarkably little interest in material production. Agriculture is one of the factors with which Thucydides begins the Archaeology, and seaborne trade elicits additional wealth by means of some mechanism that Thucydides does not choose to describe. But Thucydides comes very close to seeing one kind of wealth, that associated with naval empires, as a kind of capital. The revenues of empire motivate Minos to clear the seas of pirates (Thuc. 1.4), but the accumulation of imperial wealth seems, in Thucydides' view, to take on a life of its own. The land-based struggles of Greece were deficient precisely in this regard, for no one power could generate any momentum for its expansion but remained bogged down in disputes with its neighbors (1.15.2). Naval empires had emerged from time to time and had acquired the greatest strength by "revenues of money (1.5.1: *chrêmatôn prosodôi*) and by the domination of others (*allôn archê*)." Moving freely about the sea they would conquer (*katesrephonto*) the islands.

At 1.19, the Archaeology climaxes with the appearance of the Athenian empire, in many ways the logical culmination of the processes examined in the previous sections: "The Athenians in time received tribute

41. See especially Scott 1985, as well as Scott 1976
42. Bourdieu 1977, 183–197.

from their subject cities with the exception of the Chians and Lesbians, and they imposed on them all monetary tribute. And so they possessed for this war far more stored wealth in their own control (*hê idia paraskeuê meizôn*) than would ever have been possible if they had expanded (*ênthêsan*) to the fullest extent of power (*hôs ta kratista*) with an ad hoc alliance."[43] This passage, like many in Thucydides, is difficult to capture in translation: Thucydides examines potential energy in Athens's *paraskeuê*, "stored wealth," a word to which Thucydides gives a new importance.[44]

But the wealth that Athens accumulates is more than just "a petrified hoard," like Pythios's millions of Darics or the precious metal that the unnamed Milesian deposits with Glaukos at Sparta. The *chrêmata* that the Athenians collect from their subjects supports the navy. The navy, in turn, can bring crushing force to bear on any who do not fulfill their obligations, and it can expand its own power base (as, on a small scale, with Melos). The Athenian empire is a machine that runs on money and that can use money to expand. The capacity—and need—to expand leads to a number of tensions within the *History*.

First, what is the source of power? Both the Spartan Sthenelaidas and the Athenian Perikles agree that human beings, in the final analysis, are the only true source of power and force. Sthenelaidas, as we will see, argues that Sparta must defend its allies, as they are its greatest strength, while Perikles repeatedly argues that the Athenians should dismiss their personal possessions and preserve the strength of the polis as a whole (e.g., Thuc. 1.143, 2.60, 62.3; cf. 2.21.2, 55.2). But Perikles urges the Athenians to give up their farms and agricultural assets, and for him such sacrifices are tactics to preserve the empire and its revenues. He can thus give up his own estates as a gesture of solidarity with the Athenian people (2.13.1) so that he may not appear to demand more than he is willing himself to do. Money, *chrêmata*, has begun in Thucydides to evolve into an autonomous source of power, to which human labor is subordinate. On the Peloponnesian side, both the Spartan king Archi-

---

43. I take αὐτοῖς here as referring to the Athenians, though it can be interpreted to describe both Athenians and Spartans: e.g., Gomme ad loc.; Allison 1989, 25–26.

44. See Allison 1989, passim; she summarizes this term on p. 5: "*Paraskeuê*, preparedness, the possession of it and the exertion of it, is precisely what it is to be powerful. *Dunamis* is purely an abstraction in the History and denotes the capability of carrying out an action. *Paraskeuê*, by contrast, is much more inclusive and so much more flexible; it includes *dunamis*." On the importance of *paraskeuê*, see also chapter 8 above and the Spartan dilemma.

damos and the Corinthian delegation emphasize that *chrêmata* is essential in naval affairs, since money commands the labor and purchases the supplies necessary to run triremes and thus to project force.[45] For Perikles, Athenian financial reserves are a strategic asset. In the end, both the Peloponnesians and Perikles argue that human qualities will be decisive—the Peloponnesians claim greater courage, Perikles points to the fact that the Athenians have a greater store of naval skill and expertise.[46]

On the other hand, the dominance of material interests is a constant aspect of Thucydidean analysis: powerful men leading pirate expeditions for their own *kerdos* and for the material support of the weak (Thuc. 1.5.1), the weaker becoming slaves to the strong for the sake of *kerdos* (1.8.3), and Agamemnon using *deos* as well as *charis* (1.9.3). In the Archaeology alone, *chrêmata* appears nine times, and *achrêmatia* ("a lack of *chrêmata*") twice.[47] From the very beginning (2.2) a surplus (*perisousia*) of *chrêmata* is the necessary, if not sufficient, condition for significant achievements. When Pindar describes wealth, he uses terms such as *ploutos* or *olbos*. He uses the term *chrêmata* only once and in a bitterly negative passage. "*Chrêmata, chrêmata* is the man," said the Argive man, "when he had lost his possessions (*kteana*) and those dear to him (*philoi*) alike" (*Isthm.* 2.11-12). Pindar deplores a condition that Thucydides uses as a central determinant in his analysis of human affairs: material possessions define one's status and one's relationship with other people. We are very close to the phenomenon that Marx deplored as "the fetishism of the commodity,"[48] where things become more important than the human beings who create them, and society is turned upside down. Thucydides does not conceptualize this phenomenon as clearly as does Marx, but Marx's analysis provides a general framework that gives greater coherence to the isolated elements in Thucydides.

Or, to follow Karl Polanyi, we might say that in the archaic Greek world, economic activities were "embedded" in larger social relationships: one exchanged things with relations or personal connections, and these material exchanges constituted a major portion of one's personal interaction with others. Monetary exchange is an end in itself and establishes no emotional bond between buyer and seller. To understand

45. The Corinthians urge using the money accumulated at Delphi and Olympia (Thuc. 1.121.3) as well as greater contributions by the Peloponnesian allies (1.121.5).

46. Thuc. 1.143.1.

47. For *chrêmata*, see Thuc. 1.2.2, 7.1, 8.3, 9.2, 13.1, 5 (twice), 15.1, 19.1; for *achrêmatia*, see 1.11.1, 2.

48. Marx 1977, 163-177.

the impact that "market exchange" and the rise of money might have on Greek society, consider the blunt analysis offered by Adam Smith in the chapter "Accumulation of Capital" in his *Wealth of Nations*: "Capitals are increased by parsimony, and diminished by prodigality and misconduct. . . . Parsimony, and not industry, is the immediate cause of the increase of capital."[49] And yet parsimony is, as we have seen, exactly what a poet such as Pindar deplores. For Smith, symbolic capital would be an oxymoron. Thus, Smith explains, "the labor of some of the most respectable orders in the society is, like that of menial servants, unproductive of any value, and does not fix or realize itself in any permanent subject, or vendible commodity, which endures after that labor is past, and for which an equal quantity of labor could afterwards be procured." In Smith's view, material wealth is a beginning and an end, with which all other concerns must be concerned. Unless material capital is preserved and augmented, society cannot function. Human beings must subordinate themselves to things, and there is little room for the ideology of *megaloprepeia* that we briefly traced earlier.

Second, military imperialism has an ambiguous relationship to economic exploitation. Thus Adam Smith argues that "the sovereign, for example, with all the officers both of justice and war who serve under him, the whole army and navy, are unproductive laborers. They are the servants of the public, and are maintained by a part of the annual produce of the industry of other people. Their service, how honourable, how useful, or how necessary soever, produces nothing for which an equal quantity of service can afterwards be procured. The protection, security, and defence of the commonwealth, the effect of their labour this year, will not purchase its protection, security, and defence for the year to come."[50] The Athenian empire, like many others, did, however, pay for itself and turn a substantial profit for the state. While their perspectives are completely different, Adam Smith and Marx both focus with equal intensity upon the production of wealth rather than on the extraction of plunder from a limited store. In this regard, Thucydides' analysis differs from both.

Third, Thucydides does, however, portray in the Athenian empire a phenomenon that qualitatively approaches the capitalist mode of production outlined by Marx more closely than does the Persian empire. On military campaigns the subjects of the Great King, like the vassals

49. Adam Smith, *Wealth of Nations*, bk. 2, chap. 3 (Smith 1979, 437).
50. Adam Smith, *Wealth of Nations*, bk. 2, chap. 3 (Smith 1979, 430).

of a feudal lord, must provide him with their labor and even their lives, but they retain control of "the means of production." The disparate nations that participated in Xerxes' invasion each participated with their own weapons, with their own officers, and with their own tactics. In the Peloponnesian League, the individual poleis provided hoplites who themselves provided their own arms and thus controlled the basic tools of their trade. Although the individual hoplite submitted to the control of superiors, hoplite armor was an expensive commodity, and the hoplite, even as he risked his life and surrendered a part of this freedom, simultaneously reaffirmed his individual status within society.

The Athenian empire begins with a phase that may be likened to the primitive accumulation described by Marx: according to Marx, capitalism could take hold only when the majority of workers lost control of the means of production, and he saw this initial or "primitive" accumulation in the expropriation of land from the many by the few. The rich "accumulated wealth, and the latter sort had nothing to sell except their own skins."[51] In Marx's analysis of capitalism, this stage initiates the alienation of workers from the forces of production and allows the capitalist to convert workers into objects with no control over their actions as workers. The psychological consequences of this alienation are substantial, for the workers, losing control over their most basic actions, lose at the same time much of their dignity. Marx had placed his finger on a source of outrage that workers felt acutely in early European capitalism.

Marx's analysis of alienation lends greater clarity to a feature that distinguished the Athenian empire from Persia or the Peloponnesian League. With the exception only of the Chians and the Lesbians, the Athenian empire alienated its subjects from the "means of production" for their defence. At an early stage, individuals poleis chose to contribute money rather than ships (Thuc. 1.99.3), but a large portion of the Athenian fleet continued to be manned by non-Athenians. The Phokaian or Andrian who once served on ships from his own island under officers of his own polis now served as a mercenary on ships owned and officered by Athenians but paid for by the tribute of his and other states. Thus Athens not only controlled the physical triremes of its fleet but had accumulated a surplus of managerial and technical expertise that is far harder to replace, while the subjects for the most part occupied the most

51. Marx 1977, 873; Halpern 1991, 64–65.

menial and easily replaced functions. The Athenian empire thus exerted a control over its subjects that qualitatively exceeded that of Persia or the Peloponnesian League and that approached the control of early capitalism, which reduced its workers from skilled individuals to replaceable parts in an industrial system.

Fourth, Athenian imperialism by its nature gravitates toward expansion. This is a central theme in Thucydides: Alkibiades justifies the Sicilian expedition by appealing to this logic as a commonly understood phenomenon,[52] and, as we will see in the next chapter, the Corinthians help precipitate the war with their analysis of Athens as an inherently expansionist power. The Archaeology, however, expresses more clearly than any other part of the *History* an acceptance, even an approval, for this phenomenon. From the opening chapter of the Archaeology, with its contemptuous dismissal of the weak and quarrelsome past, empire appears as the only hedge against chaos and random violence. The verb *auxanô*, "grow, augment," appears four times in the Archaeology. The growth of cities (Thuc. 1.2.6), of Hellas as a whole (1.12.1), of different regions (1.16), and, by contrast, the parasitic growth of individual *oikoi* (1.17) are symptoms of the health of society. The Peloponnesian War is worthy of study because it exceeded in magnitude any previous conflict. In the opening chapter, Thucydides tells us that he expected the war would be "great" (1.1.1: *megas*). It proved to be the "greatest shock" (1.1.2: *kinêsis megistê*) ever to befall the Greek world and a good portion of the barbarians. Later, Thucydides concludes his survey of early Greek history with the claim that the accumulated resources available at its start were "greater" (*meizôn*) than any sudden alliance could muster. In between, Thucydides argues his thesis that previous events were "not great" (1.1.3: *ou megala*). The term *megas* recurs fifteen times as Thucydides calculates the magnitude of one entity or another. Sparta can summon considerable military force, but Athens is clearly portrayed as the expanding power, and this expansion is linked, as we will see in the next chapter, to the accumulation of money.

Without pressing the analogy too far, the general formula for capital outlined by Marx helps frame the gap that separates the world of Pindar and his patrons from that which unfolds in Thucydides' model. The precapitalist may use money, but only as an intermediate step to acquire some necessity. Thus when the farmer sells surplus grain and uses the

---

52. Thuc. 6.18; Herodotus already attributes this pathological need to expand to the Persians: see Evans 1982, 9–40.

money to purchase a metal tool, he may get an unusually good price for the tool or he may be cheated, but the main point is that the farmer has acquired a new "use value" that he did not previously possess. The capitalist starts with money and ends with money, purchasing cotton, for example, at one price, but selling it at another. Where the farmer can exchange $10 of grain for a $10 tool, the capitalist cannot start with $10 and end with $10. Money is purely a quantitative measure, and monetary exchange does not seek something different (tools for grain), but more of the same. Thus by its nature capitalist exchange is *quantitative*: money cannot change its nature or serve qualitatively different purposes; it can change only by increasing or decreasing. Capital must generate a surplus, and the accumulation of this surplus leads inevitably toward expansion. This model helps explain the underlying logic of the unnerving energy and expansionism that Athens exhibits.

Marx's analysis allows us to proceed one additional step. Marx argued that capitalism placed things above human beings, subordinating all concerns to profit, or the quantitative increase in money.[53] Polanyi described the same general phenomenon when he argued that precapitalist exchange is embedded in a network of social ties: precapitalist exchanges serve to reinforce the personal relationships of the two parties as much as they serve the practical needs met by the exchange. At *Odyssey* 1.182–184 Athena disguised as Mentes claims to be heading to Temese to trade copper for iron. He stops at the home of Odysseus, an old *xenos*, guest-friend, secured when Mentes' father gave Odysseus poison for his arrows (263–264). The exchange cemented a social bond, and we can be sure that Mentes would have a similar *xenos* at Temese with whom to trade.[54] These personal relationships are, in fact, the substance of symbolic capital discussed earlier. Thucydides pays little attention to symbolic capital because the Athenian empire has established a system in which financial capital has taken on a life of its own. Although he had not developed a theory of capitalism such as appears in either Marx's *Capital* or Smith's *Wealth of Nations*, he sensed acutely that material forces had begun to exert a greater force than prevailing values and perceptions admitted.

53. Marx 1977, 251: "To exchange £100 for cotton, and then exchange this same cotton again for £100, is merely a roundabout way of exchanging money for money, the same for the same, and appears to be an operation as purposeless as it is absurd. One sum of money is distinguishable from another only by its amount."

54. On Homeric guest friendship, see, still, Finley 1954, 99–104; more recently, Morris 1986.

CHAPTER 7

The Rule of the Strong
and the Limits of Friendship

Bias of Priene, one of the Seven Wise Men of the archaic period, is reported to have said that one should treat friends as if they were potential enemies and enemies as if they were potential friends. The Ajax of Sophokles' play gives this saying a place in the modern academic curriculum when he attacks it in one of the most famous speeches of Greek tragedy. Ajax refuses to accept the idea that friendship—or enmity—should be limited in this fashion. For him, emotional commitments must be absolute. Concluding that the affections of the world are impermanent, he chooses a suicide that will put him and his crumbling will beyond the reach of change. His death has many causes and has evoked complex emotions, but, in killing himself, Ajax asserts, in the grandest possible terms, the importance that he attaches to reciprocal relations, whether friendly or hostile, that never fade. However ambiguous Ajax may be, this aspect of his death strikes a solid chord.

Thucydides presents a world similar to that which Ajax rejects, for, in Thucydides, as in the *Ajax*, friendship has strict limits. But where time in the *Ajax* converts friendship into enmity and enmity into friendship, the constraints in Thucydides are different. Sophokles views change as a diachronic process that transforms friendship and enmity over time. Thucydides' perspective is more synchronic: friendship is possible or impossible at any given time depending upon the relative power of two parties. If a certain level of equilibrium is lost, friendship becomes impossible.

The limits of friendship are, in Thucydides, a key corollary to the rule

of the strong: the relative balance of power sets limits within which two
parties can define their relationship—friendship is not possible between
masters and subordinates.[1] The consequences of this corollary are even
more profound than the maxim of Bias that Ajax finds so distasteful.
Bias's warning leaves room for generosity and for friendship that—although impermanent—at least temporarily links the weak and the
strong. Many hierarchical relationships in classical Greek culture (and
even between many citizens in democratic Athens) were tolerable only
if they could be represented as friendships based on reciprocity. Thus,
in epinician poems, Pindar asserts his own importance at least in part
because he thus validates the praise that he offers. Pindar is not simply
the "hired gun," paid to deliver a commissioned poem, but a friend of
the patron who thus freely confers earned praise. By contrast, Thucydides' speakers—even when they contemplate reciprocal friendship—constantly advert to the inequalities of power, which are normally sup-
pressed. In *Isthmian* 2, Pindar daringly mentions the cold cash that paid
for his poem, but what is daring in Pindar becomes standard in Thucydides.

When we first encounter the rule of the strong, it is more than a
reductive heuristic that simplifies our view of a problem, allowing us to
jettison fictions about friendship and reciprocity and to uncover the underlying hierarchical relationship. Rather, having distilled a general law
from the present, Thucydides projects it backward into time and initially
uses it to breathe life into dim tradition. Early Greeks turned to piracy
(Thuc. 1.5.1), and in these actions "the strong exercise leadership for
their own profit (*kerdos*) and for the subsistence of the weak." Material
force—in men or in money, which can hire men—brings power, and
people accept domination to pursue that *kerdos* that distinguishes their
masters:

> In pursuit of profits (*kerdê*, pl.) the weak endured the slavery (*douleia*) of the
> strong, while those with more *dunamis* (*dunatôteroi*), having surpluses of
> wealth (*periousiai*) attached to themselves as subordinates (*hupêkooi*) to
> weaker city-states.
>
> Thuc. 1.8.3

Thus, in one sentence, Thucydides states the fundamentally hierarchical dynamic that governs interpersonal and interstate relations alike.
The impact of this principle, when applied, is significant. The world

---

1. For a somewhat different view of this "pathology of power," see Immerwahr 1973.

of "things," *erga*, is more real than that of "language," *logos*. Our human judgments and feelings—whatever we may choose to think—are ultimately subordinate to *erga*, the "objective realities" of the situation. All human beings, whether they admit it or not, understand this principle. *Charis* in its narrow sense of gratitude and earned loyalty is ultimately less powerful than fear. Thus Thucydides reinterprets the Trojan War as a kind of martial corvée, extracted from the Greeks by the domination of Agamemnon rather than elicited by moral hegemony. Agamemnon had strength (Thuc. 1.9.3: *ischus*), and he naturally "assembled the army less by means of *charis* than through terror (*phobos*)." Broadly speaking, Thucydides comes very close to the belief, once common in Marxist thought, that the "economic base" directly determines the intellectual superstructure.[2] For Thucydides, material relations—who is more powerful and controls resources—shape social relations.

The superiority of interest and the subordinate status of moral considerations pose an intellectual problem with which Thucydides' small and midsize states wrestle in their speeches. The Melians, of course, provide the classic example of a small state that refuses to acknowledge the Thucydidean rule that the weak must submit to the strong. The Athenians base their argument to the Melians on the consequences of this rule:

> We hope that you, instead of thinking to influence us by saying that you did not join the Lakedaimonians, although their colonists, or that you have done us no wrong, will aim at what is within your power (*dunata*), in accordance with those things that we each truly think. You know as well as we do that justice (*dikaia*) in human analysis (*anthrôpeios logos*) only gets considered in a relationship based on equality (*apo tou isou*), while the strong do what is within their power (*dunata*) and the weak acquiesce.
>
> Thuc. 5.89.1

Human beings are limited to what is possible, *dunata*—that is, those things that they possess the *dunamis*, power, to achieve. Those who have sufficient force impose their will, and those who cannot stop them must accept the situation as naturally as they must accept the cold winds of winter or the heat of the summer. Justice is not a universal, transcendent quality but a thing contingent for its existence upon the proper circumstances. If the gap in power between two agents is too large, then according to the *anthrôpeios logos*, "the analysis of human beings," there

---

2. For a recent discussion of this general topic by a classicist, see Rose 1992, 6–12.

is not even any point in determining whether an action is just or unjust—
the issue is irrelevant, because the weaker party is powerless to respond.

Thus Melian anxiety that surrender should convict them of "ignoble
behavior" (*kakotês*) and "cowardice" (*deilia*) wins nothing but scorn
from the Athenians (Thuc. 5.100). If the Melians use *sôphrosunê*, "self-
control"—a classic virtue in fifth-century society—then they will recognize that this is not a "game (*agôn*) between equals (*apo tou isou*)
about manly worth (*andragathia*) and that the penalty is not shame
(*aischunê*)" (5.101). The issue is raw survival, and in this situation,
moral labels cease to have meaning.

In Thucydides' text, language—and with it all those qualities that
exist only in language—is hard put to compete with physical reality.
This is a point with which the Athenians open and close their debate
with the Melians. The Athenians disdain to employ any "noble terms"
(*onomata kala*) on their own behalf (Thuc. 5.89), and they implore the
stubborn Melians not to draw fate upon themselves "through the power
(*dunamis*) of a seductive name (*onoma*)" or "overcome by spoken language (*rhêma*) in real deed (*ergon*) and of their own volition to suffer
catastrophes that cannot be repaired." The debate turns on this moral
interpretation of objective power. The Melians refuse to accept the Athenian deduction, and they suffer a very physical, biological death because
they place the realities of language above those of "objective reality."

It is important to emphasize that neither Thucydides nor his Athenians argue that all human beings treat one another according to some
generalized, objective set of principles. Thus the Athenians argue that
their treatment of Melos has no effect upon the risk that they run if they
subsequently fall to Sparta:

> The end of our rule (*archê*), if end it should, does not frighten us. For those
> who exercise rule (*archontes*) over others, as do even the Spartans (and, in
> any event, our struggle is not really with the Spartans), are not as terrible to
> the vanquished as if the subjects (*hupêkooi*) should themselves attack and
> overpower their rulers (*hoi arxantes*).
>
> Thuc. 5.91.1

Humans are grouped in two basic classes, those who exercise rule
(*archê*) and those who are subjects (*hupêkooi*). The true struggle goes
on between the rulers and the ruled. Thus the Athenians will show no
mercy toward the inferior Melians, but they can expect that the shared
status of power will prevent the Spartans from being equally brutal to
them. There are many historical parallels for this attitude. Students of
American history might compare the fear of slave revolt that haunted

antebellum Southerners and the summary execution that they often dealt during the war to the African-American Union soldiers they captured.

MYTILENE

The debate between Kleon and Diodotos about the fate of the Mytileneans is one of the most closely studied portions of the *History*.[3] Like the Melian debate, it finds its way outside of classics into many courses, on topics such as political science and international relations. Before they revolt, the Mytileneans themselves deliver one of the most important—and overlooked—speeches in Thucydides.[4] In a few brief pages (Thuc. 3.9–14), they raise crucial questions about considerations of friendship and justice in a world dominated by power politics. In justifying their actions according to traditional values, they indicate that those values have taken on an almost entirely new and grim meaning.

Like the Corcyraeans, these would-be allies must demonstrate both that they have something to offer and that their character is trustworthy. As C. Macleod pointed out, this defence of character became a topos for all speeches soliciting an alliance.[5] The Mytileneans, however, face an even more daunting task of defending their character than did the Corcyraeans. By rebelling against their ally Athens, they have called into serious question their own moral worth, and hence their value as allies. They specifically confront this problem and declare that they will make their case on the grounds of *to dikaion*, "justice," and *aretê* (Thuc. 3.10.1)—both of which they, by some standards, abandoned when they abandoned Athens in wartime. They agree with the traditional assumption that friendship must rely on "an *aretê* that is obvious to each other and on similar habits in other regards."

But, contrary to traditional thought, the Mytileneans argue that such friendships depend upon a stable balance of power.[6] Affection and loy-

---

3. E.g., Andrewes 1962; Lang 1972; Kagan 1975; Cogan 1981a, 50–65; Cogan 1981b; Connor 1984, 79–81; for further bibliography (with useful comments), see Hornblower 1991, 421–422.
4. Connor (1984), for example, leaves this speech out of his discussion as a whole; see, however, Cogan 1981a, 44–49, and now Orwin 1994, 64–70; see also Macleod 1978, 64–68; Macleod argues that "Thucydides deliberately presents his speakers getting entangled in their own arguments," primarily because they, "like Cleon later on, try to maintain that their action is both just and expedient" (p. 66).
5. Macleod 1978, 64; he cites *Rhetorica ad Alexandrum* 1424b37: δεικνύναι τοὺς τὴν συμμαχίαν ποιουμένους μάλιστα μὲν δικαίους ὄντας
6. Cf. Thucydides speaking in propria persona about the origins of the war at 1.23.6.

alty are secondary factors in their view (Thuc. 3.11.1). "Balanced fear
(*to antipalon deos*) is the only sure basis of an alliance (*summachia*): he
who would like to transgress in some respect is then deterred by the fact
of not being superior (*prouchein*)." Athens had, however, grown pro-
gressively more powerful and had reached the point where it could strip
Mytilene of its independence:

> Had we all been still independent (*autonomoi*), we could have had more faith
> in their not attempting any change; but the greater number being in their
> power (*hupocheirioi*), while they associated with us on the basis of equality
> (*apo tou isou:*), they would naturally (*eikotôs*) chafe with us alone still
> confronting them as equals (*ant-isoumenou*) in contrast to the majority that
> gave way (*eikon*); particularly as they daily grew more powerful
> (*dunatôteroi*), and we more alone.
>
> Thuc. 3.11.1

The Mytileneans appeal to "common sense": the Athenians would
naturally (*eikotôs*) press their advantage. Once they had acquired more
dunamis (i.e., were *dunatôteroi*), then they were no longer equal, *isos*,
to the Mytileneans, and no one could expect that they would long tol-
erate a relationship predicated on equality. The material realities of the
situation would ultimately assert themselves as naturally as geological
pressures lead to an earthquake, and the coming realignment would
inevitably push Mytilene into an inferior position. The Mytileneans
never even consider the possibility that the Athenians might find the
current arrangement useful in itself even if it no longer reflected their
true relative status. The will to power inexorably exerts pressure until
external dealings reflect the true balance of force.

The Mytileneans then move from this imbalance to its grotesque consequences, which invert the proper relationship between friends. The
respect that they paid each other ceased to reinforce their mutual affection and to keep alive the social bonds that connected them, and became
instead a cynical practice whereby each maneuvered for advantage and
for the ultimate chance to strike. Thus the Mytileneans explain away
the honors that Athens conferred upon them:

> Again, if we were left independent (*autonomoi*), it was only because they
> thought they saw their way to rule (*archê*) more clearly by speciousness
> (*euprepeia*) of language and by the paths of policy (*gnômê*) than by those of
> strength (*ischus*). Not only were we useful as evidence that powers who had
> votes, like themselves, would not, surely, join them in their expeditions,
> against their will, without the party attacked being in the wrong; but the
> same system also enabled them to lead the stronger states against the weaker

first, and so to leave the former to the last, stripped of their natural allies, and less capable of resistance.

Thuc. 3.11.3–4

As Simon Hornblower points out in his note on Thucydides 3.11.3, the Mytileneans are on shaky ground here, for, according to Thucydides, they had sent reinforcements to help Athens put down Samos—formerly one of the "free" allies (Thuc. 1.116.2, 117.2). They thus imply that they helped the Athenians under duress, and direct toward the Athenians the charge of hypocrisy to which they themselves are open. The Athenians, they claim, exploit language when they feel that it can help them expand their rule (*archê*) better than the application of strength (*ischus*). The alliance with Mytilene was useful for propaganda and helped Athens prepare for absorbing Mytilene as well in the end.

Once the Mytileneans have lost their faith in Athens and the spirit of the relationship has, in their minds, been corrupted, they reply in kind:

> The court that we paid (*therapeia*) to their general populace (*to koinon autôn*) and those who were also becoming its protectors (*tôn aiei proestotôn*) also helped us to maintain our independence.

Thuc. 3.11.7

The Mytileneans cynically pay court to the common people of Athens and to whatever leaders emerged as their *prostatai*, champions. Their favors, however, did not set out to reinforce a firm and lasting friendship but were a mere expedient of the moment:

> However, we did not expect to have the power to do so much longer, if this war had not broken out, following the examples that we had had of their conduct to the rest. Was this friendship (*philia*) or freedom (*eleutheria*) here worthy of trust? In this, we accepted each other against our judgment (*para gnômên*). They, on the one hand, paid court (*etherapeuon*) to us during the war because they were afraid (*deidiotes*; cf. *deos*), and we did the same thing to them during the quiet times. Goodwill (*eunoia*) most of all establishes trust (*pistis*) of others. For us, it was terror (*phobos*) that made them reliable (*echuros*), while we were retained as allies (*summachoi*) more by fear (*deos*) than by friendship (*philia*). To whichever of us security (*asphaleia*) should provide the boldness (*tharsos*), these would be the first to attempt some transgression.

Thuc. 3.11.8–12.1

Even as they allude to goodwill (*eunoia*), the Mytileneans imply that *eunoia* has no inherent value but exists only within narrow tolerances.[7]

---

7. Compare the similar fashion in which the Athenians treat the *eunoia* enjoyed by Sparta at 1.77.6.

Theirs is a world in which even closest allies cannot be trusted and in
which friendship has become a thin disguise for deadly competition. The
values of the archaic world—with its countless alliances, limited competition, and relatively flat hierarchies—no longer function for them.
Symbolic capital depends for its existence upon trust and upon the certainty that good services to an individual will be repaid in kind. The
good services that the Athenians and Mytileneans confer upon each
other have no future. They establish nothing.

The Mytileneans conclude this portion of their argument by inverting
the language of reciprocal gift exchange in spectacular fashion:

> So that if we seem to anyone to act unjustly (*adikein*) by revolting ahead of
> time (*proapostantes*) because of their delay of dreadful things against us,
> ourselves not waiting in turn (*antanameinantes*) to know clearly if any of
> these things would have taken place, he does not consider (*skopei*) properly.
> For if we had the power (*dunatoi*) on the basis of equality (*apo tou isou*) to
> plot in turn (*antepibouleusai*) and delay in turn (*antimellêsai*), why should it
> have been necessary for us—in a state of parity (*apo tou homoiou*)—to be
> at their mercy (*ep' ekeinois*). Since the initiative was always on their side,
> preemptive defence (*proamunasthai*) must belong to us.
>
> Thuc. 3.12.2–3

In a relationship of ritualized friendship, gift matches countergift, as
the partners compete with one another in terms of generosity. In this
case, however, the two parties compete with one another for advantage,
and even the idealized relationship is twisted. The Mytileneans no longer
dream of matching gift with gift or of competing with the Athenians in
public demonstrations of generosity to one another, but they still express
themselves in the language of reciprocity. The verbal prefix *anti-* indicates that an action mirrors something that has previously taken place,
and commonly appears when speakers wish to stress the reciprocity of
what they are doing. The Mytileneans use the prefix three times in this
paragraph. They lament that they cannot match the Athenians in staying
power (*ant-anameinantes*), match plot with plot (*ant-epibouleusai*), or
match their ability to delay action (*anti-mellesai*), as they could if they
were acting "on the basis of equality" (*apo tou isou*) or "in a state of
parity" (*apo tou homoiou*). Even as they express a viable model of
friendship with the linguistic tags of reciprocal action, they have turned
the spirit of friendship upside down.

At this point, we might briefly recall the ethnographic literature discussed in chapter 4. The spirit of the gift was crucial in archaic Greece,
as in so many other societies. The exchange of gifts or ritualized tokens

of respect could not simply be empty but served as signs and substance
at once of a larger social relationship. The Greek term *charis*, in part,
represents such concepts as "the 'money of fame,'"[8] the "spirit of the
gift,"[9] and Bourdieu's "symbolic capital." In chapter 4, we saw not only
that both the Corcyraeans and the Corinthians based their pleas to Athens on this system of gift and countergift, but that the Athenians had
no interest in such arguments. They ultimately choose a course that was
meant to harm both Corcyra and Corinth as much as possible. Thus,
on one level, Athens's decision to aid Corcyra reinforces the Mytilenean
argument: the Athenians cannot, in fact, be trusted to support their relationship with Mytilene, because they have no interest in the general
scheme of embedded social relations. The Athenians do not believe in
the "spirit of the gift."

The Mytilenean plea for help, however, is also problematic. Reconciling justice with expediency is tricky,[10] but the main difficulty in this
speech is more tightly linked to traditional social practices of the archaic
period. If "balanced fear" is the only basis for a relationship, then there
is little room in *any* relationship for "goodwill" (*eunoia*) and "friendship" (*philia*), since these are strong words for affection. Goodwill and
friendship only come to the test when one party falls upon hard times
and seeks help from its friends. According to the Mytileneans, trouble
for one party would involve an automatic change in the relationship,
with the powerful seeking to exploit the weakness of its fallen (and
therefore former) friend. Similarly, the statement at Thucydides 3.12.7
that Mytilene had cultivated the Athenians does indeed, as Gomme suggests, "amount to a damaging admission," but not just or primarily
because this behavior had implicated Mytilene in Athenian policy. The
subsequent defence does much more harm. The Mytileneans had begun
this part of their argument by suggesting that they needed to demonstrate their *aretê* (Thuc. 3.10.1), which here denotes their "honesty" or
basic moral worth. Yet, in denying their former friendship with Athens,
they demonstrate that they really cannot be trusted. Their actions do
not reflect their feelings. Even as they struggle to frame their needs in
terms of *philia*, *eunoia*, and *aretê*, they have sketched a system of forces
that leaves no room for these qualities, since friendship, goodwill, and

---

8. Mauss 1990, 44.
9. See the essay by that title at Sahlins 1972, 149–183.
10. So Macleod 1974, but note Hornblower 1991, 391–392, which qualifies Macleod's
analysis.

aretê are meaningful only if they endure *despite* external conditions. Furthermore, if Mytilene wholly subordinates its actions to circumstances, then its alliance is good only so long as Sparta remains useful to it, and friendship with Mytilene is not nearly as valuable—that is, expedient—as it might otherwise be. The Mytilenean speech demolishes its own premises, for it shows that the speakers have little moral worth and consequently offer a good deal less practical advantage.

The Mytilenean speech is in many ways a pivotal passage and connects with a number of other sections. In chapter 3, I analyzed the relationship between Sparta and Tegea as it appears in Herodotus. This relationship seems to have stood as the central paradigm for all bilateral relationships with Sparta: those who acknowledged Sparta's superiority would not be degraded but would, despite their inequality in military power, enter into a partnership based on mutual respect. Thus even small states could define their alliance in similar terms and at least pretend that they, like the Tegeans, received honor and respect from Sparta. Sparta depended for its position, as we saw earlier, on the shared assumption that the powerful would not overwhelm the weak. The Mytilenean speech baldly drags the general principle involved out into the open and denies an assumption by which the Peloponnesian allies listening to them at Olympia maintained their allegiance to Sparta. I will conclude by comparing the Mytilenean sentiments with the defence of Athenian imperialism at Sparta, but first I must sketch the implications of the Mytilenean speech for the evolution of language in the description of stasis at Corcyra, for Kleon's later demand that the Mytileneans be exterminated, and for Sparta's offer of peace in book 4.

First, the Mytilenean affair (like the other great episode in book 3, the fall of Plataia) sets the stage for the dismal analysis of civil strife and its effect upon human behavior at Corcyra. Thucydides begins this excursus by stating two conditions for such savage internal conflict: the presence of war and the opportunity to bring in a great power as ally. The Mytileneans tried to argue that those with common habits (see *homoiotropoi* at Thuc. 3.10.1) could establish a firm friendship, but their own argument makes it clear that material considerations, such as relative power, are more important than personal habits. Ulimately, the Athenians come to make democrats their allies, and oligarchs consistently turn to Sparta (3.82.1).[11]

11. On this, see Cogan 1981b.

When the Mytileneans offered their inverted model of friendship, in which the parties hold each other at bay with the threat of reciprocal violence, they anticipate a general linguistic phenomenon that Thucydides deplores in his analysis of stasis at Corcyra:

> In their own judgment (*dikaiôsis*), people exchanged (*antêllaxan*) the accustomed evaluation (*axiôsis*) of words (*onomata*) with regard to deeds (*erga*) Reckless audacity (*alogistos tolma*) came to be considered the courage of a loyal ally (*andreia philetairos*), and prudent hesitation (*mellêsis promêthês*) was thought specious cowardice (*deilia euprepes*). Self-restraint (*to sôphrôn*) became a cloak for unmanliness (*to anandron*); ability to see all sides of a question, inaptness to act on any. Frantic violence (*to emplêktos oxu*) became the attribute of a true man; plotting (*to epibouleusasthai*) from a position of safety (*asphaleia*), a creditable pretext (*eulogos prophasis*) for self-defence.
>
> Thuc. 3.82.4

In the following sections, Thucydides develops this idea at even greater length. As the grim details pile up, the general principle remains consistent: trust and good nature withered in the savagery of civil war, and as human behavior became more brutal, language changed to reflect the new reality. Those noble concepts that remained uncorrupted were "laughed out of existence" (Thuc. 3.83.1), and those terms that previously had denoted generous virtues shifted to describe grotesque inversions of their former selves. The dismal, Hobbesian view of friendship that the Mytileneans put forward neatly illustrates how, on the other side of the Greek world from Corcyra, the meaning of one fundamental quality had already begun to change. Furthermore, the Mytileneans conclude the defence of their own action by anticipating exactly the final statement in the paragraph quoted above. Both they and the Athenians, they claim, were maintaining their charade of friendship and goodwill only until a position of safety (3.12.1: *asphaleia*) would provide one or the other with the courage so that they could be first to transgress against their supposed friendship. Once they had the opportunity, they not only "plotted against" the Athenians (cf. *antepibouleusai* at 3.12.3 and *to epibouleusasthai* at 3.82.4) but took preemptive action as well. The creditable pretext (*eulogos prophasis*) for self-defence mentioned at 3.82.4 perfectly describes the Mytilenean defence at 3.10–12 and especially 3.12.1–3.

Second, so many readers of Thucydides have focused on the dramatic confrontation between Kleon and Diodotos that little attention has been paid to the relationship between the Mytilenean speech at Thucydides

3.9–14 and Kleon's denunciation of Mytilene at 3.37–40. The Mytileneans, for example, admit that they had been friendly toward the champions of the common people at Athens. Their tokens of respect
constituted nothing but a tactic by which they could buy time (Thuc.
3.11.7). When the Mytileneans revolted, those champions of the people
who had also championed the Mytileneans must have been placed in a
difficult position. Kleon was the most famous *prostatês* of the Athenian
people of the time, and, for all we know, the Mytilenean revolt may have
personally embarrassed him. Whatever his relations with Mytilene, his
speech demands the execution of all Mytileneans and bases its argument
in large measure upon the peculiar relationship between Athens and
Mytilene. He thus develops a major theme presented in the Mytilenean
speech.

Kleon's speech picks up two of the themes that the Mytileneans introduce and that become part of the general case study of civil strife at
Corcyra. The Mytileneans are acutely conscious that their status with
respect to Athens is almost unique—only the Chians remain as free allies
(Thuc. 3.10.5). They offer their uncertain position as a pretext (*prophasis*) to justify their revolt (3.9.1, 13.1). Thucydides describes later
how desperate men justified such plots by using self-defence as a creditable pretext (*eulogos prophasis*) (3.82.1). Kleon analyzes the Mytilenean revolt in the same way. He demands severe retaliation against Mytilene so that no one in the future will "revolt on some small pretext"
(*bracheia prophasis apostêsesthai*). Furthermore, according to the Mytileneans, each side constantly plotted against the other (*antepibouleusai*; see 3.12.3 and *to epibouleusasthai* at 3.82.4). Kleon shares with the
Mytileneans the idea that they have engaged in plotting, but fastens
upon this term and gives it considerable prominence. He uses *epibouleuô*
and various derivatives five times in his speech (3.37.2 twice, 39.2, 40.1,
40.5).

Kleon does more, however, than echo the term *epibouleuô*. He combines plotting with the assumption that different power relationships
justify different kinds of behavior. But where the Mytileneans had used
this principle to bolster their own moral position—they were so much
more powerful than we that we had to take action—Kleon makes it a
linchpin for his attack:

> I proceed to show that no one state has ever injured you as much as Mytilene.
> I can have forgiveness (*sungnômê*) for those who revolt because they cannot
> bear our rule (*archê*), or who have been forced to do so by the enemy. But
> these possessed an island with fortifications, could fear our enemies only by

sea, and they had their own force of triremes to protect them. They were independent (*autonomoi*) and shown honor (*timê*) to the highest degree by you. These people have not revolted—revolt is the act of those who have suffered violence (*biaion ti*). Rather, they have hatched plots (*epebouleusan*) and stabbed us in the back.[12] They sought to stand at the side of our bitterest enemies and to destroy us. Indeed, this is more serious than if they had acquired power (*dunamis*) by themselves and confronted us in war (*antepolemêsan*).

Thuc. 3.39.1–2

The Mytileneans had feared degradation to the status of subject ally, but this change had not taken place. Where the Mytileneans stress the difference in real power, Kleon—with at least as much and probably more validity—points to the actual state of affairs. The Mytileneans were in fact still independent (*autonomoi*), and they did receive unusual honor (*timê*) from Athens. Those who had "suffered some act of violence" (*tôn biaion ti paschontôn*) might revolt, and for them there could be forgiveness (*sungnômê*), because they returned no more than they had received. (The logic of reciprocity that Kleon applies is, it should be noted, opportunistic—at Thucydides 5.91.1, the Athenians imply that savage retribution is more suitable when chastising subjects than when vanquishing equals.) The Mytileneans were not, however, under Athenian rule (*archê*), and the Athenians had never brought any act of violence (*biaion ti*) to bear against them. The high status that the Mytileneans had enjoyed meant that their act was simple treachery rather than the desperate rebellion of an oppressed subject.

Kleon, however, argues on both sides of the question. He states that the Mytileneans deserve to die because they acted as if they were friends but betrayed the Athenians. At the same time, however, he shares the Mytileneans' grim view of human relationships. Acts of kindness have at best no value in themselves and, for an imperial power, are self-defeating:

The Mytileneans should long ago have received from us no honor (*timê*) distinguished from the rest, and they never would have given in to hubris to this extent, for human beings (*anthrôpos*) tend by nature to despise that which pays court (*therapeuô*) and to feel awe (*thaumazein*) before that which does not yield (*to mê eikon*).

Thuc. 3.39.5

---

12. This attempts to capture the pungency implied by the Greek ἐπανέστησαν μᾶλλον ἢ ἀπέστησαν on which, see Hornblower 1991, ad loc.

Kleon does not believe that it is possible to accumulate any positive symbolic capital with subordinates. Kind actions appear as a sign of weakness. There is no room in his view for patrons and clients, only masters who squeeze as much as they possibly can from resentful slaves.

The honor that Athens had conferred upon Mytilene therefore did not win corresponding respect but instead inflamed the Mytileneans with hubris. Kleon brackets the speech with attacks against any notion that the Athenians can accumulate a store of *charis* with their allies. "You do not realize," he says at Thucydides 3.37.2, "that your softness (*to malakizesthai*) will contribute to your danger and not to the *charis* felt by your allies. . . . The allies will not obey you because you—harming your own selves—stored up *charis* (*charizesthe*)." Toward the end (Thuc. 3.40.4), he says: "To sum up in brief, I say that if you follow my advice you will do what is just (*ta dikaia*) toward the Mytileneans, and at the same time expedient (*ta sumphora*); while by a different decision you will not store up *charis* with them so much as pass sentence upon yourselves."

But, like the Mytileneans, Kleon does still understand the world in terms of balanced reciprocity even as he dismisses the possibilities of effective friendship between Athens and its allies:

> It is just that compassion (*eleos*) be given in return (*antididosthai*) to one's peers (*hoi homoioi*), and not to those who will never pity us in return (*antoiktountes*) but are constituted of necessity our eternal enemies: the orators who charm us with sentiment may find other less important arenas for their talents, in the place of one where the city pays a heavy penalty for a momentary pleasure, themselves receiving fine acknowledgments for their fine phrases; while indulgence (*epieikeia*) should be shown toward those who will be our friends (*epitêdeioi*) in future, instead of toward those who will remain just what they were, and as much our enemies (*polemioi*) as before.
>
> Thuc. 3.40.3

This passage, in the conclusion of Kleon's argument, pulls together several themes that we have discussed. First, it asserts again the priority of an objective reality whose influence inexorably determines the overall character of human relations. The Mytileneans are constituted as enemies of the Athenians. A product of necessity (*anankê*), this condition is permanent. No compassion (*eleos*) or pity (*oiktos*) conferred upon the Mytileneans will ever convert them from enemies to friends. No relationship with the Mytileneans can base itself on exchanges of kindness and good feelings. Mytilene is far weaker than Athens, but it comes as close to being a peer as any of Athens's allies. If Mytilene is so inferior that it cannot maintain true friendship with Athens, then Athens is truly alone. It has no friends, only allies. Those who concern themselves with fine language can develop brilliant verbal arguments to the contrary, but they cannot change these objective realities, and they only endanger the city by obscuring the real situation. Language, properly used, mirrors the true situation. Gifts, honors, and words alike are vapid epiphenomena. The relative balance of power alone matters.

Kleon develops his argument from the premise that Athenian *archê* is a *turannis* (Thuc. 3.37.2). The opening of Kleon's argument is a dense network of ideas that relates now familiar terms for friendship and treachery to the condition of tyranny:

> Because your daily life is free from fear (*adees*, lacking in *deos*) and not filled with plotting (*anepibouleuton*) against each other, you feel just the same with regard to your allies and never reflect that the mistakes into which you may be led by listening to their appeals, or by giving way to your own compassion (*oiktos*), are full of risk (*kindunos*) for yourselves and bring you no thanks (*charis*) from your allies for your weakness; entirely forgetting that your empire is a *turannis* and your subjects are plotting against you (*epibouleuontas*) and subject to your rule (*archê*) against their will. These men will not obey you because of those things that you—although doing injury to yourselves—store up as *charis*, but by the superiority given you by your own strength (*ischus*) and not their goodwill (*eunoia*).
>
> Thuc. 3.37.2

Athens is a democracy, and its citizens live a daily life that is free from fear (*adees*, lacking in *deos*) and not filled with plotting (*anepibouleuton*). But Athenian rule (*archê*) is a *turannis*—a domination based on force, pure and simple. Thus compassion (*oiktos*), *charis*, and goodwill (*eunoia*) are meaningless concepts, and any trust put in their influence brings with it risk (*kindunos*). The allies eternally plot against their masters. In the world of friendship and trust, symbolic capital maintains stability and lends to human relationships an on-going momentum through time. In Kleon's world, the *turannis* maintains its position by the constant possession of *ischus*. Once the Athenians lose their material superiority, they will plummet downward like a bird that has ceased beating its wings.

Kleon's speech thus reinforces an idea expressed by the Mytileneans. Differences in power prevent Greek states from being peers. A powerful state such as Athens inevitably bends its subordinates to its will and exercises the greatest possible control. In such a world, affection is possible only between peers. The Athenians do not exercise hegemony but domination pure and simple. Kleon has no use for a conciliating ideology that seeks to justify Athenian prominence and to evoke any emotions other than fear from the allies. The Athenians had treated the Mytileneans with honor, but the Mytileneans had not reciprocated this respect and had acted as hostile subordinates, eager to strike those above them.

SPARTAN TRADITIONALISM

Appeals to generosity and to "the spirit of the gift," as it were, never succeed in Thucydides, but they can be quite eloquent. Book 4 contains perhaps our best statement from the fifth century on the "war with warre," which redirects competition from warfare to peaceful spheres. After Sphakteria, the Spartans do not offer terms for peace or even for alliance (surprising as that itself may have been).[13] They insist on embedding the peace within a broader social bond:

> The Lakedaimonians accordingly invite you to make a treaty and to end the war, giving (*didontes*), on the one hand, peace and alliance and, besides, substantial friendship (*philia*) and intimacy (*oikeiotês*) between us; and, on the other hand, asking in return (*antaitountes*) for the men on the island, thinking it better for both parties not to hold out until the end, on the chance of some favorable accident enabling the men to force their way out, or of their being compelled to succumb under the pressure of blockade.
>
> Thuc. 4.19.1

The Spartans strike a posture that is almost statuesque. They propose to establish this new relationship with the classic technique of a gift exchange: in the Greek the *men . . . de* ("on the one hand . . . on the other") reinforces the interlocking "we give" (*didontes*) and "we ask in return" (*antaitountes*) by which the Spartans define the suggested transaction. They propose not only peace and an alliance, but friendship (*philia*) and *oikeiotês*, the latter a difficult term that literally describes the intimacy of those who share a common *oikos*, "household." Friendship and especially *oikeiotês* imply trust and affection. The agreement is not to be a cold and businesslike diplomatic contract, but the beginning of a broader, more complex relationship warmed by social and emotional ties. Finally, this passage captures one of the cornerstones of Spartan diplomacy as represented in Herodotus: the limitation of goals.

13. So Connor 1984, 112 n. 10.

As we saw in chapter 3, the Spartans become preeminent in Greece when they give up hopes for domination and seek instead hegemony.

The Spartans do not belittle the enmity that has separated them from the Athenians, nor do they conceal that their own interests will be served:

> Indeed we believe that great enmities (*echthrai*) find the most secure resolution—not when someone defending himself in turn (*antamunomenos*), gaining the upper hand for the most part of the war, and imposing oaths by necessity (*ananke*), does not conclude an agreement on the basis of equality (*apo tou isou*), but when, although it is possible to do this very thing, with an eye to generosity (*to epieikes*) and having conquered him by means of *aretê*, someone accords a peace on moderate terms (*metrios*) contrary to what was expected.
>
> Thuc. 4.19.2

Although the Greek is tortured and convoluted, as is characteristic of Thucydides, the ideas expressed elegantly sketch the etiquette of gift exchange. The Spartans freely concede that the Athenians currently have the upper hand, and they ask them to come to terms without pressing home their advantage. In acting with moderation (*metrios*) and generosity (*to epieikes*), the Athenians will defeat their Spartan adversaries with *aretê*. Thus if they do not force the Spartans to accept terms, but show generosity now, they will transform the competition between themselves and the Spartans from an exchange of slaughter to a contest of generosity and high-mindedness:

> For the opponent then owes a debt not to defend himself in his turn (*antamunesthai*), because he had submitted to violence (*biastheis*), but to give back in return (*antapodounai*) *aretê*. He is more inclined by a sense of shame (*aischunê*) to adhere to the terms to which he agreed.
>
> Thuc. 4.19.3

The Athenians would place the Spartans in a debt that is public—*aischunê*, "shame," describes the inhibitions felt before others. Self-respect, rather than driving the Spartans to even the score for a humiliating defeat, would force them to match Athenian *aretê* with similarly generous behavior. In typically Thucydidean fashion, these Spartans do not simply assert that such behavior will take place, but relate it to the behavior natural for any human:

> Human beings tend more to do this with respect to their greater enemies than with respect to those with whom their differences are moderate (*metria*). For

men are naturally inclined (*pephukasi*) to yield in return (*anthhêssasthai*) to those who give way of their own free will, but to endure every risk even contrary to their own best judgment (*gnômê*) when confronting those who are arrogant.

Thuc. 4.19.4

This statement is the precise opposite of the statement Kleon makes at Thucydides 3.39.5. Given the problems of Kleon's argument, such a contradiction only strengthens the credit owed this noble offer.

After all the savagery and social decay that Thucydides has included in his narrative—plague and moral collapse at Athens, the Mytilenean debate, the siege of Plataia and juridical massacre of the survivors, civil strife and even worse moral collapse at Corcyra—this is an extraordinary speech. Scholarly reaction has, predictably, been mixed, although many analyze the Spartan offer of peace without reference to this elaborate speech. De Romilly accuses the Athenians of "bad faith" and of being "devoid of any justification" when they reject this offer,[14] and, more recently, T. E. J. Wiedemann has argued that Thucydides himself believed that the Athenians had made a great mistake in rejecting the Spartan offer of a compromise peace.[15] For Marc Cogan, "this is an extremely intelligent and decent speech,"[16] which fails, in his view, because, after six years of war, it is too reasonable. Gomme, on the other hand, had only scorn for the moral arguments of the Spartans,[17] and Lowell Edmunds characterized this speech as "more a sermon on tyche than a suit for peace."[18]

In their offer of peace, the Spartans declare their faith in symbolic capital and the traditional rhetoric of gift exchange that the Athenian delegates at Athens, the Mytileneans at Olympia, and Kleon, demanding vengeance, have abandoned. The Spartans appeal to *aretê* and to that spirit of friendship that exchange engenders. Their argument is almost

---

14. De Romilly 1963, 172.
15. Wiedemann 1982, xxix.
16. Cogan 1981a, 75.
17. Gomme on 4.20.4: "Their offer on this occasion, militarily speaking worth nothing, except in the moral effect of its having been made at all, demanded not only a generosity of feeling and a far-sightedness on the part of Athens which they had no reason and no right to expect (and no country can throw a stone at Athens for that), but an even greater generosity, μεγαλοψυχία on their own, to accept the Athenians' gesture and forget their own disgrace"; Kagan (1969) concludes that the Spartans had not yet reached the frame of mind where they could truly give up the idea of defeating Athens; Cartledge (1979, 242) follows Gomme and terms this "an empty and, almost certainly, a vain offer."
18. Edmunds 1975a, 100.

a textbook-perfect appeal to the "war against warre," for they explicitly challenge the Athenians to shift the locus of competition from war to *aretê*.[19] The Athenians hold the advantage and can compel Sparta to compete with them in generosity rather than in arms. The Spartans, therefore, recall the traditional arguments that we encountered in the programmatic debate between Corcyra and Corinth. If anything, the Spartans are more high-minded, engaging in less scolding and implied threats and placing greater relative emphasis upon the positive acquisition of friendship, the value of *aretê*, and generosity (including that generosity implied by their own willingness to settle). With their rational explanations for the psychology of gift exchange, they are almost too explicit. They are not just oddly "rhetorical."[20] They sound like an idealized ethnographic informant, ready to explain local practices in terms familiar to the inquiring anthropologist.

But the Spartan offer, even when it directly contradicts Kleon's analysis (Thuc. 4.19.4 vs. 3.39.5), is at least partially consistent with the views of human relations expressed by the Mytileneans, Kleon, and the Athenians at Melos. The Spartans conclude their offer by linking the promise of *charis* with the material basis for cooperation:

> While the issue is still in doubt, and you have reputation (*doxa*) and our friendship (*philia*) in prospect, and for us the disaster may be moderately (*metriôs*) settled before any disgrace (*aischron ti*), let us be reconciled. For ourselves let us choose peace instead of war, and let us fashion a pause from troubles for the rest of the Hellenes. In this matter, they will think that you are more responsible (*aitiôteros*). The war that they labor under they know not which began, but once the peace, over which you have authority (*kurioi*), has come into being, they will contribute their *charis* to your account.
>
> Thuc. 4.20.2

Inscribed within this Spartan offer is an inflammatory assumption. Sparta and Athens are two states set apart. The rest of Greece must wait for the decision these two parties make between themselves. If Athens comes to terms with Sparta, then Athens and Sparta will generously grant peace to the rest of the Greek world—whether Sparta's allies are ready for peace or not. The Spartans generously offer to accept a settlement in which they will not only themselves incur a debt of *aretê* and

---

19. Not all have read the Spartan speech this way: Strauss (1964, 173) suggests that the Spartan emphasis on Athens's good fortune makes their offer "underhanded and grudging," and observes that "their lack of frankness and of pride is not redeemed by graciousness."

20. Hunter 1973, 74.

commit their friendship, but in which the watching Hellenes will confer far more of their *charis* upon the Athenians. But if Sparta accepts a relative decline in its prestige, the decline is not so quantitatively great that it leads to a qualitative change. Sparta remains in the same class as Athens, as one of the two "superpowers" of the Greek world. This assumption, which begins to materialize in the previous section, becomes explicit as the concluding argument of their speech:

> [3] By such a decision you can become firm friends with the Spartans at their own invitation, impelled by *charis* far more than by violence. [4] And from this friendship consider the good things that are likely to follow: know that when we and you have the same wishes, the rest of Hellas, being inferior (*hupodeesteron*), will confer honor (*timê*) upon those who are greatest.
>
> Thuc. 4.20.3–4

The idea that Athens and Sparta should make up their differences and collaborate as leaders of Greece seems to have been topical. Trugaios in Aristophanes' *Peace* suggests that Athens and Sparta should jointly exercise rule (*archê*) over Hellas (*Pax* 1080–1082). According to Thucydides, Sparta's more powerful allies feared such an accommodation (Thuc. 5.29.3–4), and Sparta's assumption that it could make peace on behalf of all caused it considerable trouble in the years after the Peace of Nikias.

Thucydides' Spartans portray their own traditional position in Greece with typical Thucydidean reasoning. Where Trugaios speaks bluntly of shared rule (*archê*), Sparta refers only to the honor (*timê*) that the two will receive. But the Spartans leave no doubts about what guarantees this honor. The rest of Greece is "inferior" (*hupodeesteron*) to Athens and Sparta combined (Thuc. 4.20.4). Athens and Sparta will receive honor from the rest of Hellas because they are "the greatest" (*ta megista*). Sparta explicitly bases its offer to Athens on the preponderant coercive power that an Athenian-Spartan alliance could exert.

The conclusion of Sparta's argument contains several assumptions. First, unlike the Mytileneans or Kleon, it bases international relations on the exchange of *charis* and on self-conscious restraint in the application of power. This first assumption comes at the end and serves to reinforce a second assumption, which provides the dominant logic that makes peace reasonable: Athens and Sparta can come to an understanding because they are, as the Athenian delegates at Melos observe (Thuc. 5.91.1), comparable. The Mytileneans' critique of their own friendship with Athens did not apply, because no gross disparity in power made Sparta fear Athenian friendship. The opening sections of the Spartan

speech focus upon the uncertainty of fortune (4.17–18): Athens holds
the upper hand at present, but the situation may change, and Athens
should convert its material advantage into a more permanent increase
in prestige and symbolic capital. Sparta is willing to make a settlement,
however, because even a temporary setback with Athens does not per-
manently affect its position. Third, Thucydides informs us after the
speech (4.21.1) that the Athenians had previously "longed for a treaty"
and would—so the Spartans thought—eagerly snatch up the offer. Thus
although the Spartans called attention to the fact that they were in a
weaker position and would have to seek peace at a loss, they still felt
themselves to be in control of the situation. They were able to make the
generous offer they did because they remained confident in their fundamentally strong position.

Thus even the Spartan speech, which brilliantly commands the rhetoric of generosity, leaves open some questions as to the nature of the offer.
First, Spartan friendship may be firm, but only as long as the material
conditions keep the two powers within the same relative status. Given
the ultimate reference to power, the contest of *aretê* between Athens and
Sparta is contingent on the continued parity between the two sides.[21]
Second, the years of warfare have resolved nothing. The Athenians remain what they were. The Spartans do not address the grievances, past
or present, of the Corinthians or any other allies. Sparta had begun its
war in large measure because a failure to act would have gutted the trust
and symbolic capital that the Spartans enjoyed with allies whom they
could not afford to lose.[22] This offer of peace, which dismisses allied
concerns and deals with none of the underlying issues, is anachronistic.
It appeals to Athens as if Athens really were a comparable power, although the narrative up to this point has elaborately portrayed Athens
as different and incompatible with a traditionalist state such as Sparta.
However noble or, for the moment, heartfelt the Spartan sentiments may
be, no lasting peace can come of this.

The limits of Spartan loyalty appear most dramatically in the Melian
affair (Thuc. 5.104–111). The Melians are colonists, *apoikoi*, of Sparta
and thus have an unusually strong claim to Spartan support. They argue

21. On this, see Strauss 1964, 239, near the conclusion of his analysis of Thucydides:
"The order of cities which is presupposed in the most noble Spartan proclamations is
altogether impossible, given the unequal power of the different cities which inevitably
leads to the consequence that the most powerful cities cannot help being hegemonial or
even imperial."

22. On the dilemma facing the Spartans, see chapter 8 below.

that Sparta will have to come to their defence if only to preserve its credibility, but the cynical Athenians prove correct in asserting that the Spartans have an extremely narrow view of their interests and are loath to undertake actions in support of anyone other than themselves. Corinth could, by throwing a diplomatic tantrum at 1.68–71, rouse Sparta. Melos, *apoikia* or not, was not a great power or vital material interest. The Spartans, according to Thucydides, do not lift a finger to help them.

The narrative has, however, already given a less dramatic but equally revealing example of Sparta's limited commitments, when Sparta and its allies finally capture Plataia.[23] The Spartans framed their response in a fashion that conflicts with the traditionalist posture they present to the Athenians. Plataia had been the site of a critical Greek victory under Spartan leadership, and Plataia had subsequently become a kind of Panhellenic sanctuary, with a special relationship to Sparta (whose dead lay buried on Plataian ground). The Plataian speech to the Spartans takes as its main point the special obligations that this bond places upon Sparta. The Spartans, by contrast, frame the situation in a brutally simple fashion (Thuc. 3.52.4). They refuse to acknowledge any prior obligations, nor do they level any accusation of wrongdoing (*katêgoria*). "They called upon the Plataians and asked them this much only: whether they had done the Spartans and their allies any good in the current war." The Plataians (3.53–59) and Thebans (3.61–67) in the end might as well have said nothing, for the Spartans simply continue to press the same question upon the Plataians (3.68.1). They methodically posed this question to each Plataian and then executed them all.

The criterion that the Spartans choose is revealing because it rejects a fundamental principle of exchange. By insisting on good services rendered in the present war, the Spartans turn their back on the permanent and timeless nature of *charis*. Euripides composed suppliant plays that linked Athenian services in mythological times to present politics. In their speech at Athens, the Corinthians demanded a return on aid rendered before the Persian Wars (Thuc. 1.41.2). The Spartans, however, coldly exclude from consideration any obligations based on the battle at Plataia. Furthermore, although the Plataian case is not without problems (they had killed Theban prisoners and had rejected a handsome offer from the the Spartan king Archidamos), they can claim the high moral ground on at least one issue: they, unlike the Mytileneans, had

---

23. For an even harsher analysis of Spartan dealings with Plataia, see Badian 1989.

refused to abandon their friends the Athenians: "We now fear to perish by having again acted on the same principles [as in the defence against Xerxes], and chosen to act justly (*dikaiôs*) with Athens rather than with an eye to our profit (*kerdaleôs*) with Sparta" (3.56.6). Although the Plataians could claim that they had stood by their friends the Athenians to the bitter end, the Spartans give this no weight at all. The Spartans had demanded the Plataians be neutral and, once that demand had been refused, felt that they could do with the Plataians as they saw fit (3.68.1). Thucydides offers his own interpretation of Spartan motives:

> The Spartans had adopted such a recalcitrant position with respect to almost the entire business about the Plataians for the sake of the Thebans, for they thought that the Thebans would be useful (*ôphelimoi*) for the war that had just then broken out.
>
> Thuc. 3.68.4

Thucydides' reasoning picks up the language of the Spartan query. The Spartans demand to know what the Plataians have done for them in the present war, because their real concern is the potential service of Thebes in the same period. Whatever moral claims the Spartans might make, or whatever generous postures they might strike, the advantage of the present ultimately outweighed the debts of the past. They pursue traditional values, but only to a degree.

The Plataian debate obviously cries out for comparison with the Mytilenan debate that so closely precedes it. The Athenians at the last minute chose not to execute all of their prisoners. Sparta went forward and killed all the Plataians.[24] But this is not the only point of comparison. The Plataian debate also reveals that when their interests are at stake, the Spartans are as indifferent to *charis* and symbolic capital as the Athenians showed themselves after the debate between Corcyra and Corinth. In both cases, Athens and Sparta act as if the speeches had never been delivered. In both cases, Athens and Sparta pursue that course that serves their immediate interest. The Spartans, however, make a mockery of traditional gift exchange, truncating the time frame within which they will consider good services. Both of the preeminent powers in Greece, in the final analysis, placed their immediate interest above the obligations of *charis* or loyalty. Sparta made a greater attempt to maintain appearances—the old Spartan king Archidamos, for example, made a decorous offer to Plataia at Thucydides 2.72 and gave the Plataians a

---

24. For a discussion of the limits of this comparison, see Cogan 1981b, 7.

way out (provided that they would abandon the Athenians). But the Spartans still leave themselves open to cynical interpretations, and their actions at Plataia have drawn almost universal disdain from historians. Such questionable behavior is especially damning because the Spartans owe so much of their position to moral authority. The Spartans, however, occupy a precarious position in any event (at least in Thucydides' scheme of the Greek world), and it is to the dilemmas that confront them that we will now turn.

CHAPTER 8

Archidamos and Sthenelaidas

The Dilemma of Spartan Authority

Before shifting the focus away from Thucydides' engagement with the traditional discourses of the archaic world, I wish first to trace some of the complexities in his account of Sparta, the leading state of the old world. In chapter 1, I began by contrasting the different models of Spartan prestige that informed Herodotus and Xenophon. For Herodotus, Sparta's position was provisional. Its unique way of life and military prowess were necessary but not sufficient conditions for Spartan leadership. Herodotus carefully stresses the limits of Sparta's ambitions and the legitimacy that Sparta received from Apollo's oracle at Delphi. In effect, Sparta could command leadership by force. A combination of force and moral posturing allowed other Greeks to concede to Sparta a preeminent position. Xenophon, by contrast, lays much greater stress upon Sparta's ability to project physical violence. The Spartan way of life is impressive because it was responsible for Sparta's position. Xenophon's Spartans fashioned not only themselves but their own status in the world at large. For Herodotus, Spartan status is the product of a complex negotiation between the Spartans and the larger Greek world. Xenophon's Spartans could—even in the fourth century—always, it is felt, reassert their ancient glory if they could strictly adhere to their way of life and thus return to the battlefield with their former strength. Herodotus, on the other hand, makes it clear from the start that excellence at home and military power abroad never by themselves constituted a sufficient basis for hegemony.

The same dichotomy between Sparta as autonomous and Sparta as

the product of a wider consensus informs the debate in book 1 between
the two Spartans Archidamos and Sthenelaidas. The two argue about
how to confront Athens. Like much else that takes place in the opening
book, their speeches are programmatic, for they illustrate the insoluble
problem that Athens poses for the Spartans and thus dramatize the confrontation between old and new that underlies so much of the *History*.

Both speakers trace part of a dilemma. Sparta could not confront
Athens without developing naval power and the regular financial resources that ships required, but to do so would require Sparta to change,
to become more like Athens, and in so doing to give up the position
upon which its prestige depended.[1] In the end, Sparta succumbed to this
dilemma, conquering Athens, but becoming as hated as the Athenians
had been and never again quite regaining the status that it had enjoyed
in the late 430s. Thucydides' Archidamos and Sthenelaidas allow us to
see the new world through the eyes of the old. I do not propose to offer
a comprehensive analysis of Thucydides' Spartans—such an examination would comprise a study in itself. Rather, I will concentrate on the
two very different Spartans who step forward to give complementary
views of their city and its position, and measure the claims of these men
against subsequent Spartan behavior described in the *History*.

Archidamos and Sthenelaidas develop the picture of Spartan character presented by the Corinthians, rejecting some characteristics and
appropriating and reinterpreting others. Archidamos and Sthenelaidas
allow us to see from the start that although there may be a Spartan
national character, characteristic Spartans can be very different in outlook and manner. These two speakers do not so much contradict as give
depth to the two-dimensional picture sketched by the Corinthians. For
all of their differences, Archidamos and Sthenelaidas are variations on
a single theme, and each offers a different and only partial analysis of
Sparta's position. These speeches do not explain why Sparta ultimately
was victorious but rather, by their complementary limitations, frame the
problem of Sparta's victory with greater clarity.

The style of the two speeches could hardly be more distinct: the
thoughtful analysis by the old king Archidamos gives way to a fiery
harangue by the ephor Sthenelaidas. With only a few exceptions,[2] readers have expressed broad admiration for Archidamos and his speech.
"Archidamus' quiet dignity and old-fashioned poise, his balance of mind

---

1. On this, see chapter 4 above.
2. Most recently, Pelling 1991.

and unconcern with any emotional appeal, his blend of valor and sound judgment, make him the paragon of the age-old tradition of the Spartan warrior king."[3] He is a "wise and experienced statesman,"[4] "the voice of reason,"[5] "credited with statesmanship of almost Periclean quality,"[6] and his speech is "masterful."[7] One leading expert on Sparta states that if Archidamos really "counselled caution," as he does in Thucydides, "he was prudent," for

> the Archidamian War cruelly exposed Spartan deficiencies in many areas: manpower shortage, inability to respond swiftly or fully enough to changes in tactics by land and sea, rudimentary "system" of public finances, incompatibility between a Spartan upbringing and the requirements of a prolonged foreign command, internecine behind-the-scenes struggles for power and influence at Sparta, failure to retain the loyalty of some of her prominent Peloponnesian League allies, and, not least, the constant threat posed by the enemy within, the Helots, lying in wait for and (as in 425) seizing upon their collective master's misfortune. In the end it was not so much that Sparta had won the war as that Athens had lost it.[8]

Thucydides certainly does nothing to undercut this favorable impression of Archidamos's character, introducing him with the specific comment that the king was a man "who appeared to be intelligent (*sunetos*) and possessed of self-control (*sôphrôn*)" (Thuc. 1.79.2).

By contrast, the short and biting speech of Sthenelaidas at Thucydides 1.86 has encountered more than its share of criticism: its "shallowness is evident in the jingles and equivocations of the language."[9] Sthenelaidas's appeal has struck many as irrational and emotional;[10] at best it is considered a rhetorical tour de force that cozens its audience into action.[11] "On the heels of Archidamos' speech, Sthenelaidas' words sound naive and misguided; indeed he seems to miss the point."[12] In the end, Sthenelaidas, irrational or not, carries the day, and the Spartans

---

3. Wassermann 1953, 194–195.
4. Connor 1984, 38.
5. Stahl 1966, 54.
6. Westlake 1968, 125.
7. Bloedow 1981, 135; for additional references praising Archidamos, see Pelling 1991, 122.
8. Cartledge 1987, 408.
9. Connor 1984, 38.
10. Finley 1942, 135–136; Stahl 1966, 57: "Sparta entscheidet sich gegen die Vernunft"; Immerwahr 1973, 24; Bloedow 1981, 142–143; Bloedow 1987, 66.
11. Stahl 1966, 56: "ein Musterstück raffinierter Rhetorik"; Allison 1984 explores the rhetorical effectiveness of the speech.
12. Kallet-Marx 1993a, 86.

vote decisively that the Athenians had broken the treaty (Thuc. 1.87). Most modern critics, however, have rejected the content, much as they have despised the manner, of his speech.

Sthenelaidas's rhetorical task was not as formidable as might at first appear. Effective as Archidamos's speech may have been, the majority of Spartans began the meeting convinced that "the Athenians were in the wrong and that they needed to go to war as quickly as possible" (Thuc. 1.79.2). Sthenelaidas had only to "recover the emotional state of the assembly which existed before Archidamus spoke."[13] Nor was Archidamos's speech, thoughtful and attractive as it may have been, necessarily the best policy at the time—"The proposals of Archidamus were altogether in accord with the views expressed by the Athenian ambassadors in the Spartan assembly."[14] Nevertheless, the question remains: Why was Sthenelaidas more persuasive than Archidamos? Or, to put it another way, why has Archidamos's speech been so much more persuasive to readers of Thucydides' *History* than to its original audience?

Most critics have traditionally sided with Archidamos or Sthenelaidas, and in this they have accepted the dialectic premise, with its tendency to endorse one side and reduce the other to rubble. Both speeches, I believe, are insightful and capture much of the Spartan dilemma. Each is—and can only be—a partial analysis, for, in Thucydides' analysis at any rate, there is no real solution to Sparta's problems. The world is changing. Sparta may defeat Athens, but its victory is problematic at best. Furthermore, most examinations of these speeches have concentrated on the speeches themselves and taken relatively little account of the larger context.

ARCHIDAMOS

Archidamos's speech consists of two basic sections. The first (Thuc. 1.80–82) is a cool estimation of Sparta's relative weaknesses in a war against Athens. Athens is a qualitatively different kind of power, against which Sparta cannot bring to bear its usual overwhelming force (80.3). Sparta is inferior to Athens in ships and especially in financial resources (80.4). Athens can survive land invasions by importing what it needs by sea (81.2), and Sparta will have to have its own navy if it is to break up the Athenian empire (81.3). For these reasons, Archidamos urges cau-

13. Allison 1984, 14.
14. Kagan 1969, 304.

tion. The Lakedaimonians should temporize, neither threatening war too clearly nor implying that they will accept arbitration (82.1). Two or three years would put them in a much better position for war, and they should in the meantime play for time. If Athens should choose to resolve matters diplomatically in the meantime, so much the better (82.2).

In at least one regard, Archidamos's speech views the world from a typically Thucydidean perspective. The Spartan king is obsessed with *paraskeuê*, a concept to which Thucydides gave great emphasis. An entire monograph has been devoted to this term, which describes both the process of accumulating power and the accumulated power itself.[15] Thucydides uses the verbal form *paraskeuazo* substantially more frequently (163 examples) than Xenophon (149 examples), Plato (121), or Demosthenes (121), each of whose surviving opus is larger than Thucydides' *History*. Most striking, though, is Thucydides' interest in the noun *paraskeuê*. The verb tends to be very concrete: one "prepares" a march (e.g., Hdt. 1.71.2), a feast (Hdt. 1.126.2), or 200 triremes (Hdt. 5.32.1). The noun, however, can stand by itself without a concrete object to supplement its meaning, not "preparation *for*" but simply "the accumulated power that allows one to take action." The noun *paraskeuê* appears in Thucydides 104 times as opposed to 12 times in Xenophon, 23 times in Plato, and 44 times in Demosthenes.[16]

Thucydides found the term *paraskeuê* useful because Athenian power increased over time. Where the Peloponnesians could conduct a rapid levy en masse and descend with crushing force upon an opponent, they were less well prepared to maintain such a force—their troops needed to return and maintain their homes. As long as their financial resources lasted, the Athenians, by contrast, could maintain their forces in the field. And, unlike the resources of their Peloponnesian adversaries, Athenian financial resources could grow with each year's tribute. Archidamos establishes a clear hierarchical relationship between military force and financial power: "War is not so much an issue of arms as it is of the expense (*dapanê*) on account of which arms are of help" (Thuc. 1.83.2). The Athenians "have outfitted themselves excellently in all things: they have . . . ships, horses, arms, and a swarm of men greater than any single polis contains." Badly outclassed at sea, the Peloponnesians are even more inferior to Athens in monetary resources, *chrêmata* (1.80.4). Above all, the Athenians have "wealth (*ploutos*), both private and pub-

15. Allison 1989, 30–38.
16. For these and other figures, see the table on p. 29 in Allison 1989.

lic" (80.3), and from this flows all of Athens's material advantages. The Athenians have just as many allies as do the Spartans, but their allies contribute money (80.3, 83.2), whereas the Peloponnesian allies neither have a common store of wealth nor readily contribute money from their own individual resources (80.4). If the Peloponnesians cannot cut off the flow of money to Athens from its empire, then in the coming war, Archidamos argues, "we will only do ourselves greater harm."

Later in book 1, the Corinthians and Perikles would, in their curious, oblique "debate," each point out that the Peloponnesians could, if pressed, commandeer the financial resources stored at Olympia and Delphi (Thuc. 1.121.3, 1.143.1). Archidamos's speech, however, focuses on the general difference between the accumulated power of Athens and that of Sparta and its allies. The Spartans should avoid the fate of the clever fool who "in his analysis neatly scorns the *paraskeuai* [plural] of his enemies and then falls short when it comes time for action (*ergon*)" (1.84.3). Twice Archidamos implores his fellow citizens not to rush into this war *a-paraskeuoi*, "without sufficient *paraskeuê*"(80.3, 84.1). The Peloponnesians must take time to develop their own counter-*paraskeuê* by building a navy (80.4: *antiparaskeuasometha*). Once they begin serious preparations for war, the Peloponnesians will be able to back their words with their *paraskeuê*, and the Athenians may choose to yield (81.3). The king exhorts his fellow Spartans to follow their natural tendencies: "We always make our preparations (84.4: *paraskeuazometha*) on the assumption that their adversaries are also making careful plans." Archidamos concludes his speech by arguing that the Spartans should give diplomacy an opportunity to work, but "at the same time, prepare for the war" (85.2: *paraskeuazesthe*).

Thus Archidamos, at least in part, analyzes the war in Thucydidean terms, and his argument accepts the fundamental categories that Thucydides introduces in the Archaeology. War with Athens will turn on monetary and material advantages. The Spartans can control the Peloponnesians and their neighbors because "our strength is similar." The Athenians are a naval power, and their true strength—subject lands across the sea—is inaccessible to Peloponnesian attack (Thuc. 1.80.3). "This war" that confronts the Spartans is the subject for calculation, which one should "reason through in a self-possessed fashion (*sôphronôs*)" (80.2). How many ships are available? How long can they be supported? The sums and figures of empire, by an accountant's logic, determine whether or when the Spartans should or should not fight. War is not a good thing, and diplomacy is preferable; if diplomacy does not succeed, wait until the balance of power tilts in our favor and then attack.

We have discussed Pindar's second Isthmian ode and its exploration of the theme "money, money, makes the man" (Pind. *Isthm.* 2.11: see chapter 3 above). Money determines the social position of an individual, Pindar's speaker bleakly fears, and Archidamos applies a similar principle to the affairs of city-states. In war, "money, money, makes the state." When Archidamos argues that any allies, Greek or barbarian, will suffice if they bring with them "the power of money" (Thuc. 1.82.1: *chrêmatôn dunamis*), he embraces that aspect of monetary exchange most antithetical to social continuity: money overcomes any social obstacle and gives power to anyone, whatever their background.[17] Archidamos largely subordinates his foreign policy to the calculus of power. In so doing, he accepts a materialistic perspective that terrified the old elites of the archaic period. The Spartans had defined themselves, at least in part, by rejecting the symbols and practices by which money sought to transmute itself into prestige. To fight Athens, Archidamos argues from a paradigm that was ultimately corrosive to the Spartan mirage. Archidamos's arguments could win the war but destroy the delicate environment in which the Herodotean Sparta could prosper. Some observers (such as Xenophon; cf. *Lak. Pol.* 14) might argue that this is precisely what did happen.

But Archidamos himself is acutely sensitive to the true source of Spartan authority, and he develops his argument further in the second section of his speech (Thuc. 1.83–85). Archidamos's speech is remarkable in that it attempts to synthesize the calculus of power with the traditional, antimonetary, socially embedded values upon which Sparta's preeminent position within the Greek world rested. The shrewd gambits to win time and the inexorable accumulation of *paraskeuê* are tactics that, in Archidamos's hopeful analysis, touch only the surface of things, like the feigned panics at Thermopylai with which they tricked their opponents (Hdt. 7.211). Archidamos uses his speech to present, with great eloquence, a vision of the Spartan character that proudly rejects the criticisms of the Corinthians and anticipates the proud exposition of Athenian character in the Funeral Oration. The Spartans may dissemble, temporize, collect money from any source—even from non-Greeks (the Persians at Thuc. 1.82.1)—but the core of the Spartan soul remains

17. Kurke 1991, 240–256.

untouched and in fact demands the stratagems that Archidamos outlines.

Archidamos opens his speech by recalling his own extensive experience in past wars. Neither he nor any of his contemporaries have any illusions about warfare or, he implies, any need to prove their valor with a new conflict (Thuc. 1.80.1). The Corinthians in their speech scourged their Spartan allies, harshly goading them into action. They castigated them for being sluggish. Archidamos confronts this charge directly: "If you undertake the war without proper *paraskeuê*, you may by rushing only delay its conclusion" (84.1). Twice elsewhere he implores his audience not to "rush off without the proper *paraskeuê*," with no clear basis for confidence (80.3), or goaded by the accusations of their allies (82.5). "Let us not," he insists at 1.85.1, "make our plans about many men, monies, and cities, rushed in the brief space of a day."

Archidamos does not restrict himself to defending his position. Those who wish for war, he counters, have let their feelings cloud their judgment. Three times he implores his fellow Spartans not to let their emotions "get the better of them" (*epairesthai*, a very negative term). "Let us not be carried away (*epairômetha*) by that hope, at any rate, that the war will end quickly" (Thuc. 1.81.6). The seductive power of *elpis*, hope, and its ability to draw mortals on to destruction is a familiar theme in archaic literature. A few sentences later, Archidamos enjoins his fellows: "Let us not be carried away (*epairômetha*) too soon by the arguments of our allies" (83.3). In the following chapter, he reminds them of traditional Spartan behavior: "We are not carried away (*epairometha*) with pleasure" (84.2).

Although Archidamos's arguments may not convince the Spartans, the Corinthians in their next speech address the fear that Sparta might be "carried away." They seek not only to deflect this criticism, but to appropriate it for their own purposes and to use it to help justify war. They concede that no one should be "carried away (*epairesthai*) by good fortune in war" (Thuc. 1.120.3), for the one who glories in such good fortune "does not understand that he is carried away (*epairomenos*) by a boldness that deserves no trust" (120.4). This war, they argue, has been forced upon them and is not the product of temporary excitement.

Appeals to calculation and morality run throughout Archidamos's speech, but about halfway through, Archidamos begins to shift the focus of his argument to a defence of Spartan character. Having opened his speech by alluding to his own solid military record, he returns at Thucydides 1.83.1 to the theme of courage: "Let no one think that the many do not immediately attack a single city because of cowardice (*anandria:*)." At 83.3, he undercuts the appeals of the allies: "Since we shall, for better or worse, end up with the greater share of the responsibility for whatever happens, let us be the ones to consider ahead of time any of these things in a calm fashion (*kath' hêsuchian*)." The Corinthians can demand rapid action because they do not have primary responsibility for its consequences. Spartan caution and calculuation are products of Spartan authority.

The Lakedaimonians can dismiss the criticisms of their allies because "we inhabit a city that is in every way free (*eleuthera*) and possessing the best reputation (*eudoxôtatê*)" (Thuc. 1.84.1). Archidamos's language here is forceful and slightly poetic.[18] At first, he accepts negative terms to describe Spartan caution, thus setting his initial defence in the framework set by the Corinthians: "Do not," he argues, "be ashamed of the 'slowness' (*to bradu*) and 'hesitancy' (*to mellon*), for which they blame us the most" (84.1). He then goes on to redefine this Spartan quality, defining it in his own terms:

> The quality that they condemn is really nothing but *sôphrosunê* lodged within the mind (*emphrôn*); on account of this, we alone do not become insolent in success and give way less than others in misfortune. If people cheer us on with praise (*epainos*), we are not carried away by the pleasure to risks that our judgment condemns; nor, if someone goads us into action with an accusation (*katêgoria*), are we any the more convinced because we have been exasperated.
>
> Thuc. 1.84.2

Archidamos lays claim to *sôphrosunê*, "self-possession," that is based on good sense (*emphrôn*). This quality is internal and allows the Spartans to construct their view of the world and their reactions from the inside out. Neither good fortune (*eupragiai*) nor disasters (*sumphorai*) can overcome this self-possession, and the Spartans maintain their equilibrium under all circumstances. Likewise, Archidamos claims that Spartans are immune to social pressures and that their values are not, as one might now put it, socially constructed. The Spartans decide what to do based on their estimation of the situation and without regard to the praise or blame that others may lay upon them. Archidamos does not claim that the Spartans are insensitive to these emotions. Rather, he

---

18. See Hornblower's (1991) notes ad loc. on ἐλευθέραν and καὶ εὐδοξοτάτην.

states that whether they feel pleasure, *hêdonê*, or are annoyed, *achthes-thentes*, they are nevertheless able to come to the best decision.

The Spartan character, as outlined by Archidamos, refines and inten-sifies general qualities for which archaic Greek sources express admi-ration. In discussing the speech of the Corinthians, we touched upon the mistrust of haste and rushing that appears in archaic literature. "Do not," Theognis urges Kyrnos, "rush anything too much (*mêden agan speudein*). Of all things, those in the middle are best, and thus, Kyrnos, you will possess *aretê*, which is difficult to acquire" (Theog. 335–336). And again: "Do not rush too much (*mêden agan speudein*). Timing is the best in all mortal affairs. Often a mortal rushes after *aretê*, seeking profit, but a god (*daimôn*) eagerly leads him astray into a great error (*amplakia*) and makes what is good seem bad to him and what is bad good" (Theog. 401–406). Solon mocks the insatiable rush of humankind after profit (frag. 13.43ff., 71ff. [= Theog. 227–232] West).

Likewise, the even judgment of which Archidamos boasts is a prized quality, as a fragment of Archilochus illustrates:

My heart, my heart (*thumos*), that are confounded with troubles that are beyond help (*amêchanoi*), defend yourself . . . standing securely near to the foe. Do not exult openly if you are victorious, and if you are not victorious, do not fall down in your home and weep. Do not rejoice overmuch in delightful things nor be vexed overmuch in troubles, knowing what sort of condition possesses human beings!

Archil. frag. 128 West

This even temperament wins praise elsewhere in archaic literature (e.g., Theog. 657–658). Its roots lie in the oppressive sense of *amêchania*, the "helplessness" of all mortals before the rise and fall of fortune. "What is Zeus doing?" Aisop reportedly asked Chilon of Lakedaimon, one of the Seven Wise Men of Greek tradition. "He is bringing low the lofty humble, and raising high the humble," came the answer (Diog. Laert. 1.69). The rise and fall of humans is one of the most pervasive themes of archaic literature (e.g., Archil. frag. 130 West). Human beings have no control over their external condition: prosperity or death can arrive without warning.

Mortals can, however, define their own internal states. If they cannot control what the external world does to them, they can determine their own reactions. The individual agent contains a moral space that is au-tonomous. For Archidamos, the true locus of control resides within hu-man beings. What happens to them—even death—are mere epiphenom-

ena that cannot touch this secure core. Herodotus's picture of Kroisos
on the pyre is perhaps the most extreme example.[19] Herodotus distinguishes his account sharply from that which appears in Bacchylides. In
that poem, written for the Sicilian tyrant Hieron, Apollo spirits Kroisos
away to a life among the Hyperboreans that extends into eternity the
luxurious existence that Kroisos had enjoyed among mortals. The
wealthy despot shares his material prosperity with Apollo, who repays
his mortal benefactor in kind. In Herodotus, Kroisos receives no such
reward from Apollo. In Herodotus, Kroisos ascends the pyre a defeated
king and descends it as a sage who has faced a terrible death and, in
that instant, received a flash of insight and understood that his earlier
perceived good fortune had been an illusion.

In Thucydides, of course, malicious divinities do not lurk immediately
beneath the surface of human misfortunes. Archidamos's Spartans base
their character on *sôphrosunê*, the autonomous, internal quality of self-
possession:

> We are both warlike (*polemikoi*) and wise (*eubouloi*) because of our sense
> of order (*to eukosmon*). We are warlike because *sôphrosunê* is the greatest
> part of shame (*aidôs*), and a sense of shame (*aischunê* = *aidôs*) is the greatest
> part of courage (*eupsuchia*).
>
> Thuc. 1.84.3

The language is, as often in Thucydides, slippery, but the argument
is clear. The Spartans have *sôphrosunê*, or self-control, and *sôphrosunê*
provides the main foundation for *aidôs/aischunê*, the shame that we feel
before others.[20] This sense of shame, in turn, provides the foundation
for courage, for it keeps us from running away or shirking duty in war.
The distinction is subtle but important: the Spartans are not brave simply because they fear what their fellows may say of them. The sense of
shame depends on *sôphrosunê* lodged in the Spartan heart. *Sôphrosunê*
thus radiates outward from the central core of the Spartan character and
makes possible shame, which in turn grounds courage.

Archidamos also attributes the wisdom of the Spartans (*eubouloi*) to
sôphrosunê, but he reverses the relationship of internal and external.
Spartans are not good at war because they fear what others might say
or do, but they are wise because of what others have in the past said or
done to them and because of the harsh experiences they have endured:

---

19. On this, see Flower 1991.
20. On the precise meaning of this passage, see Hornblower (1991, ad loc.), who agrees
with the interpretation of Nussbaum 1986, 508 n. 24.

And we are wise (*eubouloi*), because we are educated with too little learning
to despise the laws, and with too much emphasis on self-control
(*sôphronesteron*) to disobey them, and are brought up not to be too knowing
in useless matters—such as the knowledge that can give a specious criticism
of an enemy's plans in theory but fails to assail them with equal success in
practice—but are taught to consider that the schemes of our enemies are not
dissimilar to our own, and that those accidents that occur are not
determinable by calculation. [4] In practice we always base our preparations
against an enemy on the assumption that his plans are good; indeed, it is
right to rest our hopes not on a belief in his blunders, but on the soundness
of our plans. Nor ought we to believe that there is much difference between
one person and another, but to think that the superiority lies with the one
who is reared in the severest school (ἐν τοῖς ἀναγκαιοτάτοις παιδεύεται).

Thuc. 1.84.3–4

The Spartan upbringing does not make its products so clever that
they disdain customary usages. The harshness of this education prepares them for the "freaks of chance" that defy rational planning and
make them independent of their adversaries. They do not need to depend upon the mistakes their enemies will make. They can focus their
attention on their own plans, and if these are good enough, then all
will be well. In effect Archidamos argues that the Spartans do not depend upon misfortune striking others, but they do expect such misfortune to transpire. Their unflappable ability to function in the face of
adversity means that the unexpected will affect them less than it does
their adversaries and that this self-possession will allow them to prevail. Harshness in the past has thus rendered them more "self-possessed" (*sôphronesteron*), and this added *sôphrosunê* is the tough core
on which they rely. Thus they are wise for the same reason that they
are warlike, because their internal character renders them as autonomous of external events or stresses as possible.

Archidamos does not present a picture of universal success in the
short term. Courage does not guarantee victory, and Archidamos inte-
grates the unpredictable nature of events into Spartan ideology. The
Spartans may lose a particular battle or suffer setbacks, but the Spartan
character, tough and self-possessed, cannot be defeated. Archidamos's
speech thus gives a rationale for Demaratos's warnings to Xerxes about
Spartan valor a half-century before (Hdt. 7.101–104). Xerxes may overwhelm the Spartans in the end, but he will have to kill them all. He
cannot subjugate them and make them bow to his will. In the *Prometheus Bound* and in the plays of Sophokles, conventional *sôphrosunê*
implies accommodation and a willingness to yield to circumstances that

the hero despises. Archidamos's speech, by contrast, is important not least because it allows us to see *sôphrosunê* as a resilient, heroic quality and to understand why it could exercise such a fascination.

The opening chapters of Archidamos's speech (Thuc. 1.80–82) display "simplicity and directness . . . both in thought and expression in marked contrast with the elaboration of the Corinthian, as well as the Athenian" speeches,[21] and Daniel Tompkins has recently pointed out that the speech as a whole seems to "portray a character who is not only cautious and prudent but who to some extent does not participate in the major stylistic changes of the late fifth century."[22] Archidamos's analysis of *sôphrosunê* at 84.2–3 has, indeed, been criticized for "its unrealistically intellectual form,"[23] and the most recent commentator has endorsed the view that 1.84 is "undisguisedly the product of the sophistic age."[24] Certainly, the style of Archidamos's speech belongs to Thucydides—as does that of every speech, even the "Lakonic" harangue of Sthenelaidas. The reasoning of 84.2–3 is dense, and the language slippery.

Nevertheless, it is important to stress that what Archidamos says and the role that he assumes are both deeply conservative. Archidamos is playing a well-known, traditional role in Greek literature, that of the "warner," a wise individual whose advice will be ignored (cf. the following in Herodotus: Solon at 1.29–33, Artabanos at 7.10, Artemisia at 8.68).[25] The dense and aphoristic reasoning may reflect sophistic influence, but it belongs to a venerable tradition of authoritative moral speech. The first book of Diogenes Laertius, for example, preserves dozens of pithy aphorisms attributed to the various wise men of the early sixth century. In reply to the question "Who is fortunate (*eudaimôn*)?" Thales answered: "The one who is healthy in body, well equipped with respect to his *psuchê* and well trained with respect to his nature (*phusis*)" (Diog. Laert. 1.37). Pittakos, the tyrant of Lesbos more than a century and a half before the Peloponnesian War, is associated with decidedly Archidamian sentiments. "It is characteristic of wise (*sunetoi*) men that, before difficulties should arise, they foresee how they should not take

21. Gomme on 1.85.2.
22. So Tompkins 1993a, 110.
23. Westlake 1968, 124.
24. Hornblower 1991, 125, citing Hussey 1985.
25. On this, see Lattimore 1939.

place, and of courageous (*andreioi*) men that they set these difficulties right once they do occur" (Pittakos at Diog. Laert. 1.78). Likewise, Bias of Priene is reported to have said: "Be slow to take a hand in affairs, but whatever you choose, watch over it securely and stay with it through to the end" (Diog. Laert. 1.87). The denser the saying, the better. "Know yourself" (*gnôthi seauton*) and "Nothing in excess" (*mêden agan*) are only the most famous; others include "Love intelligence" (Diog. Laert. 1.88: *phronêsin agapa*), "Master pleasure" (Diog. Laert. 1.92: *hêdonês kratein*), and "Profit is shameful" (Diog. Laert. 1.97: *kerdos aischron*). A statement such as "*Sôphrosunê* is the greatest part of shame (*aidôs*), and a sense of shame (*aischunê* = *aidôs*) is the greatest part of courage (*eupsuchia*)" may extend, but nevertheless falls squarely within, this linguistic tradition.[26]

The content of Archidamos's analysis is even more important than the style. Gorgias's *Helen* is perhaps the classic example of sophistic logic, for it uses argumentation to stand traditional values on their head. Archidamos subjects Spartan character to analysis, but, as we have already noted, the Spartan character has firm roots in traditional values. Archidamos may well agree with Demokritos and "take education to be the more important, and [be] optimistic about its capacity to provide a firm foundation for civic life,"[27] but the Spartans based their prestige to an extraordinary degree on their peculiarly demanding way of life. An admiration of Sparta assumed, explicitly or not, that society could decisively shape human character. It is more likely that Demokritos bolstered his argument by the example of Sparta than that Archidamos—even Thucydides' Archidamos—needed to draw upon Demokritos.

The qualities of *aidôs* and *sôphrosunê* are often found associated with one another (e.g., Pl. *Leg.* 772a; Isoc. 1.15; Xen. *Cyr.* 8.1.31; Arist. *Eth. Eud.* 1234a32). When, however, Archidamos defines the relationship between these two qualities and states that *sôphrosunê* is largely responsible for *aidôs*, he seems to be presenting a conventional idea of the time. The dramatic date of Plato's *Charmides* is the same as that of Archidamos's speech, the beginning of the Peloponnesian War. In the dialogue, Sokrates and the handsome youth Charmides explore the meaning of *sôphrosunê*. When asked to define *sôphrosunê*, Charmides

---

26. On the traditional foundations for many sophistic mannerisms, see still Finley 1967, 55–117.

27. Hussey 1985, 123.

replies: "Well, I think . . . that *sôphrosunê* makes people feel a sense of shame (*aischunesthai*) or be bashful (*aischuntelos*), and that *sôphrosunê* is the same as *aidôs*"(*Chrm.* 160e). Charmides' position (which Sokrates immediately makes him abandon) is clearly presented as a piece of conventional wisdom. Archidamos is not presenting a new or unexpected interpretation of *sôphrosunê* but uses a well-known idea associated with *sôphrosunê* as part of an argument to praise the Spartan character. The authority of Archidamos's argument flows, at least in part, from the traditionality of its individual sentiments.

Overall, the speech of Archidamos is a brilliant response to the equally brilliant attack of the Corinthians. On the one hand, the Corinthians have complained: "Your customs are old-fashioned (*archaiotropa*) when compared to them" (Thuc. 1.71.2). The "unchanging customs" (71.3: *akinêta nomima*) of Sparta are no longer adequate. The time has come for "innovation" (*epitechnêsis*). Archidamos does not deny but urgently affirms the fact that the Athenians are a qualitatively different kind of enemy. Archidamos pushes his analysis even farther in one direction than do the Corinthians, who, after chastising the Spartans for being old-fashioned, call for an "antediluvian" reaction, a traditional invasion of Attika:[28]

> In a struggle with Peloponnesians and neighbors our strength is of the same character, and it is possible to move swiftly on the different points. But a struggle with a people who live in a distant land, who have also an extraordinary familiarity with the sea, and who are in the highest state of preparation in every other department; with wealth private and public, with ships and horses and heavy infantry, and a population such as no one other Hellenic place can equal, and lastly a number of tributary allies—what can justify us in rashly beginning such a struggle?
>
> Thuc. 1.80.3

The Spartans and their allies are woefully behind Athens in two major categories: ships and money. Archidamos exhorts the allies to play for time and put off war for two or three years, but only so that they can make up this shortfall in named, "material" resources. The Spartans must raise money from any and all quarters, build ships, and learn how to use these ships in war, but this process will take time (1.80.4). But if Archidamos recognizes a difference between his own people

28. Pelling 1991, 123.

and the Athenians, he does not represent it in the same way as the Corinthians. The Corinthians had based their critique on the difference between Athenian and Spartan temperaments. The Athenians simply viewed the world in a more aggressive, risk-taking, and dynamic fashion than their opponents, and this habit of thought ultimately produced the accumulated power at Athens's disposal. The Spartans need, according to the Corinthians, in some degree to match Athens's peculiar strengths of character if they are going to defeat the Athenians.

Archidamos, however, locates the crucial advantage of Athenian power in externalized factors such as money, ships, and the skill to sail them. The Spartans do not need to change their character. They need a navy and the wherewithal to support it. Arms, not the man, are the problem, and once the Spartans and their allies have built the ships, piled up the silver, and learned the new tactics of war, they will be more than ready. Archidamos concedes Spartan disadvantage but then turns this concession into a calculating argument for delay and a springboard to his main point, the vindication of Spartan character and the implicit legitimacy of Sparta's claim to a preeminent position in the Greek world. The proud analysis of *sôphrosunê* and Spartan power at Thucydides 1.84 rejects the notion that Spartan character is a weakness, and boldly claims that this character, once it has at its disposal the new tools of conflict, will prove a fundamental and decisive advantage.

Thus Archidamos climaxes his argument with an appeal to the ancestral values of the Spartans:

> These practices, then, which our fathers have handed down to us, and by whose maintenance we have always profited, must not be given up. And we must not be hurried into deciding in a day's brief space a question that concerns many lives and fortunes and many cities, and in which honor is deeply involved—but we must decide calmly. And this course is possible for us more than for others on account of our strength.
>
> Thuc. 1.85.1

Archidamos thus dismisses out of hand the claim that Sparta's customs are "old-fashioned" or obsolescent. They should above all hold fast to the practices, *meletai*, that their fathers have given them, for these habits have been the source of their strength. Archidamos reaffirms with all the force at his disposal the theme that we saw already in Herodotus, that Sparta owed its preeminence less to its raw ability to project force than to the peculiar character that it had developed.

Why then does Archidamos's speech fail?

STHENELAIDAS

Sthenelaidas's speech is remarkable for its brevity. This short, "laconic" performance is, as Gomme observed, "perfectly in character" for the crusty Spartan. In less than a page, Sthenelaidas demolishes, even when he does not answer, Archidamos's case, and the Spartans enthusiastically affirm the consensus with which they had opened the meeting, that Athens had violated the treaty and that war was inevitable (Thuc. 1.79.2, 87). The brevity of Sthenelaidas's speech has perhaps disturbed American scholars less than others, for the most famous speech in American political rhetoric, Lincoln's Gettysburg Address, was comparable in length to Sthenelaidas's harangue and, like Sthenelaidas's harangue, was delivered after a long, eloquent speech by a revered elder (the famous orator and former Eliot Professor of Greek at Harvard Edward Everett, who spoke for more than two hours). Nevertheless, few would compare Sthenelaidas's apoplectic energy with Lincoln at Gettysburg. Scholars have, as we have already noted, generally shaken their heads at the irrational decision that the Spartans ultimately do take.[29]

Angry as its tone may be, Sthenelaidas's speech is deceptively subtle. Sthenelaidas, by his brevity and his words alike—by his practice as well as by what he says—not only attacks Archidamos's arguments but, at least as important, undermines the king's authority:

> The long speech of the Athenians I do not pretend to understand. They said a good deal in praise of themselves but nowhere denied that they are injuring our allies and the Peloponnesians. And yet if they behaved well against the Mede then, but ill toward us now, they deserve double punishment for having ceased to be good and for having become bad. [2] We meanwhile are the same then and now and shall not, if we are wise, disregard the wrongs of our allies or put off till tomorrow the duty of assisting those who must suffer today.
>
> Thuc. 1.86.1–2

Sthenelaidas claims, in essence, that he, not Archidamos, is truer to the Spartan character. He distinguishes himself sharply from those who have preceded him by dismissing the "long speech of the Athenians," striking the pose of hard Spartan taciturnity. Where Archidamos eloquently explores the nature of Spartan constancy, Sthenelaidas bluntly asserts this quality as given and transparent and claims it as an argument for action: "We meanwhile are the same then and now," but the Athe-

29. Contrast, however, Kagan 1969, 304–306.

nians deserve to be punished twice over, not just because they are bad, but also because they ceased to be good.

Once Sthenelaidas has established his position, he goes directly to the heart of his argument. He completes a progression that began with the opening of the debate. The Corinthian speech had lamented the moral and material weakness of Sparta, as opposed to Athens. Archidamos then acknowledged the material but rejected the moral weakness. Sthenelaidas dismisses the material advantages of Athens altogether. Viciously parodying Archidamos's words at Thucydides 1.83, he urges immediate action:

> Others have much money and ships and horses, but we have good allies whom we must not give up to the Athenians, nor by lawsuits and words decide the matter, as it is anything but in word that we are harmed, but render instant and powerful help. [4] And let us not be told that it is fitting for us to deliberate under injustice; long deliberation is rather fitting for those who have injustice in contemplation. [5] Vote, therefore, Lakedaimonians, for war, as the honor of Sparta demands, and neither allow the further aggrandizement of Athens nor betray our allies to ruin, but with the gods let us advance against the aggressors.
>
> Thuc. 1.86.3–5

Sthenelaidas does not deny that the Athenians have more money and ships, but he fixes his furious glance firmly upon the true source of Spartan power, the allies that Sparta can call to its side.

Sparta is not an imperial power. Its allies emphatically do not pay monetary tribute, and even Archidamos concedes that they are not inclined to do so (Thuc. 1.80.4). Sparta owed its preeminent position both to its weakness and to its power. The Spartans could project overwhelming force, but only over a brief period of time. After absorbing Messene, they were unable to subjugate any of its neighbors. Were Sparta to "lose face," the rest of the Greeks could withhold the honor and prestige that they, for the most part, freely bestowed upon Sparta. If we view the Peloponnesian League as a firmly defined political entity, Archidamos's advice is extremely cogent. A delay of two or three years would not affect the Peloponnesian League and would allow the allies to accumulate the necessities of war. But if we view "the Spartans and their allies" as a much looser aggregation, Archidamos's policy risked utter destruction, for the alliance itself could collapse. The Corinthians conclude their angry and bitter speech with an open threat:

> Here, at least, let your procrastination end. For the present, assist your allies and Poteideia in particular, as you promised, by a speedy invasion of Attika,

and do not sacrifice friends and kindred to their bitterest enemies, and drive the rest of us in despair to some other alliance. [5] Such a step would not be condemned either by the gods who received our oaths or by the men who witnessed them. The breach of a treaty cannot be laid to the people whom desertion compels to seek new relations, but to the power that fails to assist its confederate. [6] But if you will only act, we will stand by you; it would be unnatural for us to change, and never should we meet with such a congenial ally.

Thuc. 1.71.4–6

If Sparta does not do something and do it immediately, Corinth threatens to make the best deal that it can get in an alliance with some other power. The scholiast suggests that Corinth has Argos in mind, but the obvious implication is that Corinth would strike a deal of some kind with Athens.[30]

Perhaps this was an idle threat.[31] We have, however, already emphasized the importance that Corinth attached to its colonial connections. Athens had decisively eliminated Corinthian influence in Corcyra and was engaged in breaking Corinth's relationship with Poteideia. If the Corinthians viewed their status among their colonies—and the prestige that such status assured among other Greeks—as an attractive luxury that they could, of necessity, forgo, then they could well, if pressed, stand by and watch Poteideia—and their own reputation—collapse. We cannot assume that the Corinthians interpreted their "vital interests" in the deceptively modernist terms of a Thucydides. If the Corinthians saw in the traditional status of *metropolis* an end rather than a means, and a goal to which their economic and military power was subordinated rather than vice versa, if customs such as dispatching yearly magistrates to Poteideia were what defined Corinth's sense of itself as a polis, then they needed an alliance—any alliance—which could preserve this status for them. Under these circumstances, an accommodation with Athens—whatever its complications—was a desperate but logical response. Neither the Athenians nor the Spartans were, after all, going to seize the Acrocorinth. Corinth needed stability overseas, and an alliance that could not provide that stability was of little use.

---

30. Sthenelaidas may hint at such an interpretation when he argues that the Spartans have "good allies whom we must not hand over to the Athenians" (1.86.3); Ste. Croix 1972, 59–60.

31. See, for example, Pelling 1991, 125: "It is hard to believe that the Corinthians would actually go over to the Athenians, whatever else they may do"; also Kagan 1969, 292; Gomme mentions only the scholiast's suggestion of an Argive alliance; Salmon (1984, 299) simply alludes to the "threat to join a different alliance" and does not speculate about the possible new allies.

We cannot, of course, be sure to what extent Corinth meant its threat to seek a new alliance. The complicated diplomatic maneuvers after the Peace of Nikias that weakened the "Peloponnesian League" suggest that this entity was indeed fragile. But it is hard to see how Corinth could have been more emphatic in its demands or put its case more forcefully. Two or three years might help the Spartans and their allies prepare for war, but it could easily lose Poteideia. Poteideia might well be a "personal grievance" of the Corinthians, as Archidamos implies at Thucydides 1.82.5–6, but if the Corinthians conclude that the Spartan alliance cannot protect their private interests, and if the rest of the allies draw the same conclusion, then Sparta's position would be weakened.

Because the Spartans depend largely upon symbolic capital, the credit and the faith that others have in them, and because they do not have a complex bureaucracy of finance and power, they must above all else maintain the faith of their allies. We saw in the debate between Corcyra and Corinth at Athens that time was a fundamental element in this system. The good services that the Corinthians had rendered Athens years or even generations before remained as *charis* upon which the Corinthians felt that they could ultimately draw. A gift need not be immediately repaid, for the gift is a form of investment laid down against subsequent need. An insult or offence is, however, the inverse of a gift, and retribution, *timôria*, settles a negative account. In this exchange, however, there is less flexibility. A gift can luxuriate over years, firmly rooted in the minds of giver and recipient, maintaining a kind of intangible bond that ties one to the other. Retribution for an ongoing and pressing need—as with the siege of Poteideia—demands instant action if it is to have proper effect.

Sthenelaidas perfectly grasps this relationship and its fundamental bearing on Sparta's condition. Sparta will never be able to challenge the financial power of Athens because Sparta cannot forcibly appropriate as much wealth from its allies as can Athens. Archidamos's advice assumes a similarity between Athenian and Spartan power that is at best problematic. Were the Spartans to pursue the logic of Archidamos's speech, they would either fulfill the prophecy that the Athenian speakers make and risk becoming as oppressive and hated as the Athenians, or they would pursue half-measures and, worst of all, fight a war according to the terms set by the Athenians.

Both Archidamos and Sthenelaidas strike stylized poses that touch upon established aspects of the Spartan persona. Sthenelaidas does, in fact, respond to the urgency with which the Corinthians press their case.

He calls for immediate action. He brushes aside "the slowness and hesitancy" that the Corinthians condemn and Archidamos rationalizes. "At least in regard to Athens, the Spartan character has changed. A nation usually slow to move, on this occasion something has urgently driven them to decisiveness. Archidamos represents the past here, but the majority of Spartans have already arrived at a new state of mind."[32] Such a judgment is, however, only partially true. Both Archidamos and Sthenelaidas offer their own distinct syntheses, in which they seek to adapt Sparta's traditional strengths to the present situation.

Sthenelaidas's argument is, in a sense, neither old nor new. Its closest literary analogue (and perhaps a model that Thucydides had in mind) appears in the *Iliad*.[33] Feeling the absence of Achilles, the Greeks send a delegation to seek his help against their enemies. Odysseus and Phoinix deliver long, reasoned speeches (*Il.* 9.225–306, 434–605, 625–642), as do the Athenians and Archidamos. Like Odysseus in *Iliad* 9, the Athenians frame their arguments in the hard terms of self-interest. Like Phoinix, Archidamos presents the prudent council of an elder statesman. Sthenelaidas then bursts upon the stately debate in a speech that, in its bluntness and its surprising brevity, is remarkably similar to the indignant reaction of Ajax. Ajax's speech (19 lines) is one-fourth as long as that of Odysseus (82 lines) and only about one-tenth as long as that of Phoinix (172 lines). If Ajax does not bring Achilles immediately back into the war, his speech, like that of Sthenelaidas, is more effective than either of those that precede it.

Above all, Sthenelaidas and Ajax both base their arguments on the same theme: the fundamental bonds that bind human beings together. "As for Achilles," Ajax snaps, "he has rendered his great heart savage— a hard man who does not respect the friendship (*philotês*) of his companions, with which we honored him beyond others—a pitiless man!" (*Il.* 9.628–632). "Placate your heart!" he goes on. "Show respect (*aidôs*) for your home, for we from among the mass of the Greeks are under your roof. We wish to be nearest (*kêdistoi*) and dearest (*philtatoi*) to you beyond all other Achaians, as many as there may be" (9.639–642). Sthenelaidas, like Ajax, breaks through the surface of the argument.

---

32. Cogan 1981a, 32.
33. A resemblance noted elsewhere: e.g., Pelling 1991, 125; Finley (1975, 170) sees a general similarity between the Spartan assembly and Homeric debate: "My guess is that the Spartan assembly was much closer to the Homeric than to the Athenian in function and psychology. Archidamus and Sthenelaidas harangued each other before the assembled people as Agamemnon and Achilles did."

Where Ajax leaves behind Odysseus's list of material rewards and Phoinix's incomprehensible parable of Meleager, Sthenelaidas bowls over
the appeals that the Athenians and Archidamos make to expediency,
quantities of ships and wealth, and the need for cautious planning.
Sparta's personalized relationships with its allies are its strength. With
loyal allies, the Spartans can weather adversity. Without the allies, no
amount of planning or caution will help Sparta. Sthenelaidas shoulders
his way past the stately and reasoned posture of Archidamos and grasps
the essential basis for Spartan power, the loyalty of allies, a type of
motivation that preexisted and long outlived the particular Spartan mirage.

The speeches of Archidamos and Sthenelaidas reproduce different
attitudes toward Spartan authority that are already visible in Herodotus.
Archidamos most closely approaches the model of Demaratos (Hdt.
7.102, 209, 234) and the battle of Thermopylai: the Spartans define
themselves from the inside out. The Persians can kill Spartans and, with
their numerical superiority, can sooner or later crush any army the Spartans put in the field. In the end, the Persians can conceivably eliminate
all Spartan resistance, but they cannot break the Spartan will or touch
the essential character of the Spartans. Thus, according to Archidamos,
the Spartans can view conflict with Athens from a position of *ischus*,
"strength" (Thuc. 1.85.1). Neither the praise nor the blame, not even
the individual troubles, of their allies should distort their judgment. The
Spartans will not dismiss their allies (1.82.1) but will take action according to their own best plans and at the time that seems best to them.
The Spartans have the best chance of success if they hold fast to their
own understanding of the situation and to their patriarchal customs
(1.85.1). Archidamos bases his analysis on the vision of imperturbable,
serene, and self-contained power. The Greeks yield Sparta their admiration as much because of this fascinating pose—the essence of the Spartan mirage—as because of Sparta's quantitative military power.

Sthenelaidas's vision of Spartan authority, on the other hand, is much
closer to that which Herodotus sketches at 1.65–68: both are far more
sensitive than Archidamos to the contingent nature of Sparta's position
and the degree to which the Spartans depend upon the freely conferred
sanction of their fellow Greeks. Thus, as we saw in the analysis of Herodotus's account in chapter 3, Lykourgos's system has legitimacy not
simply because it had a positive impact on Spartan society, but because
the Panhellenic Greek oracle at Delphi singled out Lykourgos for approbation and established him as the lawgiver. Even Lykourgos's re-

forms—the famous Spartan system—are not alone sufficient to establish
Sparta as the preeminent power in Greece. The Spartans rise to their
dominant position only when they limit their aspirations, give up their
attempt to subjugate other Greek states, and accept the reciprocal duties
and responsibilities of patrons for the rest of the Greeks, rather than
pursuing theoretically unlimited domination such as they exercise over
the helots. Sthenelaidas concludes his harangue by urging the Spartans
first not to allow the Athenians to grow even more powerful and second
not to betray their allies.

Sthenelaidas thus develops a line of reasoning that, not surprisingly,
agrees with Thucydides' analysis at 1.23.6: the Spartans feel that they
must fight to contain Athenian power. The debate at Sparta and the
desperate Corinthian speech allow us to see more precisely what Sparta
has to fear. At the outset of the war, the Spartans "publicly announced
that they were freeing Greece" (Thuc. 2.8.4), and this official policy was
a major factor in the widespread goodwill (*eunoia*) that they enjoyed.
The Athenians had inspired rage among their subjects and fear among
those not yet under Athenian domination, and these emotions aided
Sparta.

Speaking as a Spartan among Spartans, however, Sthenelaidas demands "a double punishment" (Thuc. 1.86.1: *zêmia diplê*) for Athens
and immediate military action against them (1.86.5), but he does not
explicitly argue that the Peloponnesians will destroy Athenian power or
"free Greece" (i.e., break up the Athenian empire). Sthenelaidas does not
answer Archidamos's reasoned analysis of Athenian power, because,
strictly speaking, his goals are much more limited than those assumed
by Archidamos. Sthenelaidas argues for war, but the attack on Athens
is primarily a means to a further end, maintaining the loyalty of Sparta's
allies. Archidamos's fears about war with Athens are largely irrelevant
to Sthenelaidas. Invasions of Attika do not need to bring the Athenians
to their knees, and Athens can draw supplies from its subjects indefi-
nitely so long as the destruction in Attika satisfies the angry allies of
Sparta and keeps them loyal.

But if Sthenelaidas, as Gomme points out, "says nothing, in the Spartan assembly, about freeing Greece," we place the wrong emphasis on
this speech if we simply conclude that "only Peloponnesian interests
concern Sparta." Sthenelaidas's speech underlines Sparta's weakness and
dependence on other states, rather than Spartan cynicism (which Thucydides will explore more nastily elsewhere). Lacking the regular, administrative tools of force (such as the Athenians have in their navy),

the Spartans cannot keep allies such as Corinth loyal to them with force alone, nor is the dignity of the Spartan character enough. They must give the Corinthians concrete help to retain their loyalty. If not, Sparta risks the loss not only of a major ally, but of that reputation and trustworthiness—that symbolic capital—that holds its allies together. Crushing the Athenian empire might well be attractive to Sthenelaidas, but the goal to which he gives voice, the protection of the allies, is fundamentally defensive. So long as Sparta can maintain its own alliances intact and restrict the growth of Athenian power, then the most urgent needs expressed in Sthenelaidas's speech will be met.

The differing conceptions of Spartan power emerge from the appeals that Archidamos and Sthenelaidas make to justice. Archidamos treats with suspicion the charges (*enklêmata*) leveled by the allies, seeing in them provocations to excessive haste (Thuc. 1.82.5) that will embroil Sparta in a war from which it may not be able to extricate itself (1.82.6). At the very end of his speech, we hear that "the allies *claim* to have been wronged (*adikeisthai*)" (1.85.2). But until the Spartans know whether the Athenians will agree to some kind of terms for what they have done, it is not lawful for the Spartans to move against them "as against one who is doing wrong (*adikounta*)." Archidamos leaves the allied charges in indirect discourse. The allies may or may not have a case, but the Spartans should send embassies to the Athenians and demand some kind of satisfaction. The Spartans owe their allies diplomatic support, right or wrong, but they are not obliged to violate accepted norms of behavior and to attack Athens without first seeking a diplomatic solution.

Where Archidamos discusses both material power and the strength of Spartan character, Sthenelaidas frames his argument almost entirely in moral terms. The Athenians spent time "praising themselves" (Thuc. 1.86.1). They were good (*agathoi*) once but are now bad (*kakoi*). We, however, were the same then as we are now (86.2). We have "good allies" (86.3: *summachoi agathoi*). Above all, the Athenians are unjust, and Sthenelaidas turns five times to the verb *adikeô* (a term that Archidamos, in his much longer speech, uses just twice and both times in a single section, 1.85.2). Outrage at Athenian injustice permeates Sthenelaidas's words. Nowhere in their long-winded speech, Sthenelaidas declares, do the Athenians "deny that they are wronging (*adikousi*) our allies and the Peloponnese" (86.1). The Spartans cannot stand by as their allies "are suffering injustice" (86.2: *adikoumenous*). A few lines later, we hear again: "Let us not be told that it is fitting for us to deliberate while suffering injustice (*adikoumenous*); long deliberation is rather fit-

ting for those who intend to commit injustice (*adikein*)" (86.4). "With
the help of the gods," he concludes, "let us attack those who are com-
mitting injustice (*tous adikountas*)" (86.5). In the face of such injustice,
delay warrants contempt.

Such injustice demands instant action from the Spartans: "If we have
sôphrosunê, we will not overlook our allies, or hesitate to avenge them"
(Thuc. 1.86.2). "They must not be betrayed (*paradotea*) to the Athenians!" (86.3). "Let us not utterly betray them (*kataprodidômen*)"
(86.5). Action must be taken. "Double punishment!" (86.1). "Let us not
hesitate to inflict retribution (*timôrein*)!"(86.2). "Inflict retribution (*ti-
môrêtea*) immediately and with all possible force" (86.3). Attack now!
(86.5).

Instant action does not seem necessary to Archidamos, because Archidamos has a very different view of Sparta's position in the world.
Archidamos places great emphasis upon the peculiar character of the
Spartans and upon their ability to define themselves through their virtues. He assumes that this character provides Sparta with a certain level
of autonomy and fashions a space within which the Spartans can negotiate, play for time, resist the more extreme demands of their allies,
and pursue their goals. The Spartans, in Archidamos's eyes, ultimately
control their own destiny.

Sthenelaidas, on the other hand, has no such implicit faith in Sparta
by itself. When the allies, led by Corinth, demand action in return for
continued loyalty, there is no room for maneuver. The Spartans must
"help their friends," and it is this social necessity that makes the moral
argument cogent. In the end, Sthenelaidas argues that the Spartans must
fight because the allies are unhappy. There are no overriding principles
of justice or morality, nor any inviolable customs or procedures (such
as seeking *dikai* through negotiations). In the final analysis, the Spartans
have no control over their destiny. Their special moral qualities mean
nothing. They are creatures of circumstance. If Archidamos recalls the
proud self-possession of Solon or Kroisos as sage, Sthenelaidas acts as
if the Spartans as a whole bear out Solon's gloomy maxim: πᾶν ἐστὶ
ἄνθρωπος συμφορή , "Man is entirely a product of external circumstances" (Hdt. 1.32.4).

If Sthenelaidas's dynamism and furious energy belie Corinthian accusations of slowness and hesitancy, his strategic vision (or lack thereof)
nevertheless reinforces a more general criticism of Sparta. Archidamos
assumed that the Spartans could have an Athenian-style military while
remaining Spartan at heart. The situation, threatened by Athenian ac-

tion, should be restored to the status quo ante. Other Spartans may see things differently, but Sthenelaidas is, in his own way, as conservative as Archidamos, prizing constancy of (good) character and seeking to reproduce Greek society as it stands. Archidamos and Sthenelaidas each put their finger squarely upon problems that confront Sparta—Archidamos on the lack of modern infrastructure, Sthenelaidas on Sparta's dependence upon its allies—but each provides at best a partial vision. Neither answers the central Corinthian charge that Spartan customs are *archaiotropa*, "old-fashioned." Neither Archidamos nor Sthenelaidas offers a complete synthesis of old and new or presents a model by which Sparta can transform itself into a match for Athens without changing that essential character by which the Spartans define themselves.

ARCHIDAMOS'S VISION AND SPARTAN PRACTICE

If neither Archidamos nor Sthenelaidas articulates a satisfactory plan for Sparta, does one of the two speakers nevertheless better represent Sparta—or, at least, the Sparta that we encounter in Thucydides? More important, if each of these speakers stresses different aspects of a common Spartan self-representation, how valid does this model of Spartan character prove? A number of episodes within the *History* seem framed in such a way as to test the claims and assumptions of Archidamos and Sthenelaidas. Thucydides does not wholly reject Sparta's self-representation, but the events in his *History* and the subsequent utterances that he chooses to include qualify and constrain the Spartan model. The most famous such critique comes during the Melian Dialogue, when the Athenians correctly predict that the Spartans will not intervene and that they subordinate virtue to their own self-interest. Nevertheless, the dialectic between the pretensions of Archidamos and of Sthenelaidas and Spartan practice begins as soon as the Spartans take the field. I will concentrate upon three episodes: Archidamos's first invasion of Attika, the naval battles in the Corinthian Gulf early in the war, and the Spartan defeat at Sphakteria.

After his one page of celebrity at Thucydides 1.86, Sthenelaidas vanishes from the *History* and is never heard from again. Archidamos, however, is a major character. He leads the Peloponnesian allies on their yearly invasions of Attika in 431, 430, 429, and 428 and plays an important role in the early negotiations between Sparta and the Plataians, before he disappears from the narrative, to be replaced by his son Agis. When hostilities finally do erupt between Athens and the Peloponnesian allies in the summer of 431, Archidamos takes center stage. Thucydides introduces this section of the narrative with a "new preface," summarizing the situation at 2.7–9. At 2.10, the Peloponnesian invasion force gathers, and at 2.11 Archidamos delivers a brief speech to the chief allied officers under his command.

Archidamos's speech at Thucydides 2.11 has attracted far less attention than it deserves. H. D. Westlake, for example, dismissed Archidamos's speech as "thoroughly conventional and uninspired" and suggested that it "probably reflects the real character of Archidamos more accurately than the speech assigned to him in the first book."[34] Archidamos's remarks in book 2, however, are more than a dramatic exclamation point for the beginning of hostilities. Archidamos subtly restates and revises many of his previous assumptions and claims. His speech is remarkable both because of its similarities and its contrasts to his advice in book 1. As in the previous speech, Archidamos opens by characterizing himself as an elder statesman with experience of wars (Thuc. 2.11.1: ἡμῶν αὐτῶν οἱ πρεσβύτεροι οὐκ ἄπειροι πολέμων εἰσίν; 1.80.1: καὶ αὐτὸς πολλῶν ἤδη πολέμων ἔμπειρός εἰμι). As before, he looks even farther backward and explicitly links present actions with the standards of "our fathers" (2.11.1, 11.2), closing his speech with an appeal to ancestral tradition (2.11.9: οἱ πατέρες ἡμῶν; 1.85.1: μήτε τῶν πατέρων χείρους φαίνεσθαι). As before, he praises caution (2.11.3: μεγίστην δόξαν οἰσόμενοι τοῖς τε προγόνοις καὶ ἡμῖν αὐτοῖς; 1.84.1: ἃς οἱ πατέρες τε ἡμῖν παρέδοσαν μελέτας), emphasizes true (rather than illusory) security, *asphaleia* (2.11.3, 5, 9; 1.80.1, 84.4), and a healthy respect for the Athenians even if the Peloponnesians are more numerous (2.11.4; 1.81.1–2).

But if the Archidamos of Thucydides 2.11 has strong links to the figure that we see in 1.80–85, his attitudes are subtly but significantly different. Where Archidamos's earlier audience consisted entirely of Spartans, he now addresses the combined Peloponnesian force. In book 2, he alludes to the public reasons for the invasion: the rest of Greece has goodwill (*eunoia*) and hopes that "we will accomplish what we plan" (Thuc. 2.11.2). Where before Archidamos scorned the excitement caused by hope (expressed by the verb *epairomai*: 1.81.6, 83.3, 84.2), he now argues that the allies must not prove inferior to their forefathers or to their own reputation, "for all Hellas has been whipped into a state

34. Westlake 1968, 126.

of excitement (2.11.2: *epêrtai*, the perfect of *epairomai*) and is focusing
its attention on us." The emotionalism denoted by the verb *epairomai*—
to be avoided by Spartans—should, we now hear, be exploited and made
to serve Spartan ends when it appears among others. Archidamos has
lower expectations for those who are not his immediate countrymen and
does not to hesitate to elicit emotions that he would deplore and seek
to suppress among his fellow Spartans.

As in the first speech, Archidamos speaks repeatedly of *paraskeuê*.[35]
The Peloponnesian force has greater *paraskeuê* than any of the numerous other expeditions that have preceded it (Thuc. 2.11.1). They should
not let themselves proceed "in a state of less careful *paraskeuê*"(2.11.3:
ἀμελέστερόν τι παρεσκευασμένους) because of their great strength.
Those who are overconfident often prove to lack *paraskeuê* (2.11.4: τὸ
καταφρονοῦντας ἀπαρασκεύους γενέσθαι). Athens itself is superbly fit-
ted out with *paraskeuê* of all kinds (2.11.6: τοῖς πᾶσιν ἄριστα παρεσ-
κευασμένη), and they should expect the Athenians to fight.

The Athenians of Thucydides 2.11 have the same *paraskeuê* to which
Archidamos alludes more extensively in 1.80–81. The Peloponnesians,
however, also still possess their own peculiar *paraskeuê*, the same inappropriate power against which Archidamos had eloquently warned.
They have acquired neither the ships nor the money that would allow
them to strike at Athens's true power, its naval empire (Thuc. 1.80.4–
81.4). They march into Attika with the same massive force that they
would wield "against Peloponnesians and their neighbors" (1.80.3), a
"force that is not comparable" to that of Athens and thus cannot strike
a mortal blow. Only one year has passed since Archidamos addressed
his fellow Spartans, and the Peloponnesian force lumbers across the Isthmus on a mission that, according to his own analysis, has little hope of
success.

Given the weak prospects, Archidamos shifts his rhetoric to reflect
his lower expectations.[36] In his first speech, Archidamos had boasted
that Spartans did not depend upon the mistakes of others. They assumed
that their opponents planned well and differed from them primarily in
training. As a consequence, they did not base their expectations on the
mistakes of others (Thuc. 1.84.3–4). In book 2, however, Archidamos
sketches the following strategy:

35. Allison 1989, 55–56.
36. On this, see Pelling 1991, 126; Schwartz (1929, 135–136) felt that the inconsistency
was due to differing and unreconciled stages of composition.

We have every reason to expect that they will take the field against us, and
that if they have not set out already before we are there, they will certainly
do so when they see us in their territory wasting and destroying their
property. [7] For men are always exasperated at suffering injuries to which
they are not accustomed, and on seeing them inflicted before their very eyes,
and where least inclined for reflection (*logismos*), rush with the greatest heat
to action. [8] The Athenians are the very people of all others to do this, as
they aspire to rule the rest of the world and are more in the habit of invading
and ravaging their neighbors' territory than of seeing their own treated in
the like fashion.

Thuc. 2.11.6–8

The Peloponnesian invasion will enrage the Athenians. Accustomed
to injuring rather than being injured, and little inclined for rational reflection, the Athenians will rush out to confront the superior Peloponnesian force. The allies, Archidamos argues, will provoke the Athenians
into a terrible miscalculation.[37] In fact, Archidamos's prediction comes
very close to being fulfilled.[38] A portion of the Athenian populace reacts
exactly as Archidamos foresees (Thuc. 2.21.3). Perikles, however, observes that the people "are enraged by what lies at hand and are not
thinking very well" (2.22.1). He thus refuses to convene the assembly,
so that "they would not go out of the city and commit an error because
of anger (*orgê*) rather than planning (*gnômê*)." Perikles' parliamentary
gambit saves the Athenians. Archidamos's plan falls short—barely perhaps, but enough. Forced to lead an expedition in which he has little
confidence, he adopts a strategy that he knows is flawed. He does the
best he can, and almost succeeds; his failure illustrates perfectly the problems that he pointed out in his earlier speech. Unable to attack the true
source of Athenian power, the Peloponnesians can only hope that their
opponents will make a mistake and give them an opening. The Peloponnesian invasions never inflict a strategic defeat upon the Athenians.[39]
   At the same time, Archidamos's Spartan character is also at least
partially to blame. His troops accused him of wasting valuable time: he
delayed at the Isthmus, moved slowly when the expedition began to
march, and then wasted the most time of all investing the border fortress
of Oinoe in Attika (Thuc. 2.18.3). Archidamos had already in his first
speech justified such a restrained pace: Attika was a hostage that the

---

37. Pelling 1991, 128.
   38. For a detailed analysis of the precision with which Archidamos anticipates Athenian reactions, see Hunter 1973, 11–21, esp. 12–13. Hunter argues that Archidamos's
insights are so precise that they must have been deduced after the fact.
   39. Hanson 1983.

Peloponnesians should spare as long as possible (1.82.4; cf. 2.18.5). The delay, however, allowed the Athenians to bring in their possessions and to evacuate the countryside (2.18.4). The invasion, when it did come, was less devastating than might have been the case. Archidamos's hesitation directly reduced his prospects for goading Athens into an ill-considered and possibly catastrophic land battle.[40] Archidamos thus shrewdly manipulated his Spartan caution to play upon Athenian nerves, and, in this, he followed the course that he himself had recommended, but this same constancy weakened his "un-Spartan" assumption that the enemy would make a mistake.

Thucydides does not hide his disdain for Spartan caution. Near the end of the *History*, Thucydides describes a prime opportunity that the Peloponnesians failed to exploit:

> But here, as on so many other occasions, the Lakedaimonians proved the most convenient people in the world for the Athenians to be at war with. For being most different in regard to character (*tropos*)—the Athenians energetic (*oxeis*), the Spartans slow (*bradeis*), the former enterprising (*epicheiretai*), the latter lacking in daring (*atolmoi*)—the Spartans proved of the greatest service, especially to a maritime empire like Athens. Indeed this was shown by the Syracusans, who were most like the Athenians in character (*homoiotropoi*), and also most successful in combating them.
>
> Thuc. 8.96.5

Like Archidamos, Thucydides concludes that the Spartans were too different from the Athenians to compete effectively against them. Unlike Archidamos (and like the Corinthians at Thuc. 1.68–71), however, Thucydides locates this essential difference in the national characters, rather than the material forces, of each side. Whatever Archidamos may say, Thucydides asserts that caution weakened the Spartans.

Thucydides, however, goes farther in his critique of Spartan character. He not only denigrates the efficacy of Spartan caution, he calls into question another prized character trait. Archidamos had boasted to his fellow Spartans of the internal consistency that they shared. The Spartan general Brasidas prefaces a successful Peloponnesian action before a much greater non-Greek force with similar claims to such discipline and steadiness (Thuc. 4.126), but elsewhere Thucydides subverts this quality. The first major sea battle of the war takes place in the Gulf of Corinth, near Naupaktos. The Athenian admiral Phormio ambushes a fleet of

---

40. See Stahl 1966, 76.

transports attempting to ferry troops into Akarnania. Phormio's twenty triremes caught the Peloponnesian fleet of forty-two heavily loaded troop ships and five fast vessels and inflicted a sharp defeat, capturing twelve ships (2.83–84). The Peloponnesians collected reinforcements and assembled a fleet of seventy-seven ships, all primed for action, to oppose Phormio's fleet of twenty—a crushing advantage if the two sides were remotely equal in skill. In this dramatic situation, Thucydides includes speeches for both sides.

Concerned with the low morale of their troops, the Spartan commanders appeal to the Archidamian vision of men who, by the strength of their inherent character, impose their will upon events. For them, as for Archidamos, the Peloponnesians, with their Spartan leadership, outstrip their Athenian opponents in moral strength, and they will thus be able to win a very material victory. The Spartan commanders mention only briefly the overwhelming superiority in numbers and instead spend most of their time arguing that the superior character of the Peloponnesian force would, in the end, prevail over the superior Athenian experience in naval warfare. Mere chance (*tuchê*) and inexperience (*apeiria*) were responsible for the previous defeat (Thuc. 2.87.2):

> It was not, therefore, cowardice (*kakia*) that produced our defeat, nor ought the determination (*gnômê*) which force has not quelled, but which still has a word to say with its adversary, to lose its edge from the result of an accident; but admitting the possibility that men may fail because of chance (*tuchê*), we should know that those who are the same in their resolutions (*gnômai*) are always properly courageous, and while they remain so can never put forward inexperience (*apeiria*) as an excuse for proving cowardly (*kakoi*). [4] Nor is your inexperience (*apeiria*) so behind the enemy as you are ahead of him in daring (*tolmê*); and although the science (*epistêmê*) of your opponents would, if valor (*andreia*) accompanied it, have also the presence of mind to carry out at an emergency the lesson it has learned, yet without courage (*eupsuchia*) art (*technê*) is powerless in the face of danger. For panic (*phobos*) takes away presence of mind, and without valor (*alkê*) art (*technê*) is useless. [5] Against their superior experience (*to empeiroteron*) set your superior daring (*to tolmêroteron*), and against the fear induced by defeat the fact of your having been then unprepared (*aparaskeuoi*).
>
> Thuc. 2.87.3–5

Unlike Archidamos, the Spartan commanders disparage the moral character of their enemies. The Athenians, we hear, have more experience in naval warfare, but they are far less courageous than the Peloponnesians. Like Archidamos, the Spartan commanders locate their greatest and ultimate strengths in their own moral strength, but they go farther than Archidamos. Technical skills, they argue, can be learned, but courage cannot, and courage is a Peloponnesian strength. Where Archidamos had stressed that all people were fundamentally similar and that only education distinguished the Peloponnesians from their opponents, these Spartan commanders appropriate a traditional boast of the Greek elites. Like the Corinthians in an earlier speech to rally the Peloponnesians (Thuc. 1.121.4), they denigrate learning and stress courage as if it were an inborn quality peculiar to the Peloponnesian side. Without courage, they argue, technical skills are forgotten in the pressure of battle. The Peloponnesians should thus, by means of their firm resolution (*gnômê*) and their courage (*eupsuchia, andreia, alkê*), break the Athenians' concentration and will to fight. When all is said and done, the Peloponnesians, cool and unflappable in battle, will be able to impose their superior will upon their enemies.

The battle that follows turns the Spartan argument on its head. The Spartan commanders do what Archidamos could not previously do—they force the Athenians to meet them on their own terms. The Spartan force threatens undefended Naupaktos, and the Athenian fleet must reluctantly send their twenty fast and maneuverable ships against the seventy-seven lumbering Peloponnesians in narrow waters (Thuc. 2.90). A swift movement by the Peloponnesians cuts off almost half of the Athenian squadron, and just ten ships escape to Naupaktos, where they form up for a final defence (2.91.1). The leading squadron of the Peloponnesian fleet—the vanguard of a force that now outnumbered the Athenians seven to one—advanced to crush the remaining Athenian ships, singing a hymn to Apollo in celebration of their victory. By any rational calculation, the Peloponnesian navy was about to annihilate Athenian naval power in the west.

But in the midst of this catastrophe, the true characters of the Athenians and the Peloponnesians came into play. One Athenian ship had not yet reached Naupaktos:

> The single Athenian ship remaining was chased by a Leukadian far ahead of the rest. [3] But there happened to be a merchantman lying at anchor in the roadstead, which the Athenian ship found time to sail round, and struck the Leukadian in chase amidships and sank it.
>
> Thuc. 2.91.2–3

Faced with destruction, the Athenians had executed an unexpected maneuver and attacked, a single ship against the outrunner of a squadron. This single, bold gesture, however, overwhelms the Peloponnesian fleet:

An exploit so sudden and contrary to plan (*para logon*) produced a panic (*phobos*) among the Peloponnesians; and having fallen out of order in the excitement of victory, some of them dropped their oars and stopped their way in order to let the main body come up—an unsafe thing to do considering how near they were to the enemy's prows; while others ran aground in the shallows, in their ignorance of the localities.

Thuc. 2.91.4

The Peloponnesians succumb to the inconstancy that their leaders had attributed to the Athenians. Where the Peloponnesians had spoken confidently of the pressure of battle, a single reverse that was minor but "contrary to plan" (*para logon*) breaks their nerve and fills them with panic (*phobos*). The Peloponnesian leaders had encouraged their men by anticipating weakness among the Athenians and their allies. "Panic takes away presence of mind," they had blithely proclaimed at Thucydides 2.87.4, but, in the event, this panic grips the Peloponnesians rather than the Athenians. Their tactical formation went to pieces, and their ships became ensnarled with one another. Even the Spartan commander of the Leukadian ship, once the vessel began to sink, gave in to circumstances and killed himself (Thuc. 2.92.3).

In the end, the Athenians demonstrate that they, not the Peloponnesians, have *gnômê* and *tolmê*. The Athenians exhibit presence of mind in the worst emergencies. Where Phormio had warned them that they were at a serious disadvantage in Peloponnesian waters (Thuc. 2.89.8), nevertheless, when forced, they did not hesitate to meet the Peloponnesians. With almost half their small squadron destroyed, the remaining ships sought a defensive position and formed up again in good order. Pressed with imminent destruction, the exposed Athenian ship had brilliantly seized an opportunity, skillfully rounding the Leukadian merchantman and seizing victory. And once the ten Athenian ships, lined up in defensive formation, saw the confusion of their enemies, all of them at once seized the opportunity, attacked the Peloponnesians, captured the nearest six vessels, and rescued those of their own ships that had not been destroyed (2.92.2).

The Athenian commander Phormio presents a different and apparently more telling interpretation of Spartan courage:

As to that upon which they most rely, the fact that they feel that it is their due to be courageous (*andreioi*), they are confident here for no other reason than because, on account of their own experience (*empeiria*) in infantry warfare, they are usually successful, and they fancy that they will achieve the same in naval warfare.

Thuc. 2.89.2

Phormio then goes on to give the other side of Archidamos's moral equation its proper due:

> But this advantage will in all justice belong to us now, if to them there; as they are not superior to us in courage (*eupsuchia*), but we are each of us more confident (*thrasuteroi*), insofar as we have more experience (*empeiroteroi*) in our particular department.
>
> Thuc. 2.89.3

Phormio, like Archidamos in book 1, assumes that the Spartans and the Athenians are fundamentally similar and differ primarily in their training (cf. Thuc. 1.84.4.). The Spartan character is not a unique quality that radiates outward from the Spartans and ultimately subjects the world to their will. The Spartans are successful at the things in which they are accustomed to succeed, and their strong qualities in traditional warfare and diplomacy do not automatically support them in different circumstances. If *gnômê* is primarily for the Spartans a moral rather than an intellectual quality, resolution and firmness of purpose rather than intellectual planning and analysis,[41] this difference emerges from the assumption, seen dramatically at Thermopylai and explicated by Archidamos, that Spartans possess an emotional space within themselves that no adversity can touch. The second battle at Naupaktos exposes the limits of this self-serving pose. Confronted with unexpected and unfamiliar circumstances, the Spartans and their allies lose control of the situation. The despairing suicide of Timokrates, the Spartan captain, at Thucydides 2.92.3 is a gesture that seeks to assert this control and to place the Spartan beyond the reach of events. By the standards of Greek culture, however, such a suicide, like that of Ajax, is at best ambivalent, a gesture of weakness rather than of self-control.[42]

The *History* as a whole at best partially confirms Archidamos's boast that "we give in to disasters less than others" (Thuc. 1.84.2). Events that are "contrary to calculation" (*para logon*) cow the Spartans. The Spartans, at one point, concluded that the Mytilenean campaign had stressed Athenian resources to the limit. The Athenians chose to disabuse the Lakedaimonians of this perception, and "they made a formal demonstration (*epideixis*)" of their power, sending 100 ships off on an expedition that made landings on the Peloponnese "wherever it pleased" (3.16.1). "The Spartans, viewing an unexpected event of this magnitude

41. Edmunds 1975a.
42. On the problematic nature of suicide, see Dover 1974, 167–168.

(*polun ton paralogon*), concluded also that the people of Lesbos"
(3.16.2), who had claimed that Athens was weak (3.13.3–4), "were lying." The other Peloponnesian allies failed to appear, and the Spartans
gave up this attempt at sending an expedition to Lesbos. The Peloponnesian fleet that did set sail arrived too late (3.29). The Spartan admiral,
Alkidas, did minor damage and butchered some prisoners that he took
along the way (3.32.1), but, once Mytilene had fallen, was mainly concerned to return home safely (3.31.2).

Later in the war, Thucydides sketches the limits of Spartan character
even more clearly. When the Athenians managed to seize the island of
Kythera, just off the coast of Lakonia, as well as a strong point at Pylos,
in Messene, the Spartans found themselves exposed to a guerrilla war
"that surrounded them on all sides, a war that was swift and against
which no guard could be set" (Thuc. 4.55.1). The number and strange-
ness of these setbacks begin to break their spirit:

> They became more hesitant (*oknêroteroi*) than ever in military matters,
> finding themselves involved in a maritime struggle, which was at odds
> with the nature of their preparation (*paraskeuê*) in its current state, and
> that against Athenians, with whom an enterprise unattempted (*to mê
> epicheiroumenon*) was always looked upon as a success sacrificed. Besides
> this, their late numerous reverses of fortune (*tuchê*), coming close one
> upon another without any reason, had imposed a tremendous shock
> (*ekplêxis*) on them, and they were always afraid of a second disaster like that
> on the island and thus became even less daring (*atolmoteroi*) with regard to
> battle but fancied that they could not stir without a blunder, for, being new
> to the experience of adversity, they had lost all confidence in themselves.
>
> Thuc. 4.55.2–4

Thucydides portrays the Spartans and Athenians in the terms that the
Corinthians had used at 1.68–71. The Spartans really are excessively
hesitant (Thuc. 1.70.4) and less daring (70.3). The Athenians really do
thrive on *epicheirêsis*, putting their hand to new endeavors (70.7). Thucydides likewise recalls Archidamos's admonitions at 1.80–82: the *paraskeuê* of the Spartans is qualitatively not suited to the kind of naval
combat prosecuted by the Athenians.

But Thucydides' analysis disproves the proud boasts of Archidamos
and the Peloponnesian commanders at Naupaktos. The Spartans are not
more resilient than others in the face of misfortune. Spartan character
is not constant, and even the relative difference between Spartans and
Athenians is a dynamic factor that changes with events. The Spartan
self, painfully constructed "in the most trying conditions" (Thuc. 1.84.4:
en tois anankaiotatois), nevertheless cannot determine its own internal

state. Reverses of fortune (*tuchê*) fill Spartans with shock (*ekplêxis*). They lose their daring (*tolmê*) and become *more* hesitant (*oknêroteroi*). Archidamos boasted that Spartan calculation was immune to the emotional swings of success and failure (1.84), but, in Thucydides' *History* at any rate, external events cloud their judgment. The Spartans have no internal core of *sôphrosunê* to which they can turn when circumstances become excessively harsh.

Two specific engagements more than any other in Thucydides circumscribe Spartan moral authority in the eyes of the Greek world. The surrender of 120 surviving Spartans on the island of Sphakteria in 425 shocked the Greeks. Thucydides describes how the Athenians wore down this force with light-armed troops who could strike at the Spartans from a distance and escape at will (Thuc. 4.31–35). Finally, the Athenians surround the Spartans.

> The Lakedaimonians thus placed between two fires, and in the same dilemma, to compare small things with great, as at Thermopylai, where the defenders were cut off through the Persians getting round by the path, being now attacked in front and behind, began to give way and, overcome by the odds against them and exhausted from want of food, retreated.
>
> Thuc. 4.36.3

Once he has made explicit the similarity to Thermopylai (where the number of Spartans engaged was roughly equivalent), readers can make their own comparison in what happens next. Where the Spartans at Thermopylai chose to die and thus to purchase with their lives immense credit for Spartan moral determination, the Spartans at Sphakteria give in and surrender to save their lives (Thuc. 4.38). "Of all the events that had taken place during the war this one was the most contrary to rational expectation (*gnômê*) for the Hellenes" (4.40.1). The Hellenes had formed a moral evaluation (*êxioun*), an *axiôsis* of the Lakedaimonians, which confirmed the ideologically charged posture that Thermopylai had dramatized and Archidamos had articulated. The other Greeks were sure that the Spartans would "surrender to neither famine nor necessity but would, as they were, fight on to the extent of their abilities."

Thucydides allows us to see how the Spartans themselves could attempt to assimilate their defeat on Sphakteria to their traditional values, and, in so doing, he departs from his normal practice and relates an aphorism framed in an anecdote. Such combinations of anecdote and aphorism are common in Herodotus, and Thucydides may well have had Herodotus's treatment of Thermopylai in mind when he chose to include such a story at this point in his narrative. After describing the battle, Herodotus reports that the Spartan Dienekes "is generally agreed to have been the best (aristos)" (Hdt. 7.226.1). Dienekes does not, however, earn this distinction by his outstanding valor during the fighting—how he saved one of his fellows or cut down an exceptional number of the enemy. Rather, Dienekes distinguished himself by his skillful ability to capture Spartan character in the form and content of his language alike. A terrified local from Trachis warned him that the foreigners were so numerous that their arrows would blot out the sun. Dienekes disdained the massive numbers of the Persian army and thanked the Trachinian for his good news: "If the Medes cover up the sun, then battle against them would take place in the shade and not in the hot sun" (7.226.2). Dienekes was well known and left behind "many other similar utterances as a memorial" (7.227.1). His skill with the aphorism, the pithy distillation of moral wisdom, stylistically suits his Lakonian persona. Disdainful of numbers and mere physical power, Dienekes provided a verbal tag with which to associate the moral status to which the Spartans laid claim at Thermopylai. Dienekes' fame, in turn, captures perfectly the extent to which Spartan authority was an "artificial" construct, which the admiring Greek world assembled from the poses, grand gestures, and telling remarks of the Spartans.

In the aftermath of Sphakteria, another Spartan used a pithy remark to embody his fellow Spartans' attitude. In this case, however, the Spartan is unnamed. He is not a heroic martyr, but one of the survivors taunted for surrendering:

> Indeed people could scarcely believe that those who had surrendered were of the same stuff as the fallen; and an Athenian ally, who some time after insultingly asked one of the prisoners from the island if those that had fallen were men of honor (kaloi k' agathoi), received for answer that the "spindle" (atraktos)—that is, the arrow—would be worth a great deal if it could tell men of honor (hoi agathoi) from the rest; in allusion to the fact that the killed were those whom the stones and the arrow happened to hit.
>
> Thuc. 4.40.2

The anecdote subtly deflects the question, but the Spartan's defence has disturbing implications for Sparta as a whole. If the men who did fall in defence at Sphakteria are no better than the rest, then there are no martyrs. The Spartans who surrendered may not be worse than the other Spartans who died or who were not involved, but, by the same token, the other Spartans are not better. The surrender on Sphakteria is not an exception, but a true indication that the Spartans are not inherently the heroic, self-denying figures that the rest of the Greeks assumed.

The unnamed Spartan's response contains within it, however, a more general defence. He scornfully terms the arrows with which they had been attacked "spindles," parts of the loom and thus artifacts associated with women rather than men. In so doing, he draws upon a strain of upper-class disapproval for light-armed troops such as archers, who could from a distance attack those encased in the expensive gear of a hoplite.[43] The Spartan attempts to convert his surrender into a further statement of superiority. Those who cornered the Spartans were not, he implies, their equals, nor did they dare to meet the Spartans in an even, pitched battle. "Only a challenge (or an offence) coming from an equal in honor deserves to be taken up; in other words, for there to be a challenge, the man who receives it must consider the man who makes it worthy of making it."[44] The Spartans did not push the contest to its limit and surrender their lives, because the contest was not fought between equals. The cowardly recourse to missiles such as arrows and rocks demeaned the Athenian forces, and the Spartans, it is implied, surrendered as much from disdain as from anything else. Unable to lay down their lives in the exchange of blows from one line of hoplites to another, the Spartans give up the entire contest. Thus the unnamed Spartan attempts to convert a humiliating defeat into a moral victory that asserts Spartan status.[45]

The Spartan captive's defence was sufficiently clever to find its way into Thucydides. It did not, however, convince many Greeks. The Spartans at Thermopylai had, of course, also succumbed in the end to arrows (Hdt. 7.225) and had endured the fate that their descendants on Sphakteria pretended to disdain. Thucydides makes this general loss of prestige explicit at the point where he describes its subsequent recovery in the battle of Mantinea. Here the Spartans had entered the battle "knowing that the long training (meletê) of action was of more saving virtue than any brief verbal exhortation, though never so well delivered" (Thuc. 5.69.2). This time, however, events do not contradict Spartan confidence. They win decisively and make a strong impression on the rest of the Greek world:

> The imputations cast upon them by the Hellenes at the time, whether of cowardice (malakia) on account of the disaster in the island or of mismanagement (aboulia) and slowness (bradutês) generally, were all wiped

---

43. See, for example, Lykos's speech at Eur. HF 140–169.
44. Bourdieu 1977, 12.
45. On this anecdote, see Edmunds 1975a, 102–109.

out by this single action: fortune (*tuchê*), it was thought, might have humbled
them, but in their force of resolution (*gnômê*), the men themselves were the
same as ever.

Thuc. 5.75.3

The other Greeks revise their interpretation of Sphakteria and
Sparta's general conduct of the war in the light of Mantinea. They had
come to attribute Sparta's setback on Sphakteria to *malakia*, "softness,"
a moral weakness that affected the spirit and manifested itself in actions
such as the surrender. Similarly, their view of Spartan caution had
aligned itself with that of the Corinthians at Thucydides 1.68–71 rather
than with Archidamos. The particular success at Mantinea, in a single
stroke, reversed Greek perceptions and restored Spartan prestige. The
Greeks quickly reverted to the traditional view of Spartan character:
they concluded that Spartan *gnômê*, their force of resolution, had, in
fact, not changed. The vagaries of fortune (*tuchê*) had caused a temporary dip in Spartan fortunes.

But the Greek reassessment of Spartan behavior is, within the context
of Thucydides' narrative, oversimplified. Phormio presented a better
model when he observed that the Spartans were courageous (*andreioi*)
on land because they were traditionally successful in that element (Thuc.
2.89.2). The Athenians, conversely, exhibit more courage on sea because
they have greater experience with naval warfare (2.89.2). Spartans and
Athenians alike have an equal share in courage (*eupsuchia*), but their
different backgrounds make them courageous in different contexts. The
Greek analysis of Mantinea is, thus, only partially correct. The Spartans
had, in fact, remained "the same in their firmness of resolution," for they
remained the same formidable opponents on land as before. The Greek
analysis falls short, however, in that it does not recognize Sparta's greatest weakness, its failure to change and to adapt to the new form of
warfare that a conflict with the Athenian empire demanded.

Mantinea suggests, then, that Archidamos was at least partially correct. The Spartans had constructed a peculiar self, distilled from qualities
admired by elite Greeks in general, and this Spartan self could exert an
unflappable autonomy that resisted swings in external fortune. The
myth of Leonidas and his 300, of Spartans whose spirit cannot be
crushed, has its justification, but only within certain limits. On land,
confronting their peers in the tight hoplite formation, the Spartans were
comfortable and knew what to expect. Where past experience mapped
out the future, the Spartans were ready for either of the two possible

outcomes, victory or death, and could rely upon their firmness of will to prevent them from "giving in."

But Archidamos fails to anticipate the degree to which Spartan courage and the peculiarities of hoplite warfare are intertwined. For Archidamos, the *paraskeuê* that Sparta lacks can be measured in money and ships. Neither he nor any other Spartan commander—with the possible exception of Brasidas—appreciates the truth of the urgent Corinthian advice at Thucydides 1.68–71. Sparta must adapt its character to changing circumstances. Spartan character really is limited. The Corinthians are only partially correct when they set these limitations in a chronological framework: they argue that the Spartans are old-fashioned and that their strengths do not obtain in the modern world. Chronological development is, however, uneven. Sparta remains, from Archidamos's first invasion of Attika to Mantinea, a powerful and crushing force in the traditional hoplite warfare on land. The empire that the Athenians invented and that exists side by side with the older society of the mainland is, however, alien to Sparta. Crushing material superiority at Naupaktos cannot make up for this inappropriate mentality. Alkidas's relief squadron for Mytilene makes no bold stand but runs ignominiously before the Athenians. The Spartans trapped on Sphakteria ultimately find themselves harassed by light-armed skirmishers with whom they cannot come to grips, and worn down by an extended hunger and thirst that they would not have encountered in a furious pitched battle. Demoralized by such unexpected troubles, they surrender.

In the end, Archidamos and Sthenelaidas fasten upon complementary aspects of Sparta's power. There was nothing magic about the Spartan self. Archidamos's vision of absolute Spartan constancy falls far short of reality, but Archidamos's vision was limited in scope rather than in kind. Neither Spartan power nor Spartan character was entirely an illusion, and Spartan actions did provide, however imperfectly, a base on which the ideology of Spartan hegemony could reside—as long as Sparta did not demand too much of its allies and provided enough benefits in return. Sthenelaidas, on the other hand, was correct in insisting upon the allies. Sparta did not exist as a lump of abstract but crushing force that its possessors could direct in any direction. Sparta was, to some degree, a mirage, for Sparta could fulfill its identity as the preeminent Greek state only if the other poleis of Hellas conferred that status upon it. Sparta was, to a degree, what other states thought it was. This shared reputation (*doxa*) or moral estimate (*axiôsis*) would determine who stayed loyal to Sparta and how energetic this loyalty could be. In the end, the Spartans had to fight because their allies expected it of them, and in the end, at Mantinea, they recoup their fundamental position because they remain fundamentally the same.

What we see in Thucydides is a delicate equilibrium in which Spartan character and its manifestations on the battlefield, balanced against the Greek need for some preeminent force and corresponding fear of external control, determine the final direction and extent of Sparta's power in the Greek world. Reality and mystification are inextricably mixed in a dialectic. Archidamos and Sthenelaidas each fasten their gaze upon separate forces that, by the tension between them, circumscribe and define Sparta's position. Neither Archidamos nor Sthenelaidas truly wins the debate. The Spartans enthusiastically support Sthenelaidas and vote that the Athenians had wrongly violated the treaty—thus the deceptively blunt Sthenelaidas shrewdly provokes the gesture that the allies demand. Sparta does not, however, take immediate action—Archidamos does not invade Attika until the following summer, when the Thebans attempt to seize Plataia and precipitate action. War on behalf of the allies and against Athens is a device that successfully balances the competing forces that constituted Spartan power for another generation, until an improbable victory rendered the Spartans masters of Greece—for a time.

CHAPTER 9

The Melian Dialogue

From Herodotus's Freedom Fighters to
Thucydides' Imperialists

Thucydides' Athenian speakers systematically dismiss or actively transgress the carefully wrought ideological poses that we find constructed
for Athens in other literary texts.[1] The extreme point of Athenian *Realpolitik* in Thucydides, the Melian Dialogue is often analyzed as the
climax of a process within the *History* that begins with the blunt analysis
of the Athenian delegation at Sparta and evolves through the cool as-
sessments of Perikles' first and final speeches, and the Mytilenean debate.[2] But the context for the Melian Dialogue begins before Thucydides.
In some sense, the dialogue explores at greater length the confrontations
between the ruthless strong and the helpless weak that we considered in
chapter 3: the Homeric Achilles and Lykaon, and Hesiod's Hawk and
Nightingale. For those wishing to assess the Athenian position, these
earlier episodes are as important as the Thrasymachos of the *Republic*
and the Kallikles of the *Gorgias*. Nevertheless, for all the attention that
the Melian Dialogue has attracted, apart from general references to a
sophistic calculus of power, very little attention has been paid to the
wider cultural context in which the debate is situated.[3] How would the
Athenian and Melian remarks have sounded in the fifth century?

---

1. This is the main theme of Strasburger 1958.
2. This decline is a major theme of, among others, Euben 1990b, 167–201; Deininger
1987, 113; White 1984, 84; Strauss 1964, 192; Meiggs 1972, 388–389; Cogan 1981a,
92; Pouncey 1980, 84. Connor 1984, 151 n. 32, succinctly compares the language of Thuc.
1.76.1–2 with that of the Melian Dialogue.
3. On the sophistic background, see Deininger 1987, 123–130.

Andrewes, in reworking Gomme's commentary, comments on Thucydides 5.89:

> The Athenians here allow that justice is a usable concept between cities on the same level of power: only in the case of disproportionate power it does not apply and *never has applied, and we all know that this is so.* But the open admission is abnormal, for evidence enough remains to show that the ordinary citizen, even of a great power acting arbitrarily, preferred to think that his city's action was morally justified [italics mine].

Andrewes's remarks are complex, for they address not only Thucydides, but the general human condition. The reader is told that, as "we all know," the very strong, by some law of sociological physics, abuse the very weak. If, then, we do not accept the basic assumptions of the Melian debate, we as readers are presumably foolish.

Nevertheless, although anyone can point to countless instances of gross oppression, human behavior is far more complex than such simplistic maxims would suggest. Andrewes's casual remarks are interesting because they make explicit an assumption common to many analyses of the Melian Dialogue and because they take for granted what is in fact a conclusion.[4] His assertion of universal assent is a classic case of the phenomenon that L. Althusser termed "interpellation," a subtle appeal to an apparently universal "common sense."[5] Thucydides differs, however, from many modern readers in that his Athenians would not have been quite so successful. Leo Strauss, for example, shrewdly emphasized that the Athenians on Melos "spoke indeed behind closed doors but to hear them one would believe that all Athenians shared their views. In fact however they spoke only for a part of Athens—for modern, innovating, daring Athens whose memory barely extends beyond Salamis and Themistokles."[6] Some Athenians would certainly have reacted to Andrewes's interpellating assertion with an automatic "Yes! Its true," but a considerable (and, in my view, predominant) percentage of the Athenian population would have reacted with outrage.

---

4. See, for example, a recent and provocative contribution: Bosworth 1993. Bosworth does not browbeat his readers by asserting that any reasonable person would agree with the Athenian premises, and he does maintain some distance between his own opinions and those of Thucydides. Nevertheless, he tells his readers at the outset that the Melian Dialogue "emphasizes the delusive and destructive effects of patriotic catchwords," and the article invites its readers to accept Melian foolishness as self-evident; similarly, Connor (1984, 153) remarks that whatever we may think of the Athenians, "this does not mean that we fail to see the Melians' folly in attempting to resist the power of Athens."

5. On this, see the introduction.

6. Strauss 1964, 200.

Still, more needs to be said. If there are other perspectives, what precisely might they have been? Strauss distinguishes between these fifth-century "modernists" and the inhabitants of rural Attika, uprooted from their homes by war, but a simple dichotomy, of course, is not enough. Consider the following argument, which the Melians adduce at the very beginning of the dialogue. The Athenians have just established their hard rules of debate: they will refuse to listen to "fair words," and insist that justice is not relevant when one party is vastly more powerful than another (Thuc. 5.89). To this the Melians respond:

> As we think, at any rate, it is expedient (*chrêsimon*)—we speak as we are obliged, since you enjoin us to let right alone and talk only of interest (*to sumpheron*)—that you should not destroy what is our common protection, the privilege of being allowed in danger to invoke what is fair and right (*dikaia*), and even to profit by arguments not strictly valid if they can be got to pass current. And you are as much interested in this as any, as your fall would be a signal for the heaviest vengeance and an example for the world to meditate upon.
>
> Thuc. 5.90

Critics have argued that the Melians seek here to change the rules of debate,[7] but this judgment is not strictly true. The dangers of fortune are, of course, a major theme in Thucydides—not to mention Herodotus and much of classical Greek literature. The Melians, however, take human frailty a step farther and use it as the premise for an additional conclusion: restraint in the application of power is prudent because today's master is tomorrow's victim. The Melians thus argue that what is just and fair (in this case, leaving the Melians in peace) is also expedient. The Melians do not abandon interest but argue that justice, fairness, and interest are all interlinked—the same argument with which Plato would shape the *Republic*. The underlying idea is not, however, an invention of Plato's. Rather, Plato was attempting to give more powerful expression to a very old idea, which the Melians cite in their defence.

Consider, for example, Kroisos on the pyre—the climax of the Lydian narrative that opens and sets the tone for Herodotus's *Histories*:

> When Kyros heard from the interpreters what Kroisos said, he relented and considered that he, a human being, was burning alive another human being,

---

7. E.g., Pouncey 1980, 88–89: "They first attempt to alter the rules with some redefinition"; Bosworth 1993, 35: "Interestingly the first response of the Melians is to circumvent the rules"; the scholia on Thuc. 5.90, however, stress the connection between expediency and justice that the Melians are trying to establish.

one his equal in good fortune. In addition, he feared retribution, reflecting how there is nothing stable in human affairs. He ordered that the blazing fire be extinguished as quickly as possible, and that Kroisos and those with him be taken down, but despite their efforts they could not master the fire.

Hdt. 1.86.6

Kyros suddenly changes his mind and resolves to save Kroisos because he recognizes that he too is mortal and that he too is likely to find himself a defeated man at the mercy of his enemies. The recognition of shared human frailty was a well-known concept: Achilles turns to this concept when he accepts Priam and finally lets go of his own wrath at the end of the *Iliad*. The logic of "enlightened self-interest" was well known. "In looking out for that man I help myself," Sophokles' rather hard-boiled Oedipus cries as he resolves to ferret out the murderers of Laios (*OT* 141). The notoriously diffident Deianeira sees her high spirits at Herakles' promised return evaporate as she beholds the pitiful women Herakles captured in war: she fearfully contemplates the prospect that she might find herself in a similarly grim position someday (*Trach.* 296ff.). Nor is this simply a reflection on Deianeira's sympathetic, but perhaps naive, character. Odysseus, whether drawn attractively or not, is a type for the sophisticated man of affairs. The recognition of shared risk drives the Odysseus of Sophokles' *Ajax* to show pity for Ajax (*Aj.* 121–126) and to insist on the hero's proper burial (1332–1345).[8]

Thucydides' Melians at 5.90 point directly to a topos that Herodotus and Sophokles put in the mouths of key figures in prominent passages.[9] The Melians are thus not simply changing the subject or altering the rules of the game. They are appealing to an established—and, to all appearances, broadly appealing, then as now—convention that equated self-interest with restraint. Of course, the principle of harming one's enemies and helping one's friends was important,[10] but the forbearance of Kyros and Odysseus represented a competing perspective that Herodotus and Sophokles, both contemporaries of Thucydides, took care

---

8. The background of Thuc. 5.90 has attracted surprisingly little attention; even de Romilly (1979, 153) considers only the parallel with Odysseus in the *Ajax*.

9. The Athenians also touch obliquely upon a part of this topos: Kyros resolves to save Kroisos at least in part because Kroisos had enjoyed a comparable share of good fortune and had thus been in some sense his "equal." The Athenians reject the Melian advice on the grounds that Sparta, as an equal of Athens, would show restraint—thus assuming that the Spartans would follow a logic similar to that of Kyros.

10. Plato begins the *Republic* by confronting the idea that justice consists of helping friends and hurting enemies (331e-336a). On this principle in Sophokles, for example, see Blundell 1989.

to represent. When Thucydides' Athenians reject this argument, they are not simply pursuing a path of least resistance, mouthing self-evident platitudes of power politics. They are brushing aside an appeal to an established posture of the great. The cost is not trivial: the game is for appearances—as the Athenians stress—but these Athenians, once again, show that they have no interest in accumulating the symbolic capital of generosity and greatheartedness. For them, fear and terror are the only symbolic forces worth cultivating.

I have used Thucydides 5.90 as a fairly straightforward example of the complex relationship between the Melian Dialogue and conventional Greek ideas. Now I will focus on a particular document. Perhaps the most important parallel, possibly even the model (or antimodel), for the Melian Dialogue appears in Herodotus—whose *Histories*, we must recall, are far closer in time to Thucydides than they are to the Persian Wars. The Melian Dialogue inverts the role and rhetorical stance that Herodotus attributes to Athens when it rejects an offer of friendship from Persia, perhaps its finest moment in the *Histories*.[11] I will return to the Melian Dialogue later because this exchange brings out a fundamental weakness in Athenian power politics. First, however, it is necessary to place this crucial section of the *History* more firmly in its intellectual context.

HERODOTUS'S ATHENIANS AND THE POLITICS OF HEROISM

The Athenian reply to Mardonios has attracted far less scholarly attention than the Athenian arguments to the Melians—claims to virtue evidently have less appeal than bald assertions of ruthlessness, a phenomenon that will probably not surprise students of Thucydides. The Macedonian king Alexander quotes Mardonios quoting Xerxes with an offer of peace and friendship (Hdt. 8.140). The Athenian response (8.144) is remarkable not only for its high-minded disdain for danger and material advantage but also for its formulation of "Hellenism" as a positive value worthy of defence. Thucydides composed the Melian Dialogue in large measure to counter such flattering representations of Athens as the Athenian rejection of Xerxes' offer in Herodotus. He

11. The contrast between the two has attracted relatively little attention, as scholars have focused primarily upon Thucydides in isolation; note, however, Connor 1984, 156–157.

hoped his audience would see in the Melian Dialogue a revised—and, in some sense, purified—vision of Athenian authority. Certainly, Thucydides' speakers exhibit little interest and less patience for tired Athenian claims about the Persian Wars. The Athenians have scarcely begun their first speech in Thucydides before they concede that Athenian references to the Persian Wars have grown stale (Thuc. 1.73.2). The Melian Dialogue may, for all we know, constitute a conscious response to the Athenian posturing at Herodotus 8.140ff., but whatever their relationship, the two passages warrant close comparison, for they highlight the gulf between Athenian opposition to Xerxes (which Thucydides' Athenians mention and immediately dismiss at 5.89) and Athens's current status as *turannos polis*. First, the pious rejection of Xerxes' offer and the amoral threats to the Melians are both theatrical expositions whose primary audiences are the Greeks as a whole: in framing their remarks, the Athenians, as it were, look past Alexander and the Melians to the wider Greek world. Second, in each case, the Athenians use this public forum as an arena within which to win prestige at the expense of the Spartans. The tactics are radically different—in Herodotus, the Athenians seek to outdo the Spartans in traditional virtues; Thucydides' Athenians turn to negative tools and seek to destroy Spartan credibility—but the net effect is the same.

The Athenian answer to Alexander is, however, part of a more complex exchange. A third party, a delegation from Sparta, also participates, and the Athenians answer Alexander and the Spartans separately. In book 1 of his *History*, Thucydides informs us that the Athenian delegation that participated in the debate leading up to the Peloponnesian War was present by accident—it just happened to be in Sparta on other business when the discussion took place (Thuc. 1.72). In Herodotus, however, the Spartans sent this delegation specifically to confront Alexander, and the Athenians manipulated the situation to their advantage:

> Moreover, it so fell out for both that they made their entry at one and the same time, for the Athenians delayed and waited for them, being certain that the Spartans were going to hear that the messenger had come from the Persians for an agreement. They had heard that the Spartans would send their envoys with all speed. Therefore it was of set purpose that they did this in order that they might make their will (*gnômê*) known to the Spartans.
>
> Hdt. 8.141.2

This detail brings out the self-consciously theatrical nature of this episode. The Athenians could have answered Alexander at an earlier date, but they wanted to perform their response in front of the Spartans and thus to dramatize their constancy before a deeply engaged local audience. Furthermore, once the Spartans took part, the entire negotation became doubly open. It was no longer an, at least formally private, exchange between two parties. The exchange between Athens and Persia thus contributes to Athens and Sparta's on-going competition for prestige within the Greek world as a whole.

The Spartan response to the Persian offer combines blame and an offer, but their overall goal from beginning to end is to place Sparta in a favorable light. The Spartans never speak on their own behalf: they urge the Athenians "to do nothing rash with respect to Hellas" (Hdt. 8.142.1). Accepting the Persian offer would "not be just (*dikaion*), nor would it be an ornament (*kosmos*) for any of the Hellenes" (142.2). If Athens wishes the world to see how nobly it resists Persian blandishments, the Spartans want to cut Athens down to size: the Athenians, they charge, caused this war, "but now it weighs against all of Hellas." "Above all it is intolerable that the Athenians should become legally liable (*aitioi*) that slavery (*doulosunê*) should be brought upon the Hellenes" (142.3). According to the Spartans, the Persian offer pits Athens against all of Hellas. At the same time, the Spartans—now speaking entirely on their own behalf—generously offer to care for Athenian dependents for however long the war may last. Blame they offer as humble representatives of Greece (although the Athenians hold this blame against them). The offered gift, however, is Sparta's own. Sparta lays personal and private claim to the gratitude that it deserves and to the reputation of generosity that this gesture enhances.

The Athenians' answer to Alexander constitutes a preface to their direct answer to the Spartans, since the Spartans and, by extension, the Greek allies are Athens's primary audience. Everything that the Athenians say responds to the tone and the challenges laid down by the Spartans. To Alexander, the Athenians flatly admit that they cannot compete with Persian force, but "nevertheless, longing for freedom (*eleutheria*) we will defend ourselves as best as we can" (Hdt. 8.143.1). A long as the sun remains on its present course, they will never come to terms with the Persians (143.2), and they brusquely urge Alexander to "get out of town" lest something happen to him.

Once the Athenians have established their indomitable commitment to freedom, they turn to the Spartans and lay claim to the highest ideals. There is not enough gold or land in the entire world to make Athens side with the Persians and enslave (*katadoulôsai*) Hellas. The Spartans had focused upon the disgrace that such a surrender would incur. The Athenians choose instead to construct a positive vision of a shared Hellenic identity on behalf of which they are determined to fight:

> For there are many great reasons why we should not do this, even if we so desired: first and foremost, the burning and destruction of the cult statues (*agalmata*) and temples of our gods, whom we are constrained to avenge to the utmost rather than make pacts with the perpetrator of these things, and next the kinship of all Greeks in blood and language, and the shrines of gods and the sacrifices that we have in common, and the likeness of our way of life, to all of which it would not befit the Athenians to be false.
>
> Hdt. 8.144.2

The Athenians thus portray themselves not merely as defending Hellas against slavery, but as champions of a culture that all Greeks share and that justifies any personal sacrifice. "The Athenians portray the Persian attack as an assault on their Greek identity."[12]

Finally, they respond to the Spartan offer of assistance, adroitly demonstrating their own incomparable generosity of spirit and gaining the advantage in this exchange. They graciously acknowledge the concern (*pronoia*) that the Spartans had for them (Hdt. 8.144.3). The Athenians decline the Spartan offer, but "the *charis* has been completely filled"—that is, the Spartans will receive the full measure of *charis* for their generosity, even though the Athenians will not take up their offer. In the competitive struggle of gift exchange, this is a bold riposte that attests to Athenian generosity and power.

The limitations on such proud rhetoric become clear only a few pages later, when the Athenians and Spartans again clash publicly in this mannered struggle for prestige. Having extracted from the Athenians a promise that they would not make peace with the Persians, the Spartans make no move to defend Greece north of the Peloponnese. An Athenian delegation journeys to Sparta and harshly demands immediate action (Hdt. 8.7), but the Spartans put off any response for ten days. Even Herodotus casts doubt upon Spartan motives, suggesting that they had cynically offered Athens military support they never intended to provide (8.8.2). Only when their allies pointed out that Athenian help was still crucial did the Spartans send forces out of the Peloponnese (8.9–10).

Both parties use the episode to jockey for position. The Spartans do not simply come to the aid of their Athenian allies after Xerxes' offer of

---

12. Smith 1998. On the structure of this group of speeches and Herodotus's emphatic placement of the argument about culture, see Lang 1984.

peace has been rejected. Instead, after hesitating to act and goading the Athenians beyond endurance, they attempt to recoup their weakened position with showmanship. When they finally choose to act, the Spartans send a substantial force out before dawn, but the departure was secret and calculated to trap the exasperated Athenian envoys at Sparta:

> So Pausanias's army had marched away from Sparta; but as soon as it was day, the envoys came before the ephors, having no knowledge of the expedition, and being minded themselves too to depart each one to his own place. When they arrived, "You Spartans," they said, "remain where you are! Observe your Hyakinthia and enjoy your celebrations, leaving your allies deserted. For the wrong that you do them and for lack of allies, the Athenians will make their peace with the Persians as best they can, [2] and thereafter, insofar as we will be the King's allies, we will march with him against whatever land his men lead us. Then will you learn what the issue of this matter will be for you."
>
> Hdt. 9.11.1–2

The Spartans have manipulated their rivals with great skill. Their city in desperate straits and tormented by days of inaction, the Athenian envoys abandon their unswervingly noble posture and, in their furious indignation, threaten to side with the Persians against the Spartans.

> In response to this the ephors swore to them that they believed their army to be even now at Orestheum, marching against the "strangers," as they called the barbarians. [3] Having no knowledge of this, the envoys questioned them further as to the meaning of this and thereby learned the whole truth; they marveled at this and hastened with all speed after the army.
>
> Hdt. 9.11.2–3

The Spartans are then able to cut the rhetorical legs out from under them. When the Athenians hear that a Spartan force is already en route, they forget their accusations and determine the veracity of the report. Stunned by the event, they hurry off without a word.

It is hard to overemphasize the cleverness with which the Spartans manage in the end to outmaneuver the Athenians, or the rhetorical success that they won. Even in modern times, critics have accepted the contradiction at its face value. Those who comment on the Athenian speeches at Herodotus 8.143–144 tend either to ignore the reversal at 9.11 or to elide the events of 9.1–10 that provoke this Athenian explosion. Macan, commenting on Herodotus 8.144, could not help but see in 9.11 a bitter satire directed against Athens. For Macan, the satire was unconscious—Herodotus had simply followed two separate sources and had not recognized the inconsistency. For Charles Fornara, however, in his influential book on Herodotus, the irony is intentional and bitter: "Herodotus is indeed making the Athenians contradict themselves. Even if he had not gone so far as to underscore the irony, it is clear that the brave words of the Athenians are double-edged."[13] The change from the noble words of 8.144 to the outraged threats of 9.11 did not lack motivation, and fury against the deceitful Spartans provided at least as much cause as fear for Athens. It is hard to say whether Herodotus's account as a whole does not weigh more heavily against the shortsighted and devious Spartans than against the desperate and victimized Athenians.

But, of course, the bitterest irony comes not from the text of Herodotus but from the historical context within which Herodotus's *Histories* evolved. "Herodotus' audience," Kurt Raaflaub has remarked, could not "overlook the profound and tragic irony that it is the later *polis turannos* that is justly praised above Sparta for its decisive contribution to saving the liberty of Hellas in the historian's famous personal statement at 7.139, and that so admirably defends those very principles in refusing the advantageous offer of a separate peace by Mardonios in the winter of 480/479 (8.136–44)."[14] Or, as Fornara, puts it, "When viewed from the perspective of Herodotus and his contemporaries, Athens made peace with Persia to gain land and gold. The burned shrines were rebuilt by Pericles with imperial revenues. Those common bonds linking Greek to Greek were snapped by the outbreak of war between them. These speeches can only be taken at face value by utterly divorcing Herodotus from his milieu and by assuming that he had no conception at all of the predictable thoughts of his contemporaries. That assumption is incompatible with the essence of his technique."[15]

THUCYDIDES AND THE GRANDCHILDREN OF SALAMIS

From their speech in the Spartan assembly to Euphemos's manipulative arguments at Kamarina, Thucydides' Athenians consistently disdain the lofty rhetoric that Herodotus's Athenians direct toward Xerxes and the Spartans, but nowhere do they carry this antirhetoric farther than in the Melian Dialogue. Herodotus's picture of noble Athenians, refusing the

13. Fornara 1971b, 86.
14. Raaflaub 1987, 239–240.
15. Fornara 1971b, 86.

Persian offers with high-minded rhetoric, had impressed itself deeply upon the Greek consciousness, and Thucydides included in the Melian Dialogue the same fundamental situation and many of the same arguments. A mighty imperial power confronts a weak opponent with an offer that it cannot refuse. The confrontation assumes a meaning beyond its immediate physical consequences and evolves into a paradigm for the nature of Athens. On the one hand, arguments rest upon the overwhelming disparity in *dunamis*, the conviction that an immediate victory will only put off the inevitable defeat, the ability to yield without dishonor in such a situation, and the charge that opposition at this point is a sign not of virtue but of stupidity. On the other side stand trust in the gods, shared kinship, the importance of goodwill and of symbolic capital, and faith in the institutions that held the Greek world together and gave meaning to those who lived in it. The Athenians in both feel free to draw upon traditional morality for their argumentation.

But each point of connection leads to an inversion—a Pindarist might describe Thucydides' Athenians on Melos as the negative foil of their grandparents in Herodotus. It is as if Thucydides had chosen to endow the Melian incident with such enormous significance because the Melian Dialogue would be a simple but striking transformation of the earlier stance—another comparable massacre at Skione (Thuc. 5.32) warrants no comment at all.[16] In Herodotus, Persia attacks Athens, while in Thucydides, Athens is the superpower menacing Melos, but the arguments against resistance in both are similar:

Do not oppose overwhelming force. In Herodotus, Mardonios warns the Athenians of the inexhaustible *dunamis* at his disposal (Hdt. 8.140A.3) and that an immediate success will only bring on an invasion force many times as large. Alexander repeats this theme, declaring that "the *dunamis* of the Great King is beyond that of a human being" (8.140B.2).

There are no long-term prospects for success. Mardonios warns the Athenians: "Even if you overcome and conquer us—of which, if you are in your right minds, you can have no hope (*elpis*)—there will nevertheless come another army many times as great as this" (Hdt. 8.140A.3).

---

16. The counterexample of Skione has been cited since antiquity in connection with Melos as an example both of Athenian cruelty and of Thucydidean inconsistency (e.g., Isok. 4.122, 123.4, 5.2.2, 18.8). It is worth stressing, however, that Skione was fundamentally different from Melos: Skione was an Athenian subject state that had revolted. It is thus closer to Mytilene than to Melos.

The Athenians do not even allow for much in the way of short-term success for the Melians. They scoff at Spartan action against Athens: "Some diversion of the kind you speak of you may one day experience, only to learn, as others have done, that the Athenians never once yet withdrew from a siege for fear of any. . . . Your actual resources are too scanty, as compared with those arrayed against you, for you to come out victorious" (Thuc. 5.111.1–2).

There is no dishonor in yielding. Mardonios warns the Athenians: "Do not wish to make yourselves equal beside the King, and thereby lose your land and always be yourselves in jeopardy, but make peace. This you can most honorably (*kallista*) do, since the King is that way inclined. Remain free (*eleutheroi*), and agree to be our brothers in arms in all faith and honesty" (Hdt. 8.140A.4).

The Athenians urge the Melians: "If you plan things out with self-restraint (*sophronos*), this is not a contest about manly valor (*andragathia*) on an equal footing, with honor as the prize and shame as the penalty, but a question of self-preservation (*sôtêria*) and of not resisting those who are far stronger than you are" (Thuc. 5.101).

Opposition at this point is a sign not of virtue but of stupidity. At Herodotus 8.140A.3, Mardonios berates the Athenians: "Why are you so insane (*mainesthe*) as to wage war against the King? You cannot overcome him, nor can you resist him forever. As for the multitude of Xerxes' army, what it did, you have seen, and you have heard of the power that I now have with me. Even if you overcome and conquer us— of which, if you be in your right minds, you can have no hope (*elpis*)— there will nevertheless come another army many times as great as this."

At Thucydides 5.111.2, by contrast, the Athenians level similar charges against the Melians: "But we are struck by the fact that after saying you would consult for the safety of your country, in all this discussion you have mentioned nothing that people might trust in and think to be saved by. Your strongest arguments depend upon hope and the future, and your actual resources are too scanty, as compared with those arrayed against you, for you to come out victorious. You will therefore show great stupidity (*alogia*) of judgment (*dianoia*), unless, after allowing us to retire, you can find some counsel more prudent than this."

If the arguments for capitulation are comparable, so too are the positions of Herodotus's Athenians and Thucydides' Melians. The Melians cling to the same general beliefs as did the Athenians when they resisted the Persian offer. Both Herodotus's Athenians and Thucydides' Melians, for example, trust the gods to play an active role in human events. To Alexander, the Athenians proudly reply:

> As long as the sun holds the course by which he now goes, we will make no agreement with Xerxes. We will fight against him without ceasing, trusting in the gods and the heroes as allies for whom he had no reverence (*opis*) but burned their temples and their cult statues (*agalmata*).
>
> Hdt. 8.143.2

Twice the Melians make similar appeals to divine justice:

> You may be sure that we are as well aware as you of the difficulty of contending against your power and fortune, unless the terms be equal. But *we trust in the fortune that derives from the divine* (*hê tuchê ek tou theiou*) that we will not be defeated, since we are pious (*hosioi*) men fighting against unjust (*ou dikaioi*).
>
> Thuc. 5.104

This faith in divine intervention returns as one of the fundamental bases for the Melians' final decision:

> Our resolution, Athenians, is the same as it was at first. We will not in a moment deprive of freedom (*eleutheria*) a city that has been inhabited these 700 years; but we put our trust in the fortune derived from the divine (*ek tou theiou*) that has preserved it until now.
>
> Thuc. 5.112.2

Similarly, both Herodotus's Athenians and Thucydides' Melians place tremendous weight on the common institutions of the Greek world. For the Athenians, Hellas itself—with its shared language, kinship, and religious sanctuaries—is the object that focuses their minds (Hdt. 8.144.2). The Melians also rely upon the interlocking web of obligations and expectations of the Hellenes as a whole that, in their minds, shape the actions of particular city-states (Thuc. 5.106), but their trust focuses upon a much narrower, better-defined, and, by traditional standards, reliable institution than a general Panhellenism:

> We trust that . . . what we want in *dunamis* will be made up by the alliance of the Spartans, who are bound, if for no other reasons, to come to our aid on account of our shared kinship (*suggeneia*) at least and by reason of shame (*aischunê*). Our confidence, therefore, after all is not so utterly irrational.
>
> Thuc. 5.104

Although the Athenians had already acknowledged that it would have been natural for the Melians, as colonists of the Spartans, to have

campaigned at their side (Thuc. 5.89), they scorn any notion that the
Spartans would feel compelled to live up to any reciprocal obligations
that incur trouble or risk (5.105). The Melians do not let this argument
drop, nor do they violate the Athenian injunction (5.89) that argumentation focus upon "expediency" (*to sumpheron*) and disregard "justice"
(*to dikaion*). They insist that even if expediency alone counts, the Spartans must come to their aid or risk losing the confidence of others who
depend upon them (5.106). Another scornful Athenian reply (5.107) still
cannot quell their faith in this argument. The Melians insist that, despite
Athenian command of the seas, Spartan intervention is practicable, and,
again, they insist that they themselves are particularly valuable allies
because of "our shared kinship" (5.108: *to sungenes*). Their final points
in the dialogue as a whole turn upon practical measures that the Spartans can take on both land and sea, and presuppose Spartan willingness
to act (5.110). In the end, they decide to resist and to rely upon divine
support and "on that retribution (*timôria*) issuing from mortals and
from the Spartans" (5.112.2).

Both Herodotus's Athenians and Thucydides' Melians believe that the
overarching issue at hand touches upon their own worth. Capitulation
does not simply mean a new administrative structure and the loss of
wealth as tribute. Capitulation undermines the qualities out of which
these individuals construct their self-images. Herodotus's Athenians
boast that their "spirit" (Hdt. 8.144.1: *phronêma*) would not let them
consider the King's offer. Everything about this scene as a whole is constructed so that the Athenians can strike the loftiest pose. Likewise, the
Melians cannot bear the appearance of "worthlessness" (Thuc. 5.100:
kakotês) or "cowardice" (*deilia*).

Both Herodotus's Athenians and Thucydides' Melians place a greater
value on freedom (*eleutheria*) than on any material advantage, and even
on life itself. In Herodotus, the Athenians resist because they are passionately attached to freedom (Hdt. 8.143.1: *eleutheria*), and the Spartans equate a settlement with slavery for all the Hellenes (8.142.2). Likewise, the Melians from the start see nothing but *douleia* in capitulation
(Thuc. 5.86, 92, 100) and are determined to preserve their freedom
(5.100, 112.2).

But at this point the situations of Herodotus's Athenians and Thucydides' Melians sharply diverge. In each case, the stronger party offers
its opponent something, but the offers are very different. The Great King
promises generous material reparations and additional land as well
(Hdt. 8.140A.2). Mardonios points out that the Athenians can "reach

a settlement in most noble fashion (*kallista*)" and even remain free (*eleutheroi*) (8.140A.4). The Great King himself, Alexander argues, is willing to make concessions so that he may become "a friend to the Athenians alone among the Hellenes" (8.140B.4). The Great King and his emissaries do everything they can to embed acceptance of his authority within a dignified and even affective relationship. Xerxes works hard to help the Athenians argue that they have established a new friendship and, at worst, have accepted hegemony rather than domination. An Athenian relationship with Xerxes would, of course, be open to other, less positive interpretations, but Xerxes does everything that he can to help the Athenians justify capitulation in their own minds.

The Athenians make no such handsome offers to the Melians. From the opening of the dialogue, they repeat that the issue before the Melians is self-preservation (*sôtêria*, Thuc. 5.87, 91.2, 101, 105.4, 111.2). Melos must serve Athens or be destroyed. In conclusion, the best they can do is present the following offer:

> This, if you are well advised, you will guard against; and you will not think it dishonorable to submit to the greatest city in Hellas, when it makes you the moderate offer of becoming its tributary ally, without ceasing to enjoy the country that belongs to you; nor when you have the choice given you between war and security, will you be so blinded as to choose the worse. And it is certain that those who do not yield to their equals (*hoi isoi*), who keep terms with their superiors (*hoi kreissones*), and are moderate toward their inferiors (*hoi hêssous*), on the whole succeed best.
>
> Thuc. 5.111.4

For the Athenians, the world is a precisely hierarchical place, in which each group falls into one of three categories: equals, superiors, or inferiors. The scale is not, however, birth, mythical heritage, or even moral standing. A simple calculus of power—the lethal force that one group can project upon the other—determines rank. There are no euphemisms for the Melians, no rhetoric of friendship, no pretensions that their "freedom" will be restored or that their relationship with Athens will be a signal honor. Nothing gently mystifies the disparity in rank that would separate Athens and the Melians. The Athenians refuse to concede the Melians any but the most pitiful scraps with which to defend their self-respect.

Indeed, the Athenians, in their analysis of the Melian position, turn upside down the arguments that their grandfathers had made in 480/479—it is almost as if they are arguing against their own prior selves. They mock the Melians' claim to divine support: "When you mention

the favor (*eumeneia*) of the divine (*to theion*), we may as fairly hope for
that as yourselves; neither our pretensions nor our conduct being in any
way contrary to mortal belief about the divine (*to theion*) or practice
among the gods themselves" (Thuc. 5.105.1). According to these Athenians, gods and mortals alike conform to the general rule that the strong
dominate the weak. Power, uninhibited by moral restraints, seeks its
natural equilibrium in the divine and the mortal sphere (5.105.2).

The Athenians in Thucydides can draw upon traditional morality
when it suits them, but they skillfully manipulate the old ideas to serve
their own interests. They warn the Melians against reliance upon hope
(*elpis*), a convention of archaic Greek thought:

> You are weak and hang upon a single turn. Do not choose to suffer (*pathein*,
> from *paschô*) this nor to become like the many (*hoi polloi*), who, while still
> able to save themselves, once evident reasons for hope (*phanerai elpides*) have
> abandoned them and they are laboring, turn to hopes with no visible support
> (*hai aphaneis*), such as divination and oracles and however many other
> things, accompanied with hopes, inflict abuse.
>
> Thuc. 5.103.2

The rebuke has a sharp edge to it—the Melian representatives are,
we know (Thuc. 5.84.3), members of the local elite who have excluded
the common people from a share in the deliberation. The Melian representatives thus define themselves as the few (*oligoi*, Thucydides' term
at 5.84.3) and as superior to "the many" (*hoi polloi*). The Athenians
thus shrewdly play upon class prejudices, but they also appeal to traditional language denigrating mortal folly. Consider, for example, an
argument that appears in Pindar:

> She fell in love with what was distant—which sort of thing many (*polloi*)
> have suffered (*pathon*, from *paschô*). There is a most vain (*mataiotaton*) tribe
> among humans that dishonors what is at home and looks far away, hunting
> down empty air with hopes (*elpis*, pl.) that cannot be fulfilled.
>
> Pind. *Pyth.* 3.19–23

In both cases, *elpis* is a desire for things that are not possible, a misfortune that "many" (*polloi*) "suffer" (*pascho*). Rather than focus upon
what is at hand and obvious, they pursue "*elpides* with no visible foundation" and "look far away, hunting down empty air with their hopes."

The parallel with Pindar, however, only brings out more clearly the
harshness of the Athenian perspective. Pindar warns against those who,
dizzied by present success, let themselves become carried away. His particular exemplum is Koronis, who had slept with Apollo and conceived

the child of a god, but then gave in to her passions and slept with another mortal before she became married (24–30). The Melians, however, are not basking in good fortune. Their outrageous ambition is to maintain themselves as a small but free state. The Melians do not attempt to rise above their positions as mortals, but to preserve their status as free Greeks. The Melians want nothing more than to maintain the traditional semiautonomous status that all Greek city-states expected and that was a fundamental principle in archaic Hellas. Thus even when they turn to a traditional moral argument, the Athenians twist it in ways that transgress traditional sensibilities.

Nevertheless, for all their differences, in some ways, the Athenians in Herodotus and in Thucydides are similar. Both perceive themselves as actors in a drama performed to impress a wider audience. In Herodotus, the audience (the rest of Hellas) is implicit, but fundamental. The Athenian stance justifies, in part, their leading role after Plataia. The Melian Dialogue plays a similarly fundamental role in defining Athens's position sixty years after Plataia. Thucydides' Athenians, however, explicitly mention the gaze of the outside world. Melos has no material consequence but is crucial as a *paradeigma*: "Your hostility (*echthra*) cannot so much hurt us as your friendship (*philia*) will be an argument to our subjects of our weakness, and your hatred (*misos*) of our power (*dunamis*)" (Thuc. 5.95). The argument turns on how the other Greeks will interpret events at Melos: the Greeks will consider what is reasonable and not expect you to treat us like your own *apoikoi* or conquered rebels (5.96). The Athenians respond that the rest of the world thinks that power and terror (*dunamis* and *phobos*) alone constrain Athenian actions (5.97). The Melians warn that the Athenians will make enemies of all remaining neutral (5.98). The Athenians shrug this off: the Greeks on the mainland are free and have no reason to worry about the Melians; the islanders who are under the Athenian yoke are most likely to give in to desperation and attempt something rash (5.99). The Melians believe that the Spartans will have to come to their aid because those Hellenes who are friendly to the Spartans will otherwise deem them "people who do not warrant trust" (5.106: *apistoi*).

Similarly, different as their Athenians may be, both Herodotus and Thucydides wrote, at least in part, to illustrate a critique of the Athenians that must have been especially common in the later fifth century. We have already examined the impact that Herodotus's account—composed in the second half of the fifth century, when the Athenian empire was at its height—must have had. Even Herodotus concedes that most of his audience in the Greek world has become hostile to Athens and resents accounts that glorify even prior Athenian virtues (Hdt. 7.139.1).

Thucydides' Athenians, of course, have changed positions. No longer freedom fighters, they are now imperialists, and they thus undermine the moral authority that they won in opposing Xerxes. Thucydides even provides us with a glimpse of how Greeks in the later fifth century turned Athens's behavior against Persia against it. As Sthenelaidas observes in the debate at Sparta, "If they were good (*agathoi*) against the Mede then, but bad (*kakoi*) toward us now, they deserve double punishment for having ceased to be good (*agathoi*) and for having become bad (*kakoi*)" (Thuc. 1.86.1). Athens's noble past, now two generations old, lends to the Melian Dialogue an even more intense "profound and tragic irony" than that which readers have seen in the contrast between Herodotean Athenians and the realities of the empire.[17]

But in Thucydides' account the Athenians are arguably not the biggest losers in terms of moral standing. They are closer to the much-admired Neoptolemos than to the calculating Odysseus of Sophokles' *Philoktetes*. Neoptolemos has no qualms about using force to achieve his goals—his only objection is to deceit (*Phil.* 86–95). The Athenians may be harsh, but they are explicit in their goals, and they stand by their word. Neither can be said for the Spartans. When the Athenians deny—correctly—that the Spartans will aid their Melian colonists, the implications of their argument are subtle, but far-reaching. In Herodotus, the Athenian response to the Persians is part of an ongoing contest with the Spartans for prestige among the Greeks, and Herodotus does, I believe, poke some fun at Sparta's shifty maneuvers for prestige (Hdt. 9.11), but the Melian Dialogue is more pointed. Symbolic capital depends upon a central assumption: exchanges implicate their participants in a social relationship that endures over time. One can build up such symbolic capital only if both sides believe that a present investment, namely, a good service of some kind, will be returned in the future. Thus the Spartans and Athenians struggle to increase this capital or to demonstrate their trustworthiness. The Athenian answer to the Persians itself promulgates the idea that no danger or material reward will compel the Athenians to abandon their moral commitments to the Greek world. Faced with an unbearable combination of threat and promise, the Athenians are unmoved. The Spartans attempt to undercut the Athenian po-

17. The phrase is from Raaflaub 1987, 239–240.

sition by pointing out that the Athenians are responsible for Xerxes' invasion and by offering, as a particular gift of Sparta, aid to the Athenian dependents (Hdt. 8.142). The Athenians contrive to threaten Alexander while still parading their commitment to *charis*—they hope that Alexander, their friend and *proxenos*, should suffer nothing *acharis*, "lacking or contrary to that *charis*"that should bind them (8.143.3). The Athenians then acknowledge the generosity of the Spartans—and trump it by giving them the *charis* as a gift that they chose not to accept (8.144.3–4).

If the competition for symbolic capital shapes much of what Herodotus's Athenians say, Thucydides' Athenians devote much of their intellectual energy critiquing such intangible wealth. For these Athenians, personal feelings such as affection, loyalty, goodwill, or the quest for moral virtue operate at the margins of human behavior and are relevant only when two parties are roughly equal in strength. Should the disparity in power grow too great, then such sentimental qualities count for nothing, as relative power seeks, by universal law, its equilibrium. Spartan ties of kinship mean nothing when set beside Athenian force. The Melians simply do not matter enough for the Spartans to incur the risks involved in confronting the Athenians (Thuc. 5.105, 107, 109, 111). If the Spartans had a tremendous material advantage, they might then perceive intervention to be in their interest (5.109). Loyalty and faithfulness can, according to these Athenians, exist only within narrow tolerances imposed by external conditions. All human virtues are, in this view, contingent. All human actions, virtues, and even feelings depend upon the given situation and must give way to external circumstances.

The Athenians in Thucydides are as concerned as those in Herodotus to publicize their consistency of purpose, but Athenian consistency in Thucydides fundamentally differs from that in Herodotus. Herodotus's Athenians prove that they are masters of their actions—Xerxes can kill them all, but they will never surrender. Thucydides' Athenians wish to convey the idea that they have a cool appreciation for the calculus of power and that they will impersonally pursue the course that this logic determines. Herodotus's Athenians are reliable because they would rather die than betray Hellas and their friends. Thucydides' Athenians are predictable because they follow the logic of any given situation. In Herodotus, the Athenians develop their internal, personal qualities. In Thucydides, they point outward toward a generalized logic of human existence. The tactics differ: Herodotus's Athenians command admiration and loyalty; Thucydides' Athenians exploit fear. In both cases, however, the object is the same: to enhance their standing and to give them the greatest possible leverage in the Greek world.

Thus the Athenians do more than abandon their moral authority as defenders of Greek freedom against Persian conquest. They attack the grounds on which their previous moral authority had rested, not only rejecting the role of heroic resistance but even denying the practical existence of such a role. Even if Thucydides' Athenians were once again to become liberators, these Athenians could not deliver the speeches that we find in Herodotus 8.143–144, because they have rejected the premises on which those speeches depended. They have thus not simply exchanged roles but have redefined the rules of the game itself and rendered the old system irrelevant.

But if Thucydides' Athenians deny much, their position is far from being entirely negative. It is not strictly true to say that the Athenians assure the Melians that "the rule of law is not applicable to them."[18] The Athenians dismiss justice and conventional morality, but they put in their place a new, almost scientific law based on power and, as they insist, empirical truth. The breadth of vision is similar to that of Achilles when he confronts Lykaon in book 21 of the *Iliad (Il.* 21.54–63)—and the Athenian position is in its own way, as Brian Bosworth has most recently argued, humane (the terrified Lykaon would have been delighted to accept Athenian terms: surrender and be spared).

Even the concept of symbolic capital has not so much been abandoned as redefined. For all the talk of power politics and the concentration on force—who can deploy the most ships and men and ultimately cut the most throats—the Athenians never pretend that Melos is a materially important site. The Melians have no money, men, ships, or other tangible strength with which either to help or to hurt Athens. The Melians are important only because they have symbolic value (Thuc. 5.95). The Athenians scorn as naive any faith in human loyalty, but they take very seriously revenge and threats of force. Athens offers little in the way of friendship but seeks to represent itself as utterly reliable as an exponent of violence. The Athenians wish to conquer Melos to prove that they will always bend the weaker to their will. If the Athenians on Melos are the evil twins of their counterparts in the Persian Wars, on the one hand, and of the idealized Spartans in whom the Melians put such faith, on the other, they are the only agents in Thucydides' bleak world who

18. Bosworth 1993, 30.

base their actions on any consistent, objectified intellectual framework. Athenian domination is the mirror of archaic generosity, and the two are linked, just as the exchange of gifts is linked with its opposite, the chain of vengeance. For all that he throws away, Thucydides and his Athenians still attempt to rebuild from the old patterns. Now let us consider the limits with which they struggled and the distinctions that the historian drew between his own voice and that of his creations.

CHAPTER 10

Athenian Theses

Realism as the Modern Simplicity

We have examined the differences between Thucydides' Athenians at Melos and Herodotus's Athenians after Salamis and before Plataia. The Athenian attack upon the Melians has long been recognized as a climax of Athenian ruthlessness, and the *History* clearly invites us (e.g., Thuc. 2.65) to understand that Athens has undergone a steady moral decline throughout the war. Nevertheless, it is also important to recognize that this qualitative change reflects a quantitative intensification of trends among the Athenians. Before the war even begins, the Corinthians paint a striking picture of the insatiable energy and acquisitiveness of the Athenians (1.68–71), and as I argued in chapter 4, the debate between Corcyra and Corinth (1.31–45) serves, in part, to dramatize the degree to which Athens had drifted away from the old values inherent in aristocratic exchange and alliances.

Let us consider further the way in which the Athenians theorize their own position. We might note at the outset that the most famous remarks of the Athenians have acquired a conventional name, "the Athenian thesis." At Thucydides 1.76, in their first speech in the *History*, they argue that fear, honor, and advantage drive all people and that those who act in accordance with these values simply pursue their innate "human nature." This triad of motivations in particular deeply impressed Hobbes (who published a translation of Thucydides' *History*), and they reappear in the much-studied thirteenth chapter of *Leviathan* as "competition," "diffidence," and "glory." The Athenian thesis has attracted the attention of political theorists ever since.[1] But if the Athenian thesis has attracted support from Hobbes onward, the "realism" of Thucydides' Athenians proves deeply problematic. Thucydides offers us a real world that can be as elusive as that sketched by such recent critics of realism as Richard Ashley and James Der Derian.[2]

Harsh and disturbing as the Athenians may be at times, they nevertheless do have a positive, if rather bleak, project. The Athenians at Sparta, Perikles, Kleon, Diodotos, the Athenian commissioners at Melos, Nikias, Alkibiades, and Euphemos all, in differing ways, struggle to articulate a new framework that not only explains but in its own manner justifies domination and empire. Different as they may be, these speakers share an arresting candor that, as Herman Strasburger demonstrated,[3] stands in sharp contrast to the way in which the Athenians normally seem to have represented themselves. But if Thucydides' Athenians give up the more extravagant claims that other Athenians regularly make, they formulate a new, ostensibly more defensible, but, in some ways, far bolder position. "It is above all by the amazing frankness with which they defend the Athenian acquisition of empire that they reveal Athenian power, for only the most powerful can afford to utter the principles which they utter."[4] These Athenians seek to place themselves beyond reproach for hypocrisy—no one can charge them with actions that they do not themselves acknowledge. They ostentatiously claim to eschew any "false consciousness" by which the powerful mystify their privileges. They attempt to transcend ideology and confront what we might term "the real world."

Thucydides' Athenians shrewdly exploit this candor to balance old values with contemporary rationalism. If the brutality of the times "annihilated and laughed to scorn that ancient simplicity of which nobility so largely consists" (Thuc. 3.83.1), and if Thucydides' Athenians may abandon that ostentatious generosity that prose authors called *megalophrosunê* or *megalopsuchia*, they nevertheless lay claim to an honesty—a modern simplicity—with which no member of the Greek elite could find logical fault. Kallikles in the *Gorgias* and Thrasymachos in

1. Orwin (1994) gives a central role to the Athenian thesis: see, for example, pp. 75–86, 90–96; Johnson (1993, 3) introduces the Athenian thesis in the opening paragraph of her book and spends much of her time analyzing it; see also Strauss 1964, 171–172.
2. See Ashley 1986 and 1995; Derian 1995b.
3. Strasburger 1958.
4. Strauss 1964, 172.

the *Republic* assert that "might is right,"[5] but their values were not, as I argued in chapter 3, as innovative as some have thought. In the archaic Greek world, where the good were expected to "harm their enemies and help their friends," a clear line needed to be drawn between friends and enemies, and against such a background Athenian candor emerges as a sterling quality. Thucydides' Athenians, in an act of moral triage, salvage what they can from the old, giving up claims to generosity but retaining a strong claim to that honesty that the archaic system demanded.

Thucydides' speakers are acutely sensitive to the pitfalls of manifest hypocrisy. The Athenians at Sparta briefly state that "openly lawless pursuit of greed" excites relatively less resentment than domination mixed with the appearance of fairness (Thuc. 1.77.3). Later in the *History*, Brasidas—the one Spartan whose intelligence and far-sighted self-interest Thucydides singles out for praise—expresses the dangers that the Athenians, from their opening speech in book 1 to Euphemos in book 6, so skillfully avoid. The Spartans would not, he insists, come as liberators and then enslave the Greeks:

> This would be heavier than the rule (*archê*) of a foreign people; and we Spartans instead of receiving *charis* for our toils (*ponoi*) should, instead of honor (*timê*) or reputation (*doxa*), receive blame (*aitia*). We would show the charges with which we make war against the Athenians to be more hateful if we incurred them than if we had never made any pretensions to *aretê*. [6] It is more shameful (*aischion*) for persons of character (*axiôma*) to take what they covet by specious deceit (*apatê euprepês*) than by open violence (*bia emphanês*). The latter attacks according to its judgment of the strength that fortune has given it, and the former through plotting (*epiboulê*) an unjust (*adikos*) intelligence.
>
> Thuc. 4.86.5–6

Here Brasidas alludes to a criticism commonly leveled against the Athenians: they had come as liberators from Persia and had then exploited their position to become masters as harsh and unjust as the Persians. The Athenians at Sparta, however, make no such heroic claims to virtue. They not only acknowledge their imperial status; they even accept, at least for the sake of argument, the allied criticism that they take advantage of their position so that the law—supposedly common to all—from time to time serves their interests more than it should (Thuc. 1.77.1–3). They claim not that they are perfect, but that they could be

5. See Hornblower 1987, 185–186.

a great deal worse and that they deserve credit for the privileges of power
that they forgo.

Thucydides' Athenians have had a grim appeal for political realists
and classicists alike. They successfully defend themselves without the
traditional euphemisms and self-serving fictions with which dominant
groups—and not only in archaic Greece—so often strive to transform
their selfish interests into high-minded ideals. The Athenians' position
has historically seemed natural to many readers of Thucydides. As Eduard Schwartz put it, for example, "The Athenians defend themselves
not before Sparta but before the court of rational political thought."[6]
De Romilly, however, has been perhaps the most eloquent expositor of
the scientific Thucydides. In her eyes, Thucydides transcends the particular conditions of his age and begins to work with the unchanging truths
of the human condition. For de Romilly, Thucydides is a kind of heroic
realist and pioneering antecedent to the modern, scientific mind:

> Thucydides is here dealing with a whole line of political development which
> no longer belongs to the present and which no longer involves any choice; it
> is shown as made up of good and bad elements which are indissolubly linked
> together by the very necessity of this development. Thucydides takes note of
> this development and explains it; and, in his *impartial, theoretician's mind,*
> *the particular case brings out the general law.* This *scientific detachment,* on
> which Thucydides' impartiality is based, enables him to understand, and
> consequently to justify, without prejudice and without illusions. The defense
> of Athenian imperialism thus rests upon *a profoundly realistic attitude.* And,
> at the same time, as the analysis rises to consider the very nature of Athenian
> imperialism as a particular experience given to the scientist to study, so the
> philosophical ideas begin to appear. *Realism becomes a moral attitude,* and,
> as the facts stand out in their eternal essence, we begin to see, beyond the
> individual whose acts are described, the *naked principles of justice and force.*[7]

This is an excellent representation of Thucydides and a brilliant exposition of the traditional humanist, who shares with a kindred intellect
of the past a common view. As Thucydides' "analysis rises to consider
the very nature of Athenian imperialism," de Romilly rises to appreciate
Thucydides.

Much of the best Thucydidean scholarship in the past century has
constituted a reaction against the idea of a detached Thucydides. Almost
all readers now acknowledge that the dispassionate language of Thucydides constitutes a self-conscious, minimalist style designed to bring

6. Schwartz 1929, 106.
7. De Romilly 1963, 272 (italics mine).

out the pathos of events. Connor has perhaps been the most prominent
exponent of this view, but he has hardly been alone.[8] But if Connor has
argued that "objectivity was for Thucydides not a principle or a goal
but an authorial stance, a device, a mode by which the author presented
himself to the reader,"[9] he has also taken for granted a crucial Athenian
assumption. Thus he contrasts the "old-fashioned and rather naive
ideas" of the Melians with the Athenian dialogue as "the culmination
of the hard-headed realism so often encountered in Athenian argumentation."[10] Whatever the morality of the Athenian position, they have a
more sophisticated view of events.

Certainly, in this, Connor aptly describes a motivation that drives
Thucydides' Athenians. They attempt to rise above the ideology, and to
see the world "as it really is." The Athenians brush mere verbal constructs aside and base their worldview not on some ludicrous self-serving
morality tale, but on the objective reality to which all humans are equally
subject. For them, power is neither good nor bad, but an end that they
feel compelled to pursue.[11] They do not abandon so much as transcend
the morality of the archaic world. In their cool appraisal of the situation,
they lay claim to the higher moral position of the nineteenth-century
scientist, the neoclassical economist, or the old-fashioned Marxist revolutionary. They are, in a sense, Plato's parents, already groping for
some position from which an absolute truth is visible.

But, of course, objectivity as a goal has proven a good deal less
compelling than it was even a generation ago. The reaction against the
objective Thucydides has tended to focus upon the compassion and
emotion that Thucydides' text, with its disingenuous appearance of
neutrality, evokes in so many of its readers.[12] The issue before us is
not, however, whether Thucydides is objective, but whether his Athenians have somehow attained a higher level of understanding that frees

8. The most famous statement of this position is Connor 1977a; cf. Hunter 1973;
Hornblower (1987, 196) argues that Thucydides practices so effectively on our emotions
because the mask of objectivity so rarely slips; see also Walker 1993; note as well Connor
1984, 4ff., for a useful discussion of how the old "scientific" historian affected scholarship
in the 1950s.

9. Connor 1984, 6.

10. Connor 1984, 153.

11. Erbse 1989, 106: "Power is not only a relative, but also a neutral quantity (*Größe*):
it can accomplish good and deal out bad, depending upon the attitude with which one
unleashes it."

12. E.g., Connor 1977a; Badian (1990, 47–48) emphasizes that this vision of Thucydides' work as "highly personal and committed" was present in earlier twentieth-century
criticism.

them from the self-serving rhetoric and the half-truths to which their adversaries are prone.

Ideology is not, however, a fog that prevents us from gaining unmediated access to the "real world." Events simply cannot "speak for themselves," because the reporters inevitably select—and thus give shape to—their material.[13] Many have commented on the irony that Athens, the progressive sea power, should have lost and that the obsolescent Sparta should emerge as victor, but the Athenian intellectual adventure is perhaps even more bitter. Thucydides' Athenians give up all of their claims to virtue and traditional morality in return for a purer, unassailable position. The single greatest Athenian virtue is that they reject cheap, self-serving rhetoric. The irony is that they do not, of course, escape ideology. They simply replace one ideology with another. As Althusser has argued, ideologies may come and go, but ideology itself has no history. Ideology has no outside. If we argue that they have escaped ideology and that we have finally and fully perceived the world as it really is, then we have, in effect, constructed a new ideological position.

We will begin by articulating the model that the Athenians sketch in their problematic speech at Sparta in book 1. Harsh and disturbing as their remarks may be, they nevertheless represent a serious intellectual attempt to understand the position of domination in human affairs. For Thucydides' Athenians, as for Thucydides himself, domination is an inevitable part of a universal condition. Suggestions to the contrary are, for the Athenians, idle propaganda and merit contempt. Nevertheless, Thucydides' Athenians do not simply give in to the unrestrained hunger for power. They seek to establish a space within which limited but tangible moral behavior is possible. Turning archaic Greek morality on its head, they argue that they, as masters, are models of moderation and that those who seek freedom from human domination are deluded, carried away by their excessive good fortune.

There are further problems with the Athenian position to explore here. Both Euphemos's speech at Kamarina and the Athenian argument with the Melians demonstrate the limits of rational self-interest: they indicate in each case, but from opposite positions, that although human behavior may always be in some sense rational, there is often more than one rational response to a given situation. In this, the rationalizing Athe-

13. Although this remains a goal for many ancient historians: see, for example, Badian 1990, 47; Fornara and Samons 1991, xvii; the boldest exploration of such selectivity and its possible operation in Thucydides remains Hunter 1973.

nians, the first fully developed political realists in surviving European tradition, dramatize the ambiguities of that faith in fundamental human rationality with which their successors wrestle to this day. Thucydides' Athenians argue, first, that each party pursues its best interest and, second, that the strong dominate the weak, but neither assumption in practice proves to be valid. Self-interest is—as the Herodotean Kroisos had already observed—ambiguous. The powerful take risks that even they should recognize as foolhardy, and the weak do not always give way to the strong.

The Melian Dialogue is a complex document with many intertwined themes, but at least one major point, I believe, deserves more attention than it has received. The Athenians must kill the Melians because the Melians are living proof that the rule of the strong is not universal law. Force can kill, but it cannot dominate over the long term. Domination requires complicity between ruler and ruled, for the ruled can almost always, in the final analysis, evade domination through suicidal resistance. Thucydides never makes it quite clear whether we are to view the Melians as fools or tragic heroes,[14] but his Melians are important for a very different reason. The Melians prove that all human beings do not accept the calculus of power, and the Athenians, I argue, annihilate the Melians as a corrupt scientist might destroy a troubling experiment. But if the Melians are liquidated, their resistance and refusal to accept Athens's logic remain inscribed in Thucydides' "possession for all time."

THE ATHENIANS AT SPARTA: OLD VICTORIES, NEW LESSONS

Consider the first speech that Thucydides attributes to his Athenians. The scene is a congress of the Peloponnesian League at Sparta. A furious Corinthian delegation has just demanded immediate action against Athens from Sparta and its allies. The Corinthians show themselves to be deeply enraged, and they demand war in the most stinging possible terms. Thucydides makes it clear that the Athenians do not want war with Sparta—they choose to speak, "thinking that the Spartans would as a result of their arguments be more inclined toward inaction than toward war" (Thuc. 1.72.1). The anonymous delegates are in an ideal

14. For "rationality" as a common assumption among political realists, see chapter 2.

position to make an Athenian case for peace and to capitalize on the aggressive, scornful remarks of the Corinthians. A discreetly flattering speech (such as that which the Spartans at 4.17–20 in fact make to the Athenians) might have been ideal.

But the Athenians are not flattering. They are not even discreet. Almost all of those who have commented upon the Athenian speech have remarked on its harsh tone. The Athenian speakers exhibit "aggressiveness" and are "tactless."[15] "The effect is a devastating portrayal of the Athenians as self-confident to the point of arrogance, immune to pressure, certain that they were in control of everything."[16] "Provocative" is a favorite term in analyses of this speech. "The difficulty of their speech (besides the lack of any reference to it by Archidamos) lies in its tenor. Taken by itself it would seem to have been purposely provocative. . . . One would have expected the Spartans to have been sooner stirred to anger by the provocative irony of the Athenians than to shame by the *psogos* [blame] of the Corinthians."[17] "The most difficult problem of all has been to decide on the purpose of the speech, for it has seemed to many to be deliberately provocative and calculated to bring on the war, yet Thucydides clearly believed the contrary to be true."[18] "The speech was provocative to the Spartans, but it was not meant by the Athenians to be provocative."[19]

Complex and problematic as their speech may be, the Athenians at Sparta have also attracted their share of admiration. A. E. Raubitschek saw in this Athenian speech "a moral justification of Athenian Democracy. A comparison of the Athenian speech at Sparta with the speeches of the Athenian generals at Melos and of Euphemus at Kamarina shows clearly the difference between the cynicism of an Alkibiades and the idealism of a Pericles. This means that we possess in the speech of the Athenians at Sparta an authentic statement on the glory and virtue of the Athenian Empire in the days of Pericles."[20] Recently, Hartmut Erbse has argued that this speech lays the moral groundwork for the Funeral Oration: "The clever linking of power and justice gave to the Athenians

15. Hornblower 1987, 55; Hornblower takes issue with interpretations based on this tactlessness, but not with the tactlessness itself.
16. Cogan 1981a, 28.
17. Gomme 1945, 1: 253–254.
18. Kagan 1969, 294–295
19. Raubitschek 1973, 48.
20. Raubitschek 1973, 48.

of the Periklean age the right in their own eyes to feel that they were the
'school of Hellas' (cf. 2.41.1: *tês Hellados paideusis*) and to point to
their own laws as exemplary (2.37.1)."[21] But although such judgments
capture much of the spirit of this speech, they blunt the sharp edge of
its reasoning. These Athenians appropriate to themselves certain traditional positions even as they subvert the basic assumptions out of which
these positions evolved. In a few brief paragraphs, the Athenians present
an analysis of human behavior that renders impossible the kind of limited, euphemized hegemony that the majority of Greek states were traditionally willing to accept.[22]

Two complementary strategies shape the Athenian argument. First,
the style the Athenians adopt subtly reinforces their overt message: the
Athenians are bluff, even tactless, but they thus affect an ingenuous pose.
Because they obviously do not aim to please, they invite an added measure of credence. Second, the Athenians argue that their city is indeed
powerful and that its strength is no self-serving illusion or fragile cloud
of mystifications. Their emphasis upon strength and Athens's ability to
assert control over the external world inverts the normative analysis of
Spartan power that Herodotus offered in the opening of his *Histories*.
Herodotus pointedly structures his account to show that Lykourgos's
reforms were not, in themselves, sufficient to make Sparta the preeminent power in Greece. The sanction of Delphi, the limitations on Spartan
ambitions, and the associated complicity of the rest of the Greek world
were all essential to Sparta's position, because this position rested as
much upon the tacit consent of other Greek states as it did upon Spartan
power. Thucydides' Athenians, by contrast, may depend upon their allies
for strength, but they have allies and empire because of their unique
character—their empire is an effect rather than a cause. The Athenians
thus differ from Herodotus's Spartans even as they anticipate the Spartans of Xenophon, whose power and prestige radiate outward from their

21. Erbse 1989, 112.
22. Connor (1984, 37) suggests that "up to this point the analysis has been based
almost entirely on the quantifiable factors of—above all, ships and money." For him, the
four speeches at Sparta contrast with what follows, explicating the "less tangible considerations, the morale and the determination of the belligerents." I would suggest that there
is less contrast than synthesis: Thucydides allows us to see the complex symbiotic relationship between determination and the material attributes of power. For Thucydides'
speakers (including Sthenelaidas who recognizes the importance of Sparta's allies), moral
considerations are only important insofar as they affect the ability to project physical
power.

dynamic way of life. Herodotus's Sparta required the guidance of Delphi to establish itself.[23] Athens defied the Persians, both alone at Marathon and in partnership with the other Greeks during Xerxes' invasion. Thucydides' Athenians thus methodically ignore the assumptions that Herodotus so carefully worked into his introduction of Sparta.[24]

The Athenians open their speech with a curt statement that the Peloponnesians have no jurisdiction over them (Thuc. 1.73.1). The Athenians assert that they are not speaking in their own defence, but seek only to prevent the Spartans from acting too hastily. This argument reappears at the conclusion of the speech (1.78) and plays to the caution that the Corinthians have just vilified (1.68–71, esp. 70) and that Archidamos would in the following speech defend (1.80–86, esp. 84). The Athenians proceed to introduce the praise of their city in particularly confrontational language:

> The story shall be told less as a *paraitêsis* than as a testimony and demonstration about the kind of polis with which this contest of yours shall take place if you do not plan well.
>
> Thuc. 1.73.3

This is a harsh statement, because it frames the situation in extreme terms, leaves no doubt that the Athenians resent the discussion, and brusquely suggests that Sparta should back off. The term *paraitêsis* means "request," but it is quite a strong word: people seek a *paraitêsis* only from someone who has them at their mercy.[25] If the Athenians were offering a *paraitêsis*, such a role would imply a position of powerlessness—as if they had been called on the carpet by their Peloponnesian masters. More diplomatic speakers might have stressed the at least titular friendship between Athenians and Peloponnesians and sought to maintain the fiction of amicable relations. These Athenians instead shift directly from confrontational remarks about their supposed weakness to threats. The Persian Wars are proof that Athens is a formidable city. A struggle between Athens and Sparta could take place only if the Spartans do not properly analyze this evidence and thus "do not plan well."

---

23. On the representations of Spartan power in Herodotus and Xenophon, see chapter 3 above.

24. For the strain that Athenian power placed upon Sparta, see chapter 8.

25. See, for example, the use of the verb at Thuc. 5.63.3, where Agis begs to avoid a harsh penalty from his enraged countrymen; see also Hdt. 1.24.2, 3 (Arion begs for concessions before his shipmates cast him overboard), 1.90.2, 3 (Kroisos begs a favor of Kyros), etc.

Even when the Athenians locate in the Persian Wars the ultimate paradigm of Athenian worth (Thuc. 1.73.2), they affect a no-nonsense tone. Conventional as references to Marathon and Salamis may have been, Thucydides' Athenians elsewhere pass quickly over, or even mock, such boasts (5.89, 6.83.2). Even at Sparta, when they expand upon this theme at greater length than anywhere else in the *History*, they cannot help apologizing for what they admit to be a hackneyed claim: "As for the Persian Wars and all the things that you yourselves already know, even though we ourselves are sick of dragging it out, nevertheless it is necessary to discuss them again" (1.73). After almost fifty years, everyone in Greece must have been tired of hearing the Athenians praise their own valor at Marathon and Salamis. Bluntness is one of the features that defines Athenian rhetoric in Thucydides, and the Athenians open this section by admitting the groans, spoken or silent, that this well-worn argument would provoke.

But such bluntness is, of course, a studied pose, for in wielding it the speaker implicitly claims a certain honesty and invites trust. If we are so tactless and confrontational, the Athenians thus suggest, then surely you can take our arguments at face value. In fact, Athenian candor can, as I will argue in discussing the speech of Euphemos, be profoundly deceptive. The Athenians are most subtly manipulative when they acknowledge moral complaints against them and claim that they have nothing to hide. In book 1, the Athenians imply that they are straightforward even as they give the old argument a nontraditional slant.

The Athenians quickly move on to their second and main thesis: their city is "worthy of consideration" (*axia logou*). But although many scholars have expressed surprise at the tone of the speech, virtually none have remarked upon its perhaps even more unconventional argument. Athenian self-praise may have been common enough, and the Athenians clearly loved to dilate upon their successes against the Persians, but Thucydides' Athenians trample upon conventions as heavily as Aeschylus' Agamemnon does upon propriety when he steps out onto his purple robe. They affect to direct against themselves a mixture of "realism" and the same gruffness that they directed against Sparta. From the very start of this speech, the Athenians have as little interest in "fine words" as their counterparts who bar such arguments from the Melian Dialogue (Thuc. 5.89). These Athenians attribute their valor in the Persian Wars to advantage rather than to any more glorious ideal. "When we took action," they continue at 1.73.2, "risks were run for advantage (*ôphe-*

lia)." Since the Athenians took part with the Spartans in "the actual work" (*to ergon*) and since their actions "were of some advantage" (*ei ti ôphelei*), they deserve part of the "verbal reputation" (*logos*). Thucydides' speakers subordinate language to the "real world" of *erga* and tangible advantage.

The Athenians continue pointing to past *ôphelia* with one hand while they shake their rhetorical fist with the other. They defeated the Persians at Marathon (Thuc. 1.73.4), but, more important, they played the pivotal central role at Salamis, which, they argue, was the decisive battle of the war (1.73.4–5). In elaborating on their contributions (1.74.1), they expand upon the theme of *ôphelia*, "concrete advantage," and boast that they provided "the three most advantageous things" (*ôphelimôtata*) for the victory: the greatest number of ships, the most intelligent (*sunetôtatos*) leader, and the most unhesitating enthusiasm (*prothumia aoknotatê*). They adduce these factors to support their general argument: "We declare that you have not provided greater advantage (*ôphelêsai*) to us than you have yourselves encountered." The material power, cleverness, and aggressive courage of the Athenians are important because they are profitable.

But this sleight of hand between debts of the past and threats for the immediate future distracts our attention from a fundamental omission. De Romilly, for example, found the measured self-praise of the Athenians so compelling and so close to her own taste that she did not realize that Thucydides' Athenians fundamentally transform their self-eulogy. In Thucydides, the Persian Wars are not relevant because the Athenians showed themselves to be, like the Spartans, masters of complex aristocratic values, which combine both symbolism with martial prowess. The Persian Wars are important because they are past proof of permanent Athenian valor. Sparta should avoid war because previous experience shows that Athens would be a formidable opponent. But by insisting that the war was fought for *ôphelia*, material advantage, they lay an at best limited claim to "moral superiority." They do not represent their formidable performance as a heroic or grand gesture.[26]

The Athenian rejection of fair words conforms so closely to the con-

---

26. De Romilly (1963, 244–250) cannot praise this speech too highly: e.g., "It represents everything which a sympathetic view can accord to Athens, but nothing that goes beyond this. . . . When the Athenians describe the service which they rendered to the whole of Greece, they are clearly doing nothing more than stating the truth" (p. 246).

ventions of political realism that it is hard to appreciate how daring their approach is.[27] Thucydides' Athenians are bold in their restraint. The conventional claims that they do not make speak loudly by their absence. I have already discussed the extreme and perhaps pointed contrast between the Athenian response to Persian overtures for peace (Hdt. 8.143–144)—with its devotion to an idealized Hellas—and the Athenian arguments in the Melian Dialogue, but the contrast with Herodotus's Athenians is already strong in this, the first Athenian speech in Thucydides. In answering Xerxes, the Athenians speak boldly and without reserve, asserting that they will never make peace with Xerxes and that they will trust in the aid of their gods and heroes (Hdt. 8.143.2). The reply that Herodotus's Athenians direct to the Spartans contrasts sharply with the words of their grandchildren in Thucydides:

> It was most human (*anthrôpeion*) that the Spartans should fear our making an agreement with the barbarian. We think that it is an ignoble thing to be afraid, especially since we know the Athenian temper to be such that there is nowhere on earth such store of gold or such territory of surpassing fairness and excellence that the gift of it should prevail upon us to take the Persian part and enslave Hellas.
>
> Hdt. 8.144.1

The appeal to what is human anticipates a major theme in the Athenian speech at Sparta, but the Athenian defence at Sparta reverses the main thrust of the Herodotean passage. In Thucydides, the Athenians declare that all actors in the Persian Wars simply pursued *ôphelia*. In Herodotus, they grandly reject material reward as a motivation. In Thucydides, money—the accumulated silver of the empire—is the Athenian trump card, and even the Spartan king Archidamos stresses its importance. The "Athenian temper" is restlessly acquisitive. In Herodotus, that very Athenian spirit—Athenian *phronêma*—makes the Athenians dismiss the value of any material reward, be it precious metals or land, when compared with the freedom of Hellas. Herodotus's Athenians are willing to lay down their lives to the last person in order to defend the shared customs, sanctuaries, and language that define the Greeks as a people (Hdt. 8.144.2–3). Greek culture is treated as a thing—"reified"

---

27. Virtually no one has considered how unconventional this argument based on advantage really is; those few who even cite it generally take it for granted: e.g., Pouncey 1980, 62–63; Cogan (1981a, 25), however, stresses another neglected oddity of the Athenian speech, the fact that the Athenians do not respond to particular grievances but produce instead a model of empire in general; likewise Ste. Croix 1972, 13.

in the jargon of academia—and this invention is so real that it becomes more important than gold, land, or even human life. For Thucydides' Athenians, the balance has shifted entirely. The concepts embedded solely in *logoi* mean nothing when set beside tangible *erga*. Culture in Thucydides is almost an epiphenomenon: interesting, attractive, but wholly secondary to harsh material considerations.

Thucydides' Athenians do indeed boast at 1.75.1 of their "energy (*prothumia*) and the intelligence of [their] planning (*gnômês sunesis*)" during the Persian Wars, but they carefully justify this value in utilitarian terms. The term *prothumia* regularly designates eagerness and energy in war,[28] but the combination of *prothumia* and intelligence does not constitute a bold claim to "moral superiority," and these Athenians self-consciously abstain from more presumptuous terms. They tie their boasts to tangible phenomena, as if, paradoxically, their greatest fear were ridicule.

Even in Thucydides, of course, all speakers are not indifferent to moral virtue. The Corinthians and Corcyraeans argue about *aretê* (Thuc. 1.33.2, 37.2, 37.5), the Mytileneans fret about their own perceived lack of *aretê* (3.10), and the Spartans speak loftily of *aretê* when they offer peace (4.19.2, 3).[29] In one crucial section of Thucydides, *aretê* is a dominant motif: Perikles' Funeral Oration, in its own peculiarly Thucydidean fashion, presents an idealized Athens. The term *aretê* defines the excellence of those who died for their city—thus those who fell at Marathon were buried on the spot because they exhibited such transcendent *aretê* (2.34.5). It is quite fair to say that the *aretê* of the dead is the explicit theme that dominates and shapes Perikles' remarks. Twelve times in this one speech, Perikles points to *aretê*[30]—of the total of forty-three instances of this word in Thucydides' text, more than one-fourth occur in this one brief passage.

The Athenian speech at Sparta belonged to a very different genre than the Funeral Oration at Athens—the first was part of an actual political debate, while the second belonged to a more literary genre of oratory in which abstractions and high-flown rhetoric were expected. Nevertheless, the two passages are, in fact, connected, for it is the Athenians at Sparta who deliver the praise of Athenian valor against the Persians that by

---

28. E.g., Thuc. 1.118.2, 2.71.3, 3.56.5 (where Crawley translates it "patriotism"), etc.
29. See chapters 4, 7, and 8.
30. Thuc. 2.35.1,. 2.36.1, 2.37.1, 2.40.4 (twice), 2.42.2 (twice), 2.43.1, 2.45.1, 2.45.2 (twice), 2.46.1.

convention belongs to the Funeral Oration. Each year, someone was chosen to eulogize Athens's war dead, and the few surviving examples indicate that such speeches followed a conventional outline.[31] Many scholars have observed that Thucydides' Funeral Oration leaves out the Persian Wars (a favorite topic of this ritualized speech), because the Athenians had, as it were, already given this part of the funeral oration when they discussed the Persian Wars at Thucydides 1.73–74. Thucydides thus distributes the usual topics into two places and, in a sense, maintains the integrity of the funeral oration by including the Persian Wars at an earlier stage of his text as a whole.

Nevertheless, the Athenians at Sparta are a far cry from the idealizing Perikles of the Funeral Oration, and in putting the Persian Wars in the mouth of the one rather than the other, Thucydides has done more than change speakers. The Persian Wars should be a clarion instance of Athenian *aretê*, and thus a demonstration that Athens adhered closely to that shifting combination of courage, generosity, and vainglory that we find in such works as Euripides' suppliant plays. In Aristophanes' *Clouds*, the "Just Argument" declares (*Nub.* 986) that his values had educated the Marathonomachai, "Marathon Fighters," and these old-fashioned virtues, associated with the earlier Athens, oppose the "Unjust Argument," whose harsh, amoral arguments come close to the tone of the Athenians at Sparta. In the *Knights*, the idealized Demos is restored to the genteel condition that he enjoyed in the days of Aristides and Miltiades (*Eq.* 1325).

In the surviving funeral orations, the rhetoric is consistent, and it is easy to see how even the speakers could find the praise tiresome. The funeral oration of Lysias, to take one example, laboriously used history to prove that Athenians were *andres agathoi*, "real men, and good ones too" (Lys. 2.8). At Marathon, the Athenians had shown their *aretê* as they struggled against tens of thousands of Persians "on behalf of all Greece" (2.20). Because they were *andres agathoi*, they preferred *aretê* to personal safety and fought at Marathon (2.25). Salamis had demonstrated the *aretê* of the Athenians when they defended Greek freedom (2.41, 43). Likewise, in Plato's *Menexenus*, the Persian Wars are a paradigm of Athenian *aretê* (*Menex.* 239d, 240d). The Persians had already enslaved a great part of the Greek world and wished to conquer the rest,

---

31. For this, Loraux 1986a has become the standard work, but Ziolkowski 1981 remains a more succinct and accessible introduction to the main points.

but the Athenians valued Greek freedom more than their own lives (240e). Demosthenes passes more quickly over the Persian Wars, but he is careful to praise the Athenians' *aretê*, nobility (*eugeneia*), and defence of freedom (Dem. 60.12). Marathon, above all, is the paradigmatic proof of Athenian heroism.[32]

By contrast, Thucydides' Athenians not only disdain to posture about Athenian *aretê* but base no moral claims on the Persian Wars—insofar as they lay claim to justice, they do so in the second half of the speech. In the first speech of the debate (Thuc. 1.69.1), the Corinthians accuse the Spartans of standing by after the Persian Wars while Athens enslaved the Greeks and stripped them of freedom (*eleutheria*). The Athenians do not rebut this—they do not even refer to their claim to have helped liberate Greece, and no form of the word "freedom" even appears in their speech. In the final segment of the debate, Sthenelaidas builds his case around what *agathoi*, "good men," should and should not do (1.86.1, 2, 3). The Athenians have nothing to say about what is or is not *agathos*. Thucydides' Athenians dutifully touch upon the basic facts of the case—Marathon and Salamis, the Persian threat and Athenian contribution—but the spirit with which they portray these events could not be farther from that which we find in Herodotus, the funeral orations, or Aristophanes.

Thucydides' Athenians thus use history first and foremost to advertise their abiding power. The Persian Wars are important only because of what they reveal about Athenian character, but Athenian character is important only because it explains Athenian strength, and this Athenian strength should deter Spartan action:[33] the Athenians still have the largest navy, and even the Corinthians, their bitterest enemies, have marveled at Athenian energy (e.g., Thuc. 1.70). If Athens had Themistokles in the past, it had Perikles at the start of the war (and, in case this similarity was not obvious, Perikles' first speech in Thucydides is preceded by the story of Themistokles). Athenian valor remains central but becomes a means rather than an end. Even as they turn to the old, ostensibly tired example of the Persian Wars, the Athenians put their past successes in a very different light than we might expect.

---

32. On Marathon's special place in the funeral orations, see Loraux 1986a, 155–171.

33. Strauss (1964, 171) surprisingly argues that no part of the speech praises Athenian power.

"MORE JUST" RATHER THAN "JUST": JUSTICE AS A ZERO-SUM GAME

Once the Athenians have finished with the Persian Wars, they do move
on to justify their current position, but it would overstate the case to
say that "justice" plays in the second part the same central role as
"power" does in the first.[34] These Athenians do not celebrate justice like
a Theseus or Demophon in the Theater of Dionysos. They demystify
and subvert it, defining its limits rather than trumpeting its importance.
The Athenians thus, in a sense, complete their inversion of the Herodotean perspective. Where Herodotus, in his introduction of Spartan
preeminence, subordinates power to religious sanctions and the restraint
of aggression, Thucydides' Athenians move from the praise of power to
weak praise for an optional justice that is a luxury of the strong. Their
arguments do not depend upon any transcendent, generalized pattern
of behavior. The Athenian speech, in fact, ignores any notion of *ison-
omia*, "equality before the law." The Athenians certainly do not turn to
the gods and heroes or seek legitimacy from any supposed service to a
greater Hellas (as they do at Hdt. 8.143–144).[35] Instead, they assume
that the relative power of, and opportunities that present themselves to,
an agent sets definite constraints on its behavior.

First, they did not seek *archê* but received it when the Spartans gave
up the struggle and the allies personally sought Athenian help (Thuc.
1.75.2):[36] "From this very material condition (*ergon*) we were compelled
(*katênankasthêmen*, i.e., suffered *anankê*) at the start to convert this
[i.e., rule, *archê*] into the present situation, most of all under the influence of fear, then also of honor (*timê*), and later also of advantage (*ôphelia*)" (1.75.3). Fear, presumably of Persia, was the initial cause for the
Delian League. Then Athens felt a thirst for public respect, *timê*, and,
in the end, a desire for some concrete advantage took over. Thucydides'
Athenians thus clearly distinguish between symbolic and material re-

---

34. Erbse 1989, 109.

35. Note, however, that the Athenians are not entirely immune to calling upon the
gods to make a rhetorical point: at the conclusion of the speech they call upon the *theoi
hoi horkioi*, "the gods of oaths," as witnesses if the Spartans attack without seeking negotiations first (1.78.4).

36. Note that the verb that the Athenians use at 1.75.2 (*elabomen*, aorist of *lambanô*:
"we took" our *archê*) does not specify whether the *archê* was freely offered or seized by
force. By using the term *dechomai*, the Athenians could have implied from the start that
their rule was a gift freely offered. Only later do the Athenians resolve this ambiguity,
using instead the verb *dechomai*, and describe their *archê* as a "gift freely given" (*archê
didomenê*). On the drama and importance of "acceptance," see chapter 4 above.

wards for leadership and see the two as distinct stages (at least in the case of Athenian rule).[37] Above all, they argue that their acquisitiveness is natural when human beings find themselves in a position such as that of Athens after the Persian Wars.

After having accounted for the historical development from the Persian Wars to the present, the Athenians move on to the second point. They claim now to be prisoners of history. They assert that no one can be reproached if "they maximize for themselves those things that are expedient concerning the most important risks" (Thuc. 1.75.4). Circumstances thus force the Athenians to maintain their empire. Some of the allies had already revolted and been brought under control by force. Virtually all of the allies hated the Athenians. The Spartans were no longer friendly but suspicious and quarrelsome, and those who revolted attempted to side with the Spartans. "It no longer," the Athenians conclude, "seemed safe . . . to relax our grip and incur risk" (1.75.4).

The Athenians go on to set up two foils with which to put their own behavior into perspective. Ultimately, they develop a brilliantly unconventional case against their own allies' thirst for freedom, but they first take aim at the Spartans themselves. The Athenians deny the Spartans a uniquely selfless position or superiority over the Athenians. They brush aside any fictions about Spartan hegemony and declare flatly: "You, at any rate, Lakedaimonians, exercise leadership, having organized the city-states in the Peloponnese in accordance with what is advantageous to you (to humin ôphelimon)" (Thuc. 1.76.1). The Spartans are no different than the Athenians and would, if they had retained their hêgemonia over the Greeks, have ultimately "been forced either to rule by means of superior force (archein enkratôs) or themselves to incur risk (kinduneuein)"—precisely the same dilemma that the Athenians now face.

The Athenians assert that behavior must be judged relative to the agent's position and that no large, transcendent scheme of justice is im-

---

37. A few sentences later, the Athenians restate these three motives, but not in quite the same order: at 1.76.2 they state that they were ""overcome by timê, deos, and ôphelia. If these three were to be chronological, then we might have to interpret the timê as the pleasure that the honor of leading the Delian League brought and the deos as the subsequent fear of breaking up the league. The fact that these two qualities are reversed in this second reference suggests that chronology, at least for the first two items, was not primary in the speaker's mind. The fear probably was generally that of Persia, of sullen allies, and of simply losing control. Note, however, that ôphelia caps both lists. Thucydides does, I think, clearly imply that Athenian rule evolved and that ôphelia became more important as time progressed.

mediately applicable: "We have done nothing shocking (*thaumaston*) or contrary to human character (*ho anthrôpeios tropos*)" (Thuc. 1.76.2). The Spartan foil serves to illustrate that Athenian behavior was natural and thus should not provoke outrage or shock—at least from the Spartans. Here, as later in this speech, the Athenians charge that no one can blame them, since they have not fallen below normal standards of human behavior. Unless their accusers can plausibly claim some distinct moral advantage, there are no grounds for complaint. Certainly, if the struggle is between Athens and Sparta, then the contest is pointless, because circumstances would ultimately force the Spartans to behave in the same way as the Athenians, and the Greeks would only replace one master with another.

The Athenians then move on to a third reason for their behavior, the standard Thucydidean principle that we have discussed so far and that the Athenians themselves cite:

> We were not indeed the ones who were instigators of such behavior.[38]
> Rather, it has always been the case that the weaker was constrained
> by the more powerful (*dunatôteros*, i.e., person with more *dunamis*).
>   Thuc. 1.76.2

The Athenians are the first speakers to introduce this principle into a debate, and they develop it in their first speech to a unique degree. Because they have acted in accordance with this principle, they can claim that they had only "followed their human nature (*hê anthrôpeia phusis*)" (Thuc. 1.76.3).

Not content with describing what would have happened if Sparta had remained as leader of the Greeks, the Athenians shift their attention to a putative future when Sparta would replace Athens. "Others would, we think, best demonstrate by taking over our position whether we show restraint," they sourly remark at Thucydides 1.76.4. A few sentences later, they move from barbed suggestion to direct attack:

> If you were to succeed in overthrowing us and exercise rule (*archê*), you
> would speedily lose the goodwill (*eunoia*) that fear (*deos*) of us has given
> you, if your policy of today is at all to tally with the sample that you gave
> of it during the brief period of your leadership against the Persians. Not only

---

38. Note that the verb *huparchô* appears only infrequently with the genitive in Thucydides and Herodotus and, when it does, indicates the actor has initiated an unjust act; Hdt. 1.5.3: Kroisos was the first who *huparxanta adikôn ergôn es tous Hellênas*, "instigated unjust acts against the Hellenes"; Hdt. 7.9 (another programmatic section): a Persian refers to *Hellênas huparxantas adikiês*, "the Hellenes who instigated injustice."

is your life at home regulated by customs (*nomima*) incompatible (*ameikta*) with those of others, but your citizens abroad act neither on these customs nor on those that are recognized by the rest of Hellas.

Thuc. 1.77.6

This criticism attacks the Spartans on several points. As often, Thucydides only introduces a positive emotion so that he can draw an overall negative conclusion.[39] His Athenians grudgingly acknowledge the *eunoia*, that goodwill that the Spartans enjoy, and even then do so only because they wish to discredit it. The goodwill toward Sparta has no solid foundation but results from a negative quality, *deos*, the fear that the Greeks have of Athens. There is thus no positive basis for this *eunoia* or for Sparta's leadership in Greece. The rest of the paragraph goes on to develop this notion: Sparta had already made itself unpopular even during its brief leadership during the Persian Wars, and it is likely that the Spartans would be as unsuccessful in the future. The Athenians base this observation on a double critique that strikes at two of Sparta's most prized qualities.

First, the Spartans were renowned for their unique lifestyle and customs, but this lifestyle enjoyed its prestige because it refined and extended values that all Greeks shared. The "Spartan mirage," as it has been called, exerted its hold on the Greek imagination because many wanted to believe in tough, fearless Greeks for whom physical pleasures and material considerations were unimportant. People admired the Spartans on the grounds that they were different—but different only in the degree to which they supposedly put common values into practice, not in kind. The Spartans were not foreign, but champions of Hellenic values.

The Athenians, however, simply describe the Spartan customs as *ameikta tois allois*, literally, "not susceptible to being mixed with others." The Spartans are not the truest exponents of Hellas. They are simply incompatible with their fellows. They are not purified exemplars of the familiar. They are simply "other." This seems to have been traditionally a sore point. According to Herodotus, the Spartans had, in fact, once been "poor at mixing with outsiders" (Hdt. 1.65.2: *xeinoisi aprosmiktoi*), a term that contains the same verbal root as *ameikta*. Herod-

---

39. Compare the manner in which the Mytileneans acknowledge the good treatment and respect that they have received from their Athenian allies at 3.11–12. They also see in *eunoia* a weak emotional force, contingent on external circumstances (in this case, relative balance of power).

otus, however, pointedly assigns this quality to Sparta's benighted past. His praise of the current Sparta contains the prescriptive assumption that the Spartans are now different and able to interact with other Greeks. This praise is thus not just a statement of "fact," but a condition for Spartan prestige.[40] The Athenians play to the same weakness and deny this prop to Spartan prestige.

Second, consistency of behavior is one of the primary elements that Archidamos stresses in his own praise of the Spartan character. The Spartans operate according to their own rules (Thuc. 1.84). Neither flattery nor scorn can affect the Spartans' judgment (1.84.2). Their self-control (*sôphrosunê*) is responsible for their military prowess (1.84.3). Thus Thucydides' Athenians charge that the Spartans lack consistency. Any Spartan who leaves his country begins to behave in a bizarre fashion that follows no established custom, whether of Sparta or anywhere else in Greece. Consistency is a central virtue in the *History*: Thucydides' Perikles bases part of his moral authority on the fact that his resolve is unchanging (1.140.1)—a feature that Kleon attempts to emulate (3.38.1). When the Athenians sneeringly suggest that the Spartans change their behavior as soon as they leave their homeland, they deny them their absolute self-possession and refuse to accept a fundamental element of the Spartan mystique.

If the Athenians disdain to assert any grandiose moral standing, they have caustic things to say about the virtue of the allies, their supposed victims. The Athenians make no attempt to say that the existence of their empire is just, but they do take care to argue that the allies, by traditional standards, are deficient. They turn two principles against their allies: the love of honor and advantage, and the rule of the strong. The Athenians are not Herodotean imperialists, intoxicated by a thirst for expansion. Instead, it is the allies whom love of honor has carried away and who have formed too high an estimate of their position. They resented Athenian rule, even though the Athenians showed restraint and did not rule as harshly as their position would have allowed. They had grown accustomed to dealing with the Athenians on an equal basis (Thuc. 1.77.3: *apo tou isou*). They did not feel *charis* for the moderation that the Athenians conferred upon them as a kind of gift-by-restraint. If the Athenians had exercised their greed, then "in that case not even they

40. Herodotus's account of Sparta is, as a whole, normative. Even when it praises Sparta, it simultaneously sets conditions to which Sparta must, at least nominally, adhere if it is to retain that praise in the future.

[i.e., the allies] would have argued that it was not right for the weaker to give way to the strong." The Athenians bracket this section by repeating their general charge: the allies are angry because they have accepted the illusion that they should deal with the Athenians *apo tou isou*, "on the basis of equality" (1.77.4).

The Athenians, although untraditional in some respects, nevertheless skillfully exploit traditional prejudices. They obliquely link the discontent of the allies to a typical human failing:

> At the hands of the Persians, the allies had endured suffering much more terrible conditions than the present, but our rule (*archê*) seems to them too harsh. So one would expect (*eikotôs*): the present (*to paron*) is always hard on those who are subject (*hupêkooi*).
>
> Thuc. 1.77.5

The allies are, in fact, better off now than they had been under the Persians, but they are unable to appreciate their true situation, because they have fallen into a moral trap. They "long for what they do not have"—a conventional moral weakness that is often cited in archaic Greek literature[41] and that will, in fact, drive the Athenians on to the disastrous invasion of Sicily. The allies do not appreciate the favor that the Athenians have shown them, and refuse to return Athenian consideration with the *charis* that it deserves (Thuc. 1.77.3). They have an unbalanced view of their situation, because, the Athenians remark, "they have become accustomed to associating with us on the basis of equality," whereas the Athenians are in fact far superior to them. In the Mytilenean debate, Kleon picks up on this theme, asserting that favorable Athenian treatment had driven the Mytileneans into hubris (3.39.4, 5). The Athenians at Sparta disdain any such explicitly negative terminology (as they disdain references to their own *aretê*), but they implicitly attribute hubris to the allies all the same. The allies are morally deficient because they fall into the common trap of misrecognizing the present and longing for what they cannot have. The Athenian argument is a daring mixture of old and new, brilliantly twisting a traditional notion to attack the credibility of their accusers.

The broad material determinism, denial of special qualities to the Spartans, and dismissal of allied moral authority combine to make one central—if obliquely expressed—point. Interstate relations in the archaic

---

41. Cf. Thuc. 5.103.2 (discussed in the previous chapter), where the Athenians make similar charges against the Melian elite with whom they negotiate.

world had, as I argued earlier, laid great stress upon the obfuscation of power relations, had emphasized hegemony rather than domination, and had provided a framework in which each state could make the strongest possible claim that it was free and independent. The weak and the strong cooperated to blur the hierarchical relationships that did exist. In this their first speech, the Athenians construct a vision of the world where such polite fictions are impossible.

When the Athenians argue that they have treated their subject allies too well, they impudently apologize for having acted deceptively. They apologize because they have not more fully exploited their disproportionate strength. The Athenians submit themselves to the same rule of law that they impose upon the allies (Thuc. 1.77.1), but this common submission to law confuses the allies and obscures the issue. On the contrary, so the Athenians claim (1.77.2), those who simply base their rule upon the application of violence (*biazesthai*) have no need of legal proceedings (*dikazesthai*) and incur less criticism. If the Athenians were to "put aside custom (*nomos*)" and "openly pursue their greed," then even the allies would have to agree that the weak must give way to the strong (1.77.3). The outrage that the allies feel is an effect of good treatment by the Athenians, and this present discontent illustrates a general rule of human behavior:

> Human beings, it seems, become more angry when they suffer legal wrong (*adikoumenoi*) than when they are the victims of superior force (*biazomenoi*). The first looks like the pursuit of greed (*to pleonekteisthai*) in a relationship of equality (*apo tou isou*), the second like the application of necessity (*ananke*) by one more powerful.
>
> Thuc. 1.77.4

The Athenians are so committed to law and so disinclined to base their dealings on the application of force that their allies completely misinterpret their situation. The Athenian empire thus mistakenly allows its allies to think that they are Athens's equals. If, on the other hand, the Athenians exerted their full force, then the allies would not object, because they would acknowledge the natural rule of the strong.

This is an extraordinary argument. It turns the fictions of the archaic world upside down. The hundreds of jealous, quarrelsome city-states had done everything that they could to maintain their at least putative freedom and autonomy—thus providing a standard according to which the great and the small could be equal. A greater portion of the Greek world had united against Xerxes than at any time since the Trojan War so that the Greeks might preserve this fragmented freedom.

The Athenians, however, blithely state that the appearance of equality causes, rather than solves, problems. The illusion of equality is a "false consciousness" that allows Athens's subjects to level unjustified criticisms. Of course, Athens is a dominant force—the Athenians have the power to exert control, and, by an almost Newtonian law, their power achieves equilibrium by exerting control over the weak. The over-generous behavior of the Athenians obscures this truth. The best way to win the willing acquiescence of one's subjects is to be ruthless and always to apply overwhelming force.

But, of course, the Athenians do not pursue this logical course, and, in the end, they establish their own peculiar claim to moral authority. They exploit an old topos about wealth and power. "We received this *archê* not by force," they say at Thucydides 1.75.2, "but because you were not willing to remain through the end against the remaining forces of the foreigners and because the allies came to us and themselves asked us to be their *hêgemones*." A few sentences later, they conclude this section of their argument by declaring that they had done nothing surprising or unnatural "if we accepted *archê* that was given to us (*didomenê*)" (Thuc. 1.76.2).[42] Already in Hesiod, we find the distinction between that which is acquired as a gift and the product of violence: "A gift (*dôs*) is a good thing, what is taken is evil—a giver (*doteira*) of death" (*WD* 356). Solon prays for wealth, but not if it is acquired unjustly (frag. 13.7–8). Only wealth freely given by the gods rests upon a sure foundation (9–10). That which mortals acquire through hubris follows unwillingly. Thucydides' Athenians, in their secular and devious way, play upon this idea. Their rule was a gift, not the product of conquest or theft. They must hedge a bit about their subsequent behavior and explain why they would not return the gift, but gift it was at the start, and this lends a measure of traditional legitimacy to their possession.

The Athenians fashion for themselves a justification that can be paralleled in the epinician poets—whose mystifications for power these Athenians resolutely avoid. The concept of *phthonos*, "jealous ill will," is central to epinician poetry.[43] The victor incurs the enmity and ill will

42. On the traditional fiction of equality and hard limits on hegemony, see chapters 3 and 8 above; Raaflaub (1979, 251) accepts the Athenian argument here: the previous fiction of equality rendered Athens much more vulnerable to the charge of tyranny when the league evolved into an empire.

43. A simple word search of Pindar or Bacchylides will turn up the dense references to *phthonos* and its linguistic derivatives; for one recent survey, see Bulman 1992; Kurke (1991) is especially good at revealing the ways in which these poets sought to resolve the tensions between victor and community.

of his small-minded neighbors because of his great good fortune, and the poet attempts to assuage such jealous feelings (thus by begging off resentment the poet simultaneously dramatizes the good fortune that incurs this resentment). *Phthonos* is not a particularly prominent concept in Thucydides as a whole, but the Athenians cite it twice. They open the justification of their present position by stating that they do not "warrant the *phthonos*"that they have acquired (Thuc. 1.75.1: expressed rather torturously by making the adjective *epiphthonos* part of a rhetorical question). A few sentences later (1.75.5), they turn to the same concept again: minimizing the most important dangers is natural and "does not warrant *phthonos*"(*anepiphthonos*). *Phthonos* is a small-minded, negative quality. In the ideology of the archaic and classical elite, the great suffer envy and slanders from their inferiors but are expected themselves to be immune to such pusillanimous feelings.[44] In attributing *phthonos* to their critics they simultaneously accuse them of pettiness. The idea that external circumstances determine human behavior was popular among the sophists (who could use it to justify almost anything—including Helen of Troy), but Thucydides' Athenians frame this sophistic argument within the traditional rhetoric about *phthonos*.

Finally, the Athenians do make their own peculiar claim to moral authority. The Athenians portray a world in which certain principles (avoiding dangers, the rule of the powerful) dictate the general outlines of human behavior. But these general outlines still leave a limited space for individual action. Having established this space, the Athenians then make their own peculiar claim to moral authority:

> Praise (*epainos*) is due to all who, following their human nature (*anthropeia phusis*) to exercise rule (*archê*) over others, yet are *more just* (*dikaioteroi*) than is in accordance with the power (*dunamis*) at their disposal. Others, we suppose, would, if they took over our position, best demonstrate whether we are showing any moderation (*ti metriazomen*). Instead, an evil reputation (*adoxia*) rather than praise (*epainos*) has accrued to us even from our sense of fairness (*to epieikes*)—and this is not reasonable (*ouk eikotôs*).
>
> Thuc. 1.76.4

The Athenians have the *dunamis* to exert far greater control than they do. They can, so they claim, rule by means of violence, but their

---

44. Thus one of the most damning charges that Otanes directs against tyrants is that although they possess the greatest power and wealth of any men, they are at the same time obsessed with *phthonos* and envy (Hdt. 3.80.4); cf. also Herodotus's story of Thrasyboulos's advice to Periander (5.92z).

sense of fairness or equity (*to epieikes*) restrains them. They forgo a measure of their power, and this forbearance constitutes a net "gift," but the Athenians also demand in return to receive corresponding *epainos*, "praise," as a countergift. The Athenians do not discard the logic of reciprocity so much as the fictions of equality. Significantly, they do not claim to be "just," for, in their view, absolute justice is unrealistic. The Athenians claim instead to be "more just" (*dikaioteroi*) than they need, because they have deviated from a natural course and not allowed their power to reach its natural equilibrium (which would reduce Athens's allies to a much more abject state). Within this scheme, the Athenians can claim to "exercise moderation" (*metriazomen*) like the most austere Spartan. They are moderate toward their allies (Thuc. 1.77.2), and if the allies do not recognize this, it is because they fail to make the proper comparisons with other imperial powers.

At the beginning of their speech (Thuc. 1.73.1), the Athenians had declared that they would "show that what we have acquired we do not possess without good reason (*apeikotôs*)," and the importance of this appeal to reason now becomes clear in the latter portion of the speech. If material conditions dominate human decisions and if there is thus no universal standard of justice, then if justice can be said to exist at all, it constitutes at best a relative concept, a deviation from "natural" behavior (i.e., the tendency of force to dominate weakness). Each action must be evaluated according to the situation and the ordinary limitations of human behavior. Neither the allies nor the Spartans have any claim to special moral authority—their "subject positions," to use a now popular term, simply differ from that of Athens. The Athenians already lay claim to a degree of "justice" greater than that which they attribute to their opponents. Since the Athenians are already moral equals if not superiors, neither the allies nor the Spartans have any right to criticize the Athenians or to demand more from them.

The Athenian speech thus sketches for justice and moderation an outline that takes into consideration the selfishness inherent in human behavior. There are no heroic standards such as "Greece," "justice," or "honor" that are so important that they are worth the highest sacrifice. All agents pursue their interests and avoid catastrophe. But within this framework, the Athenians become again a paradigm of moderation. The Athenians fail to euphemize their position or to make it possible for the allies to accept their situation. The fault, however, lies not with Athenian high-handedness, but with the small-mindedness of the allies. Ideological mystification does not work, but instead of stressing the bluntness of Athenian rule, this speech gives the Athenians credit for sustaining the fictions of equality with their allies even as the Athenians disdain the high rhetoric of other sources. Thucydides systematically takes to pieces the Athens of Theseus and of Demophon that we find in Euripides—there is no *charis*, no *aretê*, no grand, unselfish gesture on behalf of Hellas. But Thucydides' Athenians nevertheless erect from the rubble an empire that is more just than it needs to be. In this world of limited moral expectations, the Athenian empire proves an ongoing theater of Athenian generosity lavished upon unworthy allies.

The Athenian speech at Sparta allows Thucydides to rewrite, in a comparably programmatic section of his own history, several of the major themes in the Kroisos logos that opens Herodotus's work. First, I have already suggested that Thucydides' Athenians invert the norms by which Herodotus shapes his account of Spartan power in book 1. Second, in subordinating human behavior to external forces, Thucydides' Athenians approach a central idea of the Herodotean Solon: "A human being is entirely a product of outside forces" (Thuc. 1.32.4: *pan esti anthrôpos sumphorê*). Third, this subordination to larger forces in both cases demands that human beings show consideration and understanding for one another, basing their judgments not on some impersonal principle but on the fact that today's judges may in the future find themselves in a similar position. Thucydides' Athenians, as we noted above, make constant reference to such "humanist" logic. Likewise, when Kyros learned from Kroisos what Solon had said, he "changed his mind and recognized that he, being also himself a human being, was burning alive another human being who had been no inferior to him in good fortune. He ordered that the fire that was now beginning to burn be extinguished and Kroisos as well as those with Kroisos be brought down from the pyre" (Hdt. 1.86.6).

Herodotus's Kroisos had, however, played counterpoint to the Kroisos of Bacchylides and to that poet's positive representation of material wealth.[45] Thucydides' Athenians, on the other hand, reverse this slant. Herodotus had explicitly condemned Kroisos as an imperialist who imposed tribute on the Greeks (Hdt. 1.6). The Herodotean Kroisos was a straw man, who naively equated "prosperity" and material wealth. Not only was Kroisos unable to answer Solon; he did not even appreciate the crushing rhetorical defeat that he had suffered—until the flames lick-

45. See Crane 1996c.

ing at the pyre recall Solon's words to his mind. The Athenians extracted tribute from the same Greeks, but they are unabashed imperialists, who defend their position with vigor. They avoid the boorish shortsightedness of the Herodotean Kroisos, who naively equated wealth with good fortune, but they also do away with the elegant and skillful postures that the epinician poets fashioned for people such as the Syracusan tyrant Hieron. At the same time, Thucydides' Athenians extend a process that began in Herodotus. Apollo whisks Bacchylides' Kroisos off to his eternal paradise among the Hyperboreans. The gods still take an active role in Herodotus (Hdt. 1.87.2, 91.2), but Kroisos's fate is secular: he lives on as a wise man at the Persian court. Thucydides' Athenians, however, have no interest in divine intervention at all. Theirs is a world in which humans confront an impersonal and almost Newtonian system of behavior.

PROBLEMS IN THE DATA: EUPHEMOS AT KAMARINA AND THE MELIAN DIALOGUE

Thucydides defies convention—modern and ancient—in selecting materials for his *History*. Religion, women, and kinship are only some of the elements that Thucydides pushes to the margins of his account. Nevertheless, we can still often see in Thucydides' own text indications of the things that he has excluded.[46] It is, however, even easier to see in Thucydides' text the limitations on that realism that his speakers so often espouse and toward which the historian's voice aspires. Two famous passages demonstrate the fundamental problems for Athenian realism: Euphemos's speech at Kamarina and the Melian Dialogue. Each dramatizes a major obstacle to one of the realisms that I outlined in chapter 2. Euphemos's speech reflects the weakness of "scientific realism": in manipulating the facts, this crafty Athenian unwittingly speaks the truth and in so doing foreshadows, with almost Oedipodean heavyhandedness, the Athenian disaster to come. The Athenians at Melos reach the limits of that "ideological realism" that seeks to charm or cozen obedience through appeals to "sweet reason." The calculus of self-interest varies depending upon one's subject position and upon the values

---

46. See, for example, Hornblower (1992), who uses Thucydides' own text to show that he underrepresents the importance of religion; on topics excluded by Thucydides generally, see Crane 1996a.

that agents bring with them, and the Melians reveal the hollowness of Athenian power.

Before moving on to these two specific debates, let us consider, however, the general problem of language in Thucydides. The Athenians, for example, assume a fundamental distinction between *erga*, "real things," and *logoi*, "words," with the *erga* constituting reality and *logoi* a kind of secondary epiphenomenon.[47] At Corcyra, the "accustomed valuations" of words were changed so that terms for virtues were applied to vices, but this represented a perversion of language: the "real" values remained unchanged, even if the vocabulary was perverted. Or, to put it more succinctly, signifiers may shift, but that which is signified remains untouched.[48]

But speech is an act, and *logoi* are, of course, themselves *erga*—that is why the perversion of language at Thucydides 3.82 is so terrible. A hierarchical model that places one above the other is untenable. Thucydides' narrative itself is *logos*, and it brilliantly records the influence of spoken *logoi* upon human events. Much as Thucydides strives to efface himself during the narrative portions of the *History*, the meanings of *erga* are not transparent to those who make decisions in the *History*. Actors in this history perceive *erga* through the *logoi* of public debate and private discussion. If the meaning of *erga* were perfectly transparent, then best interests would be obvious, and Athenian policy, to take one instance, would not have changed after Perikles' death. Hence, the "objective" historian of the narrative includes a set of speeches that all argue according to similarly idiosyncratic Thucydidean principles. As Cogan argues, the speeches are there because Thucydides saw in debate a true cause for historical events. If we wish to understand why things happen, we have to know what people thought.[49]

Thucydides is acutely aware of the tension between language and the world. The speech of Euphemos at Kamarina gives bitterly ironic expression to the ambiguous ties between the two. The consequences of this ambiguity are profound: the calculus of interest depends upon a clear recognition of what is or is not advantageous. What happens to Athenian ideology, with its emphasis on "realism," if the real is itself ambiguous? Thucydides' *History* is not a celebration of realism but an arena in which many realisms compete for dominance.

47. On this, see Euben 1990b, 169–171; White 1984, 59–92; Parry 1981.
48. See Wilson 1982.
49. Cogan 1981a, esp. 234–254.

At the beginning of the Sicilian campaign, the Syracusan leader Hermokrates attacks Athenian motives in a debate at Kamarina (Thuc. 6.76–80). He excoriates the Athenians as cynical hypocrites, who exploit fine concepts such as affection for their kindred (6.76.1: *to suggenes kêdesthai*) as a pretext (6.76.2: *prophasis*) to embroil themselves in Sicilian affairs. The Athenians seek only a fair-seeming justification (6.76.3: *aitia euprepês*) to conquer Sicily. He uses manifest Athenian hypocrisy as a tool to discredit Athens's supposedly limited goals in Sicily and to dramatize the danger of Athenian conquest.

Euphemos, the Athenian representative who answers Hermokrates, delivers a speech that parallels—and on a number of occasion echoes—that of the Athenians at Sparta. The two clearly balance one another, and Euphemos's speech occurs at the outset of the Sicilian expedition, just as the Athenian speech at Sparta precedes the beginning of the first phase of the war.[50]

Hermokrates played directly into Athens's rhetorical strengths. Whatever words they may actually have expressed, Thucydides' Athenians have little use for conventional moralizing. With the partial exception of the Funeral Oration, every Athenian speech from the beginning of the *History* has undercut charges of such naive hypocrisy. Euphemos thus argues that Athens's interests pit it against Syracuse but prevent it from extending its domination to Sicily:

> Besides, for a man who is a *turannos* or a city-state that exercises rule (*archê*), nothing is unreasonable if expedient (*sumpheron*), nor is there anything of personal interest (*oikeion*) that is not worthy of trust (*piston*). In all cases one must be a friend or an enemy in accordance at the proper time (*meta kairou*). Here, in Sicily, it gives us advantage (*ôphelei*) not if we weaken our friends, but if our enemies become lacking in power (*adunatoi*, lacking in *dunamis*) because of the martial strength (*rhômê*) of our friends. Why doubt this? In Hellas we treat our allies as we find them useful (*chrêsimoi*).
>
> Thuc. 6.85.1–2

Euphemos airily dismisses all higher principles. The Athenians are like a *turannos*, but he argues that this is, in its own way, an advantage to third parties. Athens's status as *turannos polis* makes its motives transparent. The Athenians are thus as reliable (or at least predictable) as if they adhered to a traditional code of ethics. What is expedient (*sumpheron*), what gives advantage (*ôphelei*), and what is useful (*chrês-*

---

50. For comparisons, see de Romilly 1963, 243–250; Rawlings 1981, 117–122.

mon) absolutely constrain Athenian behavior. If something is in their interest, then it is expedient. If something touches their personal interest (*oikeion*), then they may be relied upon to pursue it. Euphemos perfectly expresses the logic that statesmen of the major powers openly follow. The sentiments expressed above would excite little comment if they appeared in a *New York Times* news analysis—except that these principles would appear so obvious that the editor would probably excise or shorten them.

The general gap between *erga* and their proper *logoi* provides the rhetorical basis for Euphemos's argument. Objective realities determine actions, and thus the Athenians can be trusted because restraint in Sicily is in their interests. The same argument, however, also renders Euphemos's words problematic for two reasons. First, he is lying. His admission that Athens is a *turannos* and pursues its interests may be true, but not in the fashion that he claims. As Strasburger pointed out a generation ago, this kind of false candor is subtle and devious, for the speaker only pretends to "lay all his cards on the table."[51] Thucydides has left us in no doubt that the Athenians did indeed intend to conquer all of Sicily. Hermokrates' accusations are completely correct.[52]

Second, Euphemos's speech is bitterly ironic, for in lying Euphemos really does, at least in Thucydides' eyes, describe Athens's best interests. The Athenians would have been much better off if they had in fact the limited goals that Euphemos ascribes to them. Thucydides did not think it impossible for the Athenians to conquer Syracuse (Thuc. 2.65.11), but the post-Periklean Athenians were unable to achieve even this goal, and Perikles' emphatic advice not to expand in the face of Spartan power was clearly superior (1.144.1, 2.65.7). The Syracusan demagogue Athenagoras ironically has a much clearer vision of Athenian interests than do the Athenians themselves:

> Now it is not likely that they would leave the Peloponnesians behind them, and before they have well ended the war in Hellas wantonly come in quest of a new war quite as arduous, in Sicily; indeed, in my judgment, they are only too glad that we do not go and attack them, being so many and such great cities as we are.
>
> Thuc. 6.36.4

51. Strasburger 1958, 521.
52. Book 6 opens with an explicit statement that the Athenians planned to conquer Sicily (see 6.1.1).

The violent and malevolent Athenagoras, who resembles no one so much as Kleon, nevertheless grasps a central principle of Periklean strategy. One of the great ironies that runs throughout Thucydides' *History* is that reality is ambiguous and that actors cannot, in fact, determine their own best interest. Even the wisest and most clearheaded planners cannot eliminate risk and anticipate the operation of chance—this is practically the first thing that Perikles says in his opening speech (Thuc. 1.140), and the plague appears as if to bring home the limits of rational planning.[53]

The idealized dominance of *erga* over *logoi* is not simply an issue of academic concern to the actors in Thucydides' *History*. The calculus of power is not, in fact, natural but proceeds only insofar as participants accept it as natural. The strong can kill, but they cannot dominate without developing a consensus with the weak. In dragging the calculus of power out of the shadows, the Athenians change the system. Euphemisms and fictions limit power and protect the weak. The calculus of power eliminates ambiguities and raises the stakes for strong and weak alike—one is either equal, master, or slave. But this stark system has its own ideological logic that serves the interests of the strong. Resistance is futile. Only fools struggle. True wisdom dictates submission. The strong thus seek the same advantage that they received under a more ambiguous scheme: they provide the weak with a moral (or perhaps transmoral?) argument by which to justify their own submission.

Hence the Melian Dialogue and its prominence. This debate is not simply important because it documents the ruthlessness with which Athenians exercise their power or the worthlessness of Sparta's commitment to even its closest allies. The debate is important because the Melians simply refuse to make their actions conform to this calculus of power. They face the full wrath of Athenian power, discuss the matter at length with implacably logical Athenians, and simply do not agree. Objective realities may dominate the fictive constructs—the desperate hopes (*elpides*), the wish for what is noble (*to kalon*), the fear of shame (*aischunê*), may well be poor helps. Yet the Melians stubbornly cling to these ideas, fictive constructs though they may be.

And so the Melians must die. The Athenians explain themselves clearly. The hatred of the Melians harms them less than their friendship; for friendship would imply that Athens was unable to crush the Melians,

53. The limits of rationality in Thucydides have, of course, been the subject of extensive debate; see Stahl 1966; Edmunds 1975a.

while the hatred of the Melians would be a public demonstration (*paradeigma*) of Athens's *dunamis* to all its subjects (Thuc. 5.95). No one, according to the Athenians, pays any serious attention to justice or issues of morality:

> As far as justification (*dikaiôma*) goes, they think one has as much of it as the other, and that if any maintain their independence, it is because of power (*dunamis*), and that if we do not molest them, it is because of terror (*phobos*); so that besides extending our rule (*archê*) we should gain in security by your subjection; the fact that you are islanders and weaker than others rendering it all the more important that you should not succeed in baffling the masters of the sea.
>
> Thuc. 5.97

The whole Greek world fixes its gaze upon Athens. The Athenians on Melos are, as I argued above, not so different from the earlier Athenians who refused the Persian offer of peace before Plataia. Both act on their own immediate behalf, but also, and more important, both seek with their actions to impress their worth upon the Hellenes. The Athenians before Plataia will do anything to serve their objectified vision of Hellas. The Athenians on Melos are equally ready to do anything to advance their *archê*. The Athenians before Plataia are willing to fight to the last person; their grandchildren at Melos, to the last Melian. The Athenians may have shifted the burden, but they remain equally ruthless.

Most important, the Athenians at Melos may claim to have set aside all moral considerations, but the vision of the world they seek to advance is as artificial and, at least in its extreme form, as much an invention as the idealized Hellas of Herodotus 8.144. The Athenians at Melos claim that they must demonstrate their own strength, but in fact they need to do more. They need to convince the world that the strong really do rule the weak, that the calculus of power is a universal phenomenon, and that in yielding the weak follow a higher natural law. The Athenians have not abandoned morality. They have replaced it with a new, supposedly more sophisticated system to justify their position.

The Melians must die, but not because their defiance implies Athenian weakness—any comparison between Athenian and Melian strength is ludicrous. In this famous section of the *History*, the Athenians show an unease about their empire and its stability[54]—surprisingly, given that the war has, at least temporarily, come to an end. But the Athenian position

---

54. On this change of attitude, see Cogan 1981a, 92; Macleod 1974, 392.

has less to do with particulars of empire than with the need to impose their vision on the world. The Melians must die because they are an embarrassment to the universal calculus of power. Their resistance challenges not only the particular strength of a particular imperial power, but, more important, the fiction that all human beings recognize the "rule of the strong" as "natural." If the Athenians can convince all of their allies that this principle is a kind of natural law, then they can argue, as they do to the Melians, that there is no dishonor—indeed, there is a kind of cool rationality—in submitting to an overwhelming force (Thuc. 5.89, 111).

The Athenian arguments at Melos are thus just as ideological as the Spartan claims to virtue. The Spartan mirage allowed other Greeks to accept Spartan leadership, because they attributed to Sparta virtues that all admired and they did not need to fear Spartan expansionism. The Greeks did not, in a sense, even follow the Spartans per se, but the *nomos*, "general law," that guided the Spartans (Hdt. 7.104.4–5). The Spartans were not absolute masters, but first among equals, because—and provided that—they subordinated themselves to this overarching concept. Athens demands far more of its subordinates than Sparta did of its allies, but, if it abandons the old rhetoric, it does not abandon ideology. When the Athenians assert that the "rule of the strong" is a natural law to which all (including the Athenians) are subject, they adopt the same strategy as the Spartans before them. The Spartans and Greeks together had created the Spartan mirage, the image of Sparta as military and most widely recognized moral leader in Greece, because the Spartan mirage helped all parties justify to themselves Sparta's leadership. Greeks did not admire the Spartans per se, but the *aretê* that their idealized Spartans had, at great personal cost, cultivated. The Athenians attempt to place their own much more dominant position in a similarly impersonal framework. Submission to Athens is not so much a personal surrender as the recognition of a universal truth, that the powerful dominate the weak. For the time being at least, Athens is strong, Melos is weak, and each party should recognize as simple reality the inevitable subordination of the one to the other.

Melian resistance is thus the Athenian nightmare in small. The Athenians cannot—even if they had the resources to do so—kill all of their subjects, for they function as a superpower only because the subjects are alive and, however reluctantly, choose to lend their support. The allies could always choose the alternative and resolve to "live free or die." In this sense, rule is always a negotiation between the weak and the strong.

From a practical point of view, the reductio ad absurdum is improbable—the entire *archê* never did rise in rebellion, and Athenian domination was not so harsh as to provoke all its subjects to risk death. Of course, the Athenians must maintain a certain level of power to balance that of their adversaries. And Athenian power is more than an illusion—as many of allies learned to their cost, when they underestimated Athens's remaining power after the Sicilian catastrophe (Thuc. 2.65.12). Once Sparta crushes the Athenian navy at Aigospotamoi, the rest of Athenian power collapses.

Nevertheless, the calculus of power is, in the pure form that the Athenians give it, an ideological fiction that enhances Athenian control and augments the net sum of Athenian *dunamis* by holding back, perhaps, a few allies who might otherwise revolt. It is thus a classic example of an Althusserian ideological state apparatus that augments the power of raw force and oppression.[55] The Athenians butcher the Melians so that they can support the fiction of realism and so that such brilliant readers as de Romilly would believe that "realism becomes a moral attitude"—if Athens's view is not "real," then this moral attitude becomes just another self-serving posture. The clarity of purpose must seem to melt away the haze of interpretation so that "as the facts stand out in their eternal essence, we begin to see, beyond the individual whose acts are described, the naked principles of justice and force."[56]

The Melians are the statistical outlier, the experiment that does not match the theory. The Athenians are in the end not realists. They are not even objective scientists, because they doctor the evidence to fit their own theory. The Athenians destroy the Melians as a corrupt scientist might destroy inconvenient evidence.

Thucydides' *logoi*, however, changed the Melian "incident" forever, for representation can transform an event. A savage beating by Los Angeles police in 1991 would have gone unnoticed and unpunished, but it was captured on videotape, and in that vivid medium it attained a reality and exerted an impact that would otherwise never have been possible. In the Peloponnesian War, the massacre at Skione (Thuc. 5.32.1) passes with little comment. It can slide past as a grim reality, but also as an

55. Althusser 1971, 142: "In order to advance the theory of the State it is indispensable to take into account not only the distinction between State power and State apparatus, but also another reality which is clearly on the side of the (repressive) State apparatus, but must not be confused with it. I shall call this reality by its concept: *the ideological state apparatuses.*"
56. De Romilly 1963, 272.

abstraction without substance for most Greeks. Skione was the cleanest demonstration of power, in that it called little attention to its grim details. The events at Melos, however, are different, because the issues are inscribed in Thucydides' text. The arguments remain fixed forever in the public display of a text that has in fact transcended barriers of time and space. Like Sisyphos rolling his stone forever in Hades, the Athenians must forever recite their failed ideology of power to each reader who passes his or her eyes across the text. For in killing the Melians, the Athenians prove that they are wrong. The weak do not always yield to the strong.

CHAPTER 11

Conclusion

Thucydidean Realism
and the Price of Objectivity

We have explored the problems inherent in the realism that Thucydides' Athenians claim for themselves. Their "real world" proves ambiguous, their claim to abstract knowledge a self-serving fiction, their candor simply another ideological gambit. But what of the realism that Thucydides' text claims for itself? We cannot assume that the Athenians or anyone else in the *History*—not even Perikles—simply reflects the ideas of Thucydides himself.[1] Indeed, many have concluded that Thucydides never resolved on a single position,[2] and we are safer, by and large, to think in terms of Thucydidean voices rather than a single, monolithic authorial voice. Our analysis of Thucydidean realisms in chapter 2 concentrated primarily on those few passages in which the writer purports to make his judgments most explicit—the Archaeology and methodological chapters, and the descriptions of plague at Athens and civil war at Corcyra. Nevertheless, Thucydides' practice has its own consistent patterns, and what Thucydides actually does is at least as enlightening as what he claims to do. I have stressed so far primarily the ambiguities that Thucydides brings out in the positions of his characters: the dissonance between the expectations of states such as Corinth, Corcyra, Plataia, and Melos and those of the two "great powers," Athens and Sparta; the changing nature of power, which is prefigured in the Archaeology and

---

1. Hornblower (1987, 155–190) goes into the problems of isolating Thucydides' own ideas at length.
2. E.g., Pouncey 1980, ix–x; similarly, Connor 1984, 249–250.

which culminates in the Athenian empire; the irresolvable dilemmas with which this new power confronts Sparta; the Athenian attempt to reformulate and come to grips with their position.

But Thucydides, for all his insight, also faced the same pressures as did his Athenians. Let us return here to three of the assumptions common to political realists, ancient and modern, that we considered in chapter 2: first, that the rules governing international affairs are essentially constant if we move across time or from culture to culture; second, that the group, not the individual human being, is the proper unit of analysis; third, that the pursuit of power is a fundamental human motivation. Each of these assumptions is critical to Thucydides' method— as it has been to that of many who have come after him. If Thucydides had not exploited these ideas with such vigor, his work would never have achieved its peculiar character or earned such a degree of success. At the same time, each of these assumptions limits Thucydides' view, blinding him to many factors at work and constricting his intellectual range. Together, they constitute a part of that general paradigmatic quality, common to all realisms, that I discussed in chapter 2, and that directs the inquirer's gaze toward some phenomena and away from others.

ESSENTIALISM, HISTORY, AND IDEOLOGY IN THUCYDIDES

First, political realists, with their emphasis on the constants of human nature or society, have often had trouble accounting for major historical changes, since the emphasis on continuity and on common factors can, at the least, distract from the very real differences that appear as we move, either through time or space, from one cultural context to another.[3] Early Greek thought, in fact, identified this general problem very early on when it wrestled with the issue of unity and change. The sixth-century Milesian intellectuals Thales, Anaximander, and Anaximenes had all struggled to reconcile diversity with similarity, postulating fundamental elements from which all things were fashioned. In the fifth century, Parmenides, Empedokles, Demokritos, and others developed

---

3. E.g., Cox (1986, 243), who criticizes Morgenthau and Waltz for being "ahistorical" and insensitive to change; Ruggie (1986, 141–152) argues that Waltz's systemic view is not very successful at explaining a major transformation such as that from the medieval to the modern state; the essays critiquing realism in Wayman and Diehl 1994 do not have much to say about its weakness in accounting for change because these studies concentrate on the modern political arena and make little attempt to deal with different systems.

this problem even further. Thucydides' subject—human affairs—was both more complex and more manageable than these cosmological speculations. Rather than turn to water, "the infinite," air, the four elements, or atoms, Thucydides based much of his historical method on a single fundamental assertion, that, in the end, there exists an unchanging human nature, an *anthrôpeia phusis*.[4]

A constant human nature is hardly by itself a revolutionary concept in Thucydides—Herodotus uses the same phrase (Hdt. 3.65.3), and the traditional Greek exhortation that mortals should "think mortal thoughts" (*thnêta phronein*) assumes that all mortals, male and female, slave and free, Greek and non-Greek, share some broadly defined but single and unified position. The emphasis on cultural difference seems not to have developed until the fifth century, no doubt gaining particular impetus from the traumatic encounter in mainland Greece with the non-Greek Other, in large numbers, during Xerxes' invasion.[5] Thucydides himself prods his fellow Greeks, reminding them that the prized distinction between Greeks and non-Greeks was comparatively recent: he stresses that the term "barbarian" does not appear in Homer (Thuc. 1.3.3; cf. also 1.6.5–6).

But if the constancy of human nature was not an idea peculiar to Thucydides, Thucydides nevertheless exploited the principle with a consistency and brilliance unattested before and rarely equaled since. Thucydides felt that he could work with partial or conflicting sources precisely because a certain number of major trends—the constant pull of human ambition, the tendency of the powerful to dominate the weak, for example—shape human behavior, and the historian can turn to these constants in order to unmask hidden motives, fill in gaps, and push beyond the surface of the evidence. Thucydides used his analysis of the

4. On this, see now Johnson 1993, 61–62; a political philosopher, Johnson contrasts Hobbes with Thucydides. Thucydides' Athenians and Hobbes both argue that interest dominates events, but Thucydides' narrative contains numerous episodes that reveal the inadequacy of such a universalizing deterministic viewpoint. Nevertheless, Thucydides differs not because he does not believe in a stable human nature but because, as the product of classical Greek culture, he believes that chance is too unpredictable and events too ambiguous to allow humans to behave predictably. There is a rich literature on chance and intelligence in Thucydides: see, for example, Cornford 1907; Stahl 1966; Edmunds 1975a.

5. Thus Hall 1989, 54–55; on Herodotus's view of the Other, the classic study is Hartog 1988.

present to "predict" the past. It is easy to speak condescendingly of hidden or unexamined assumptions in authors, but Thucydides was often quite conscious of his own limitations and advertised them as dramatically as he could.

By opening the *History* with the Archaeology, his revisionist picture of the ancient past, Thucydides confronted his readers with the implications of a constant "human nature" by showing concretely how such an assumption could turn the past upside down. The Kretan ruler Minos—famous in mythology as an icon of tyranny, the man who handed the young people of Athens over to the Minotaur, and villain of Bacchylides 17—becomes an agent of civilization, able to bring order and tranquillity and to suppress piracy (Thuc. 1.4, 8.2–3). Thucydides represents the distinction between Greeks and foreigners—which Euripidean drama shows to have been a prominent part of popular culture[6]—as a recent phenomenon, still irrelevant in the Homeric epics (1.3, 1.6). The Trojan War, far from being a major enterprise, was a primitive affair, hardly comparable to the events of the fifth century (1.10–11). Thucydides develops a fairly extensive argument that even Agamemnon based his power less upon the gratitude and honor of his allies than upon his overwhelming military power and the consequent intimidation (1.9). One particular configuration of forces drives the progress—and progress it clearly is as far as Thucydides is concerned—of human civilization: "The weak, hungering for profits (*kerdê*), endured slavery (*douleia*) to the powerful, while those with greater force, because they enjoyed a surplus of wealth, used to acquire weaker city-states as subjects" (1.8.3). The compulsive and unbounded quest for power and profit that Solon had described at the opening of the sixth century and of Athenian recorded history (frag. 13 West) becomes in Thucydides, almost two centuries later, a unifying force that drives the weak and the mighty alike.

The belief in a stable and even transcendent human nature runs throughout the *History*.[7] The speeches that Thucydides includes and

6. This is not to say that Euripides endorsed Greek chauvinism: see, for example, Eur. *Med.* 534–538, which cannot even win tepid ambivalence from the Chorus (cf. 576–578); the non-Greek appearance of Dionysos is a major theme throughout the *Bacchae*; the degraded picture of Helen's Phrygian servants is one of the ugliest elements in an ugly play (Eur. *Or.* 1369ff.); on the representation of non-Greeks in tragedy, see Hall 1989.
7. Ste. Croix 1972, 29.

that illustrate the very different subject positions of participants in the war return again and again to the universal laws that affect behavior.[8] Thucydides' Athenians, of course, appeal to a vision of natural law throughout. In their opening speech, they argue that no one should feel resentment (*phthonos*) against those who "make the best arrangements for themselves when it comes to the most serious risks" (Thuc. 1.75.5). The "Athenian thesis" articulated at 1.76 presupposes a constant human nature. If the Athenians have acquired an empire, they have only exhibited "human behavior" (1.76.2: *anthrôpeios tropos*), and no one has any right to quarrel with them on these grounds, least of all the Spartans, who follow the same principles of self-interest (1.76.1, 4). If Athens's subjects feel resentment, this is also a natural but irrational phenomenon: if the Athenians ruled by pure force, their subjects would, we are told, feel less oppressed. The restraint of Athenian rule provokes paradoxically greater anger—but such anger, though paradoxical, is represented as predictable, a consequence of universal human psychology (1.77.2–4). In book 6, Euphemos portrays Athens as a tyrant city that, as such, must subordinate its affections to its interests (6.85). Circumstances, he argues a bit later at 6.87.2, force the Athenians to develop their empire: "We assert that we are rulers in Hellas in order not to be subjects; liberators in Sicily that we may not be harmed by the Sicilians; that we are compelled to interfere in many things, because we have many things to guard against." The Syracusan leader Hermokrates, terrified at the threat of Athenian expansion in Sicily, nevertheless strikes a similarly dispassionate pose. He takes it for granted that human beings seek power and that they will pursue aggression to gain their ends (4.59.2). A few paragraphs later he remarks that "it is human nature (*pephuke to anthrôpeion*) to rule the one who yields and to defend onself against attack" (4.61.5).

According to Thucydides, Hermokrates and his fellow Syracusans are similar in nature to the Athenians (Thuc. 6.20.3, 7.55.2, 8.96.5), but such generalizing thought is not confined to the Athenians and those like them. Thucydides' Peloponnesians are equally prone to such universalizing arguments. The Corinthians, arguing before the conservative Spartans, assert, for example, that "it is characteristic of the self-possessed (*sôphrôn*) to remain quiet unless they suffer injustice, and it is characteristic of the brave (*agathoi*) to exchange war for peace when

---

8. See, for example, de Romilly 1990, 61–104; Hammond 1973.

they suffer injustice and then, when the chance presents itself, to replace war with a settlement" (1.120.3). The Corinthians do not prob-
lematize the complex terms *sôphrôn* and *agathos* but represent them as
constant values from which predictable lessons may be drawn. Even
Thucydides' Spartans are prone to such universalizing reflections on human nature:[9]

> Indeed if great enmities are ever to be really settled, we think it will be, not
> by the system of revenge and military success, and by forcing an opponent
> to swear to a treaty to his disadvantage, but when the more fortunate
> combatant waives these his privileges, to be guided by gentler feelings,
> conquers his rival in generosity, and accords peace on more moderate
> conditions than he expected. [3] From that moment, instead of the debt of
> revenge that violence must entail, his adversary owes a debt of generosity to
> be paid in kind and is inclined by honor to stand to his agreement.
>
> Thuc. 4.19.2–3

The Spartans offer as universal a system in which gift demands countergift, and rivals compete in a theater of generosity. Although we may
historicize the Spartan assertions and insist that such behavior is not
universal, Thucydides' Spartans offer no such conditions. Thucydides,
of course, is deeply sensitive to the limits of *megalophrosunê*, "greatheartedness," and, as argued above in chapter 7, the *History* provides
ample material with which to critique the Spartan arguments, but the
appeal to the universal—rather than the debatable content of this particular appeal—is ubiquitous in Thucydides. Gnomic wisdom and aphorisms are, of course, traditional in formal Greek speech, but Thucydides develops such generalizing maxims with an intensity surpassed by
none of his contemporaries whose works have survived.

Not simply characteristics that Thucydides attributes to his speakers,
references to human nature are a recurrent heuristic by which he shapes
his own narrative. At 2.50.1, he remarks that the plague at Athens was
"almost too harsh for human nature (*hê anthrôpeia phusis*)". At
4.108.4, he sourly observes that the restive Athenian allies overempha-
sized Brasidas's prospects, "for human beings (*hoi anthrôpoi*) are accustomed (*eiôthotes*) to entrust to an unexamined hope what they desire
and to use sovereign reason to thrust aside what they do not fancy." At
5.68.2, he frets about a numerical estimate "because of the human ten-

---

9. Besides the passage quoted here, note also the rather surprising intellectualism of
the Spartan king Archidamos at Thuc. 1.84; on the relationship between sophistic thought
and the remarks attributed to Archidamos, see Hussey 1985.

dency toward boastfulness (to anthrôpeion kompôdes) with regard to
their own side." His analysis of the effect of civil war on society at
Corcyra is one of the most famous (if also one of the most complex)
passages in the *History*. There, Thucydides makes explicit why his analysis of events on a particular island at a particular time is of transcendent
importance:

> The sufferings that revolution entailed upon the cities were many and terrible,
> such as have occurred and always will occur as long as the nature of human
> beings (*phusis anthrôpôn*) remains the same.
>
> Thuc. 3.82.2

The possibility of a change in human nature would seem, at best,
remote in Thucydides' relentless narrative of greed, fear, and warfare.
He argues that human nature, at some level, remains unchanged and
that there is, as we might now term it, an "essence" of common humanity
that all biological human beings possess. This essential humanity allows
Thucydides' work to exert an appeal that transcends its particular time
and origin. The stability of human nature lies behind and validates Thucydides' famous claim that his work will be a *ktêma es aiei*, "a valuable
possession for all time" (Thuc. 1.22.4).

Thucydides' argument is a strong one. The rising cycle of brutalization that he explored at Corcyra seems grimly applicable to the savagery
that has unfolded in the late twentieth century in Cambodia, Guatemala,
Nicaragua, Armenia, Bosnia, Somalia, Rwanda, and other places. Death
squads and other mechanisms of internecine slaughter do indeed transcend any one culture, religion, or ethnic group—there are good reasons
why Thucydides retains a foothold in many curricula as a kind of patron
saint of power politics. Thucydides becomes the first surviving author
in European literature who gave written expression to the world "as it
really was" and made it possible for us to take human nature into proper
account as we structure our dealings with one another.

But nothing is ever simple in Thucydides. Different readers have established very different visions of Thucydides—Der Derian, surveying
realist thought, refers to "the eternal return of the ghost of Thucydides"[10]
—but almost all of those who have studied him closely have sensed in
his text dramatic and unresolved tensions. As Peter Pouncey put it, "The
real difficulty in locating the whole of Thucydides lies in the fact that
there is genuine ambivalence in the man, especially on questions con-

10. Derian 1995b, 382.

nected with the pursuit of power, and the abuses to which its exercise can lead. Reticent but also self-aware, he makes room in his history for arguments that speak to each side of this ambivalence. But I do not believe that he ever fully resolved it, and the interpreter must resist the inclination to impose solutions on him."[11] Sophokles, by contrast, seems to have thrived on ambiguity—his plays glory in their lack of closure, their resistance to any fixed or stable reading. Thucydides, on the other hand, concentrated the full power of his mind on the problem of establishing a settled account, a transparent window onto what really happened, and a history that answered more questions than it raised. And yet Thucydides never came close to such a goal. Not only did he leave his work only three-quarters complete (the narrative breaks off in 411), but his model of history implied that Athens, not Sparta, should have won the war.

Even the essentialism that shapes Thucydides' *History*—the assumption that human nature was stable and historical inquiry thus possible—is problematic. Immediately after his reference to "the nature of human beings" at 3.82.2 (quoted above), Thucydides qualifies this remark:

> [Human nature] is sometimes more [harsh] and at other times more peaceful and distinct in its manifestations (*eidê*, pl. of *eidos*), depending upon how all the vicissitudes of events bear upon it. In peace and prosperity, states and individuals have better sentiments, because they do not find themselves suddenly confronted with imperious necessities; but war takes away the easy supply of daily wants, and so proves a rough master that brings most people's characters to a level with their fortunes.
>
> Thuc. 3.82.2

Thucydides thus appeals to the stability of human nature as a necessary tool with which to tell his story—and yet the theme of his story is not stability but change. He describes not only the battles, the victories, the shifts in advantage, and other events of the war but also the qualitative impact that these events had upon human life. The Corcyraean civil war is important because its effects upon Corcyraean society were devastating. The murderous power struggles there shattered the assumptions and bonds that had previously maintained stable human relations.

Thucydides describes the plague at Athens not only because such a disease—whatever it was—might strike again but because he wanted to

---

11. Pouncey 1980, ix–x; similarly, Connor 1984 249–250.

show how the terrible sufferings—"almost too harsh for human nature (*anthrôpeia phusis*)" (Thuc. 2.50.1)—broke down the restraints imposed by society and devastated the moral behavior of Athenian citizens. Athens itself fell in the end because, after Perikles' death, it could no longer find leaders who had the intellectual power or moral vision to lead the city (2.65). Thucydides does not tell the story of traditional values validated. The assumptions of his class—the international Greek elite, with its supranational loyalties, countless and overlapping personal alliances, its conventions of what constituted appropriate behavior—all seemed to have collapsed around him, and Thucydides wanted to understand how this had happened. If Thucydides posited an essential, transhistorical human nature, this was not an easy, conventional idea, but a bold and determined assertion that flew against many of the experiences through which he felt that he had lived.

The tension between change and continuity runs throughout the *History*. The apocalyptic description of plague at Athens gives way to a narrative that, after Perikles' final response, resumes its course and makes surprisingly few references to the ongoing devastation in the city.[12] The Athenians act brutally at Melos, but the logic of their reasoning remains consistent with that which they express at the prewar conference at Sparta. Although Thucydides constantly uses a timeless human nature to explicate events, both past and present, he uses this timeless human nature to explain why human society had so radically changed. Of course, one can argue that human nature and human society are distinct, but, in practice, Thucydides treats both as if they were orthogonal. Like a Renaissance painter who represents children as dif-

---

12. At the conclusion of his description of the plague, Thucydides reports the rumor that the Peloponnesians shortened their invasion of Attika because of the plague, but he then concedes that, in fact, the Spartans made their longest invasion (forty days) during the first plague year (2.57). Athenian reinforcements to Poteideia prove counterproductive because they brought the plague with them to the Athenian army in northern Greece (2.58), but it is at least surprising that the Athenians managed to send any reinforcements (or even had any functioning foreign policy) after the apocalyptic description of chaos and anarchy at Athens. Perikles' final speech responds to the plague (2.61.3, 64.1), but the plague then plays very little role in the narrative. Thucydides mentions it again in book 3, explaining that the plague preoccupied the Athenians and prevented them from paying as much attention to Mytilene as they might otherwise have done (3.3), but military operations proceed for the most part as normal. At 3.87, Thucydides focuses again, although briefly, on a resurgence of the plague, citing the loss of 4,000 hoplites and 300 cavalry (a tremendous blow to Athenian labor power), but he does not subsequently integrate the ravages of the plague into his narrative, and, indeed, there does not seem to be a reference to the plague in his account of the following year.

ferent in size but not in kind from adults, Thucydides conflates psychology and sociology.[13]

Thucydides' *History* relates two simultaneous stories. First, warfare, civil strife, and plague had shattered human society. Second, things had always been pretty much the same: thus even Agamemnon, when he mustered the Greek expedition upon Troy, really depended upon intimidation rather than loyalty (Thuc. 1.9). The entire Archaeology proceeds from the assumption that Thucydides can apply the same heuristics to ancient times as to the present. Thucydides thus describes history as a process of dramatic, often corrosive change, but he does so by assuming that human beings think and react much the same way at all times and in all places. If history charts a consistent process in which humans rise from squalor into ever larger and more secure groups (like Minos and the Athenian empire), then why did this natural process miscarry, brutalizing Greek society and handing victory to Sparta? Although we can, of course, develop arguments to reconcile this tension between change and stability, Thucydides did not. This unresolved conflict between the two tendencies that Thucydides observed contributes much to the tension and nagging lack of closure that have struck so many readers of the *History*.

THE CITY AND MAN

Strauss entitled his famous collection of essays on Aristotle's *Politics*, Plato's *Republic*, and Thucydides' *History* (in that reverse chronological order) "The City and Man." He drives home the significance of this choice, asserting, on the first page of the introduction, that "the theme of political philosophy is the City and Man." Thucydides certainly shared this view. As I pointed out in chapter 2, almost all political realists have traditionally worked with groups rather than with individuals. Most students of international affairs have tended to concentrate on nation-states, since these have been the conventional dominant structures of European diplomacy since the Peace of Westphalia over 300 years ago, but analysts readily concede that fiefdoms, tribes, and city-states would be more appropriate in other historical circumstances. Thucydides' focus upon the polis thus places him squarely in the tradition

13. So Hunter 1989; Morrison 1994.

of realist thought. When he attributes speeches (and the points of view
that they inscribe) to aggregates such as the Corcyraeans (Thuc. 1.32–
36), Corinthians (1.37–43, 68–71, 120–124), Athenians (1.73–78), Plataians (2.71, 3.53–59), Mytileneans (3.9–14), and Thebans (3.61–67),
he has, like any analyst, self-consciously reduced and simplified his data.
Such simplifications are necessary in realisms as in any paradigms. The
exclusion of some details can be justified by the increase in focus, and
the exchange, in theory at least, helps us see much more than we lose.
And, of course, we must reduce and simplify if we are to get anywhere—
as our colleagues in cognitive science have shown, we cannot perceive
anything unless we apply patterns to fields of detail. All that we can do
is strive for the most finely meshed and insightful patterns.

Thucydides, however, narrows his intellectual focus to an extraordinary degree. I have elsewhere explored at length the extent to which he
marginalizes in his work not only religion and women (as often, the
realist voice is also distinctly masculine),[14] but all kinship ties and social
bonds.[15] Thucydides' simplified model of the world systematically minimizes all relationships that intervene between the city, on the one hand,
and individuals, on the other. Against speeches by the "Athenians," "Corinthians," or other groups stand speeches by individuals such Archidamos, Sthenelaidas, Perikles, Kleon, Diodotos, Nikias, Alkibiades,
Hermokrates, and Euphemos, to name only the most prominent.

This extreme dualism reflects the most dynamic thought of the fifth
century. Although the Platonic corpus, as we have it, begins with Euthyphro, earnestly intent upon prosecuting his own father for a dubious
case of accidental homicide, this young man's unreflective moralism has
made it difficult to appreciate the underlying strength and idealism of
his position.[16] In Sophokles' *Antigone*, Kreon's character proves so brit-
tle and his fate so catastrophic that few have recognized what (I at least
would argue)[17] is the idealism that marks much of his opening speech:
when Kreon publicly values the polis above his family and friends (*Ant.*
163–210) and then maintains this stance against his own niece, he espouses a dramatically radical principle that the Thucydidean Perikles

---

14. Compare Tickner 1995.
15. This is one of the major themes of Crane 1996a. For an interesting survey of how
this narrowing of perception affects the rise of political thought generally in the fifth and
fourth centuries, see Saxonhouse 1992, which treats Thucydides only in passing.
16. Saxonhouse (1992, 93–101) locates Euthyphro's position in the development of
progressive political thought.
17. On this, see Crane 1989.

vigorously advances as well (see esp. Thuc. 2.60). Protagoras may have done most to articulate this subordination of individual to state, but the historical Perikles seems to have contributed to it as well: Plutarch (*Per.* 7) reports that as soon as Perikles entered public life, he ostentatiously cut himself off from all of his social ties. Where the aristocratic Kimon exploited a network of personal friendships and familial alliances, Perikles devised a lifestyle that would dramatize that nothing could distract him from his devotion to the state.[18] Thucydides exploits the importance of subordinating individual to state by its converse: he does not object to the Greek tyrants because they were harsh rulers who took away freedom, but because they subordinated the polis to—indeed, treated the polis as an extension of—their own *oikos*.[19]

Here as elsewhere, Thucydides' practice as an historian runs parallel to the reported practice of Perikles as statesman.[20] In this case, however, the results are at best problematic. In focusing on states and individuals, Thucydides imposes on his material an idealized view of the world that often did not fit events. His representation of Alkibiades makes this point, but much of what can be said about it could be extended to the complex diplomatic maneuvers of book 5 and especially to the events of book 8, where personal machinations and rivalries often drive the actions of states.

The confrontation between Nikias and Alkibiades establishes the latter as a brilliant and charismatic figure, but Thucydides pushes his Alkibiades to an extreme. Alkibiades, like Perikles before him, appears as an isolated individual, and the friendships and alliances—which were a crucial source of his power—receive little emphasis, appearing only when necessary to explain particular events and never identified as a general source of Alkibiades' power. From the opening of this confrontation (Thuc. 6.15.2), Thucydides contrasts Alkibiades' "political differences" (*diaphoros ta politika*) with his "private" good fortune (*ta idia*). Again, at 6.15.4 we hear that Alkibiades had an outstanding record in his public (*dêmosiai*) conduct of the war, but that his private (*idiai*) lifestyle offended his fellow citizens. The spotlight shines on Alkibiades alone, and Alkibiades reinforces this as soon as he begins speaking:

---

18. Kleon too is reported to have repudiated his friends to dramatize his devotion to the state: Plut. *Mor.* 806F; Connor 1992, 91–94.

19. Thuc. 1.17; on this, see chapter 6.

20. On this, see chapter 2.

Athenians, I (*moi*) have a better right to command than others—I must begin
with this as Nikias has attacked *me* (*mou*)—and at the same time I believe
myself to be worthy of it. The things for which I am abused bring fame to
my (*mou*) ancestors and to *myself* (*emoi*), and to the fatherland (*patris*) profit
besides.

                                                                          Thuc. 6.16.1

Alkibiades argues that he has benefited his fatherland—a logical assertion given that he is trying to persuade his fellow citizens. Alkibiades
even refers to his own family, but only, it should be noted, to the dead
and not to any of the many kin to whom he was related. His household,
extended family and friends, pale before the lone figure brilliantly illu-
minated in the textual spotlight. Inflected forms of the first person singular pronoun *egô* appear four times in the first sentence. Thucydides
presents Alkibiades, like Perikles, as a charismatic figure who acts alone
and influences events with the force of his personality. But if the Thucydidean Perikles is also fond of the first person pronoun and tends to
depict a world in which the only major players are himself and the polis,
Alkibiades reverses the polarity in this exchange, placing himself, not
the state, in the dominant role. Where Perikles asserts that the individual
is nothing without the state (Thuc. 2.60.2–4), Alkibiades, in his arresting
definition of "patriotism" (*to philopoli*), argues that the state counts for
nothing if it does not support him as an individual (6.92.2–5).

Alkibiades, of course, mattered little as an isolated individual, and he
would never have risen so far at so young an age had he not been born
into an important family and inherited a network of preexisting connections, but Thucydides systematically minimizes in his *History* the role
of such personalized alliances—or, more properly perhaps, from the Archaeology and Corcyraean debate onward, he minimizes these alliances
when they work properly, so that gratitude is stored up, loyalty repaid,
and ritualized friendship effective. Thus Thucydides has much more to
say about Alkibiades' enemies (who provide a major theme of his speech
at Thuc. 6.16–18) than about the widespread and influential friends who
clearly helped Alkibiades rise to power, provided him with the levers
that he needed to manipulate events outside of Athens, protected him
during his exile, helped engineer his return to Athens, and allowed him
to withdraw from Athenian affairs one final time. The importance of
these relationships shows through from time to time. We hear, for example, that Alkibiades had persuaded the Mantineans and Argives to
contribute major forces to the Sicilian expedition, but this corporate
aspect of Alkibiades' position occurs only in passing, when Thucydides

explains the caution with which the Athenians recall him (6.61.5). When the Athenians initially take him into custody, Thucydides remarks that not only Alkibiades but "those who had been verbally attacked along with him" (6.61.6) set sail for Athens. The subsequent escape is a collective one—the Athenians search for "Alkibiades and those with him" (6.61.7)—but these unnamed extras quickly disappear. In the very next sentence, Thucydides turns his attention to "Alkibiades, now being an exile," and his passage back to the Greek mainland. Thucydides drops this thread of the narrative for a bit, and Alkibiades' "fellow exiles" reappear briefly (6.88.9), but again immediately drop from sight.

When Alkibiades is summoned to Sparta, his extraordinary defence of his actions drives home, even more forcefully, his isolation:

> It is necessary first to speak to you of the *prejudice against me (tês emês diabolês)*, in order that suspicion may not make you disinclined to listen to *me (mou)* upon public matters. [2] The connection with you as your *proxenos*, which the ancestors of our family by reason of some discontent renounced, *I personally (autos egô)* tried to renew by my good offices toward you, in particular upon the occasion of the disaster at Pylos. But although *I (mou)* maintained this friendly attitude, you yet chose to negotiate the peace with the Athenians through *my enemies (tois emois echthrois)*, and thus to strengthen them and to heap discredit upon *me (emoi)*.
>
> Thuc. 6.89.1–2

There are only two active parties here: Alkibiades and the Spartans. Alkibiades refers to the prejudice against *himself*, demands that the Spartans listen to *him*, claims that *he personally* reestablished the *proxenia* with the Spartans, defends *his* goodwill with the ingratitude of the Spartans. He continues in the next section (Thuc. 6.89.3) to speak of how *he*, in the singular, managed to influence the Mantineans and Argives— as if he had direct and unmediated access to both these groups and did not have to work through a network of friends and allies at each of these city-states. If Alkibiades pictures individual Spartans, they appear as an indistinct "someone" (*tis*). When he portrays his political status at Athens, he speaks of how *he* as an individual was attached to the common people (*dêmos*) as an undifferentiated group. At 6.89.4–6, he briefly widens the focus, shifting to "we," but only because for the moment he wants to lessen his personal responsibility.

If Alkibiades at Sparta concludes the political speeches of the *History*, the solipsistic patriotism that he articulates shapes almost all of the subsequent events that Thucydides describes in the home theater of operations. Once the Sicilian expedition has been treated in book 7, events in

book 8 disintegrate, and Thucydides' realist inclination to analyze human beings in groups breaks down. The struggle between oligarchs and
democrats at Athens is a major theme of the book, but this internal
dissension continues to spread throughout the Greek world (e.g., Chios
[Thuc. 8.9.3]). Civil war has scattered exiles other than Alkibiades
throughout the Greek world, and these seek help against their home
governments wherever they can (8.6.1). The Athenians, their prestige
damaged, cannot even trust those allies who serve with them (8.10.2).
Thucydides cites the ritualized friendship that binds Alkibiades and the
Spartan ephor Endios (8.6.3), but only because this traditional Greek
institution helps Alkibiades play a more effectively divisive role in Spartan affairs (8.12.2). Likewise, we hear that Alkibiades was "a close associate (*epitêdeios*) of the leading men in Miletos" (8.17), but only so
that we may better understand how Alkibiades sought to manipulate
this relationship to his own personal advantage. The Athenian commander Phrynichos chooses to betray Athens so as to damage Alkibiades
(8.50).

Neither the conservative Spartans nor the imperial Persians can escape this fragmentation. We hear that Agis had plenary powers while
operating near Dekeleia and that, "in a word, the allies at this point in
time were subject to Agis rather than to the Spartans at home, for the
force that he had with him made him feared wherever he went" (Thuc.
8.5.3). The Persian empire is no Greek city-state, in which the people or
a small elite share power: the Great King presides as absolute ruler, his
domain is an extension of his personal household, and all his subjects
are (at least as the Greeks see it) his personal slaves. Nevertheless, even
Persia ceases to function as a unit, as Tissaphernes and Pharnabazos,
the two Persian governors adjacent to the Greek world, compete with
one another and pursue actions designed to promote their own immediate interests rather than those of the empire as a whole (e.g., 8.5.5,
8.6.1).

The focus upon Alkibiades as an individual and upon his private
advantage thus reflects a larger theme in Thucydides' *History*: the failure
of leadership and concomitant decline of Athens after Perikles. Thucydides sums up this process in his overview of Perikles:

> Perikles told them to wait quietly, to pay attention to their navy, to attempt
> no new conquests, and to expose the city to no hazards during the war and,
> doing this, promised them a favorable result. What they did was the very
> contrary, allowing private ambitions (*idiai philotimiai*) and private interests
> (*idia kerdê*), in matters apparently quite foreign to the war, to lead them into

projects unjust both to themselves and to their allies—projects whose success would only conduce to the honor and advantage of private persons, and whose failure entailed certain disaster on the country in the war.

Thuc. 2.65.7

Alkibiades, for all his brilliance, belongs to this group of politicians who subordinated the interest of the state to their own (see 6.15.2–3). He is thus an example of change and a symptom of Athenian decline.

But decline from what? If Alkibiades reflects a decline from Periklean leadership, Perikles, and not Alkibiades, constituted the anomaly. The Alkibiades of book 6 is no innovation. He is—and is feared as—a classic figure of the archaic Greek world. When he claims credit for having sponsored four chariot teams at the Olympic games, he appeals to the same system of prestige through which the patrons of Simonides, Pindar, and Bacchylides had, in the first half of the fifth century, sought to win Panhellenic distinction for themselves, their families, and their homelands (Thuc. 6.16).[21] At the same time, this traditional pattern has its drawbacks: two centuries before, Kylon had effectively opened Athenian history by becoming first a victor at Olympia and then by trying to make himself a tyrant.[22] The Athenians of the late fifth century had not forgotten this collocation of lavish expenditure and tyrannical ambitions: according to Thucydides 6.15.4, the people feared that Alkibiades wanted to make himself the new *turannos* of Athens. While this speech contributes to the thread of disarming Athenian candor, real or affected, that runs throughout the *History*,[23] the ideas expressed are not new. Far from being an innovative figure, Alkibiades hearkens back to the aristocratic world whose demise Thucydides seems to record.[24] Neither Alkibiades nor the general infighting that fills book 8 constitutes a decline from normal standards, except if viewed in comparison with the earlier books of Thucydides. Both reflect the resurgence of traditional figures and politics, but Thucydides has relatively little sympathy for charismatic masters of competitive generosity and even less for the networks of loyalty strengthened by the exchange of favors.

Decline is a major theme in Thucydides[25]—Alkibiades is no Perikles,

---

21. Kurke 1991, 171–177; Forde (1989, 186) suggests that Alkibiades differed from the traditional tyrants only in the single-minded extremism of his pursuit of "honor."

22. Hdt. 5.71; Thuc. 1.126.3.

23. So Orwin 1994, 125.

24. One of the best treatments of Alkibiades' attitude toward the state remains Pusey 1940.

25. So Euben 1990b, 167–169.

and Melos is worse than Mytilene—and Athens, along with the world, clearly did not stay the same, but Thucydides' narrative, by its own biases, exaggerates and distorts this change. In Thucydides, *stasis* destroys politics—or, to be more precise, the politics officially sanctioned by the city-state[26] —but it might be more accurate to state that politics remained as important as before, shifting its locus from citizen and city-state to the complex webs of ritualized friendship, political clubs, family connections, and ideological alliances.

Thucydides' concluding segment has earned, and for good reason, a reputation as "the least satisfactory of his books."[27] Its narrative is fractured, covering too much ground in too confusing a manner for the tastes of most readers. Thucydides mentions too many individuals in too brief a space.[28] There are no speeches, although a number of the events—especially the revolution and counterrevolution at Athens—would readily lend themselves to such extended treatment. Consider the conclusion of Pouncey, whose book on Thucydides concentrates heavily on book 8:

> I believe that the importance of the eighth book has so far been neglected. It is clear to me that in this book Thucydides finally settles on a pessimistic view of human nature that is applied not merely in ominous isolated episodes but fairly systematically through the narrative, and shows the basic level at which it operates and the basic tendency it has. The basic level is the individual, and the basic tendency is towards aggression. Various speakers in the war have complacently conceded this, but Thucydides now seems to insist that at least under circumstances of continued pressure, the primary aggression is applied for oneself, at the expense of any claims from any society or institution to which one belongs. The pessimism at the end seems to override any of the more positive strands we had noted earlier in the work, and the possibilities of collective action recede. The bonds between human nature and war and *stasis* are now complete.[29]

This is, like much in Pouncey's book, a very perceptive reading of the *History*. At the same time, however, this judgment, valid as it may be for the text at hand, derives from a weakness in Thucydides' outlook and the distortions that this weakness introduced. The basic unit of measure does indeed shift from the larger group, at the opening of the

---

26. Orwin 1994, 182.
27. Connor 1984, 230.
28. Pouncey (1980, 39 n. 11; pp. 173–174) relays statistics developed by Kenneth Rothwell about how many more individuals Thucydides names in book 8 than in other books.
29. Pouncey 1980, 42–43.

History, to the atomized individuals of book 8. Thucydides truly did study the city and man, as Strauss believed. The problem for Thucydides was that his method, because it consistently reduced too much of human affairs to this simple dichotomy, was ill equipped to capture and assess the many more complex ties that enmeshed anyone prominent enough to warrant mention in the *History*—not just Alkibiades but Phrynichos, Agis, Tissaphernes, and the mere names who appear briefly to push their schemes.

Book 8 has proven unsatisfactory to so many readers because it is unfinished, but I suspect that it is unfinished because Thucydides found the material too unsatisfactory. Almost ninety years ago Francis Cornford aptly observed that "the eighth book is a mere continuation on the old chronological plan, unfinished, dull, and spiritless."[30] When Thucydides is no longer able to describe "the Athenians as a unit in civic or collective narrative, or to select one or two individuals whose ideas and policies eventually shape civic action," then a "narrative convenience" indeed disappears,[31] but the consequences go beyond this. Thucydides' intellectual approach thrashes in book 8 like a machine digesting material that is too coarse or too fine. Thucydides' *History*—at least such of it as he managed to complete—works best when a small number of intellects, whether individual or collective, guide events according to large ideas. Thucydides could not properly describe the forces at work in book 8 unless he returned to its proper place, and gave full credence to, that ancient simplicity that made personal alliances possible and without which these grasping schemers could not have undermined the interests of their state.[32] Thucydides gives us no reason to assume that Peisistratos and his sons, who spent years in the mid-sixth century building up alliances in the Greek world so as to seize power one more time in Athens, would have felt out of place if they had found themselves transported a century and a half later into the Ionia of book 8.

Nevertheless, Thucydides' least satisfying book is more influential than the best work that most of those who followed him ever produced. Successful historians (and scientists) create engaging stories to account for events, and the idea of Athenian moral decline appeals to scholarly pessimism better than the notion that Greek politics in book 8, to a

---

30. Cornford 1907, 244.
31. Connor 1984, 214.
32. By contrast, Plato recognized that personal justice and public corruption were not incompatible: see *Rep.* 351c-352a.

great degree, returned to their customary fragmented state. Certainly, the values and assumptions prevalent in the Greek world changed during a generation of near-continuous warfare, but Thucydides, in emphasizing the consistency of human nature, failed to give proper emphasis to the continuity that bound individuals such as Alkibiades and Phrynichos to Peisistratos and Isagoras in the sixth century. If the ancient simplicity were as defunct as Thucydides argues, then the Athenians, Spartans, Chians, Milesians, and Persians of book 8 would have had far less opportunity to pursue their divisive courses of action. If we have only in recent years begun to recognize the degree to which fifth-century politics was in many ways as complex and stylized as the politics of Homer,[33] the elegance of Thucydides' idealizing emphasis on individual and state bears much of the responsibility. If an overemphasis on unitary groups and on isolated individuals is a common danger for all political realists, Thucydides led the way here as elsewhere.

THE FUNERAL ORATION AND THE PRICE OF OBJECTIVITY

We shall conclude with, by most standards, the least "realistic" document in Thucydides, the self-consciously idealizing Funeral Oration, because this speech captures one of the great tensions within the *History*. The Funeral Oration presents us with an Athens that not only balances the interests of city and man but also addresses a more historically contingent problem. It establishes a delicate synthesis that combines the values of the traditional Greek elite with those of a democratic society. Of course, the description of the plague, which follows almost immediately, betrays the fragility of Athenian society and undermines much of what Perikles says (although it is important to remember that Perikles delivers his heroic final speech *after* the section on the plague and Perikles, not the plague, has the final word). In at least one regard, however, Perikles anticipates the problems that will occur, for, in the final analysis, it is Athenian power that commands the respect and love of its citizens, and Perikles thus bases much of his argument on a motivation that virtually all realist thinkers have stressed:[34] the love of power, which emerges as a fundamental human trait in the Archaeology and continues

33. See, for example, Herman 1987, which surprised many of us by showing how pervasive the "archaic" system of ritualized friendship remained in the classical period.
34. See chapter 2.

to shape events through all eight books. The Thucydidean Perikles thus builds his idealizing vision[35] on a sound realist base and defends it against that scorn that would bring down the "ancient simplicity."

At the same time, however, the emphasis on power is itself inconsistent with Perikles' larger project, for the values of the traditional Greek elite, as a particular historical system, depended for their survival upon the at least partial mystification of power and especially upon embedding power within affections and social bonds. Thus even in the Funeral Oration itself, the problems of Thucydides' outlook appear, for the realism that Thucydides takes for granted renders the Periklean synthesis unstable. Even if the *History* had broken off after the Funeral Oration, and there had been no description of the plague, no Mytilenean debate, no slaughter of the Plataians, no Melos, even so the Funeral Oration would have given up fundamental principles upon which that ancient simplicity had depended.

First, in the Funeral Oration the Thucydidean Perikles articulates a vision of democracy that synthesizes qualities that elsewhere clash, for the greatness of the Athenian polis makes aristocrats of all its citizens:[36] in normal language, the "good and the beautiful" (*kalos kagathos*) designated the persons and values of the upper class. Elsewhere, the Thucydidean Kleon also attempts to unify society when he daringly appropriates for "the more common sort" (Thuc. 3.37.3: *hoi phauloteroi*) that moderation, *sôphrosunê*, by which the elite defined themselves. In the Funeral Oration, on the other hand, the aristocratic Perikles pushes in the opposite direction, assimilating the common people upward into the elite: all Athenians, rich and poor, are champions of "greatheartedness," which can lavish favors on friends without expecting anything in return (2.40.4). In the Funeral Oration, every Athenian—and especially those who lay down their lives for the community, whatever their private faults (2.42.3)—can share in the *aretê* of the city. In the Funeral Oration, all Athenians, because they are not afraid to die, fashion their own freedom (2.43.4).

35. I take this speech to be an attempt to visualize Athenian democracy as it could be. Like all such praise it is prescriptive as well as descriptive, for, to the extent that the speech is specific, it challenges the recipient to live up to those claims made for it. Here, if nowhere else, Thucydides provides us with a vision of that "ancient simplicity" as it might exist in his modern, Athenian world. On the ideology of the funeral oration as an Athenian genre, Loraux 1986a has become the standard work, but Ziolkowski 1981 remains a useful and often more usable starting point.

36. See, for example, Edmunds and Martin 1977.

The democratization of aristocratic values is a major theme of the Funeral Oration. A single passage will suffice to illustrate this. In this passage, Perikles notes that great families could erect imposing burial monuments to their dead, but all those who give their lives for Athens receive a far greater honor:

> For this offering of their lives made in common by them all they each of them individually received that renown that never grows old, and for a tomb, not so much that in which their bones have been deposited, but that noblest of shrines wherein their reputation (*doxa*) is laid up to be eternally remembered upon every occasion on which deed or story shall fall for its commemoration. [3] For famous men have the whole earth for their tomb. Not only do inscriptions on stone columns (*stêlôn epigraphê*) serve as their memorial (*sêmainei*), but even in lands beyond our control there resides in every breast a memory unwritten (*agraphos mnêmê*) more of their resolve (*gnômê*) than even of their accomplishment (*ergon*).
>
> Thuc. 2.43.2–3

This extraordinarily dense passage builds upon and extends the ideologically charged imagery of aristocratic burial. On the one hand, the Athenian state conventionally erected as funeral monuments stone slabs (*stêlai*) that listed the names of those Athenians and even their allies who had fallen in battle.[37] At the same time, wealthy Greek families had, in the archaic period, erected imposing funeral monuments to their dead. Not only were some of these still visible,[38] but, starting in about 430— roughly the dramatic date of Perikles' Funeral Oration—there was a change in fashion at Athens, and Athenians began once again to lavish large amounts of wealth on impressive burial monuments.[39] Such private burial monuments defined status and highlighted social stratification— that was, in fact, their purpose, for the rich chose to convert their wealth into visible symbols of their position.

Perikles, however, daringly converts this divisive practice into a unifying image—the boldness of this paradoxical maneuver is comparable to that of Diodotos, when he accepts the terms of debate imposed by Kleon. *All* of those who give their lives for Athens receive an imposing tomb—indeed, a tomb that is far more imposing than any material

---

37. For examples, see Meiggs and Lewis 1988, nos. 33, 48; no. 35 lists Argives who died fighting alongside the Athenians at Tanagra; Crawford and Whitehead 1983, no. 127, translates the opening of Meiggs and Lewis no. 33.

38. For a survey of these archaic funeral monuments in Attika, see Richter 1962; it is not clear how many of these early monuments would have survived the raids and destruction of the Persian Wars.

39. For the implications of this, see Morris 1994.

monument ever could hope to be. The richest aristocrats must content themselves with physical monuments that are, however splendid, fixed in place. The Athenian dead, by contrast, not only have their state monument but have achieved a reputation that travels far beyond Athens and its possessions.[40] This is a well-known convention: the poet Pindar, for example, boasts that his work is no statue, rooted to the ground, but can travel freely in every ship that floats (*Nem.* 5.1–3). But for Athens this idea has an added force: however far Athenian power may have extended the city's possessions, the memory of these individuals will travel even farther. Loved or hated, they will be remembered far beyond the spatial and temporal limits of Athenian domination. Where the realist Thucydides resolutely champions the importance of *erga*, real accomplishments, his Perikles strikes an aggressively idealistic pose: these individuals will be remembered not so much for what they have done but for *gnômê*, their moral resolve.[41]

Perikles, in good Thucydidean style, forcefully grounds the idealism of this speech on realist foundations. Perikles' remark at the opening of Thucydides 2.41—where he calls Athens "the school of Hellas"[42]—has become famous, not least because Athens actually did, after the fall of the Athenian empire and especially during the Roman Empire, develop into the cultural center of Greece. The proof that Perikles adduces for this has, however, attracted less attention. Athens has not become the school of Hellas because Perikles filled the city with spectacular architecture (most Greeks would have preferred Delphi or Olympia) or because Athenian literature was preeminent (Athenian drama was still primarily a local literary form written by and for Athenians) or because Athenians were the greatest philosophers (Plato had not yet been born, and Sokrates was still just a local eccentric) or because the Athenians excelled at history (Herodotus, sympathetic as he may have been to Athens, was not Athenian, and Thucydides had scarcely begun work in 430). Athens is the school of Hellas because it has more power than any other state.

Nor is this Athenian power subtle or understated: the Spartan military power partakes, I have argued, largely of bluff; for the Spartans,

---

40. I take this to be the force of ἐν τῇ μὴ προσηκούσῃ: not simply beyond Attika, but in land that is beyond Athenian control.

41. On the role of *gnômê* in the Funeral Oration as a whole, see Edmunds 1975a, 44–70, esp. 68, where Edmunds stresses that it is the fact that these men chose to give their lives that makes their sacrifice a triumph of will and freedom over chance.

42. On this phrase, see Hornblower 1991, ad loc.

with their fixed numbers, could not even annex Tegea, and although they (when reinforced by their allies) may be irresistible in a single battle, they cannot project their force over a long period of time. Spartan power has much in common with Foucault's invisible, pervasive discipline, for Spartan leadership depends upon moral leadership and symbolic capital that, as I pointed out in chapter 8, places serious constraints on their action. On the other hand, Foucault's "spectacle of the scaffold," the public, dramatized display of power—the ability to inflict tangible violence upon the physical bodies of their opponents—constitutes the Athenian power that Perikles celebrates. If Athens is the school of Greece, then the Athenians can be grim schoolmasters. Melos and Skione, of course, lay in the future, as did that Athenian mercy that restricted executions on Mytilene to 1,000 men and gently reduced the remaining population to serfdom (Thuc. 3.50).[43] But many of those who listened to Perikles would have served under him when he had brought Athenian power to bear and crushed the revolt of Samos a decade before. Thucydides' text, at least as it stands now, had already included a summary of the Samian revolt (1.115.2–117).[44]

The Athenian citizens are, we hear, uniquely accomplished. A symbiotic relationship links the excellence of individual Athenians to the power of their city as a whole: in this, the Thucydidean Perikles is surely appropriating for Athens a claim usually made for the Spartan way of life in the fifth century.[45] He goes on to develop his vision of Athenian power:

> And that this is no mere boast thrown out for the occasion, but truth of deeds (ergôn alêtheia), the power (dunamis) of the state acquired by these habits proves. [3] For Athens alone of its contemporaries is found when tested to be stronger (kreissôn) than its reputation and alone gives no occasion to its assailants to blush at the antagonist by whom they have been worsted, or to its subjects to question its title by merit to rule.
>
> Thuc. 2.41.2–3

43. On the size of this number and the severity of this punishment, see Connor 1984, 86–87, with nn. 18 and 19.

44. Duris of Samos (Plut. Per. 28) went farther and attributed to Perikles a spectacular ferocity: Perikles reportedly led the ship captains and marines into the marketplace of Miletos, crucified them, let them hang exposed for ten days before ordering their heads to be broken, and—worst, perhaps of all, to Greek sensibilities—had their bodies cast out without burial. Even Plutarch expresses his doubts about Duris's reliability, however, and suggests that he may have added this detail to help slander the Athenians. Such a punishment was, however, standard for traitors, and Duris's account may be at least partially true: on this, see the note at Stadter 1989, 258–259.

45. Cf. the opening section of Xen. Lak. Pol., discussed in chapter 3.

Perikles is not content to make pious statements. He insists that Athens's position is *real*, it is the "truth," *alêtheia*, of "actual deeds," *erga*. Athens is so powerful that no one exaggerates its accomplishments. It is so great that those whom it crushes in the field depart without loss of dignity. The reality of Athenian power is its anchor, now and in the future:

> Rather, the admiration of the present and succeeding ages will be ours, since we have not left our power (*dunamis*) without witness but have shown it by mighty proofs; and far from needing a Homer for our panegyrist, or other of his craft whose verses might charm for the moment only for the impression that they gave to melt at the touch of fact, we have forced (*katanankasantes*) every sea and land to be the highway of our daring and everywhere, whether for evil or for good, have left imperishable monuments (*mnêmeia*) behind us. [5] Such is the Athens for which these individuals, in the assertion of their resolve not to lose it, nobly fought and died; and well may every one of their survivors be ready to suffer in its cause.
>
> Thuc. 2.41.4–5

Perikles leaves no doubt as to the nature of Athenian power, and thus of the source of Athens's position. The Athenians have brought the world to its knees—they have pushed themselves onto every sea and land. Nothing can stand in their way, and they have covered the world with "imperishable monuments" of their accomplishments. The boasts of the statesmen merge with those of the historian (cf. Thuc. 1.21): the Athenians have no need for the seductive fantasies of the poets, because their power is real and, being not "without witness," can be confirmed despite hostile scrutiny. At the center of Athenian identity stands the power to compel and, if necessary, to destroy. It was not for some vague ideal or empty platitude but for this power that these individuals fought and died.

A few sentences later, Perikles returns to this theme, arguing that it is power that renders Athens an object deserving of adoration and worthy of every sacrifice. This is one of the few places where a speaker—especially an Athenian speaker—moves away from immediate self-interest and urges subordination of the self to some other goal. The dead deserve praise because they appreciated the city for what it was:

> So died these men as became Athenians. You, their survivors, must determine to have as unfaltering a resolution in the field, though you may pray that it may have a happier issue. And do not consider with words (*logos*) alone the advantage (*ôphelia*) that is bound up with the defence of your country, though this would furnish a valuable text to a speaker even before an audience so alive to them as the present. Rather, you must yourselves day by

day gaze upon the power (*dunamis*)—power in real fact (*ergon*)—of Athens
and become its lovers (*erastai*). And then when the city seems to you to be
great (*megalê*), you must reflect that it was by daring (*tolmôntes*), recognizing
those things that had to be done, and a keen sense of shame (*aischunomenoi*)
in action that mortals won all this. Whenever in any attempt they met with
failure, they nevertheless resolved not to deprive the city at least of their own
aretê but laid it at the city's feet as the most noble (*kalliston*) contribution
that they could offer.

Thuc. 2.43.1

The language is typically Thucydidean. There is the familiar, obsessive
contrast between language (*logoi*) and material advantage (*ôphelia*). In
the translation above I have also tried to bring out the force of *dunamis*
as it is modified by *ergon*. Furthermore, these dead Athenians clearly
resemble the Athenians of the Corinthian speech at Thucydides 1.68–
71: they exhibit boldness (*tolmê*), forge ahead to do what they must,
and let nothing stop them.

The most striking element of this passage, however, is the term *erastai*,
"lovers" (pl. of *erastês*, "lover"). The Athenians who are still alive are
supposed to gaze upon Athens and fall in love with their city. The language is quite strong, since an *erastês* is one possessed by *erôs*—erotic
love. The Athenians are not supposed to feel a kind of sublimated, chaste
love for a high ideal. Perikles frankly eroticizes the polis, making it an
object that commands sexual desire.

Sexual passion for the city would not have struck Athenians at the
time as a strange metaphor, for it seems to have been a topos in the later
fifth century.[46] Thus, when Cloudcuckooland in Aristophanes' *Birds* becomes a smashing success, the Herald declares: "You do not know how
much honor this city earns among mortals / or how many *erastai*, 'lovers,' of this land you have" (*Av.* 1278–1279). A few lines later (1316),
the Chorus glories that "passionate desires (*erôtes*) for my polis prevail!"
In the *Acharnians*, the Thracian Sitalkes is described as *philathenian*.
He was, one character tells the Athenians, "your *erastês*"(*Ach.* 143) and
scribbled "Athens is beautiful" graffiti on walls, as a man would do for
some sexual favorite. The *Knights* makes great play out of this image.
Kleon appeals for help from Demos, "The People," "because I love you,
O Demos, and I am your *erastês*"(*Eq.* 732). The claim is funny—not

---

46. On this passage and its implications, see now Monoson (1994), who argues that
by presenting the city as a lover rather than a nurturer, Perikles stresses the reciprocal
nature of citizenship.

because it is absurd to claim to be a lover of the Athenian demos, but because the age and appearance of Demos in this particular play render the profession of love absurd. Men were expected to become *erastai* of beautiful young boys, not of old men.[47] Nor is this metaphor restricted in the fifth century to comedy: in Euripides' *Phoinician Women*, Polyneikes, who in this play is a relatively sympathetic character, tells the Chorus that "all men must feel *erôs* for their fatherland" (*Phoen.* 358–359). At Plato *Gorgias* 481d, we hear of men who declared themselves the *erastai* of the Athenian demos in order to win their favor. Elsewhere (*Alc.* 1.132a), Sokrates warns Alkibiades not to become a *dêmerastês*, "an *erastês* of the *dêmos*."

Perikles' picture of the *erastês* transfixed with desire and awe for the *erômenos*, the object of desire, belongs to a larger tradition of depicting erotic possession. About 600 B.C., roughly the same period when Solon instituted his reforms at Athens, Sappho composed a poem describing the intense feelings of the lover's gaze (frag. 31). At the sight of the beloved sitting with a man, and the sound of "her sweet voice and lovely laughter," the poetic narrator loses her voice. A flame runs beneath her flesh. She sees nothing, and her ears hum.

Perikles does not here call upon the Athenians to love Athens for its physical charms or for its generosity or even for the advantages that it confers upon them and the security it provides their families. He explicitly tells his listeners to "fasten their gaze" (*theômenous*, from *theaomai*, another strong word) upon the power (*dunamis*) of the city, and this power is supposed to fill the Athenians with erotic love. Thucydides imagines his listeners contemplating the city in their mind's eye not because it is good or even because it is, in some personified form, beautiful but because it is great (*megalê*).

The open worship of power had serious consequences for Greek culture. Consider, for example, the following passage from Euripides' *Phoinissai*. In this play, Eteokles is the villainous brother who has cheated Polyneikes out of his position and refuses to deal reasonably with him. Confronted by his mother, Jokasta, Eteokles offers the following explanation:

> I will tell you this, Mother, without any concealment: I would go to the rising
> of the stars and the sun, [505] or beneath the earth, if I were able so to do,

---

47. On this passage, see Dover 1978, 146.

to win Tyranny, the greatest of the gods. Therefore, Mother, I will not yield this blessing to another rather than keep it for myself; for it is cowardly to lose the greater [510] and to win the less.[48]

Eur. Phoen. 503–510

The love of power leads here to the glorification of tyranny, absolute domination at home. Four times Athens itself is characterized as a *turannos* over other cities,[49] and it is to Athens's dominant position that Perikles here directs the gaze of his audience. But if the Athenians surrender themselves to their infatuation with Athenian power, then what is to prevent them from seeking their own private power at the expense of others and the state as a whole? This is, in fact, precisely what Thucydides reports to have happened (Thuc. 2.65) and what we can see happening as events splinter into small actions and feuds in book 8. Perikles gave eloquent expression to the importance of the state, especially in his heroic final speech, but his ideas lost force after death removed his personal authority from the scene.

The glorification of power is not simply problematic because it helps produce an Alkibiades. The Thucydidean Perikles anticipates Plato in the *Symposium* and especially the *Phaedrus*, where true love reacts not to the physical person but to the abstract qualities that the *erômenos* embodies. In the *Phaedrus*, Sokrates explains true love as a force that draws the incorporeal "soul," *psuchê*, to it. True love inflames mortals with a kind of madness, *mania*, but this madness is a good thing (*Phdr.* 249d). This occurs when the soul of the lover sees *to kallos*, "physical beauty" (but also, in other contexts, "nobility"), on earth and, through this vision, recalls the "true" *kallos* (*to alêthês*). For Plato, justice (*dikaiosunê*) and self-control (*sôphrosunê*) constitute true beauty and inspire desire (250b–d). The true lover does not exploit the object of his desires for the sake of pleasure and pursue mere sexuality (250e). True passion touches body and spirit equally:

> When he sees a godlike (*theoeides*) face or form that is a good image of beauty (*kallos*), he shudders at first, and something of the old awe comes over him. Then, as he gazes, he reveres (*sebetai*) the beautiful one as a god, and if he did not fear to be thought stark mad, he would offer sacrifice to his beloved

48. This translation is based on that of David Kovacs, published both in Crane 1996b and in the Loeb edition.

49. At 1.124.3, the Corinthians label Athens as *turannos polis* (cf. 1.122.3); the other three speakers are Athenians: Perikles (2.63.1–2), Kleon (3.37.2), and Euphemos (6.85.1). This phrase has attracted considerable attention: see, for example, Hunter 1973/4; Connor 1977b; Raaflaub 1979; Raaflaub 1987, 226.

as to a cult statue (*agalma*) or a god. And as he looks upon him, a reaction
from his shuddering comes over him, with sweat and unwonted heat; for as
the effluence of beauty (*to kallos*) enters him through the eyes, he is warmed.

Pl. *Phdr.* 251a-b

The physical symptoms are similar to those in Sappho, but Plato has
subordinated the physical to another—in his scheme, higher—sphere.
Love, in this view, is a personal submission to some transcendent, ultimately impersonal quality, but the experience remains deeply physical:
trembling, sweat, and heat transfix the very corporeal sensations of the
lover even as he senses through his equally fleshly beloved the grand,
transcendent qualities that give this love its true meaning. The flesh remains as a barrier, but as a barrier that, with all its limitations, constitutes a kind of lens that gives shape to the very emotions that look
beyond this world.

In Thucydides, by contrast, the object of erotic desire has no physical
being. Athenian power has many proofs, but these are signs that point
to a quality that is seductive but impersonal. This adoration of power
constitutes, like the aggressive candor of Thucydides' Athenians, a thoroughly modern simplicity, for it openly declares itself and does not hide
behind hypocritical fictions. Perikles is in fact attempting to resolve a
problem of Athenian nature. I have argued that the Athenians refuse
from the Corcyraean debate onward to embed their dealings with others
in affective ties, and in so doing they have set themselves apart from the
Corinthians, Corcyraeans, Plataians, and other more traditional Greeks.
Perikles attempts to re-embed the crucial relationship between the city
and man. The realist's love of power drives the idealist's selfless patriotism.

Contrast this vision of the Athenian polis with that of Hannah
Arendt. Confronted with the twin barbarisms of Nazi Germany and
Stalinist Russia, Arendt turned to the Greek polis as a space for "human
plurality." Totalitarian regimes had attempted to destroy individuality
and render each person—even Hitler and Stalin themselves—the anonymous representatives of transcendent historical forces.[50] The fundamental equality and tangible distinctness of human beings combined to
render each human life special, make possible interaction between people, and allow each of us to "insert ourselves into the human world"—
to "act," as Arendt interprets the term.[51] We are, in Arendt's view, human

50. Arendt 1973; Canovan 1992, 17–62.
51. Arendt 1958, 175–176.

only insofar as we "act," setting into motion by our words and deeds—
even by our birth—further trains of consequences that no one could
predict. But we can act in this way only in the presence of other, distinct
human beings: the people who witness our actions and feel their consequences provide these actions with their meaning. More than once
Arendt quotes the Thucydidean Perikles to help explain this humanistic
vision.[52]

But if the Funeral Oration—with its grand vision of a democratic
society where all citizens share rights and responsibilities—provides
Arendt with a starting point for her work, Thucydides and his Perikles
reveal a habit of thought that would develop into the totalitarianism
that haunted Arendt. When Perikles calls upon the citizens of Athens to
lose themselves in their adoration of the polis, he undermines the distinctness of its citizens. Athens becomes an embodiment of power, and
this power seduces each subject into the same position of submission
and adoration. The power that makes of each Athenian an *erastês* foreshadows the ideological schemes and historical necessities that would
make the supporters of Hitler and Stalin sacrifice their lives as well as
their individuality to a truth that supposedly transcended human values.

But if the Thucydidean Perikles at his best reveals a potential for
totalitarianism, his aristocratic vision paved the way for atomizing the
citizens and for transforming them into what Arendt would call a mob.[53]
While Perikles lived, he could, by the force of his will, twist the love of
power to the city's advantage, but the lover's adoration, which inspires
the individual to give up everything for the city, faded after his death.
After Perikles was gone, "personal ambitions and personal profits"
(Thuc. 2.65.7: *idiai philotimiai kai idia kerdê*) drove subsequent leaders
to undertake projects that were not in the interests of the state. The
grand exemplar of this attitude is, of course, Perikles' own kinsman,
Alkibiades, who is, more than anyone, the dominant personality in the
last three books of the *History*. Where Kleon had been a would-be Perikles, the more able (at least in Thucydides) Alkibiades approached this
level and fashioned himself as a kind of anti-Perikles.[54]

Alkibiades' speech at Sparta (Thuc. 6.89–92) occurs more than two
books before the *History* breaks off, but in several ways it marks an

52. Arendt 1958, 197, 205.
53. Arendt 1973, 305–326.
54. Rawlings (1981, 122–125) compares Alkibiades' speech at 6.89–92 with that of
Perikles at 1.140–144.

end. This, the final political speech in the *History*, balances the first
Athenian speech, which also was delivered at Sparta. More important,
Alkibiades articulates both the collapse of the Periklean ideal (and thus
the decline that Thucydides cites at 2.65 and 8.89.3) and the resurgence
of a traditional elite disdain for the state (of which Thucydides, as I
argued in the previous section, has less to say and which he distorts
according to his own prejudices). Consider Alkibiades' famous enunci-
ation of patriotism near the conclusion of the speech:

> I hope that none of you will think any the worse of me if after having hitherto
> passed as a lover of my country, I now actively join its worst enemies in
> attacking it, or will suspect what I say as the fruit of an outlaw's enthusiasm.
> [3] I am an outlaw from the iniquity of those who drove me forth, not, if
> you will be guided by me, from your service: my worst enemies are not you
> who only harmed your foes, but they who forced their friends to become
> enemies; [4] and love of country is what I do not feel when I am wronged,
> but what I felt when secure in my rights as a citizen. Indeed I do not consider
> that I am now attacking a country that is still mine; I am rather trying to
> recover one that is mine no longer; and the true lover of his country is not
> he who consents to lose it unjustly rather than attack it, but he who longs
> for it so much that he will go all lengths to recover it.
>
> Thuc. 6.92.2–4

K. J. Dover, in his commentary on this passage, labeled the above
reasoning "a sophistry that is obscure and lame." Of course, it is sophistic—almost everyone in Thucydides speaks in sophistic terms, and
Alkibiades was himself a product of the later fifth-century intelligent-
sia—but I do not think that the reasoning would have seemed either
"obscure" or "lame." Nathan Marsh Pusey was closer to the mark when
he stressed that patriotism was, at least among the Greek elite with their
many international connections, hardly universal.[55] Alkibiades is simply
restating the deeply traditional Greek commonplace that one should
harm enemies and help friends. The Athenians, who should have been
his friends, have harmed Alkibiades, and Alkibiades thus has a right—
even a duty—to retaliate in kind. The strong ahistorical streak in the
History that was the focus of the beginning of this chapter has correspondingly deflected attention from the traditional aspects of Alkibiades' position. No doubt, Peisistratos, during his long years of exile from

---

55. Pusey 1940; note, for example, that when Kimon reportedly sought, during his
ostracism, to fight alongside the Athenians at Tanagra, he was rebuffed: the Athenians
thought that he was at least as likely to be working for the Spartans, with whom he had
close ties (Plut. *Kim.* 17).

Athens more than a century before, presented his case in a similar fashion as he prepared his return to power. Plato's prestige has made famous
the attitude of his Sokrates, who in the *Krito* allows his homeland, however unjustly, to take his life, but the Platonic dialogue itself is hardly
the norm. Rather, it constitutes itself an attack upon the far less selfless
norms of his time (doubtless obliquely defending Sokrates against his
association with Alkibiades himself).

At the same time, the emphasis of Alkibiades' speech has a decidedly
modern—"Athenian" would perhaps be a better word—slant. All of his
relationships seem contingent upon his immediate condition. Athens has
harmed him, and he is thus now its enemy. He will aid the Spartans
because they, although also his enemies, have wronged him less than the
Athenians. He makes no attempt to establish a new, ongoing relationship with the Spartans: Alkibiades—in reality, the master of aristocratic
alliances inside and beyond Athens—has, in Thucydides, no use for the
rhetoric of gift exchange and of symbolic capital that permeates the
Corcyraean debate in book 1, the Mytilenean speech and the Plataian
defence in book 3, and the Spartan offer of peace in book 4. Like the
Athenians after the Corcyraean debate and the Spartans at Plataia, Alkibiades lives in an eternal present, always ready to serve his immediate
interests, loyal only to those who can help him in the future, mindful at
best of advantages conferred in the immediate past. Alkibiades—energetic, insatiably acquisitive—may be the anti-Perikles, but he perfectly
embodies the Athenian character that the Corinthians sketched at Thucydides 1.68–71, almost two decades before. Alkibiades has, if anything,
refined the vision of the selfless lover that Perikles sketched at 2.41, for,
pushing the city aside and concentrating on his own self, he remains true
to the quest for power and advantage that Perikles situated at the core
of his Athens.

If Thucydides set out, as I believe that he did, to reconstitute the
ancient simplicity—the ideology of the elite into which he had been born
and of which he was a product—and to reconcile what we might now
call the real with the ideal, he failed. The irresistible desire for power
promised but ultimately failed to deliver a calculus of advantage with
which to measure each human action. If modern realists have at times
been more optimistic in their faith that scientific knowledge can change
the world, is this because they have proven more insightful or more
knowledgeable than Thucydides, or that the twentieth century provides
more room for hope than did democratic Athens? No one in the Greek
world—with the possible exception of Aristotle and his school—would

achieve this goal or fail with such brilliance. Plato could answer individuals such as Kleon with the *Republic* and Alkibiades with the *Krito*, but he had to leave the realist program behind, disdaining mere advantage and seeking to ground his reasoning in the good. The Greek mathematicians, such as Euclid and Archimedes, would push human understanding as far toward "true knowledge" as any single body of thinkers ever has, but they too had to leave the human world behind and entered an ideal geometrical world of their own fashioning. Thucydides refused to make such compromises. He remained with the savageries and horrors of his time. A failed general, he nevertheless kept his gaze fixed upon events in which he no longer had a part. Whatever the strengths and weaknesses of his work—and they are both great—the struggle to "save the phenomena," to synthesize the tangible with the ideal, continues now, as it will doubtless always continue. Thucydides contributed to this practice at an early stage of European culture, as ideas and writing began to evolve together. "With all his rationalism, Thucydides is equally on the side of the active life, no matter what its disappointments, and in the active life the prize is not truth, though there may be truth, but immortality."[56]

---

56. Edmunds (1975a, 214), who cites 1.22.4, along with 2.41.4, 43.2.

Bibliography

Abu-Lughod, L. 1986. *Veiled Sentiments: Honor and Poetry in a Bedouin Society*. Berkeley and Los Angeles: University of California Press.

Adcock, F. E. 1963. *Thucydides and His History*. Cambridge: Cambridge University Press.

Adkins, A. W. H. 1975. "The Arete of Nicias: Thucydides 7.68". *GRBS* 16: 379–392.

Allison, J. W. 1983. "Review of *Past and Present in Herodotus and Thucydides*, by V. Hunter. *AJP* 104: 298–301.

———. 1984. "Sthenelaidas' Speech: Thucydides 1.86". *Hermes* 112: 9–16.

———. 1989. *Power and Preparedness in Thucydides*. Baltimore: Johns Hopkins University Press.

Althusser, L. 1971. *Lenin and Philosophy and Other Essays*. New York: Monthly Review Press.

Andrewes, A. 1962. "The Mytilene Debate". *Phoenix* 16:64–85.

Arendt, H. 1958. *The Human Condition*. Chicago: University of Chicago Press.

———. 1973. *The Origins of Totalitarianism*. New York: Harcourt Brace.

Ashley, R. K. 1986. "The Poverty of Neorealism". In *Neorealism and Its Critics*, edited by R. O. Keohane, 255–300. New York: Columbia University Press.

———. 1995. "The Powers of Anarchy: Theory, Sovereignty, and the Domestication of Global Life". In *International Theory*, edited by J. D. Derian, 94–128. New York: Macmillan.

Austin, M. M., and P. Vidal-Naquet. 1977. *Economic and Social History of Ancient Greece: An Introduction*. London: Batsford.

Badian, E. 1989. "Plataea between Athens and Sparta". In *Boiotika*, edited by H. Beister and J. Buckler, 2: 95–111. Munich: Editio Maris.

———. 1990. "Thucydides and the Outbreak of the Peloponnesian War: A Historian's Brief". In *Conflict, Antithesis, and the Ancient Historian*, edited by J. W. Allison, 46–91. Athens: Ohio State University Press.

————. 1993. *From Plataea to Potidaea: Studies in the History and Historiography of the Pentecontaetia*. Baltimore: Johns Hopkins University Press.

Barthes, R. 1982. "Le discours de l'histoire". *Poetique* 49: 13–21.

Beaumont, R. L. 1936. "Greek Influence in the Adriatic". *JHS* 56: 159–204.

Bernadete, S. 1969. *Herodotean Inquiries*. The Hague: Martinus Nijhoff.

Bizer, F. 1937. *Untersuchungen zur Archäologie*. Tübingen: Postberg.

Blainey, G. 1988. *The Causes of War*. New York: Macmillan.

Bloedow, E. F. 1981. "The Speeches of Archidamus and Sthenelaidas at Sparta". *Historia* 30: 129–143.

————. 1987. "Sthenelaidas the Persuasive Spartan". *Hermes* 115: 60–66.

Blundell, M. W. 1989. *Helping Friends and Harming Enemies: A Study in Sophocles and Greek Ethics*. Cambridge: Cambridge University Press.

Boedeker, D., ed. 1987. *Herodotus and the Invention of History*. Arethusa. Baltimore: Johns Hopkins University Press.

Boer, W. d. 1977. *Progress in the Greece of Thucydides*. Amsterdam: North-Holland.

Bohannen, P. 1955. "Some Principles of Exchange and Investment among the Tiv". *American Anthropology* 57: 60–66.

Bosworth, A. B. 1993. "The Humanitarian Aspect of the Melian Dialogue". *JHS* 113: 30–44.

Bourdieu, P. 1977. *Outline of a Theory of Practice*. Cambridge: Cambridge University Press.

Boyd, R. 1991. *Introductory essay to The Philosophy of Science*, edited by R. Boyd, P. Gasper, and J. D. Trout, 3–23. Cambridge, Mass.: MIT Press.

Brenner, R. 1987. "Feudalism". In *The New Palgrave: A Dictionary of Economics*, edited by J. Eatwell, M. Milgate, and P. Newman, 170–185. New York: W. W. Norton.

Bulman, P. 1992. *Phthonos in Pindar*. Berkeley and Los Angeles: University of California Press.

Burkert, W., ed. 1990. *Herodote et les peuples non Grecs: Neuf exposés suivi de discussions*. Entretriens sur l'Antiquité Classique. Vandoeuvres-Geneva: Fondation Hardt.

Canovan, M. 1992. *Hannah Arendt: A Reinterpretation of Her Political Thought*. New York: Cambridge University Press.

Carr, E. H. 1949. *The Twenty Years' Crisis: 1919–1939*. London: Macmillan.

Carter, L. B. 1986. *The Quiet Athenian*. Oxford: Clarendon Press.

Cartledge, P. 1979. *Sparta and Lakonia: A Regional History, 1300–362 B.C.* London and Boston: Routledge and Kegan Paul.

————. 1987. *Agesilaos and the Crisis of Sparta*. London: Duckworth.

————. 1993. "The Silent Women of Thucydides: 2.45.2 Re-Viewed". In *Nomodeiktes: Greek Studies in Honor of Martin Ostwald*, edited by R. M. Rosen and J. Farrell, 125–132. Ann Arbor: University of Michigan Press.

Castriota, D. 1992. *Myth, Ethos, and Actuality: Official Art in Fifth-Century B.C. Athens*. Madison: University of Wisconsin Press.

Chiasson, C. C. 1986. "The Herodotean Solon". *GRBS* 27: 249–262.

Church, W. F. 1973. *Richelieu and Reason of State*. Princeton: Princeton University Press.

Clark, M. T. 1993. "Realism Ancient and Modern: Thucydides and International Relations". *PS: Political Science and Politics* 26 (3): 491–494.

Cochrane, C. N. 1929. *Thucydides and the Science of History.* Oxford: Oxford University Press.

Cogan, M. 1981a. *The Human Thing: The Speeches and Principles of Thucydides' History.* Chicago: University of Chicago Press.

———. 1981b. "Mytilene, Plataea, and Corcyra: Ideology and Policy in Thucydides, Book Three". *Phoenix* 35: 1–21.

Cohen, I. B. 1985. *Revolution in Science.* Cambridge, Mass.: Harvard University Press.

Cole, T. 1967. *Democritus and the Sources of Greek Anthropology.* Atlanta: Scholars Press.

Collingwood, R. G. 1946. *The Idea of History.* Oxford: Clarendon Press.

Compagner, R. 1988. "Reciprocità economica in Pindaro". *QUCC* 58: 77–93.

Connor, R. 1977a. "A Post-Modernist Thucydides". *CJ* 72: 289–298.

———. 1977b. "Tyrannis Polis". In *Ancient and Modern: Studies in Honor of G. F. Else,* edited by J. H. D'Arms and J. W. Eadie, 95–103. Ann Arbor: Center for Coordination of Ancient and Modern Studies.

———. 1984. *Thucydides.* Princeton: Princeton University Press.

———. 1992. *The New Politicians of Fifth-Century Athens.* Indianapolis: Hackett.

Cook, A. 1985. "Particular and General in Thucydides". *ICS* 10: 23–51.

Cooper, G. L. 1981. "A Neglected Idiom of Fear and Implied Causality in Thucydides". *CJ* 76: 200–222.

Corcella, L. C. a. A. 1983. "Review of *Past and Present in Herodotus and Thucydides,* by V. Hunter. *Phoenix* 37: 166–168.

Cornford, F. M. 1907. *Thucydides Mythistoricus.* London: Arnold.

Cox, R. W. 1986. "Social Forces, States, and World Orders". In *Neorealism and Its Critics,* edited by R. O. Keohane, 204–254. New York: Columbia University Press.

Crane, G. 1989. "Creon and the "Ode to Man" in Sophocles' *Antigone. HSCP* 92: 103–116.

———. 1992a. "Fear and Pursuit of Risk: Corinth on Athens, Sparta, and the Peloponnesians (Thucydides 1.68–71, 120–121)". *TAPA* 122: 227–256.

———. 1992b. "Power, Prestige, and the Corcyrean Affair in Thucydides 1". *Classical Antiquity* 11: 1–27.

———. 1993. "Politics of Consumption and Generosity in the Carpet Scene of the *Agamemnon. Classical Philology* 88: 117–136.

———. 1996a. *The Blinded Eye: Thucydides and the Invention of History.* Lanham, Md.: Rowman and Littlefield.

———. 1996b. *Perseus 2.0: Interactive Sources and Studies on Ancient Greek Culture.* New Haven: Yale University Press.

———. 1996c. "The Prosperity of Tyrants". *Arethusa* 29: 57–85.

Crawford, M., and D. Whitehead. 1983. *Archaic and Classical Greece: A Selection of Ancient Sources in Translation.* Cambridge: Cambridge University Press.

Croix, G. E. M. d. Ste. 1972. *The Origins of the Peloponnesian War*. London: Duckworth.

———. 1980. *The Class Struggle in the Ancient Greek World*. Ithaca, N.Y.: Cornell University Press.

Darbo-Peschanski, C. 1987. *Le discours du particulier: Essai sur l'enquête Hérodotéenne*. Paris: Seuil.

Deininger, G. 1987. *Der Melier-Dialog*. New York: Garland.

Demont, P. 1990. *La cité grecque archaïque et classique et l'idéal de tranquillité*. Paris: Les Belles Lettres.

Derian, J. D., ed. 1995a. *International Theory: Critical Investigations*. New York: Macmillan.

———. 1995b. "A Reinterpretation of Realism". In *International Theory*, edited by J. D. Derian, 363–396. New York: Macmillan.

Dewald, C. 1981. "Women and Culture in Herodotus' *Histories*. *Women's Studies* 8: 93–127.

———. 1987. "Narrative Surface and Authorial Voice in Herodotus' *Histories*". *Arethusa* 20: 147–170.

———. 1993. "Reading the World: The Interpretation of Objects in Herodotus' *Histories*. In *Nomodeiktes: Greek Studies in Honor of Martin Ostwald*, edited by R. M. Rosen and J. Farrell, 55–70. Ann Arbor: University of Michigan Press.

Dewald, C., and J. Marincola. 1987. "A Selective Introduction to Herodotean Studies". *Arethusa* 20: 9–40.

Dijksterhuis, E. J. 1987. *Archimedes, with a New Bibliographic Essay by Wilbur R. Knorr*. Princeton: Princeton University Press.

Dodds, E. R. 1951. *The Greeks and the Irrational*. Berkeley and Los Angeles: University of California Press.

———. 1973. *The Ancient Concept of Progress and Other Essays on Greek Literature and Belief*. Oxford: Oxford University Press.

Dolin, E. 1983. "Thucydides on the Trojan War: A Critique of the Text of 1.11.1". *HSCP* 87: 119–149.

Donini, G. 1968. "Review of Stahl 1966". *CP* 63: 225–227.

Donlan, W. 1985. "Pistos Philos Hetairos". In *Theognis of Megara: Poetry and the Polis*, edited by T. J. Figueira and G. Nagy, 223–244. Baltimore: Johns Hopkins University Press.

Dover, K. J. 1973. "Thucydides". *Greece and Rome: New Surveys in the Classics* 7: 1–44.

———. 1974. *Greek Popular Morality in the Time of Plato and Aristotle*. Berkeley and Los Angeles: University of California Press.

———. 1978. *Greek Homosexuality*. Cambridge, Mass.: Harvard University Press.

———. 1983. "Thucydides as "History" and "Literature"". *History and Theory* 22: 54–63.

Doyle, M. 1990. "Thucydides and Political Realism". *Review of International Studies* 16 (3): 223–237.

Dubois, P. 1988. *Sowing the Body: Psychoanalysis and Ancient Representations of Women*. Chicago: University of Chicago Press.

Duhoux, Y. 1983. *Introduction aux dialectes grecs anciens*. Louvain: Peeters.

Dumont, L. 1970. *Homo Hierarchicus: An Essay on the Caste System*. Chicago: University of Chicago Press.

Edelstein, L. 1967. *The Idea of Progress in Classical Antiquity*. Baltimore: Johns Hopkins University Press.

Edmunds, L. 1975a. *Chance and Intelligence in Thucydides*. Cambridge, Mass.: Harvard University Press.

——. 1975b. "Thucydides' Ethics As Reflected in the Description of Stasis". *HSCP* 79: 73–92.

——. 1987. "The Aristophanic Cleon's "Disturbance" of Athens". *AJP* 108: 233–263.

——. 1993. "Thucydides in the Act of Writing". In *Tradizione e innovazione nella cultura greca*, edited by R. Pretagostini, 2: 831–852. Rome: GEI.

Edmunds, L., and R. Martin. 1977. "Thucydides 2.65.8: *eleutherôs*". *HSCP* 81: 187–193.

Edwards, M., and S. Usher. 1985. *Greek Orators I:Antiphon and Lysias, Translated with Commentary and Notes*. Chicago: Bolchazy-Carducci.

Ehrenberg, V. 1947. "*Polypragmosynê*: A Study in Greek Politics". *JHS* 67: 46–67.

Ellis, J. R. 1991. "The Structure and Argument of Thucydides' Archaeology". *Classical Antiquity* 10 (2): 344–375.

Elshtain, J. B. 1995. "Feminist Themes and International Relations". In *International Theory*, edited by J. D. Derian, 340–360. New York: Macmillan.

Erbse, H. 1989. *Thukydides-Interpretationen*. Berlin: Walter de Gruyter.

Euben, J. P. 1990a. "Review of *The Ambition to Rule*, by S. Forde. *The Journal of Politics* 52 (3): 996–1000.

——. 1990b. *The Tragedy of Political Theory: The Road Not Taken*. Princeton: Princeton University Press.

Evans, J. A. S. 1982. *Herodotus*. Boston: Twayne.

——. 1990. "Six New Studies on Herodotus". *AJP* 111: 92–104.

——. 1991. *Herodotus, Explorer of the Past: Three Essays*. Princeton: Princeton University Press.

Fehling, D. 1989. *Herodotus and His "Sources": Citation, Invention, and Narrative Art*. Leeds: Francis Cairns.

Ferrill, A. 1985. *The Origins of War, from the Stone Age to Alexander the Great*. London: Thames and Hudson.

Figueira, T. J. 1981. *Aegina: Society and Politics*. New York: Arno Press.

Fine, A. 1986. *The Shaky Game*. Chicago: University of Chicago Press.

Finley, J. H. 1942. *Thucydides*. Cambridge, Mass.: Harvard University Press.

——. 1967. *Three Essays on Thucydides*. Cambridge, Mass.: Harvard University Press.

Finley, M. I. 1954. *The World of Odysseus*. New York: Viking Press.

——. 1975. *The Use and Abuse of History*. London: Penguin.

Flory, S. 1980. "Who Read Herodotus' *Histories*?. *AJP* 101: 12–28.

——. 1987. *The Archaic Smile of Herodotus*. Detroit: Wayne State University Press.

——. 1988a. "*Pasa Idea* in Thucydides". *AJP* 109: 12–19.

———. 1988b. "Thucydides' Hypotheses about the Peloponnesian War". *TAPA* 118: 43–56.

———. 1990. "The Meaning of *to mê muthôdes* (1.22.4) and the Usefulness of Thucydides' *History*. *CJ* 85: 193–208.

Flower, H. 1992. "Thucydides and the Pylos Debate". *Historia* 41: 40–57.

Flower, M. A. 1991. "Revolutionary Agitation and Social Change in Classical Sparta". In *Georgica: Studies in Honour of George Cawkwell*, edited by M. A. Flower and M. Toher, 58: 78–97. London: Institute of Classical Studies.

Foley, J. M. 1992. "Word-Power, Performance, and Tradition". *Journal of American Folkore* 105: 275–301.

Forde, S. 1989. *The Ambition to Rule: Alcibiades and the Politics of Imperialism in Thucydides*. Ithaca, N.Y.: Cornell University Press.

———. 1992. "Varieties of Realism: Thucydides and Machiavelli". *Journal of Politics* 54: 372–393.

Fornara, C. W. 1971a. "Evidence for the Date of Herodotus' Publications". *JHS* 91: 25–34.

———. 1971b. *Herodotus: An Interpretive Essay*. Oxford: Oxford University Press.

———. 1981. "Herodotus' Knowledge of the Archidamian War". *Hermes* 109: 149–151.

Fornara, C. W., and L. J. Samons. 1991. *Athens from Cleisthenes to Pericles*. Berkeley and Los Angeles: University of California Press.

Fritz, K. v. 1967. *Die griechische Geschichtsschreibung*. Berlin: Walter de Gruyter.

Fuller, J. F. C. 1957. *Grant and Lee: A Study in Personality and Generalship*. Bloomington, Ind.: Indiana University Press.

Garst, D. 1989. "Thucydides and Neorealism". *International Studies Quarterly* 33 (1): 3–28.

Geertz, C. 1973. *The Interpretation of Cultures*. New York: Basic Books.

Gildersleeve, B. L. 1897. "A Southerner in the Peloponnesian War". *Atlantic Monthly* 80 (September): 330–342.

———. 1915. *The Creed of the Old South, 1865–1915*. Baltimore: Johns Hopkins University Press.

Gilpin, R. 1981. *War and Change in World Politics*. Cambridge: Cambridge University Press.

———. 1986. "The Richness of the Tradition of Political Realism". In *Neorealism and Its Critics*, edited by R. O. Keohane, 301–321. New York: Columbia University Press.

Glatthaar, J. T. 1985. *The March to the Sea and Beyond: Sherman's Troops in the Savannah and Carolinas Campaigns*. New York: New York University Press.

Goldhill, S. 1990. "The Great Dionysia and Civic Ideology". In *Nothing to Do with Dionysos*, edited by J. J. Winkler and F. Zeitlin, 97–129. Princeton: Princeton University Press.

Gomme, A. W. 1945. *A Historical Commentary on Thucydides*. 3 vols. Oxford: Clarendon Press.

Gould, J. 1989. *Herodotus.* New York: St. Martin's Press.

Graham, A. J. 1964. *Colony and Mother City in Ancient Greece.* New York: Barnes and Noble.

Graham, A. J., and G. Forsythe. 1984. "A New Slogan for Oligarchy in Thucydides 3.82.8". *HSCP* 88: 25–45.

Gramsci, A. 1971. *Selections from the Prison Notebooks.* New York: International Publishers.

Grant, J. R. 1972. "Review of *Herodotus: An Interpretive Essay*, by C. Fornara. *Phoenix* 26: 92–95.

Grene, D. 1967. *Greek Political Theory.* Chicago: University of Chicago Press.

Habermas, J. 1977. "Hannah Arendt's Communications Concept of Power". *Social Research* 44: 3–24.

Hall, E. 1989. *Inventing the Barbarian: Greek Self-Definition through Tragedy.* Oxford: Oxford University Press.

Halliday, W. R. 1975. *The Greek Questions of Plutarch with a New Translation and Commentary.* New York: Arno Press.

Halpern, R. 1991. *The Poetics of Primitive Accumulation.* Ithaca, N.Y.: Cornell University Press.

Hammond, N. G. L. 1967. *A History of Greece to 322 B.C.* Oxford: Oxford University Press.

———. 1973. "The Particular and the Universal in Thucydides with Special Reference to That of Hermocrates at Gela". In *The Speeches in Thucydides*, edited by P. A. Stadter, 49–59. Chapel Hill: University of North Carolina Press.

Hanson, V. D. 1983. *Warfare and Agriculture in Classical Greece.* Pisa: Giardini.

———. 1989. *The Western Way of War: Infantry Battle in Classical Greece.* New York: Oxford University Press.

Hart, J. 1982. *Herodotus and Greek History.* New York: St. Martin's Press.

Hartog, F. 1982. "L'oeil de Thucydide et l'histoire "véritable"". *Poetique* 49: 22–30.

———. 1988. *The Mirror of Herodotus: The Representation of the Other in the Writing of History.* Berkeley and Los Angeles: University of California Press.

Harvey, D. 1985. "Women in Thucydides". *Arethusa* 18 (1): 67–90.

Haslam, M. 1990. "Pericles *Poeta*". *CP* 85: 33.

Heath, M. 1990. "Justice in Thucydides' Speeches". *Historia* 39 (4): 385–400.

Heinimann, F. 1945. *Nomos und Physis: Herkunft und Bedeutung einer Antithese im griechischen Denken des 5. Jahrhunderts.* Darmstadt: Wissenschaftliche Buchgesellschaft.

Hereward, D. 1958. "The Flight of Demaratos". *RhM* 101: 238–249.

Herman, G. 1987. *Ritualised Friendship and the Greek City.* Cambridge: Cambridge University Press.

Herz, J. H. 1951. *Political Realism and Political Idealism.* Chicago: University of Chicago Press.

Hogan, J. C. 1972. "Thucydides 3.52–68 and Euripides' Hecuba". *Phoenix* 26: 241–257.

————. 1980. "The *axiôsis* of Words at Thucydides 3.82.4". *GRBS* 21: 139–149.

Hollingdale, S. H. 1989. *Makers of Mathematics*. New York: Penguin Books.

Hornblower, S. 1983. *The Greek World, 479–323 B.C.* London: Methuen

————. 1987. *Thucydides*. Baltimore: Johns Hopkins University Press.

————. 1991. *A Commentary on Thucydides: Books 1–3*. Oxford: Oxford University Press.

————. 1992. "The Religious Dimension of the Peloponnesian War". *HSCP* 94: 169–197.

How, W. W., and J. Wells. 1912. *A Commentary on Herodotus, with Introduction and Appendices*. Oxford: Oxford University Press.

Howard, J. E. 1991. "Scripts and/versus Playhouses: Ideological Production and the Renaissance Public Stage". In *The Matter of Difference: Materialist Feminist Criticism of Shakespeare*, edited by V. Wayne, 221–236. Ithaca, N.Y.: Cornell University Press.

Howard, M. 1983. *The Causes of War*. London: Maurice Temple Smith.

Howard, O. O. 1971. *Autobiography of Oliver Otis Howard*. 2 vols. Freeport, N.Y.: Books for Libraries Press.

Howe, P. 1994. "The Utopian Realism of E. H. Carr". *Review of International Studies* 20: 277–297.

Howie, G. 1984. "Thukydides' Einstellung zur Verangenheit: Zuhörerschaft und Wissenschaft in der *Archäologie*. *Klio* 86: 502–532.

Humphreys, S. C. 1978. *Anthropology and the Greeks*. London: Routledge and Kegan Paul.

Hunter, V. J. 1973. *Thucydides: The Artful Reporter*. Toronto: Hakkert.

————. 1973/4. "*Athens Tyrannis*: A New Approach to Thucydides". *CJ* 69 (2): 120–126.

————. 1982. *Past and Present in Herodotus and Thucydides*. Princeton: Princeton University Press.

————. 1989. "Thucydides and the Sociology of the Crowd". *CJ* 84: 17–30.

Hussey, E. L. 1985. "Thucydidean History and Democritean Theory". In *Crux*, edited by P. A. Cartledge and F. D. Harvey, 118ff. London: Imprint Academic.

Immerwahr, H. R. 1966. *Form and Thought in Herodotus*. Atlanta: Scholars Press.

————. 1973. "Pathology of Power and the Speeches in Thucydides". In *The Speeches of Thucydides*, edited by P. A. Stadter, 16–31. Chapel Hill: University of North Carolina Press.

Johnson, L. M. 1993. *Thucydides, Hobbes, and the Interpretation of Realism*. Dekalb: Northern Illinois Press.

Johnson-Bagby, L. 1994. "The Use and Abuse of Thucydides". *International Organization* 48: 131–153.

Jordan, B. 1986. "Witnesses in the Assembly: Thucydides 6.14 and [Xenophon] *Athenaion Politeia* 2.17. *CP* 81: 133–135.

Kagan, D. 1969. *The Outbreak of the Peloponnesian War*. Ithaca, N.Y.: Cornell University Press.

————. 1974. *The Archidamian War*. Ithaca, N.Y.: Cornell University Press.

————. 1975. "The Speeches in Thucydides and the Mytilene Debate". *YCS* 24: 71–94.

————. 1981. *The Peace of Nicias and the Sicilian Expedition*. Ithaca, N.Y.: Cornell University Press.

————. 1987. *The Fall of the Athenian Empire*. Ithaca, N.Y.: Cornell University Press.

————. 1988. "The First Revisionist Historian". *Commentary* 85 (5): 43–49.

————. 1995. *On the Origins of War and the Preservation of Peace*. New York: Doubleday.

Kallet-Marx, L. 1993a. *Money, Expense, and Naval Power in Thucydides' History 1–5.24*. Berkeley and Los Angeles: University of California Press.

————. 1993b. "Thucydides 2.45.2 and the Status of War Widows in Periclean Athens". In *Nomodeiktes: Greek Studies in Honor of Martin Ostwald*, edited by R. M. Rosen and J. Farrell, 133–143. Ann Arbor: University of Michigan Press.

Keitel, E. 1987. "The Influence of Thucydides 7.61–71 on Sallust *Cat.* 20–21. *CJ* 82: 293–300.

Kelly, D. H. 1981. "Thucydides and Herodotus on the Pitanate Lochos". *GRBS* 22: 31–38.

Keohane, R. O., ed. 1986a. *Neorealism and Its Critics*. New York: Columbia University Press.

————. 1986b. "Theory of World Politics: Structural Realism and Beyond". In *International Relations: Realism, Pluralism, Globalism*, edited by P. R. Votti and M. V. Kauppi, 126–167. New York: Macmillan.

Kirk, G. S. 1985. *The Iliad: A Commentary, Books 1–4*. Cambridge: Cambridge University Press.

Kissinger, H. 1994. *Diplomacy*. New York: Simon and Schuster.

Kleingünther, A. 1933. *Prôtos Heuretês: Untersuchungen zur Geschichte einer Fragestellung*. Leipzig: Dieterich.

Knutsen, T. L. 1992. *A History of International Relations Theory*. New York: Manchester University Press.

Konishi, H. 1980. "The Composition of Thucydides' History". *AJP* 101: 29–41.

Kosso, P. 1993. "Historical Evidence and Epistemic Justification: Thucydides as a Case Study". *History and Theory* 32 (1): 1–13.

Krentz, P. 1982. *The Thirty at Athens*. Ithaca, N.Y.: Cornell University Press.

————. 1989. *Xenophon, Hellenika I–II.3.10*. Warminster: Aris and Phillips.

Kuhn, T. S. 1970. *The Structure of Scientific Revolutions*. Chicago: University of Chicago Press.

Kuper, A. 1988. *The Invention of Primitive Society*. London: Routledge.

Kurke, L. 1991. *The Traffic in Praise: Pindar and the Poetics of Social Economy*. Ithaca, N.Y.: Cornell University Press.

————. N.d. "Herodotus and the Language of Metals". *Helios*, forthcoming.

Lang, M. 1972. "Cleon as the Anti-Pericles". *CP* 67: 159–169.

————. 1984. *Herodotean Narrative and Discourse*. Cambridge, Mass.: Harvard University Press.

Lateiner, D. 1975. "The Speech of Teutiaplus (Thuc.3.30)". *GRBS* 16 (2): 175–184.

———. 1976. "Tissaphernes and the Phoenician Fleet (Thucydides 8.87)". *TAPA* 106: 267–290.

———. 1977a. "Heralds and Corpses in Thucydides". *CW* 71: 97–106.

———. 1977b. "Pathos in Thucydides". *Antichthon* 11: 42–51.

———. 1985a. "Nicias' Inadequate Encouragement (Thucydides 7.69.2)". *CP* 80: 201–213.

———. 1985b. "Review of *Past and Present in Herodotus and Thucydides*, by V. Hunter. *CP* 80: 69–74.

———. 1989. *The Historical Method of Herodotus.* Toronto: University of Toronto Press.

———. 1990. "Deceptions and Delusions in Herodotus". *Classical Antiquity* 9 (2): 230–246.

Lattimore, R. 1939. "The Wise Adviser in Herodotus". *CP* 34: 24–35.

Lloyd, G. E. R. 1978. *Magic, Reason, and Experience: Studies in the Origins and Development of Greek Science.* Cambridge: Cambridge University Press.

Lloyd-Jones, H. 1971. *The Justice of Zeus.* Berkeley and Los Angeles: University of California Press.

Loraux, N. 1985. "La cité, l'historien, les femmes". *Pallas* 32: 7–39.

———. 1986a. *The Invention of Athens: The Funeral Oration in the Classical City.* Cambridge, Mass.: Harvard University Press.

———. 1986b. "Thucydide a écrit la guerre du Péloponnèse". *Metis* 1: 139–161.

Lord, L. E. 1945. *Thucydides and the World War.* New York: Russell and Russell.

Machiavelli, N. 1911. *The Prince.* London: J. M. Dent.

MacLachlan, B. 1993. *The Age of Grace: Charis in Early Greek Poetry.* Princeton: Princeton University Press.

Macleod, C. W. 1974. "Form and Meaning in the Melian Dialogue". *Historia* 23: 385–400.

———. 1977. "Thucydides' Plataean Debate". *GRBS* 18: 227–246.

Malinowski, B. 1922. *Argonauts of the Western Pacific.* London: Routledge.

———. 1978. "Reason and Necessity: Thucydides III.9–14, 37–48". *JHS* 98: 64–78.

———. 1983. "Thucydides and Tragedy". In *Collected Essays*, 140–158. New York: Oxford University Press.

Malkin, I. 1987. *Religion and Colonization in Ancient Greece.* Leiden: E. J. Brill.

Manville, P. B. 1977. "Aristagoras and Histiaios: The Leadership Struggle in the Ionian Revolt". *CQ* 27: 80–91.

———. 1990. *The Origins of Citizenship in Ancient Athens.* Princeton: Princeton University Press.

Marinatos, N. 1981. *Thucydides and Religion.* Königstein: Hain.

Marincola, J. M. 1989. "Thucydides 1.22.2". *CP* 84: 216–223.

Marszalek, J. F. 1993. *Sherman: A Soldier's Passion for Order*. New York: Free Press.

Martin, C. G. 1990. "Orientalism and the Ethnographer: Said, Herodotus, and the Discourse of Alterity". *Criticism: A Quarterly for Literature and the Arts* 32 (4): 511–530.

Marx, K. 1977. *Capital: Critique of Political Economy*. New York: Random House.

Mauss, M. 1990. *The Gift: The Form and Reason for Exchange in Archaic Societies*. New York: W. W. Norton.

McCabe, D. 1981. *The Prose-Rhythm of Demosthenes*. New York: Arno Press.

McMurry, R. M. 1982. *John Bell Hood and the War of Southern Independence*. Lexington: University Press of Kentucky.

McNeal, R. A. 1985. "How Did Pelasgians Become Hellenes? Herodotus 1.56–58". *ICS* 11–21.

Meier, C. 1987. "The Origins of History in Ancient Greece". In *Herodotus and the Invention of History*, edited by D. Boedeker, 41–57. Baltimore: Johns Hopkins University Press.

Meiggs, R. 1972. *The Athenian Empire*. Oxford: Clarendon Press.

Meiggs, R., and D. Lewis. 1988. *A Selection of Greek Historical Inscriptions*. Oxford: Oxford University Press.

Mildenberg, L., and S. Hurter. 1985. *The Arthur S. Dewing Collection of Greek Coins*. New York: American Numismatic Society.

Momigliano, A. 1990. *The Classical Foundations of Modern Historiography*. Berkeley and Los Angeles: University of California Press.

Monoson, S. 1994. "Citizen as *Erastês*: Erotic Imagery and the Idea of Reciprocity in the Periclean Funeral Oration". *Political Theory* 22 (2): 253–276.

Morgenthau, H. 1946. *Scientific Man vs. Power Politics*. Chicago: University of Chicago Press.

———. 1948. *Politics among Nations*. New York: Alfred A. Knopf.

Morris, I. 1986. "Gift and Commodity in Archaic Greece". *Man* 21: 1–27.

———. 1994. "Everyman's Grave". In *Athenian Identity and Civic Ideology*, edited by A. Boegehold and A. Scafuro, 67–101. Baltimore: Johns Hopkins University Press.

Morrison, J. L. 1986. *The Best School in the World*. Kent: Kent State University Press.

Morrison, J. S., and J. F. Coates. 1986. *The Athenian Trireme: The History and Reconstruction of an Ancient Greek Warship*. Cambridge: Cambridge University Press.

Morrison, J. V. 1994. "A Key Topos in Thucydides: The Comparison of Cities and Individuals". *AJP* 115: 525–541.

Nagy, G. 1990. *Pindar's Homer: The Lyric Possession of an Epic Past*. Baltimore: Johns Hopkins University Press.

Nussbaum, M. 1986. *The Fragility of Goodness: Luck and Ethics in Greek Tragedy and Philosophy*. Cambridge: Cambridge University Press.

Ober, J. 1989. *Mass and Elite in Democratic Athens: Rhetoric, Ideology, and the Power of the People*. Princeton: Princeton University Press.

Orwin, C. 1988. "Stasis and Plague: Thucydides on the Dissolution of Society". *Journal of Politics* 50 (4): 831–847.

———. 1989a. "Piety, Justice, and the Necessities of War: Thucydides' Delian Debate". *American Political Science Review* 83 (1): 233–240.

———. 1989b. "Thucydides' Contest: Thucydidean "Methodology" in Context". *Review of Politics* 51 (3): 345–364.

———. 1994. *The Humanity of Thucydides*. Princeton: Princeton University Press.

Osgood, R. E., and R. W. Tucker. 1967. *Force, Order, and Justice*. Baltimore: Johns Hopkins University Press.

Ostwald, M. 1988. *Ananke in Thucydides*. Atlanta: Scholars Press.

Palmer, M. 1989. "Machiavellian *virtu* and Thucydidean *arete*: Traditional Virtue and Political Wisdom in Thucydides". *Review of Politics* 51 (3): 365–385.

———. 1990. "Review of *The Ambition to Rule*, by S. Forde. *The Review of Politics* 52 (3): 469–472.

———. 1992. *Love of Glory and the Common Good*. Lanham, Md.: Rowman and Littlefield.

Parry, A. 1972. "Thucydides' Historical Perspective". *YCS* 22: 47–61.

———. 1981. *Logos and Ergon in Thucydides*. New York: Arno Press.

Pelling, C. B. R. 1991. "Thucydides' Archidamos and Herodotus' Artabanos". In *Georgica: Studies in Honour of George Cawkwell*, edited by M. A. Flower and M. Toher, 58: 120–142. London: Institute of Classical Studies.

Peristiany, J. G., ed. 1966. *Honour and Shame: The Values of Mediterranean Society*. The Nature of Human Society. Chicago: University of Chicago Press.

Plattner, S., ed. 1989. *Economic Anthropology*. Stanford: Stanford University Press.

Popper, K. 1963. *Conjectures and Refutations*. New York: Basic Books.

Pouilloux, J., and F. Salviat. 1983. "Lichas, Lacédémonien, archonte à Thasos e le livre viii de Thucydide". *CRAI* 376–403.

Pouncey, P. A. 1980. *The Necessities of War: A Study of Thucydides' Pessimism*. New York: Columbia University Press.

Pozzi, D. C. 1983. "Thucydides 2.35–46: A Text of Power Ideology". *CJ* 78: 221–231.

Proctor, D. 1980. *The Experience of Thucydides*. Warminster: Aris and Phillips.

Pusey, N. M. 1940. "Alcibiades and τὸ φιλόπολι ". *HSCP* 51: 215–231.

Raaflaub, K. 1979. "Polis Tyrannos". In *Arktouros*, edited by G. W. Bowersock, W. Burkert, and M. Putnam, 237–252. New York: Walter de Gruyter.

———. 1985. *Die Entdeckung der Freiheit: Zur historischen Semantik und Gesellschaftsgeschichte eines politischen Grundbegriffes der Griechen*. Munich: C. H. Beck.

———. 1987. "Herodotus, Political Thought, and the Meaning of History". *Arethusa* 20 (1–2): 221–248.

Rabel, R. J. 1984. "Agamemnon's Empire in Thucydides". *CJ* 80: 8–10.

Race, W. C. 1986. *Pindar*. Boston: Twayne.

———. 1987. "Pindaric Encomium and Isokrates' Evagoras". *TAPA* 117: 131–155.

Raubitschek, A. E. 1973. "The Speech of the Athenians at Sparta". In *The Speeches in Thucydides*, edited by P. Stadter, 32–48. Chapel Hill: University of North Carolina Press.

Rawlings, H. 1975. *A Semantic Study of Prophasis to 400 B. C.* Wiesbaden: Hermes Einzelschriften

———. 1981. *The Structure of Thucydides' History*. Princeton: Princeton University Press.

Redfield, J. 1985. "Herodotus the Tourist". *CP* 80: 97–118.

Reinhardt, K. 1912. "Hekataios von Abdera und Demokrit". *Hermes* 47: 492–513.

Renfrew, C., and J. Cherry, eds. 1986. *Peer Polity Interaction and Socio-Political Change*. Cambridge: Cambridge University Press.

Rhodes, P. J. 1988. *Thucydides: History of the Peloponnesian War*. Bristol: Bristol Classical Press.

Richter, G. 1962. *Archaic Gravestones of Attica*. London: Phaidon Press.

Ricoeur, P. 1988. *Time and Narrative*. Chicago: University of Chicago Press.

Romilly, J. de. 1956a. "La crainte dans l'oeuvre de Thucydide". *Classica et Mediaevalia* 17: 119–127.

———. 1956b. "L'enquête sur le passé: L'archéologie". In *Histoire et raison chez Thucydide*, edited by J. de Romilly, 240–298. Paris: Les Belles Lettres.

———. 1963. *Thucydides and Athenian Imperialism*. Oxford: Blackwell.

———. 1966a. "La condemnation du plaisir dans l'oeuvre de Thucydide". *Wiener Studien* 79: 142–148.

———. 1966b. "Thucydide et l'idée de progrès". *Annali della Scuola Normale Superiori di Pisa* 35: 143–191.

———. 1979. *La douceur dans la pensée grecque*. Paris: Budé.

———. 1984. *Réflexions parallèles chez Euripide et Thucydide*. Amsterdam: North-Holland.

———. 1990. *La construction de la vérité chez Thucydide*. Paris: Julliard.

Rosaldo, R. 1980. *Ilongot Headhunting: A Study in Society and History*. Stanford: Stanford University Press.

Rose, P. W. 1992. *Sons of the Gods, Children of Earth: Ideology and Literary Form in Ancient Greece*. Ithaca, N. Y.: Cornell University Press.

Ruggie, J. G. 1986. "Continuity and Transformation in the World Polity". In *Neorealism and Its Critics*, edited by R. O. Keohane, 131–157. New York: Columbia University Press.

Rusten, J. S. 1985. "Two Lives or Three? Pericles on the Athenian Character (Thuc. 2.40.1–2)". *CQ* 35: 14–19.

———. 1986. "Structure, Style, and Sense in Interpreting Thucydides: The Soldier's Choice (Thuc. 2.40.1–2)". *HSCP* 90: 49–76.

———. 1989. *Thucydides: The Peloponnesian War, Book 2*. Cambridge: Cambridge University Press.

Rutter, N. K. 1989. *Thucydides VI and VII: A Companion to the Penguin Translation of Rex Warner*. Bristol: Bristol Classical Press.

Sahlins, M. 1972. *Stone Age Economics*. Chicago: Aldine-Atherton.

Salmon, J. B. 1984. *Wealthy Corinth*. Oxford: Oxford University Press.

Saxonhouse, A. W. 1992. *Fear of Diversity: The Birth of Political Science in Ancient Greek Thought*. Chicago: University of Chicago Press.

Scanlon, T. 1994. "Echoes of Herodotus in Thucydides: Self-Sufficiency, Admiration, and Law". *Historia* 43 (2): 143–175.

Schaps, D. 1977. "The Woman Least Mentioned: Etiquette and Women's Names". *CQ* 27: 323–330.

Schlatter, R. 1975. *Hobbes's Thucydides*. New Brunswick, N.J.: Rutgers University Press.

Schwartz, E. 1929. *Das Geschichtswerk des Thukydides*. Bonn: Friedrich Cohen.

Scott, J. C. 1976. *The Moral Economy of the Peasant: Rebellion and Subsistence in Southeast Asia*. New Haven: Yale University Press.

———. 1985. *Weapons of the Weak: Everyday Forms of Peasant Resistance*. New Haven: Yale University Press.

Sealey, R. 1976. *A History of the Greek City States, 700–338 B.C.* Berkeley: University of California Press

Segal, C. 1971. "Croesus on the Pyre: Herodotus and Bacchylides". *Wiener Studien* 84: 39–51.

Shapiro, H. A. 1989. *Art and Cult under the Tyrants in Athens*. Mainz am Rhein: Philipp von Zabern.

Shapiro, I., and A. Wendt. 1992. "The Difference That Realism Makes". *Politics and Society* 20 (2): 197–224.

Sherman, W. T. 1984. *Memoirs of General William T. Sherman*. 2 vols. New York: Da Capo Press.

Shi, D. E. 1994. *Facing Facts: Realism in American Thought and Culture, 1850–1920*. New York: Oxford University Press.

Shimron, B. 1989. *Politics and Belief in Herodotus*. Stuttgart: Franz Steiner.

Simpson, R. H., and J. F. Lazenby. 1970. *The Catalogue of Ships in Homer's Iliad*. Oxford: Oxford University Press.

Smith, A., ed. 1979. *The Wealth of Nations, Books I-III*. New York: Penguin Books

Smith, N. 1998. *The Lettered Monument: Epigraphic Inquiry in Herodotus*. Baltimore: Rowman and Littlefield.

Stadter, P. A. 1973. *The Speeches in Thucydides: A Collection of Original Studies with a Bibliography*. Chapel Hill: University of North Carolina Press.

———. 1983. "The Motives for Athens' Alliance with Corcyra (Thuc. 1.44)". *GRBS* 24: 131–136.

———. 1989. *A Commentary on Plutarch's Pericles*. Chapel Hill: University of North Carolina.

———. 1990. "Review of *Ananke in Thucydides*, by M. Ostwald. *AJP* 111 (2): 277–279.

Stahl, H. P. 1966. *Thukydides: Die Stellung des Menschen im geschichtlichen Prozess*. Munich: C. H. Beck.

Starr, C. G. 1983. *The Flawed Mirror*. Lawrence, Kans.: Coronado Press.

———. 1988. "Athens and Its Empire". *CJ* 83: 114–123.

———. 1989. *The Influence of Sea Power on Ancient History*. New York: Oxford University Press.

Steiner, G. 1991. "Mars". *New Yorker*, 11 March, 88–92.

Stengel, P. 1910. *Die Opferbraüche der Griechen*. Leipzig: Teubner.

Stewart, A. F. 1990. *Greek Sculpture: An Exploration*. 2 vols. New Haven: Yale University Press.

Strasburger, H. 1958. "Thukydides und die politische Selbstdarstellung der Athener". *Hermes* 86: 498–530.

Strassler, R. B. 1988. "The Harbor at Pylos, 425 B.C." *JHS* 108: 198–203.

———. 1990. "The Opening of the Pylos Campaign". *JHS* 110–116.

Strauss, L. 1964. *The City and Man*. Chicago: University of Chicago Press.

Tambiah, S. J. 1990. *Magic, Science, Religion, and the Scope of Rationality*. Cambridge: Cambridge University Press.

Täubler, E. 1927. *Die Archaeologie des Thukydides*. Leipzig: Teubner.

Taylor, T. 1990. "Review of *The Mirror of the Herodotus*, by F. Hartog. *Antiquity* 64: 174–175.

Tickner, J. A. 1995. "Hans Morgenthau's Principles of Political Realism". In *Critical Investigations*, edited by J. D. Derian, 53–71. New York: Macmillan.

Tompkins, D. 1972. "Stylistic Characterization in Thucydides: Nicias and Alcibiades". *YCS* 22: 184–214.

———. 1993a. "Archidamus and the Question of Characterization in Thucydides". In *Nomodeiktes: Greek Studies in Honor of Martin Ostwald*, edited by R. M. Rosen and J. Farrell, 99–111. Ann Arbor: University of Michigan Press.

———. 1993b. "Thucydides Constructs His Speakers". *Electronic Antiquity* 1 (1).

Trédé, M. 1983. "*Akribeia* chez Thucydide". In *Mélanges Edouard Delebecque* 407–415. Marseille: Jeanne Laffitte.

Twain, M. 1992. *Collected Tales, Sketches, Speeches, and Essays, 1891–1910*. New York: Library of America.

Usher, S. 1988. *Herodotus, The Persian Wars: A Companion to the Penguin Translation of Books 5–9 from Herodotus*. Bristol: Bristol Classical Press.

Vasquez, J. A. 1990. *Classics of International Relations*. Englewood Cliffs, N.J.: Prentice Hall.

Votti, P. R., and M. V. Kauppi, eds. 1987. *International Relations Theory: Realism, Pluralism, Globalism*. New York: Macmillan.

Vretska, H. 1966. "Perikles und die Herrschaft des Würdigsten—Thuk. 2.37.1". *RhM* 109: 108–120.

Walker, A. D. 1993. "*Enargeia* and the Spectator in Greek Historiography". *TAPA* 123: 353–377.

Waltz, K. 1979. *Theory of International Relations*. Reading, Mass.: Addison-Wesley.

———. 1988. "The Origins of War in Neorealist Theory". *The Journal of Interdisciplinary Theory* 18 (4): 615–629.

Walzer, M. 1992. *Just and Unjust Wars: A Moral Argument with Historical Illustrations*. New York: Basic Books.

Wassermann, F. M. 1953. "The Speeches of King Archidamus in Thucydides". *CJ* 48: 193–200.

———. 1968. "Review of Stahl 1966". *CJ* 63: 230–231.

Waters, K. H. 1971. *Herodotos on Tyrants and Despots: A Study in Objectivity.* Wiesbaden: F. Steiner.

———. 1985. *Herodotos, the Historian: His Problems, Methods, and Originality.* London: Croom Helm.

Wayman, F. W., and P. F. Diehl, eds. 1994. *Reconstructing Realpolitik.* Ann Arbor: University of Michigan Press.

Weber, M. 1958. *The City.* Glencoe, Ill.: Free Press.

———. 1988. *The Agrarian Sociology of Ancient Civilizations.* New York: Verso.

Wendt, A. 1995. "The Social Construction of Power Politics". In *International Theory,* edited by J. D. Derian, 129–177. New York: Macmillan.

West, S. 1985. "Herodotus' Epigraphical Interests". *CQ* 35: 278–305.

Westlake, H. D. 1968. *Individuals in Thucydides.* Cambridge: Cambridge University Press.

———. 1977. "Thucydides on Pausanias and Themistocles: A Written Source?". *CQ* 27: 95–110.

———. 1980. "Thucydides, Brasidas, and Clearidas". *GRBS* 21: 331–339.

———. 1983. "Review of *Past and Present in Herodotus and Thucydides,* by V. Hunter. *CR* 33: 15–17.

———. 1989. *Studies in Thucydides and Greek History.* Bristol: Bristol Classical Press.

White, J. B. 1984. *When Words Lose Their Meaning: Constitutions and Reconstitutions of Language, Character, and Community.* Chicago: University of Chicago Press.

Wick, T. E. 1981. "The Date of the Athenian-Egestan Alliance". *CP* 76: 118–121.

Wiedemann, T. 1982. *Introduction to Thucydides Book IV,* edited by C. E. Graves, xi - xliii. Bristol: Bristol Classical Press.

———. 1983. "Thucydides, Women, and the Limits of Rational Analysis". *G&R* 30 (2): 163–170.

Wight, M. 1978. *Power Politics.* New York: Holmes and Meier.

Wills, G. 1992. *Lincoln at Gettysburg: The Words That Remade America.* New York: Simon and Schuster.

Wilson, J. 1979. *Pylos, 425 BC: A Historical and Topographical Study of Thucydides.* Warminster: Arist and Phillips.

———. 1982. "'The Customary Meanings of Words Were Changed'—Or Were They? A Note on Thucydides 3.82.4". *CQ* 32: 18–20.

———. 1987. *Athens and Corcyra: Strategy and Tactics in the Peloponnesian War.* Bristol: Bristol Classical Press.

Woodhead, A. G. 1970. *Thucydides on the Nature of Power.* Cambridge, Mass.: Harvard University Press.

Young, D. C. 1968. *Three Odes of Pindar: A Literary Study of Pythian 11, Pythian 3, and Olympian 7.* Leiden: E. J. Brill.

Zaretsky, R. 1992. "It's All Still Greek to Us: On the Timelessness of Thucydides". *The Virginia Quarterly Review* 68 (1): 54–70.

Ziolkowski, J. E. 1981. *Thucydides and the Tradition of Funeral Speeches at Athens.* New York: Arno Press.

Index

Achilles, 30–31, 72–74

Aeschines, 93

Agamemnon, 128–29; size of force of, 131, 132, 145; use of fear by, 150, 164, 174

Agis, 308

agora, 163

aidôs, 141–46, 209–10

Aigina, 156–57

Ajax, 216–17

Alexander, 241, 242, 243, 247, 249, 251

Alkibiades, 66, 70; as anti-Perikles, 322, 324; confrontation with Nikias, 305–7; politics of, 68; speech at Sparta of, 307–9, 322–24

Allison, J. W., 166n. 44, 199

Althusser, L., 8–9, 10, 292n. 55

Ameinokles, 138

anarchy, 67

Andocides, 93

Andrewes, A., 238

Archaeology (section of *History*): Athens as expansionist power in, 170; devaluation of Homer in, 59, 127, 129–34; early capitalism in, 171; Greece before the Trojan War in, 128–29; Greek tyrants in, 149–50, 162–64; human development in, 127–29, 135–37, 138; importance of sea power in, 126; lack of shame in, 141–46; origin of political power in, 148, 149–51; the polis in, 139–41; power as force in human history in, 146–47; principal points of, 126–27

Archidamos, 17, 166–67, 194–95; compared with Demaratos, 217; invasion of Attika by, 221–25; modern admiration of speech of, 197–98; on *paraskeuê*, 200–201, 223; on *sôphrosunê*,

206–8, 209, 210; on Spartan character, 202–8, 209, 210–11, 219, 235; on Sparta's weaknesses, 199–201, 211; as the "warner," 208

Archilochus, 205

Archimedes, 44, 325

Arendt, H., 10–11, 12, 321–22

aretê, 271, 272–73

Aristagoras, 85

Aristophanes, 93, 137, 191; disdain for money in, 136; old-fashioned virtues in, 272; rule of the strong in, 72; sexual passion for the city in, 318

Aristotle, 324

Athenagoras, 288–89

Athenian thesis, 64; assumption of constant human nature by, 298; in Euphemos's speech, 287–88; influence of, 258–59; as justification for behavior, 274–76, 281–82; Melian refusal to acknowledge, 174–75, 263–64, 289–93; modern assessment of, 261, 265–66, 269; in speech at Sparta, 263, 264–66, 267–71, 273–84; as unsuccessful attempt to rise above ideology, 262, 263

Athens/Athenians: alliance with Egesta of, 108; candor of, 259, 260; compared with early capitalism, 169–70; contrasted with Sparta in distant future, 150; critique of Spartan customs by, 277–78; as expansionist power, 170; generosity of, 109–10; ideology of power of, 18; lack interest in divine intervention, 251–52, 285; moral decline of, 258; plague in, 50–51, 59–60, 301–2; power of, 66–67, 262, 289, 315–18, 320; reaction to Xerxes' offer of peace, 241–43, 270; rejection of symbolic

343

Athens/Athenians *(continued)*
  capital by, 255, 256; relation with Mytilene of, 176–81; as school of Hellas,
  315–16; speech at Sparta by, 263,
  264–66, 267–71, 273; thirst for power
  of, 66–67; Thucydides vs. Herodotus
  on, 284–85; transitional position of,
  18; tribute/money as basis of, 16–17,
  121–22, 165–68, 170–71, 200–201,
  270–71; uncritical acceptance of history by, 39 *(see also* Athenian thesis);
  Melian Dialogue; Mytilenean debate;
  Persian Wars
Austin, M. M., 136n. 29
axiôsis, 177–18

Bacchylides, 152, 284, 285
barbarians, 296
Bias, 172, 173, 209
Bosworth, A. B., 238n. 4
Bourdieu, P., 111–12, 123, 155, 163
Brasidas, 225, 260
Brenner, R., 148–49
burial monuments, 314–15

capital, symbolic, 16; Athenian rejection
  of, 255, 256; distinguished from
  wealth, 154; role in archaic society of,
  155; Thucydides pays little attention
  to, 171
capitalism: Athenian empire and early,
  169–70; expansionism and, 171
Carr, E. H., 63, 69
Cartledge, P., 65, 108, 198
Catalogue of Ships *(Iliad),* 129–33
charis. See friendship
city. *See* polis
Civil War, American, 14, 33–34. *See also*
  Sherman, W. T.
Cochrane, C. N., 45
Cogan, M., 286; on Athenian speech at
  Sparta, 189, 265; on Corinthian speech
  at Athens, 94, 107n. 34, 119n. 52
Connor, R., 1–2, 45, 198; on Athenian
  speech at Sparta, 266n. 22; on Athenian thesis, 262; on Corcyreans, 94–
  95; on Melian dialogue, 238n. 4; on
  Sthenelaidas's speech, 198; on Thucydides' Book 8, 311
Cooper, James Fenimore, 40, 48
Corcyrean affair, 15; Athenian decision
  about, 122–24; Corcyrean side of,
  103–4, 106, 107, 110, 112–13, 116–
  17, 122; Corinthian side of, 97–98,
  103, 106–7, 110–12, 113–16, 117–20,
  122; language of reciprocal exchange
  in, 112, 113–15; modern views on,

93–96, 99–100; origin of, 97–100,
  103; role of status in, 110–13
Corcyra: civil war in, 32, 44, 60; sense of
  shame of, 143
Corinth: as ally of Sparta, 213–16; de-
  mands war with Athens, 264. *See also*
  Corcyrean affair
Cornford, F. M., 1, 6, 47, 311
Croix, G. E. M. Ste., 5, 77, 94, 99, 119n.
  52

death, 73–74
Deinomenes, 151
Delian League, 274, 275n. 37
Delphi, 79, 80, 81–83
democracy, 313
Demokritos, 41, 59, 209
Demosthenes, 273
Derain, J. D., 300
Diehl, P., 69
Dienekes, 232
dikê. See justice
Diodoros, 134, 160
Diodotus, 56, 66, 70, 134n. 26, 314
Diogenes Laertius, 205, 208–9
divine intervention: Athenian lack of in-
  terest in, 251–52, 285; Melian faith in,
  249
Douglas, M., 109
Dover, K. J., 323
Duris of Samos, 316n. 44

Edmunds, L., 189, 325
Egesta, 108
Einstein, A., 40
Empedocles, 41
Epidamnus, 97
epitarrhothos, 83
erastai, 318–19
Erbse, H., 262, 265–66
erga, 286, 288
Euclid, 44, 325
Euphemos, speech of, 12, 162, 263, 285,
  287, 288, 298
Euripides, 128, 134, 135, 138, 297, 319–
  20
exchange: in Corcyrean affair, 112; gift,
  109, 179–80, 215; market contrasted
  with traditional, 122; strategies of,
  123–24. *See also* capital, symbolic
expediency, 105–6, 239

Finley, J. H., 107
Finley, M. I., 216n. 33
Fornara, C. W., 90, 245–46
Foucault, M., 316
friendship: based on balanced fear, 176–

77, 180; limits of, 172–73; proposed
to Athens by Sparta, 187, 189–90, 255
Fuller, J. F. C., 14
Funeral Oration. *See under* Perikles

Gelon, 101, 102, 151, 160–61
Gildersleeve, B. L., 1
Gilpin, R., 2, 63, 70
gnômê, 43
Gomme, A. W.: on Archidamos's speech,
208; on Athenian speech at Sparta,
265; on Corcyrean affair, 98, 114,
119n. 52; on Greek warfare, 131n. 20;
on Spartan offer of peace, 189n. 17;
on Thucydides' analysis of Homer,
130; on Thucydides' treatment of Sicilian tyrants, 149n. 4
Gorgias, 209
Gramsci, A., 8n. 17, 89
Greece, Classical: conventions of war
contrasted with Civil War, 33–34; as
intermediary between modern powers
and traditional societies, 3–4; passion
for immortality in, 11; prestige in,
101–3; role of the strong in, 72–76, 87
Gudeman, S., 2
Gulf War, 3

Herakleitos, 37, 41
Herman, G., 108
Hermokrates, 287–88, 298
Herodotus: on Athenians, compared with
Thucydides, 284–85; contrasted with
Thucydides, 57; hostility of his audi-
ence to Athens, 253–54; as idealist,
46–47; on Kroisos, 206; on Persian
Wars, 101, 158, 241–48; possible criti-
cisms by Thucydides of, 39, 40; on
Sparta, 15, 76–81, 82–85, 91, 196;
Spartan character in, 277–78; Spartan
power/authority in, 217, 266–67; on
Spartans at Thermopylai, 231–32; sub-
jectivity of human experience in, 41;
on surplus wealth, 153–54
Herz, J. H., 63, 69
Hesiod, 74, 75, 125, 281
Hieron, 152, 159
Hippokrates, 135
Hobbes, Thomas: on human development, 127; impressed by Athenian thesis, 258–59; as political realist, 70; reductive analysis of, 150–51n. 7; on
war, 30, 62
Homer, 30, 83, 171, 256; rule of the
strong in, 30, 72–73; Sthenelaidas's argument modeled on *Iliad*, 216–17;
Thucydides' devaluation of, 59, 127,
129–34

Homeric Hymns, 137
Hood, John Bell, 25–26, 27–28
Hornblower, S. 13n. 30, 37, 65n. 64, 89,
178
How, W. W., 77
Howard, J. E., 8
human nature/behavior: constancy in
Thucydides of, 296–303; world of
"things" more real than that of "language," 145–46, 173–74
human development: Greek authors on,
128, 134–35, 137–38; role of polis in,
138–41; Thucydides on, 127–29, 135–
37, 138
Hunter, V. J., 45, 108–9, 129n. 15, 130,
149–50n. 4

idealism, 49
ideology, 8–9, 262, 263
immortality, 11

Johnson, L. M., 64
justice, 105–7, 142, 174–75, 274, 283

Kagan, D., 63; on Archidamos's speech,
199; on Athenian speech at Sparta,
265; on Corcyrean affair, 94, 95, 98–
99, 119n. 52
Kallet-Marx, L., 198
Kallikles, 259
katastrephô, 77
Kennedy, J. F., 62n. 53
Keohane, R. O., 63
Kimon, 305
Kirk, G. S., 130
Kleon, 55–56, 66, 183–87, 279
Kroisos, 47, 76–77, 206, 239–40, 284–
85
Kuhn, T. S., 57
Kylon, 309
Kythera, 230

language: degeneration of, 44–45, 286,
288; contrasted with "things", 174,
175, 186, 286, 318
Lazenby, J. F., 131n. 21
Lincoln, Abraham, 212
logoi. See language
Loraux, N., 110n. 42
Lord, L. E., 1
Lykourgos, 79–81, 88, 217–18
Lysias, 272

Macan, 245
Machiavelli, N., 54–55
MacLachlan, B., 110n. 42
Macleod, C., 176
Malinowski, B., 96

Mantinea, 86–87, 233–34
Marathon, 268, 269, 271, 272, 273
Mardonios, 241, 247, 248, 250–51
Marshall, G.C., 62n. 52
Marx, K., 153, 155, 167, 169, 170–71
Mauss, M., 109
megaloprepeia, 4
Meiggs, R., 120n. 53
Melian Dialogue, 64, 111; Athens's offer
  compared with Xerxes' in Persian War,
  246–56; compared to Sherman-Hood
  exchange, 24–29; issue of justice and
  expedience in, 238, 239, 240–41, 250;
  lack of shame ethos in, 144; Sparta's
  behavior in, 192–93
Melians: refuse to acknowledge the Athenian thesis, 174–75, 263–64, 289–93;
  relationship to Athens of, 119
Menestheus, 133n. 25
Messenia, 78
Minos, 138, 140, 141, 297
money: as basis of Athenian empire,
  166–68, 170–71, 200–201; loaned for
  interest in archaic Greece, 153; precapitalist vs. capitalist use of, 155, 170–71
Morgenthau, H., 2, 63, 69
Mytilenean debate, 66; balance of power
  in, 176–79; Diodotus's speech in,
  134n. 26; Kleon's speech in, 183–87;
  Mytilenean speech in, 176–79; sets
  stage for Corcyrean affair, 180, 181–
  82

Naupaktos, 225–29
Nikias, 305

objectivity, 45; Thucydides' quest for, 6–
  7, 8, 12, 13, 14, 18–19, 261–62
Odysseus, 99, 216
oikeô/oikos, 162–64
ôphelia, 269

Panathenaia, 120
Panhellenic festivals, 97, 98
paradigm, 57, 58
paraitêsis, 267
paraskeuê, 200–201, 223
Parmenides, 41
Parry, A., 46, 68
patriotism, 323
Pausanias, 151
Peisistratos, 311, 323–24
Peloponnesian War: as greatest war in
  Greek history, 42; scale of, compared
  to Trojan War, 132, 133–34; Thucydi-
  des' explanation for, 36–37
Periander, 163
Perikles, 7, 11, 59, 308–9; actions during

Spartan invasion, 224; on Athenian
  power/strength, 66–67, 315–18, 320;
  eroticization of the polis, 318, 319; Funeral Oration of, 50–51, 109, 117,
  271, 272, 312–15, 316–18, 319, 320,
  322; on gift as assertion of power, 109;
  ideological realism of, 49–52; intellectual resolve of, 42–44; as leader, 68;
  on shame, 143; as Thucydides' model
  of accuracy, 40; values of state over
  personal property and social ties, 166–
  67, 305, 306
Persian Wars: Athenian politics in, 241–
  46; Athens at end of, 274–75; as example of Athenian strength, 267–69,
  273; Herodotus on, 101, 158, 241–48;
  prestige and, 158; situation of Athens
  in, compared with Melos, 246–56
Phaeacia, 104
Phoinix, 216
Phormio, 45–46, 225–26, 228–29
Phrynichos, 68
phthonos, 281–82
Pindar, 315; on money, 167, 202; poems
  give prestige to the wealthy, 102–3,
  152, 159, 173; rhetoric of wealth of,
  156, 159; on unobtainable desires,
  252–53
Pittakos, 163, 208–9
Plataia, 34n. 29, 193–95
Plato, 8, 19, 50, 239, 324, 325; *aretê* in,
  272–73; *erastês* in, 319, 320–21; original humanity in, 134, 135, 137–38;
  polis as basic unit in, 138–39; rule of
  strong in, 72; shame and justice in,
  141–42; *sôphrosunê* in, 209–10
Plattner, S., 96
Pliny, 57
Plutarch, vi, 305
Polanyi, K., 167, 171
polis: as basic/ideal social unit, 138–39;
  differences in power between, 186–87;
  eroticization of, 318, 319; interaction
  of, 155–56; as primeval Greek social
  unit, 140–41; Thucydides' focus on,
  303–8, 311; universalism of, 10–11
Polyzalos, 151
potlatch, 151, 159
Pouncey, P.A., 300–301, 310
power: Athenian, 66–67, 262, 289, 315–
  18, 320; as force in human history,
  146–47; origin of political, 148–51;
  Spartan, 217, 266–67
prestige: importance of to Greeks, 101–3,
  157–61; as root of Corcyrean affair,
  110–13
Prometheus Bound, 59, 128, 134, 135,
  137–38

Protagoras, 41, 139, 141
Pusey, N.M., 323
Pythios, 153–54

Raaflaub, K., 77, 246
rationality, 2, 69
Raubitschek, A. E., 265
realism/realists: four characteristics of, 38; ideological, 48–56, 61; masculine bias of, 70–71; multiple types in Thucydides of, 286; paradigmatic, 56–71; political, 61–71, 261, 269–70, 303–4; procedural, 38–40; scientific, 40–48; Thucydides as, 9, 37–38, 261; unit of analysis of, 67–68, 303–4
reciprocity, 112, 113–5. See also exchange
Romilly, J. de, 45; on the Athenian speech at Sparta, 269; on the Corcyrean affair, 98, 107n. 34; on the Spartan offer of peace, 189; on Thucydides' Archaeology, 126n. 6; on Thucydides' critique of Homer, 130; on Thucydides' realism, 9, 261
Rosaldo, R., 120–21

sacrifice, 97, 98
Salamis, 268, 269
Salmon, J.B., 94, 95, 99, 119n. 52
Samons, L.J., 90
Sappho, 319
Schwartz, E., 1, 105–6, 126, 261
Scott, J.C., 165
Sealey, R., 98
shame, 141–46, 209–10
Shapiro, H.A., 150n. 5
Sherman, W.T.: compared with Thucydides, 14, 21–23, 29–30, 32–33, 34–35; evacuation of Atlanta compared with Melian Dialogue, 24–29; on war, 29–30, 31–32
Sicily, 149, 287, 288
Simonides, 152
Simpson, R.H., 131n. 21
Sitalkes, 133, 318
Skione, 247, 292–93
Smith, Adam, 168
Sokrates, 319
Solon, 47, 205, 220, 281, 284–85, 297
Sophokles, 9, 137; ambiguity of, 301; grim past in, 128; friendship in, 172; polis as basic unit in, 138–39, 304; pride in human achievement in, 59, 135
sôphrosunê, 206–8, 209
Sparta: Archidamos vs. Sthenelaidas on character of, 17–18, 197, 199–208, 209, 210–21, 235; Athenians critical of

lifestyle of, 277–78; and Athens in Persian Wars, 242–46, 254–55; basis of leadership of, 291; capture of Plataia by, 193–95; character of, 225–26, 229–31, 277–78; constancy of human nature assumed by, 299; contrasted with Athens in distant future, 150; Herodotus on, 15, 76–81, 82–85, 91, 196, 217, 266–67, 277–78; leadership, 90; limits of loyalty of, 192–93; in Melian affair, 192–93; power of contrasted with Athens, 121, 315–16; proposal for peace with Athens of, 187–92; Tegea and, 81–85, 181; weaknesses of, 199–201, 211; Xenophon on, 15, 80, 85–91
Sphakteria, 231, 232–33
Speer, A., 101
status. See prestige
Sthenelaidas, 166, 197; on Athens, 254; compared with Ajax, 216–17; modern criticism of speech of, 198–99; speech of, 212–21, 273; vision of Spartan authority of, 17–18, 217–19, 235
Strasburger, H., 259, 288
Strauss, L.: on Athens, 13–14; on Athenian thesis, 259; on the city, 10, 303; on Melian dialogue, 238, 239; on Spartan offer of peace, 190n. 19
Sulla, vi
summachia, 108, 109

Tambiah, S.J., 2
Täubler, E., 150n. 4
Tegea, 79, 81–85, 181
Thales, 208
Thebes, 194
Themistokles, 58
Theognis, 116–17, 205
Thermopylai, 231–32, 234
Thirty Years Peace, 94
Thracians, 33
Thrasymachos, 259–60
Thucydides: ambiguities in, 7; "archaic" vs. "modern" in, 5–6; Athenians of, compared with Herodotus, 284–85; basic assumptions of, 295; claim for immortality of, 11; compared with W.T. Sherman, 21–23, 29–30, 32–33, 34–35; constancy of human nature in, 296–303; deceptive familiarity of, 3–5; decline as theme in, 68, 309–10, 311–12; disdain for Spartan caution of, 225–26, 229–31; focus upon the polis of, 303–8, 311; foreignness of, 6; on friendship, 172–73; history uncompleted, 7; on human development, 127–29, 135–37, 139; humor rare in,

Thucydides *(continued)*
48; as ideological realist, 48–54, 55–
56; ideology and, 9–10; influence on
historians of, 57–58; influence on modern political thought of, 62–64; on language change, 182; as materialist, 146;
minimal role of religion in, 5; modern
interest in, 1–6; modern reaction
against "scientific" paradigm of, 12–
13, 57–61, 261–62; political realism
of, 61–71; political stability as sign of
prosperity in, 16; as procedural realist,
38–40; quest for objectivity by, 6–7, 8,
12, 13, 14, 18–19, 261–62; as realist,
9, 37–38, 261; refusal to accept surface appearances of, 37, 68–69; on
rule of the strong, 172–75; as scientific
realist, 41–48; shift from polis to individual in, 67–68, 309, 310–11; similarity to Herodotus in view of Athens's
rise and fall, 47–48; on Spartan leadership, 90; on supranational/interna-
tional power structures, 67, 91–92; on
tyrants, 149–50, 162–64; universalism
of, 10; on war, 32; women lacking in,
57, 71
Timaios, 160
Timokrates, 229
Tompkins, D., 208
trade, 137
tribute, as basis of Athenian power, 16–
17, 121–22, 165–67, 270–71
Trojan War, 128–33, 297
Tucker, R., 62
Twain, Mark, 40, 48–49, 52
tyrants: material artifacts as evidence of

power of, 151–52; Thucydides on,
149–50, 162–64; treat subjects as their
own family, 162–64

universalism, 10

Vasquez, J. A., 63n. 56
Vidal-Naquet, P., 136n. 29

Waltz, K., 63, 69
war: contrast between ancient and modern, 32–34; Greek, 131n. 20; Hobbes
on, 30, 62; spurs interest in Thucydides, 1–2; W. T. Sherman on, 29–30,
31–32 (*see also* Civil War, American);
Peloponnesian War; Persian War; Trojan War
Wasserman, F. M., 197–98
Wayman, F. W., 69
wealth: of Athenian empire, 16–17; converted to symbolic capital, 159; distinguished from capital, 154; Herodotus
on surplus, 153–54; Pindar on, 156,
157; traditional Greek, 16
Wells, J., 77
Westlake, H. D., 222
Wiedemann, T. E. J., 189
Wight, M., 63
women, 57, 71

xenia, 108–9
Xenophon, 15, 34n. 29, 80, 85–91, 106
Xerxes, 207; offer of peace by, 158, 241–
42, 251, 270; Pythios and, 153–54,
155; status and Greek responses to,
158

Printed in the United States
25938LVS00002B/91

9 780520 207899